THE BEAST

THE BEAST

NICHOLAS BRAND

White Stone Publishing

Typeset and designed by Nicholas Brand

White Stone Publishing: njcbrand@hotmail.co.uk

Unless otherwise indicated all scripture quotations are from The Holy Bible, the Revised Standard Version.

Dedicated to my parents

Adam and Prudence

HEBREW/GREEK-ENGLISH TRANSLITERATION

The Greek letters XIϚ(chi, iota, digamma/waw=616) are transliterated Ch,I,V.

The following table shows the transliteration of Hebrew letters that appear frequently in this book:

616 (alternative)	תרטז	tav, resh, tet, zayin	TRTZ
616 (standard)	תריו	tav, resh, yod, vav	TRIW
therion ("beast" in Greek)	תריונ	tav, resh, yod, vav, nun	TRIWN
666	תרסו	tav, resh, samekh, vav	TRSW

Diagrams of monograms/pages	
תרטז (TRTZ=616)	67, 122, 463
XIϚ (Ch,I,V=616)	118, 463

Contents

PART FOUR SOVIET LONG-RANGE DECEPTION STRATEGY

PART FIVE MARXISM AND SATANISM

PART SIX MARXIST PERVERSION OF CHRISTIANITY

PART SEVEN CONTEMPORARY WAR ON CHRISTIANITY IN WEST

PART EIGHT SATANIC AND OCCULT SYMBOLISM OF THE RED STAR AND SOVIET EMBLEM

PART NINE THE SEVENTY WEEKS OF DANIEL

PART TEN ISLAM: MYSTERY BABYLON THE GREAT

PART 11 THE SECOND BEAST: ISRAEL AND THE FALSE PROPHET

INTRODUCTION

This book refutes the view, held widely in the Church, that Revelation is all about Rome, and that the mark of the Beast represents a Roman Emperor. Instead, this book asserts that the Beast and the Ten Horns represent the USSR.

The mark of the Beast is the Hammer and Sickle and represents the man Lenin. The emblem can be perceived as letters which represent the name "beast" (through transliteration)in the same manner that the Chi Rho symbol represents the first three letters of the name "Christ" in Greek (ΧΡΙΣΤΟΣ).

The Fourth Kingdom, the Fourth Beast seen rising out of the sea (Dan. 7:7), is Russia. (The Ten Horns serve to represent both the succession of kings of the Romanov dynasty and the Soviet Republics).

The Workers' and Peasants' Government of the Russian Soviet Republic (WPG)/Russian Soviet Federative Socialist Republic (RSFSR) is the Beast, the Little Horn of Dan. 7:8. The First Beast of Revelation and the Little Horn (of Dan. 7:8) are one and the same: the Workers' and Peasants' Government (WPG).

The eyes in the Little Horn (of Dan. 7:8) are the eyes of a man: that man is Lenin.

The Hammer and Sickle is the mark of the Beast: a monogram of the number "616" in both Hebrew (in obverse) and Greek (in reverse) letters. The emblem was intended to represent the name of the Beast: the Workers' and Peasants' Government (of the Russian Soviet Republic), but it can be construed as the monogram of the number 616 (in Greek and Hebrew.

In 1991, the Soviet Union appeared to have lost the Cold War. In fact, the collapse of the Soviet Union was engineered by Soviet strategists to trick the West into lowering its guard. The communist foe was mistaken for an ally. Only now is the West finally waking up to the predicament it has foolishly let itself get into. The West must belatedly understand that it in fact lost the Cold War as soon as it offered enthusiastic support for the deceptive "perestroika".

The USSR was the Beast that **was**. The Commonwealth of Independent States is the Beast that **is not**. The Beast **to come**, a restored USSR, may comprise of a long line of "kings" that will extend throughout the remaining final half-week of Daniel's seventieth week (which began in 1917.)

The first half-week began with the death of Jesus Christ and the fall of Jerusalem. The advent of the Little Horn (the Beast) marked the beginning of the final half-week. The saints will be given into the Little Horn's hand during this period.

According to an article entitled "The Seven Most Popular Contenders for the Title of 'Antichrist'"[1] , the following seven are the most widely identified as the Antichrist by society at large (with the most popular listed first):

1 the Pope
2 Nicolas Jetty Carpathia (*Left Behind* books)
3 Nero
4 Hitler
5 Henry Kissinger/Mikhail Gorbachev
6 Napoleon
7 an American President

It is clear from this list, that, with the exception of those who identified Gorbachev, few identify the Soviet Union as the Beast. The Pope, Nero, and the fictional character Carpathia, are misidentifications based on the misunderstanding that the Roman Empire is the Fourth Kingdom, when in fact the Roman Empire comprises part of Daniel's Third Kingdom.

For all its many failings, the Roman Catholic Church has been a beacon of light and an enemy of the Soviet Beast. Marxists within the Church however are successfully undermining the Church's stance against communism.

Napoleon has been misidentified as the Beast because his name sounds similar to Apollyon (Rev. 9:11).

---

1 Article by Joe Carter, editor of The Gospel Coalition

The fact that the President of America is routinely identified as the Beast shows how blind people are to the truth, and how the truth has become inverted. The United States was a great bastion of freedom against Soviet tyranny. Sadly, undermined by enemies from within, the United States is becoming so weakened, both militarily and politically, that it will be unable to oppose the USSR when it is restored.

The advent of the Little Horn (Dan. 7:8), into whose hands the saints are to be given, occurred in 1917. Christians stands at a critical point in time, a prolonged period of persecution when the USSR is restored. The restoration will probably occur shortly after Mikhail Gorbachev's death.

Part One

THE BEAST: THE WORKERS' AND PEASANTS' GOVERNMENT (OF THE RUSSIAN SOVIET REPUBLIC)

1

THE BEAST: THE WORKERS' AND PEASANTS' GOVERNMENT (OF THE RUSSIAN SOVIET REPUBLIC)

The Beast: the Workers' and Peasants' Government of the Russian Soviet Republic

The Workers' and Peasants' Government of the Russian Soviet Republic is the name of the Beast.

According to the Great Soviet Encyclopeia (1979)):

> [the Provisional Workers' and Peasants' Government was] the origina lname of the Council of People's Commissars, created by the Second All-Russian Congress of Soviets of Workers' and Soliers' Deputies on October 26 (November 8) 1917, "until the convocation of the Constituent Assembly". The Consituent Assembly was convened on January 5 (18), 1918. The counterrevolutionary majority of the delegates refused to confirm the Declaration of Rights of the Working and Exploited People. On January 6 (19), the All-Russian Central Executive Commitee dissolved the Constituent Assembly. On January 18 (31) the Third All-Russian Congress of Soviets con-

> firmed the dismissal of the Constituent Assembly and adopted a resolution on the elimination of all references to it from Soviet legislation. By the decree of the congress On a New Designation for the Present Supreme State Governmente the Soviet government was given a new name - "Workers' and Peasants' Government of the Russian Soviet Republic."

The October Revolution created the Workers' and Peasants' Government. This is the name represented by the Hammer and Sickle, the mark of the Beast's name.

Trotzky explained that the formula "workers' and farmers' government", which first appeared in the agitation of the Bolsheviks in 1917, represented "nothing more that the popular designation for the already established dictatorship of the proletariat". The formula indicated the need for the workers to break with all traditional parties of the bourgeoisie in order, jointly with the farmers, to establish their own power.

Just a kings rule over their people, so the dictatorship of the proletariat rules over its people and fulfils the function of a king or "**horn**".

The Bolsheviks' use of the designation "Workers' and Peasants' Government" is recorded by E.H. Carr in his book *The Bolshevik Revolution 1917-1923 (Volume One).* Carr notes that the revolution was international and took no account of national boundaries:

The Workers' and Peasants' Government had no territorial definition and designation: the ultimate extension of its authority could not be foreseen.

Article 6 of the 1918 Constitution of the Russian Federated Soviet Republic exhibits the first state emblem of Soviet Russian. It consists of a Hammer and Sickle before a kind of shield with the sun at the bottom of it, but no Red Star above it.

The hammer and sickle represent the workers and peasants respectively.

Russia is the Fourth Kingdom

> **And the ten kings that you saw are ten kings who have not yet received royal power . . .** (Rev. 17:12)

Russia, not Rome, is the Fourth Kingdom. The Fourth Kingdom is represented by the seventh head of the seven-headed Beast.

The Fourth Kingdom comprises the seventh and eighth kingdoms, the Russian Empire and the Soviet Union respectively. In Revelation, however, the term "Beast" only refers to the Soviet Union (the eighth kingdom), not the Russian Empire.

The division of the Fourth Kingdom into a seventh and eighth kingdom is indicated in Daniel with the use of the word "**different**". All four beasts are "**different**" (Dan. 7:3). The interpreting angel explains that the fourth kingdom shall be "**different from all the kingdoms**" (Dan. 7:23). The horn that arises after the first ten is also "**different**" (Dan. 7:24)from the other horns.

To a great extent, the Soviet Union was a continuation of the Russian Empire given the preeminence of the Russians over the other nationalities that comprised the Soviet Union. It is for this reason that the seventh head of the Beast represents both kingdoms, the Russian Empire and the USSR.

In Revelation, the term "Beast" can refer to either the Little Horn (Dan. 7:8) itself or to the Beast's kingdom formed when the Ten Horns (the Soviet Republics) hand over their authority to the Little Horn. In other words, sometimes the Beast is distinguished from the Ten Horns, sometimes it is identified with them.

The Russian Soviet Federative Socialist Republic is the Little Horn. The other Soviet Republics are the Ten Horns.

During the period of the Russian Empire, the subject peoples were aliens and had "**not yet received royal power**" (Rev. 17:12). It was only after the Russian Revolution in 1917 that these nationalities became independent for a brief period of time ("**one hour**"). As Soviet Republics, these nationalities became nominally recognized as equal partners with Russia.

Brief period ("one hour") of independence after Russian Revolution

> **. . . but they [the Ten Horns] are to receive authority as kings for one hour, together with the beast.** (Rev. 17:12)

For a period of a few years after the February and October Revolutions of 1917, some of the former subject peoples of the Russian Empire enjoyed a short period of independence before they were merged into the Soviet Union. The Bolsheviks suppressed these breakaway independence movements with the help of the Red Army(a process that is examined in detail in Richard Pipes' book *The Formation of the Soviet Union*).Even before Lenin's death in 1924 the Bolsheviks had managed to regain control over all the land that had formerly belonged to the Russian Empire, with the exception of Poland and Finland .

The Declaration of the Rights of the Peoples (2 November 1917) had recognized the equality and sovereignty of all peoples, abolished all national privileges and restrictions, and established the right to self-determination 'up to and including secession and the formation of an independent state'. In *The History of the Soviet Union*, Geoffrey Hosking writes:

> The revolution and civil war had given most of the nationalities of the former tsarist empire at least a brief experience of real independence, such as they had not known for centuries, or in some cases had never known.

Lenin had not expected the empire to fragment, so decided to rectify the situation by force. After 1921 the nationalities found themselves reintegrated into a new kind of Russian Empire.

The Ten Horns have a dual significance

> **As for the ten horns, out of this kingdom ten kings shall arise, and another shall arise after them; he shall be different from the former ones, and shall put down three kings.** (Dan. 7:24)

In the Book of Daniel, the Ten Horns represent the succession of kings of the Romanov dynasty, but in the Book of Revelation the Ten Horns represent the ten Socialist Republics who hand over their royal authority to Russia.

In other words, the Ten Horns are to be interpreted in two diffent ways depending on whether the Ten Horns are perceived as belonging to the seventh kingdom (the Russian Empire) or the eighth kingdom (the USSR). If they are considered to belong to the seventh kingdom, they represent the succession of Romanov kings.

Peter the Great was the first in this line of kings, and the first to declared Russia an empire.

The three horns that are uprooted represent the final Romanov kings (Nicholas II, his son Alexei II, and Nicholas's brother Michael II), all three of whom were assassinated by the Bolsheviks in 1918.

A horn usually represents a line of kings, but given that the Little Horn is perceived asfollowing on from a line of kings, it is clear that the Little Horn represents an individual "king" (Lenin), in the same way that the Great Horn of Dan. 8:8 represents Alexander the Great.

When the Ten Horns are considered to belong to the eighth kingdom (the Beast) they represent the other (non-Russian) Soviet Republics of the Soviet Union.

It is the Little Horn/the Beast (the Workers' and Peasants' Government (WPG)/Lenin) who uproots the three horns, and it is the WPG/Lenin to whom the Ten Horns give their royal authority in the Soviet Union

Murder of the Romanov king and heirs: the three horns uprooted by the Little Horn

> **. . . behold, there came up among them another horn, a little one, before which three of the first horns were plucked up by the roots** (Dan. 7:8)

Nicholas was forced to abdicate on 15 March [O.S. 2 March] 1917. He abdicated in favour of his son Alexei who ascended the throne under a regency (with his uncle Michael as regent). For a brief period of time (one afternoon), therefore, Alexei was Tsar (Alexei II).

Upon realization that he would be exiled after his abdication, and afraid that Alexei would not be able to survive the consequent separation from his parents on account of his haemophilia, Nicholas created a second abdication document later that same afternoon so that the throne passed to his youngest brother Grand Duke Michael Alexandrovich of Russa instead. Nicholas made it appear that this document came into effect at the earlier time when the first abdication document was made, when in fact it was actually created later in the day. Whether the change had any legal validity is open to speculation. Alexei is sometimes known as Alexei II to legitimists as they do not recognize the abdication of his father in favour of his uncle as lawful

Despite being proclaimed Emperor Michael II the next morning to Russian troops and cities throughout Russia, Michael declined to accept the throne until the people were allowed to vote through a Constituent Assembly, a referendum that was never had. Nevertheless, he did not abdicate nor did he refuse to accept the throne. His renunciation of the throne, though provisional, marked the end of the Tsarist regime in Russia.

Michael was shot by the Cheka on 13 June 1918.

Nicholas and all the members of his family were executed on 17 July 1918 by the Bolshevik secret police (the Cheka). The firing squad first killed Nicholas before the Tsarevich Alexei. Precious gems within his clothing prevented him from being killed quickly.

The Bolsheviks therefore assasinated the former Tsar Nicholas II, his sonAlexei II, and his brother Michael II. These are the three horns uprooted by the Little Horn (the Workers' and Peasants' Government of the Russian Soviet Republic).

Lenin was behind all these killings, and despite all his efforts to hide his involvement in these assassinations, his role in all this is clear for all to see.

The "eyes" of the Little Horn signifies the name "Lenin"

> **. . . and behold! , eyes like the eyes of a man were in this horn were, and a mouth speaking great things.** (Dan. 7:8, author's translation)

The two Aramaic words for "**behold! eyes**" אלו עינין (*alu aynin*) in the verse above (Rev. 7:8) may adumbrate the name "Lenin". The words may possibly also point to Lenin's real name Ulyanov (Hebrew: אוליאניב) since אלו (*alu* "behold!") also sounds similar to the first syllable of that name. These eyes are **like the eyes of a man** *ce-aynei anasha*, a phrase in Aramaic which repeats the *ay-n-n* sound, a further indication that there may be some wordplay at work here.

The Little Horn's eyes are mentioned again in Dan. 7:20 in the phrase ועינין לה (*ve-aynin lah*) "and eyes to her (the horn)". Here the syllable with the l-sound comes after the word for "eyes", but this phrase may again be wordplay on the name "Lenin".

There are a further three reasons for suspecting worplay. Firstly, there seems to be no other explanation for why the eyes are mentioned. No explanation is given to explain what they signify, unlike the Little Horn's mouth which signifies blaphemy. Secondly, the word *aru* ארו "Behold!" is used on throughout chapter 7 of Daniel (Rev. 7:2; Rev. 7:5; Rev. 7:6; Rev. 7:7; Rev. 7:13) except in this one verse (Dan. 7:8) where אלו *alu* ("Behold!") is used instead (twice). The switch from *aru* to *alu* may well be for the reason that the words "behold! eyes" אלו עינין (*alu aynin*) are indeed a play on words to signify that "Lenin" is the Little Horn. Thirdly, the word "Behold!" (*alu*) itself is wordplay on the word "eyes".

It is possible that the Aramaic word "eyes" עינין (*aynin*) is alluded to again in the Greek of Revelation when the Beast is described as the Beast "**that was and is not**": ην και ουκ εστιν. The first word in this phrase (ην "was") sound like *aynin* ("eyes") and the Hebrew for "is not" (ουκ εστιν) is *einenah* (אינּנּה). This might also be wordplay on the name "Lenin".

The eyes of the Little Horn represent a man, and that man is Lenin. He is the man alluded to in Rev. 13:18.

It was Cyrus, the initial ruler over the Medo-Persian empire whose name God foretold in Isaiah chapters 44 and 45, not the name of the final ruler of that empire.

> **Thus says the Lord to his anointed, to Cyrus . . .** (Isa. 45:1)

> **For the sake of my servant Jacob, and Israel my chosen, I call you by your name, I surname you, though you do not know me.** (Isa. 45:4)

Of course it may be futile to try and perceive from words in the scriptures any indication of the name "Lenin". The mark of the Beast does not indicate the Beast's personal name (Lenin or Ulyanov), merely the name "Beast" through transliteration. Consequently, the observations in this subsection may be based on mere coincidence.

It is clear that Lenin fulfilled all the criteria of the Beast, the primary criterion being that three of the Romanov "horns" (Michael, Nicholas, Alexei) were killed on his command in fulfilment of Dan. 7:8. Hence there is no need for his actual personal name to be prophesied. Similarly, it is clear that Jesus fulfilled all the criteria of the Messiah, despite the fact that, (as far as the author is aware) there is no prophecy that prophesies, or alludes through wordplay, to his actual personal name (Jesus).

Actions of the WPG match those prophesied of the Little Horn

> **.. [he] shall put down three kings. he shall speak words against the Most High, and shall wear out the saints of the Most High, and shall think to change the times and the law; and they shall be given into his hand for a time, two times, and half a time.** (Dan. 7:24-25)

The government of the Soviet Union have fulfilled many of the actions that are prophesied of the Little Horn.

These are not the actions of just one man. The first half-week (**time, two times, and half a time**) stretched in fact across many generations and over nearly two thousand years (from Christ's death and resurrection to the advent of the Beast in 1917). The final half-week may last just as long. The actions of the Little Horn that represents Rome (Dan. 8:9) are not confined to the actions of just one Roman. Likewise the actions of the Little Horn that represents the Soviet government do not represent the actions of just one man.

Uproot three kings

The Soviet government killed three former tsars of the Russian Empire: Nicholas II, Alexei II, and Michael II.

Blasphemed God

The Bolshevik government form the League of the Militant Godless. This magazine was full of blaphemous pictures and articles .

Wearing out the saints

The Bolsheviks persecuted the saints, murdered priests, and closed down churches and monasteries.

Changing the times and the law

The Little Horn will aspire to do things that only God can do, namely change the times and seasons, or at least will be accredited with such powers. Daniel praises God who alone has such might:

> **Blessed be the name of God for ever and ever, to whom belong wisdom and might. He changes times and seasons . .** (Dan. 2:20-21)

Stalin was acredited with the wisdom and might that only belong to God in panegyrics to him. Stalin's cult of personality effectively deified him.

In his book *Marx & Satan,* Richard Wurmbrand records the words of one particular ode to Stalin that appeared in *Pravda*, but there were many thousands of other poems made to Stalin in his honour in a similar blasphemous vein:

O great Stalin, O leader of the peoples,
Thou who broughtest man to birth,
Thou who purifiest the earth,
Thou who restores the centuries,
Thou who makes bloom the Spring,
Thou who makes virbrate the musical chords.[2]

In 1929 the Soviet calendar was changed to replace the seven-day work week with five days of work and the sixth day off. This forced people to work on Sunday instead of going to church. In 1931 six -day interrupted work weeks were implemented. In 1940 both five- and six- day work weeks were abandoned.

The Soviet government did change the times and laws, sometimes in an attempt to thwart Christians. The 25th and 26th of December were proclaimed "Days of Industrialization" and all were compelled to work on those days. The traditional Russian holiday of the New Year (the Feast of the Circumcision of Christ) was prohibited .

The Soviets adopted the Gregorian Calendar in February 1918 by dropping the Julian dates of 1-13 February 1918.

Needless to say, the Soviets tried to subvert God's laws. The Dictatorship of the Proletariat considered itself above any law, whether that law be made by God or man.

Unconstrained by any laws made priro to its existence by either God or man, the new Soviet regime committed untold horros during the Red Terror period (rougly the Civil War period). Without any proper trial, thousands were killed. Some were even crucified, boiled alive, scalped, skinned alive, and so forth by the Chekists. Most were shot. Numbers vary but perhaps as many as 100,000 may have been executed during the period of the Red Terror.

The tools of oppression were never dismantled after the Civil War so the general populace continued to live in fear of the Cheka/NKVD/KGB. Terror and killings rose again to horrific heights during Stalin's reign.

Strongly atheistic, even theomachistic, the Soviet government persecuted the religious of all faiths and tried to undermine every religion and religious institution. Morals were likened to chains, imposed upon the proletariat by a self-interested bourgeoisie.

---

2 *Pravda*, August 1936

The Beast will oppress the saints during the final "half-week"

The advent of the Beast is to roughly coincide with the restoration of the Temple service in Jerusalem which marks the mid-point of the final week (the seventieth) according to Daniel (Dan. 9:27). The discrepancy in time between these two events, the advent of the Little Horn in 1917 and the restoration of the sacrificial system that will take place in 2370, according to Dan. 8:14 (2300 years after its overthrow in AD 70), is insignificant in the light of the long periods of time involved. A similar discrepancy can be seen in the way that the Women is counted as having respite from Satan (Rev. 12:6) for the first half-week (which began with the death of Jesus Christ), despite the fact that Rome did not stop persecuting Christians for over a three hundred years after the resurrection of Jesus Christ.

The USSR will be restored

> **. . . but its mortal wound was healed, and the whole earth followed the beast with wonder.** (Rev. 13:3)

The Soviet Union will be restored. This restoration is described in Revelation in terms of a mortal wound being healed, a sword wound (Rev. 13:14). The reference to a sword refers to the Cold War, which appeared to end with the apparent death of communism in the early 1990s. All the previous kingdoms that are represented by the heads of the Beast came to an end through defeat in war. The USSR appeared to have ended in a similar way, with many in the West gloating that they had won the Cold War.

The restoration of the USSR is described in terms that identifies it with Satan. Like Satan, who will be loosed from the abyss at the end of Christ's thousand year reign to deceive the nations (Rev. 20:7), so the Beast ascends from the abyss. The bottomless pit is understood to be the resting place of the departed (Rom. 10:7), and the abode of demons (Luke 8:31). Satan himself is to be imprisoned in the bottomless pit for a thousand years after the battle of Armageddon (Rev. 20:2).

The False Prophet makes the inhabitants of the earth worship the

First Beast **whose mortal wound was healed** (Rev. 13:12). Although the "First Beast" in this phrase refers to the Soviet Empire and its restoration, in practice this worship must entail the worship of an actual human being, the final ruler of the Soviet Empire in whom this empire is embodied.

The False Prophet will insist that a statue is made to represent this great empire. The False Prophet will breathe life into the statue that is made in the image ofthe Beast (Rev. 13:15). This image will be worshipped too, and its worshippers will bear the mark of the Beast, the Hammer and Sickle.

Revelation gives no indication in fact of the names of either the False Prophet or the Beast who will both make war on the Lamb at the battle of Armageddon.

The seven heads signify kingdoms, not individuals

The seven heads of the Beast are seven mountains and also seven "**kings**" (Rev. 17:10). The word "kings" signifies kingdoms, not individual kings. At no point in chapter 13 or 17 of Revelation is there any indication that the "kings" signify anything other than kingdoms.

However, the Soviet Union was comprised of seven "kings". The fact that kingdoms are referred to as "kings" (Rev. 17: 10), rather than "kingdoms", suggests that this is not just a coincidence but yet another indication that the USSR was indeed the Beast (that was). However, despite this observation, it is important to bear in mind that the Beast's seven "heads" signify kingdoms, not individual kings. Upon its restoration, the Beast will have many more "kings".

The head wound (Rev. 13: 3) refers to the end of the Cold War, not the assassination of any individual. Its healing refers to the restoration of the Soviet Union.

2

THE SEVEN KINGDOMS OF THE BEAST

The seven-headed Beast

> **This calls for a mind with wisdom: the seven heads are seven mountains on which the woman is seated; they are also seven kings, five of whom have fallen, one is, the other has not yet come, and when he comes he must remain only a little while. As for the beast that was and is not, it is an eighth but it is one of the seven . . .** (Rev. 17:9-11, *Author's translation*)

The seven heads represent:

- The seven successive kingdoms represented by the seven heads of the four beasts of Daniel chapter 7: the Lion, Bear, and the Leopard, and the Fourth Beast. These are: Babylon, Medo-Persian, Macedonian, Syrian, Egyptian, Roman Empire, and the Russian Empire (and eight: USSR).
- The former subject peoples of the seven fallen empires (Babylon, Medo-Persian, Macedonian, Syrian, Egyptian, Roman Empire, Russian Empire) upon which Babylon the Great (Mecca/Islam) is seated. Babylon the Great is Mecca, the city which represents Islam.

The eighth kingdom, the Union of Soviet Socialist Republics, is the Beast that **was and is not and is to come** (Rev. 17:8).

The seven (eight) kingdoms of the four Beasts

The eight kingdoms are the following:

Lion (nation: Chaldea)

1. Neo-Babylonian Empire [625-539 BC]

Bear (nation: Medo-Persia)

2. Medes and Persians [539-330 BC]

Leopard (nation: Javan/Greece)

3. Antigonids/kingdom of Macedonia [306-168 BC]
4. Seleucids/kingdom of Syria [312-63 BC]
5. Ptolemies/kingdom of Egypt [305-30 BC]
6. Roman Empire [27 BC-1453]

The Fourth Beast (nations: Russia and the Ten former SSRs/member states of the CIS)

7. The Russian Empire [1478-1917)
8. USSR [1917-1991]: the Beast that **was.** The Beast that is to come is yet to arise.

While the Beast is identified with Lenin, Lenin is not the Lawless One (2 Thess. 2:8) who will be slayed with the breath of the mouth of the Lord Jesus by his appearing and coming. The Lawless One is the last of the Little Horn's kings. This book maintains that those people are mistaken who assume that the mark of the Beast must be the name of the Lawless One, the last king. The mark in fact refers to Stalin.

Seven heads but eight kingdoms

Head	Beast	Kingdoms	Order	Statue	Notes
1	Lion	Babylon	1	Gold (head)	"five of whom have fallen" (Rev. 17:10)
2	Bear	Medo-Persian	2	Silver (upper body)	
3	Leopard	Macedonia	3	Bronze (thigh and upper legs)	
4		Syria	4		
5		Egypt	5		
6		Roman Republic/ Empire	6		"one is" (Rev. 17:10)
7	Fourth Beast	Russian Empire	7	Iron (lower legs)	
		USSR "The Beast" (that was and is to come)	8	Iron and clay (feet)	

Daniel had a series of visions, each new vision building upon the previous one, to reveal the identities of the Four Kingdoms that will rule over the earth in succession. These four Kingdoms are represented in Daniel by four beasts, one of which (the Leopard) has four heads.

The Table above indicates which kingdoms are represented by the seven heads of the Beast.

The Table shows how the seven (eight) kingdoms are divided between four Kingdoms represented by the Lion, Bear, Leopard and Fourth Beast in Daniel's vision, with each beast representing a different nation.

Heads of the Beast refer to kingdoms not kings

The seven **heads** of the Beast (Rev. 17:10) refer to kingdoms/empires, not individual kings. Nowhere in Daniel does a head signify an individual king. The Beast represents an eigth kingdom, but it does not represent an eighth king/ruler. Every ruler of this kingdom represents the Beast and so can be considered the Beast, not any one particular ruler. The king who fights the Lamb at Armageddon is the Beast, but then so is every other leader of the Soviet Union.

Stalin was not an "eighth" ruler, yet the mark of the Beast does indeed signify his name. The fact that there were seven rulers over the Soviet Union is just a coincidence. (Of course even this number can be disputed.) .

Many commentators mistakenlyinterpret the phrase "**five of whom have fallen**" to signify a succession of Roman emperors and are invariably unable to match any line of emperors to the seven heads in a convincing way.

The Beast's composition of lion, bear and leopard, and ten horns, overtly points to the seven/eight kingdoms represented by the seven heads of the four beasts of Daniel. The fact that the feet and mouth are distinguished from the other parts of the Beast's body indicates that the Beast represents the Little Horn, for in a similar way its "mouth" and "eyes" were distinguished from the other parts of its body. The Little Horn (Beast) represents a succession of "kings", not just one king .Stalin, however, is identified with this line of kings or "horn" and the "eyes" of the Little Horn represent Stalin.

The interpretation of "kings" as kingdoms is also supported by the fact that the Greek word for "fallen" (*epesen*) is the same Greek word that is used in describing the fall of the great city Babylon the Great herself in the very next chapter: "**Fallen, fallen** (*epesen*) **is Babylon the great!** (Rev. 18:2). As many commentators have noted, the word *epesen* is not an appropriate word to describe the end of an individual king.

The interchangeability of "kings" for "kingdoms" is also made explicit in verses Dan. 7:17 and Dan. 7:23: '**These four great beasts are four kings who shall arise out of the earth**' (Dan. 7:17)/ '**As for the fourth beast, there shall be a fouth kingdom on earth.**' (Dan. 7:23)

Satanic nature of all seven kingdoms

> **And another portent appeared in heaven; behold, a great red dragon, with seven heads and ten horns, and seven diadems upon his heads.** (Rev. 12:3)

The satanic nature of these seven kingdoms are revealed by the portent in the prophecy of the great Red Dragon (Rev. 12:3). The fact that this Red Dragon has seven heads and ten horns indicates that Satan works through the seven heads and ten horns of the Beast. In fact, the Beast is merely a different representation of the Red Dragon, incorporating imagery from chapter 7 of Daniel to indicate what the sevens heads of the Red Dragon actually signify.

Satan works through the Beast (and the False Prophet), and so the Red Beast and the Red Dragon represent the same thing. Their colour reflects this commonality: they are both red. In fact the Beast could be called the Red Beast.

Until the period of the sixth head (the Roman Empire), there were no Christians. Till then, it was the Jews who were oppressed by the Babylonian and successive empires represented by the first five heads of the Beast.

Since the resurrection of Jesus Christ, Christians (the offspring of the Woman wrapped in the sun) have had to face the Dragon's onslaughts, being persecuted during the years of the early Roman Empire and the period of the Soviet Empire. Christians enjoyed a respite from persecution after Rome adopted Christianity as its state religion, an event represented by the Woman being given the two wings of a great eagle.

The Red Beast is the culmination of the evil empires spanning the centuries from King Nebuchadnezzar's reign in Babylon. These empires are embodiments of the Red Dragon, Satan, "**the ruler of this world**" (John 14:30):

> **For we are not contending against flesh and blood, but against the principalities, against the powers, against the world rulers of this present darkness, against the spiritual hosts of wickedness in the heavenly places.** (Eph. 6:12)

The Beast and the Ten Horns

> **And I saw a beast rising out of the sea, with ten horns ...** (Rev. 13:1)

The Beast is the Little Horn's kingdom comprising the Russian Soviet Federative Socialist Republic itself and the Ten Horns which represent the other Socialist Republics.

The USSR can be identified as the Beast through the Hammer and Sickle, its emblem, because the Hammer and Sickle is the mark of the Beast.

The Workers' and Peasants' Government incorporated the Hammer and Sickle in its emblem in the 1918 Constitution of the RSFSR. The adoption of the Hammer and Sickle as the official emblem of the USSR happened during the third session of the Executive Committee of the USSR on 12 November 1923.

Each Soviet Socialist Republic (SSR) had its own emblem adorned with the Hammer and Sickle, thereby identifying them with the Beast itself.

The Ten Kings: the line of Romanov kings AND Soviet Republics

> **As for the ten horns, out of this kingdom ten kings shall arise ...** (Dan. 7:24)

The Ten Horns of Dan. 24 arise out of the the seventh kingdom, the Russian Empire. They signify the royal succession of Romanov monarchs. The number ten is not exact, in the same way that there more than three Persian kings arose between Cyrus and Xerxes (Dan. 11:2). There were in fact over a dozen kings in the Romanov line after Peter the Great. The figure is rounded down to ten to fit the pattern found in the Statue in Nebuchadezzar's dream with its ten toes.

Lenin, the Little Horn (of Dan. 7:8, uprooted three Romanov "horns" with the assassination of Michael, Nicholas, and Alexei.

The seventh head represents two kingdoms: the seventh and eighth. With regard to the seventh, the Ten Horns signify a succession of Romanov kings. In regard to the eighth kingdom (the Beast) they signify a union of states: the USSR.

The USSR was Russian-dominated

These are of one mind and give over their power and authority to the-beast . . .(Rev. 17:13)

The USSR, despite all pretensions to the contrary, was in effect merely a sovietized Russian Empire. Russia was the hegemonic power and wielded sovereign power over the other Soviet Republics. Such sovereign power was never openly admitted by the Soviets, and the pretense that each Soviet Socialist Republic had equal authority was maintained. The fact remains however, that for the other SSRs, being a part of the USSR was not so very different from being part of the Russian Empire. The Soviet Union was dominated by Russia, the Little Horn of Dan. 7:8.

Soviet leaders asserted that bourgeois nation-states must be transformed into a single proletarian world state within which all nations will eventually lose their identity as nations and merge into a single whole. The identity of this goal was used to obscure the process by which Russian nationalism benefited at the expense of proletarian internationalism.

The proletariat as the new ruling class was predominantly Great Russian. The nub of Party authority were Great Russians, or Russified non-Russians. From the beginning, the Bolshevik Party was predominantly Russian-based. This naturally reinforced the tendency toward Great Russian control which, in any case, would have been produced by the centralized Party structure. In those instances where native Communists held the First Secretaryship in their Republics, their power was more apparent than real, with a Russian Second Secretary wielding the decisive authority..

According to Eliot R. Goodman in *The Soviet Design for a World State*:

> [By the 1930s] the only criterion for one's "internationalism" was the glorification and aggrandizement of a Russian-based and Russian-dominated Union of Soviet Socialist Republics, the nucleus and prototype of a World Union of Soviet Socialist Republics.

"Soviet man" was a member of a specific nationality, and of all these nationalities, the Great Russians maintained and strengthened their dominating position. Whoever furthered the domination of the Great Russians was considered to be advancing the cause of the Soviet world state. Such a Soviet world state would clearly be a Russian-dominated world state.

The Ten Horns

> **And the ten horns that you saw are ten kings who have not yet received royal power, but they are to receive authority as kings for one hour, together with the beast.** (Rev. 17:12)

Represented by the toes of the Statue in Nebuchadnezzar's dream, these "kings" need not number exactly ten. The numbers are fairly fluid. Azerbaijan, Armenia, and Georgia, were initially incorporated into the USSR as one Soviet Republic (the Transcaucasian SSR). A similar manoeuvre would reduce the number of horns down to ten. Removal of the three Baltic States from the count would likewise reduced the number to one approaching ten. The Ten Horns comprise of some, or all, of the following:

- Azerrbaijan
- Belarus
- Kazakhstan
- Kyrgyzstan
- Armenia
- Moldova
- Tajikstan
- Uzbekistan
- Turkmenistan
- Ukraine
- Lithuania
- Latvia
- Estonia
- Georgia

3

ROME IS NOT THE BEAST

The Roman Empire is the Little Horn of Dan. 8:9 (but NOT the Little Horn of Dan. 7:8)

> **Out of one of them came forth a little horn** . . . (Dan. 8:9)

The four horns of the He-Goat came up in place of the Great Horn (Alexander the Great) towards the *four winds of heaven*. In the verse above (Dan. 8:9), the Hebrew word for "**one**" is feminine and agrees in number and gender with the Hebrew word "**wind**" and the Hebrew word for "**them**" is masculine plural and agrees in number and gender with the Hebrew for "**heaven**".

This Little Horn (Dan. 8:9) coming forth out of one of these winds of heaven is Augustus Caesar (Lenin is the Little Horn of Dan. 7:8).

The line of Caesars (the Roman Empire) was merely a continuation of the fourth Javanic kingdom - the Roman Republic - and so both are represented by the same head of the Beast (the sixth head). (Similarly, the USSR is represented by the same head of the Beast as the Russian Empire (the seventh head).)

The phrase "**at the latter end of their Kingdom**" (Dan. 8:23) indicates that Caesar will arise when the other kingdoms have ended. August Caesar did come to power in fact with the defeat of the Ptolemies at the battle of Actium. His principate marked the end of the Roman Republic.

The casting down of stars to the earth (Dan. 8:10) echoes the verse in Lamentation about the destruction of Jerusalem at the hands of the Babylonians:

> **He has cast down from heaven to earth the splendour of Israel ...** (Lam. 2:1)

The **transgressors** who **have reached their full measure** (Dan. 8:23) are the Jews who who will be destroyed by the Romans. The Roman Empire takes away the continual burnt offering, overthrows the Sanctuary, and causes desolation (Dan. 8:11). This is the time of **indignation** (Dan. 8:19) when God's wrath will fall upon Israel.

The Romans are the kingdom **of bold countenance** (Dan. 8:23). Under the curse, a nation of bold countenance was to fall upon Israel if it failed to observe God's commandments (Deut. 28:50).

Rome rises up against the **Prince of princes** and Jesus is crucified under Pontius Pilate (Dan. 8:25). This verse is not a reference to Armageddon.

The Temple will be rebuilt and the Temple service will recommence after 2300 years (Dan. 8:14).

The Little Horn of Dan. 8:9 is not the same as the Little Horn of Dan. 7:8. The Little Horn of Dan. 7:8 is the Beast of the Fourth Kingdom. The Roman Empire is not the Beast, but one of the kingdoms of the Third Kingdom (the Leopard).

Rome is a Javanic kingdom

Rome counts as one of the four horns of the He-Goat, because the Romans are descendants of Javan. The Romans are thus not the Fourth Kingdom as is widely believed, but belong to the Third Beast (the Leopard).

The Romans count as Javanic (Greek), because they are descendants of Kittim, a son of Javan (Gen. 10:4-5). Javan was a descendant of Japheth, one of the three sons of Noah. Javan's sons are listed in Genesis, one of whom was Kittim:

The sons of Javan: Elishah, Tarshish, Kittim, and Dodanim. From these the coastland peoples spread. (Gen. 10:4-5)

The Jewish commentator Ibn Ezra considered that Rome should be included in the Third Kingdom on the grounds that they were related to the Greeks.

Kittim was a settlement in present-day Larnaca on the west coast of Cyprus, known in ancient times as Kition, or (in Latin) Citium. On this basis, the whole island became known as "Kittim" in Hebrew, including the Tanach, the Hebrew Bible. The name Kittim was often applied to all the Aegean islands and even to the West in general, especially the seafaring West.

The expression "**isles of Kittim**" (Jer. 2:10; Ezek. 27:6) indicates that this designation had already become a general descriptor for the Mediterranean islands long before the time of Josephus. Sometimes this designation was further extended to apply to Romans, Macedonians or Seleucid Greeks. For example, the beginning of 1 Maccabees that "Alexander the Great the Macedonian" had come from the "land of Kittim" (1 Macc. 1:1).

The Romans are considered to be the Kittim mentioned in Numbers 24:24. The mediaeval rabbinic compilation *Yosippon* contains a detailed account of the Kittim who are correlated to the Romans.

The Romans themselves believed that their ancestors originated from Anatolia (an area of Javan), fleeing with Aeneas from Troy, a legend told in Virgil's *Aeneid*.

The Javanic nature of the Roman Empire is quite apparent from the fact that Justinian was the last Roman emperor to speak Latin. From his reign onwards all the Roman emperors spoke Greek.

The Javanic nature of the Roman Empire is also apparent from the fact that the new Roman capital, Constantinople, is situated at the mouth to the Ionian Sea, a sea which derives its name from Javan.

Attalid kingdom of Pergamum bequeathed to Rome

The Attalid kingdom of Pergamum, one of the four Javanic horns of the He-Goat, was bequeathed to the Roman Republic in 133 BC. The Romans thereby became one of the four horns of Alexander the Great's divided empire.

The Attalid dynasty was a Hellenistic dynasty that ruled the city of Pergamon in Asia Minor after the death of Lysimachus, a general of Alexander the Great. The last Attalid king, Attalus III, died without issue and bequeathed the kingdom to the Roman Republic in 133 BC. Rome defeated Eumenes III, a pretender to the throne, in 129 BC and the former kingdom of Pergamum was made the Roman provice of Asia.

Until the Romans became the dominant power in the Mediterranean world, the Hellenistic period was essentially tripartite: Egypt, Syria and Macedonia, the kingdom of Pergamum being relatively insignificant. However, the Attalid kingdom should still be counted as one of the four horns. When the kingdom of Pergamon passed from the Attalids to Rome, this fourth horn ceased to represent the Attalids any more and represented Rome instead.

The Roman Empire is the sixth kingdom: "one is" (Rev. 17:10)

> **. . . they are also seven kings, five of whom have fallen, one is . . .** (Rev 17:10)

The interpreting angel tells John that one of the heads "**is**" and that "**five have fallen**". (Rev. 17: 10). The one that "is" can only be the Roman Empire, the empire prevalent at the time of John's prophecy.

The identification of Rome as the sixth head rules out any possibility that Rome is the Fourth Kingdom, for if one allocates the first two heads of the Beast to the Lion and the Bear respectively, the sixth head must by any reckoning be one of the four heads of the Leopard.

Even if one were to allocate two heads of the Beast to the Medo-Persian Empire (the Bear), Rome would still have to be reckoned as one of the four heads of the Leopard. It is a mistake, however, to allocate two heads to the Bear, despite the fact that the Medo-Persian Empire is represented by a Ram with two horns (Dan. 8:3). Not every horn of the Ram and He-Goat is represented by one of the heads of the Beast. This is evident from the fact that the great horn of the He-Goat which represents Alexander the Great is not represented by any one head of the Beast (but instead by the four heads of the Leopard). The seven heads of the Beast represent the seven heads of the four beasts that rise up from the sea in Daniel chapter 7, not the horns of chapter 8. The Bear (the Medo-Persian Empire) is clearly represented with only one head, for the Bear only has one mouth (Dan. 7:5).

The seventh kingdom represented by the seventh head of the Beast is to **remain only a little while** (Rev. 17:10). The Roman Empire lasted for well over a thousand years. Clearly, the Roman Empire is not the seventh kingdom represented by the seventh head.

The failure to realize that Rome is not the Fourth Kingdom is a huge stumbling block for some commentators, leading them to come to some absurd conclusions. For example, despite the fact that many correctly perceive that the seven heads of the Beast match the seven heads of the four beasts of Daniel that arise from the sea, commentators then state in their commentaries that the seven heads are not intended to represent any particular seven kingdoms. One can only assume that they arrive at this conclusion out of a false belief that the Fourth Beast was intended to represent the Roman Empire. Since the Roman Empire has fallen, they have to conclude that the seven heads of the Beast do not therefore refer to the actual kingdoms represented by the four Beasts of Daniel chapter 7.

The failure to realize that the Roman Empire is only the sixth head of the Beast has resulted in endless vain attempts to match the number of the Beast to Nero or some other Roman Emperor.

The Ottoman Empire is NOT one of the seven kingdoms

Despite being the successor to the Roman Empire through conquest, the Ottoman Empire is not to be counted as one of the seven heads of the Beast. The fall of Constantinople in 1453 at the hands of the Ottomans does indeed signify the fall of the sixth head, but the seventh head is the Russian Empire (and the subsequent Soviet Empire), NOT the Ottoman Empire.

Only collectively did the four heads of the Leopard constitute a great Kingdom (the Third). Individually, such Hellenistic kingdoms as Egypt or Macedonia did not really merit recognition as great kingdoms. It is only because collectively they comprised the former empire of Alexander the Great that they are to be counted parts of the Third Kingdom (the Leopard).

Despite the fact that it rivalled the Eastern Roman (Byzantine) Empire in size, the Ottoman Empire should not be reckoned the seventh head of the Beast. The Russian Empire soon dwarfed the Ottoman Empire in size and outlived the Ottoman Empire in the guise of the Soviet Union.

The large Turkish element in the Ottoman Empire means that the Ottoman Empire was not a Javanic empire, despite the large degree of intermarriage between the Turks and the Byzantines and despite the fact that to a certain extent the Ottoman Empire was a Turkish-Greek condominium.

4

DANIEL'S VISIONS OF THE FOUR BEASTS

Daniel's visions of the Four Kingdoms

The Statue

Daniel's first vision enabled him to interpret King Nebuchadnezzar's dream of the metallic image of a Statue of a man. The gold head represented King Nebuchadnezzar's kingdom, according to Daniel's interpretation of the dream, and hence the **Babylonian Empire**. The lower parts of the body represented successive empires.

The Statue can also be seen to represent Satan, as the seven heads of the Beast represent the seven heads of the great Red Dragon.

Four beasts rising from the sea

After this Daniel dreamed of four beasts rising from the sea: a Lion, a Bear, a Leopard, and a fearsome Fourth Beast with iron teeth and Ten Horns.

The Leopard has four heads, the other beasts have only one head. These seven heads are represented by the seven heads of the Beast (Rev. 13:1).

It can be inferred from the previous vision of the Statue that the first beast, the Lion, represents the **Babylonian Empire**.

Like the Beast of Revelation, Daniel's Fourth Beast has ten horns.

The Ram and He-goat

The third vision was of a Ram (with two horns) being trampled on by a He-goat. The interpreting angel tells us that the large horn from which spring out four more is the King of **Greece**, and that the Ram with two horns represents the kings of **Media and Persia**. From this vision we can infer that the Bear of the previous vision was therefore the Medo-Persian Empire, and that the Leopard represents the four subsequent Javanic (Greek) empires.

The two horns of the Ram indicate two kingdoms, but is represented by only one of the heads of the Beast because the Medo-Persian Empire was essentially a united kingdom. The two horns of the Ram, are a type for the ten horns of the Beast. The USSR was comprised of ten (allegedly) sovereign nations, but was ruled by just one man (or "king").

Further confirmation that the He-goat (Greece) represents the same nation as the Leopard is found in the repetition of the number four in the description of both the Leopard and the He-goat. As the leopard of the earlier vision has <u>four</u> heads and <u>four</u> wings, so the <u>four</u> horns which take the place of the he-goat's broken horn reach to the <u>four</u> winds of heaven. The four wings of the Leopard represent the four winds of heaven: "**there came up four conspicuous horns toward the four winds of heaven**" (Dan. 8:8).

Daniel identifies by name all the kingdoms that have already come into existence. Kingdoms that are yet to arise are not named, but sometimes alluded to as "king of the north" or "king of the south", for example.

The Little Horn of Dan. 8:9 is the Roman Empire, the fourth Javanic kingdom.

Daniel chapter 11 only prophesies events leading up to the fall of Jerusalem in 70AD

Chapter 11 does not touch upon the events that will occur under the Fourth Kingdom (the Beast and the Ten Horns). Those events are addressed in the Book of Revelation, and briefly in chapter 7 of Daniel.

The conclusion that the Beast is not alluded to in this chapter is supported by the fact that in chapter 10, the lead up to this chapter, the angel makes no mention of any nations other than the kingdom of Persia and the kingdom of Greece. Secondly, the angel states that he has come to make

Daniel understand what shall befall his people (i.e. the Jews) in the **latter days** (Dan. 10:14). This emphasis on the future of the Jews suggests that the "**latter days**" refers to the fall of Jerusalem rather than events which occur under the Beast which have universal significance. In coming to this conclusion, the author concurs with Philip Mauro. His book *The Seventy Weeks* is very informative regarding the history of this period, in particular the defeat of Mark Antony and Cleopatra and the fall of Jerusalem. Mauro shows how closely these events match the events prophesied in Daniel chapter 11.

Daniel chapter 11 prophesies events leading up to the destruction of Jerusalem in 70 AD at the hands of the Little Horn of Dan. 8:9, the Romans. It is solely concerned with the history of the four Javanic kingdoms and simply elucidates and builds upon the visions found in Daniel chapter 8 and 9. Neither of these two chapters touch upon events that occur under the Fourth Kingdom of the Beast. In focusing solely on the events that lead up to the fall of Jerusalem, chapter 11 of Daniel is only being consistent with the previous three chapters of Daniel: chapters 8, 9, and 10.

The desolation which the Romans bring upon Jerusalem lasts for one half-week:

> **. . . and upon the wing of abominations the one who brings desolation shall cause sacrifice and offering to cease for half of the week until the decreed pours down on the desolate.** (Dan. 9:27, *Author's translation*)

Verses in chapter 12 make it clear that there is yet a period of two half-weeks between the taking away of the "continual" (and the setting up of the abomination of desolation) and the first resurrection (Dan. 12:7, Dan. 12:11-12). It is during this period that the events that occur under the Beast take place.

There is confusion over this issue because so many commentators assume mistakenly that the Little Horn of Dan. 7:8 is the same as the Little Horn of Dan. 8:9. There are indeed similarities between these two horns, and one is surely a type for the other. Both Little Horns aggrandize themselves, both cause mass slaughter, and both rise up against the Prince of princes. However, they are not one and the same.

A further confusion is due to the fact that many commentators assume mistakenly that Rome is the Fourth Kingdom. Since Rome is the Little Horn of Dan. 8:9, and therefore the subject of much of chapter 11, it is easy to see how many conclude that verses in chapter 11 of Daniel allude to the Beast.

A brief commentary on Daniel chapters 11 and 12

The events that occur during the Persian Kingdom are quickly dismissed in one verse (Dan. 11:2).

In Dan. 11:4, the division of Alexander the Great's kingdom is prophesied in terms that are almost identical to those in Dan. 8:8. Here, it is worth pointing out that no mention is made later in chapter 11 of any Ten Horns, or of any uprooting of three of these Horns. The absence of such material is further confirmation that this chapter is not concerned with the events that occur under the Beast and the Fourth Kingdom which are prophesied in Daniel chapter 7.

The following verses (Dan. 11:5-20) deal with the Syrian Wars fought between the Egyptian Ptolemies and the Syrian Seleucids. At which precise point in Daniel chapter 11 the verses begin to refer to the Romans is difficult to pinpoint, but the author would tend to lean towards verse 21, for no other king arises to take the place of this king, whose end is alluded to in the final verse of this chapter (Dan. 11:45).

There can be no doubt that the one who profanes the Temple and who takes away the continual burnt offering (Dan. 11:31) is Rome.

The self-aggrandizement of the King (Dan. 11:36-37) is no doubt a type for the Beast himself, but refers to Rome, not the Beast. It should be remembered that the Little Horn of chapter 8 **magnified itself, even up to the Prince of the host** (Dan. 8:11). Not only did the Romans crucify Jesus, but the emperors were worshiped as gods under the imperial cult.

This king prospers **till the indignation is accomplished** (Dan. 11:36). It is plausible that this period of **indignation** endures for the entire period that the Jews are barred from their homeland in Israel. Since the "one who causes desolation" causes sacrifice and offering to cease for half a week (Dan. 9:27), it should perhaps be inferred that this kingdom ("king") will endure for the entire period of the diaspora. The Jews did not in fact begin to return to the Holy Land until around the time that the Ottoman Empire fell. The Roman Empire was indeed able to cause sacrifice and offering to cease "**for half a week**" because for much of this period, but not exclusively, the Roman/Byzantine Empire had been in control of the Holy Land.

The fact that this king becomes ruler over Egypt, Libya and Ethiopia (Dan. 11:43), again points to Rome which conquered these lands. Admittedly, Rome had become ruler of Eygpt before the overthrow of Jerusalem. These verses do not follow a strict chronological order, but are words of prophecy that are not to be mistaken for a work of modern history. Bearing this in mind, it is correct to conclude that the **prince of the covenant** who is swept away (Dan. 11:22) is the Messiah.

The fact that the Messiah is "swept away" (Dan. 11:22) may indicate that it is his end which **shall come with a flood** rather than that of the **prince who is to come** (Dan. 9:26). This would make the Messiah the most natural subject of the first verb in Dan. 9:27, the one who makes a strong covenant with many for one week (the New Covenant). If the **flood** refers to the demise of Rome, then the "flood" may be a reference to the fall of Constantinople in 1453.

Dan. 12:1 alludes to the fall of Jerusalem at the hands of the king who has set up his palatial tents near Jerusalem (Dan. 11:45). The immense suffering of the Jewish **nation** (Dan. 12:1) is alluded to. Again, this reference to the Jews points to the fall of Jerusalem, rather than the eschatological times during the reign of the Beast just before Christ's return.

The removal of the "continual" marks the commencement of the final week (the seventieth). The "continual" and the Temple service is restored 1290 days after its removal (Dan. 12:12). These 1290 days roughly coincide with the mid-point of the final week (for half-weeks in Revelation consist of 1260 days). This also concurs with Dan. 9:27 which prophesies that the "continual" will cease for half a week.

The final half-week is marked by the advent of the Little Horn (Trotzky/RSFSR), the Beast, into whose hands the saints will be given (Dan. 7:25) and by the restoration of the sacrificial system at the Temple in Jerusalem in 2370 (2300 **evenings and mornings** after the year 70 AD), shortly after this mid-point.

The first half-week of the seventieth week was a protracted half-week. Assuming that the final half-week is similarly protracted, the Beast's kingdom (a restored USSR) might endure for over a thousand years. However, since Christ warned that he would return at a time unexpected (Matt. 24:44), it would be foolish to assume that the second half-week will be of exactly the same length as the first. It may be that the second half-week reverts back to standard calendar years upon the restoration of the Temple, an event that might mark the return of the Sabbatical Year.

5

BRIEF HISTORY OF THE SEVEN KINGDOMS

Brief history of the kingdoms represented by the Beast

THE LION

1. Neo-Babylonian (Chaldean) Empire [625-539 BC]

King Nebuchadrezzar ruled for forty-four years, dying in 562 BC. His father, Nabopolassar, had founded the dynasty. There would only be six kings in total in the dynasty.

The last king, Nabonidus, appointed Belshazzar co-regent while he went off to make war. In 539 Babylon was conquered by a combined force of Persians and Medes.

THE BEAR

2. Medes and Persian (Achaemenid) Empire [539-330 BC]

Cyrus conquered Media in 550 BC with the surprise victory over Astyages, King of Media.

In 539 BC Cyrus conquered Babylonia.

The dynasty comprised eleven kings and lasted two centuries.

The Achaemenid Empire ruled over a greater percentage of the world's population than any other empire in history. Around 480 BC it ruled over 112.4 million people, 44% of the world's population.

THE LEOPARD

The four horns of the He-Goat

The four heads of the Leopard (Dan. ch. 7) equate to the four horns of the He-Goat (Dan. ch. 8).

After defeating Darius at the battle of Gaugamela in 331 BC, Alexander went on to capture the Persian capitals of Babylon, Susa, and Persepolis.

Alexander the Great's empire only lasted around ten years (332-323 BC) as he died very young, having conquered most of the known world. His heirs were murdered shortly after his death.

The division of his kingdom is prophesied in several places in Daniel:

> **After this I looked, and lo, another, like a leopard, with four wings of a bird on its back; and the beast had four heads; and dominion was given to it.** (Dan. 7:6)

The Leopard with its four heads represents the four empires that will arise out of Greece (Javan) after the fall of Alexander the Great's short-lived empire.

In a later vision, the prophet Daniel sees Alexander the Great represented as a great horn between the eyes of a He-goat. This horn is broken and in its place four more horns arise, which represent four more empires that will arise out of Greece/Javan:

> **As for the horn that was broken, in place of which four others arose, four kingdoms shall arise from his nation, but not with his power.** (Dan. 8:22)

(The division of Alexander's kingdom is again prophesied later in Dan. 11:3.)

The four horns of the He-goat, which replace of the "great" horn of Alexander the Great, come up "**toward the four winds of heaven**" (Dan.

8:8). These winds correspond to the four wings on the back of the Leopard with four heads because wings and wind are often associated together in the Bible. (For example: **. . . he came swiftly upon the wings of the wind . . .** (Ps.18:10)/**A wind has wrapped them in its wings . . .** (Hos. 4:19)/ **The wind was in their wings . . .** (Zech. 5:9)/ **. . . who ridest on the wings of the wind . . .** (Ps.104:3)).

The tripartite territorial division of the Hellenistic age was in place by the end of the Wars of the Successors (323-281 BC), with the main Hellenistic powers being Macedon under Demetrius's son Antigonus II Gonatas, the Ptolemaic kingdom under the aged Ptolemy I and the Seleucid kingdom under Seleucus' son Antiochus I Soter. All three kingdoms were eventually defeated by Rome, the fourth Javanic kingdom.

3. Antigonid kingdom of Macedonia [306-168 BC]

Succeeding the Antipatrid dynasty in much of Macedonia, Antigonus ruled mostly over Asia Minor and northern Syria. His attempts to take control of the whole of Alexander's empire led to his defeat and death at the Battle of Ipsus in 301 BC. Antigonus's son Demetrius I Poliorcetes survived the battle, and managed to seize control of Macedon itself a few years later, but eventually lost his throne, dying as a prisoner of Seleucus I Nicator. After a period of confusion, Demetrius's son Antigonus II Gonatas was able to establish the family's control over the old Kingdom of Macedon, as well as over most of the Greek city-states, by 276 BC.

The Macedonian kingdom was the first Successor kingdom to be threatened by Rome. Perseus (179-168 BC) was unable to stop the advancing Roman legions and was defeated at the Battle of Pydna in 168 during the Third Macedonian War. The Antagonid dynasty was terminated and partitioned into four republics. A pretender to the throne forced the Romans to crush a rebellion in 148 BC.

4. Seleucid kingdom of Syria [312-63 BC]

Seleucus I Nicator founded the dynasty.

Having come into conflict in the east (305 BC) with Chandragupta Maurya of the Maurya Empire, Seleucus I entered into an agreement with Chandragupta whereby he ceded vast territory west of the Indus, including the Hindu Kush, modern-day Afghanistan, and the Balochistan province of Pakistan and offered his daughter in marriage to the Maurya Emperor to formalize the alliance.

Antiochus III the Great attempted to project Seleucid power and authority into Hellenistic Greece, but his attempts were thwarted by the Roman Republic and by Greek allies such as the Kingdom of Pergamon, culminating in a Seleucid defeat at the 190 BC Battle of Magnesia. In the subsequent Treaty of Apamea in 188 BC, the Seleucids were compelled to pay costly war reparations and relinquished claims to territories west of the Taurus Mountains.

The Parthians under Mithridates I of Parthia conquered much of the remaining eastern part of the Seleucid Empire in the mid-2nd century BC, while the independent Greco-Bactrian Kingdom continued to flourish in the northeast. However, the Seleucid kings continued to rule a rump state from Syria until the invasion by the Armenian king, Tigranes the Great, in 83 BC.

The Seleucid Empire's centre was Antioch in Syria. The Maccabees fought against the Syrians for twenty-five years to obtain independence.

Seleucid attempts to defeat their old enemy Ptolemaic Egypt were frustrated by Roman demands. The Roman generals Lucullus and Pompey the Great made an end to the Seleucid kingdom. The last king was dethroned in 64 BC.

In the book of Daniel, chapter 11, the Seleucid kingdom is denoted as the "king of the North".

5. Ptolemaic kingdom of Egypt [305-30 BC]

Ptolemy was appointed satrap of Egypt after Alexander's death in 323 BC. In 305 BC, he declared himself Ptolemy I, later known as "Saviour". The Egyptians soon accepted the Ptolemies as the successors to the pharaohs of independent Egypt. Ptolemy's family ruled Egypt until the Roman conquest of 30 BC.

Alexandria was the capital of the Ptolemaic empire.

The Ptolemaic dynasty ended in 30 BC with the defeat of Antony and Cleopatra at the Battle of Actium at the hands of Octavian who shortly afterwards became the first Roman Emperor, known as Caesar Augustus.

In the book of Daniel, chapter 11, the Ptolemaic kingdom is denoted as the "king of the South". The fact that the "king of the south" refers to the Ptolemaic rulers of Egypt is made explicit in Dan. 11:8.

6. Roman Republic/Empire

Roman Republic (bequeathed the Attalid kingdom of Pergamum in 133 *BC*) [133 *BC*-27 *BC*]/Roman Empire [27 *BC*- 1453]

The Roman Republic was allegedly founded in 753 BC (*ab urbe condita*).

Although the Roman Republic had conquered the Maecdonians in the Fourth Macedonian War in 148 BC and the Achaean League at the Battle of Corinth in 146 BC , surely it can only be counted as one of the four horns that arise in place of the Great Horn that represents Alexander the Great through its inheritance of the Attalid kingdom of Pergamum in 133 BC. Initially the Romans had no part in Alexander the Great's empire nor in the Diadoch Wars fought between the Macedonian generals who had served in Alexander's army.

From the accession of Caesar Augustus to the military anarchy of the third century, the Roman Empire was a principate with Rome as sole capital.

In an effort to stabilize the Empire, Diocletian set up two different imperial courts in the Greek East and Latin West in 286. The two emperors shared rule over the Western Roman Empire (based in Milan and later in Ravenna) and over the Eastern Roman Empire (based in Nicomedia and later in Constantinople).

Christians rose to positions of power in the 4th century following the Edict of Milan of 313.

Large invasions by Germanic peoples and by the Huns of Attila, led to the decline of the Western Roman Empire.

The city of Rome had remained the nominal capital of both parts until the fall of Ravenna to the Germanic Herulians. With the deposition of Romulus Augustulus in AD 476 by Odoacer, the Western Roman Empire finally collapsed and the imperial insignia were sent to Constantinople. The (Eastern Roman) emperor Zeno formally abolished the Western Roman Empire in AD 480.

The Eastern Roman Empire, (the "Byzantine Empire"), survived for another millennium until the Empire's last remains collapsed when Constantinople fell to the Ottoman Turks of Sultan Mehmed II in 1453.

Coincidentally, the USSR (the eighth kingdom) arose in the dying days of the Ottoman Empire.

THE FOURTH BEAST: RUSSIA

7. Russia [1478-1917]

Ivan III (1462-1505) threw off the Mongol yoke and conquered most of the other Russian states. His son Vasili III completed the task of uniting all of Russia by eliminating the last few independent states in the 1520s. His son Grand Duke Ivan IV (Ivan the Terrible) was proclaimed the first Russian Tsar in 1547.

Though the empire was only officially proclaimed by Tsar Peter I following the Treaty of Nystad (1721), some historians would argue that it was truly born when Ivan III conquered Veliky Novgorod in 1478.

After the Mongol Empire, the Russian Empire was the next largest contiguous empire the world had ever seen. In 1895 it encompassed 15% of the earth's landmass, nearly five times greater in extent that the Ottoman Empire.

The Workers' and Peasants' Government (or communist government) of the Russian Soviet Republic is "the Beast that was" together with the Workers' and Peasants' Governments of the other Union Republics which are the Ten Horns.

The USSR is the eighth kingdom, the Beast that was and is not and is to come.

6

THE BEAST THAT WAS: THE USSR [1922-1991]

The Beast that was

The USSR (1922-1991) is "the Beast that **was**".

Its collapse is a deception, designed to lull the West into a false sense of security so that it reduces its expenditure on nuclear weapons and weakens its military stance. The Soviet strategists hope to destroy NATO and Finlandize the European Union.

The extent of the First Soviet Empire

The First Soviet Empire (1922-1991) was comprised of four groups:

- the USSR (the Beast and the Ten Horns);
- the Eastern Bloc states;
- Marxist-Leninist states who were allied with the Soviet Union but not part of the Warsaw Pact;
- Third World countries which had pro-Soviet governments.

The Second Soviet Empire will have complete world domination, with control over all nations of the earth.

The subject peoples and nations of these communist governments were captive in the sense that they were often not communists themselves and were deprived of any democratic rights.

The Eastern bloc countries were occupied or had a period of being occupied by Soviet Army. Their politics, military, foreign and domestic policies were dominated by the Soviet Union:

- People's Socialist Republic of Albania (1946–1991)
- People's Republic of Bulgaria (1946–1990)
- Czechoslovak Socialist Republic (1948–1990)
- German Democratic Republic (1949–1990)
- Hungarian People's Republic (1949–1989)
- Polish People's Republic (1947–1989)
- Socialist Republic of Romania (1947–1989)
- Federal People's Republic of Yugoslavia (1948–1991)

Marxist-Leninist states who were allied with the Soviet Union:

- Democratic Republic of Afghanistan (1979–1987)
- People's Republic of Angola (1975–1991)
- People's Republic of Benin (1975–1990)
- People's Republic of China (1949–1991)
- People's Republic of the Congo (1969–1991)
- Republic of Cuba (1960–1991)
- Provisional Military Government of Socialist Ethiopia, then People's Democratic Republic of Ethiopia (1974–1991)
- People's Republic of Kampuchea (1979–1989)
- Democratic People's Republic of Korea (1945–1991, also allied with China)
- Lao People's Democratic Republic (1975–1991)
- Mongolian People's Republic (1924–1991)
- People's Republic of Mozambique (1975–1990)
- Somali Democratic Republic (1969–1977)
- Tuvan People's Republic (1921–1944)
- Democratic Republic of Vietnam (1945–1976), then Socialist Republic of Vietnam (1976–1991)
- People's Democratic Republic of Yemen (South Yemen) (1967–1990)

Third World countries with pro-Soviet governments:

- Algeria (1962–1990)
- People's Republic of Bangladesh (1971–1975)
- Burkina Faso (1983–1987)
- Burma (1962–1988)
- Cambodia (1975–1979)
- Cape Verde (1975–1990)
- Chile (1970–1973)
- Egypt (1954–1973)
- Ghana (1964–1966)
- People's Revolutionary Government of Grenada (1979–1983)
- Guinea (1960–1978)
- Guinea Bissau (1973–1991)
- Equatorial Guinea (1968–1979)
- India (1971–1989)
- Indonesia (1959–1965)
- Iraq (1958–1963; 1968–1991)
- Libya (1969–1991)
- Democratic Republic of Madagascar (1972–1991)
- Mali (1960–1968)
- Nicaragua (1979–1990)
- Peru (1968–1975)
- Sao Tome and Principe (1975–1991)
- Seychelles (1977–1991)
- Somali Democratic Republic (1969–1977)
- Sudan (1968–1972)
- Syria (1955–1991)

Brief history of "the Beast that was" (the USSR)

The USSR was formed on 28 December 1922 when delegations from the Russian SFSR, the Transcaucasian SFSR, the Ukrainian SSR and the Byelorussian SSR approved the Treaty on the Creation of the USSR and the Declaration of the Creation of the USSR.

The Bolsheviks had established the Soviet State on 7 November [O.S. 25 October, hence the phrase "October Revolution"] 1917. (During the period between the revolution of February 1917 and the revolution of November 1917, the former Russian Empire was known as the Russian Republic.)

Initially, the Soviet state did not have an official name. Some coined the mocking label "Sovdepia" for the nascent state of the "Soviets of Workers' and Peasants' Deputies". On 10 July 1918, the Russian Constitution of 1918 renamed the country the Russian Socialist Federative Soviet Republic (formerly, the Soviet Russian Republic).

For most of the Soviet Period there were in fact fifteen Soviet Socialist Republics, three of which were the illegally occupied Baltic States (Lithuania, Latvia and Estonia) which some states did not recognize as Soviet Republics.

The Soviet Republics were:

- Azerbaijan SSR
- Belarus SSR
- Kazakhstan SSR
- Kyrgyzstan SSR
- Armenia SSR
- Moldova SSR
- Russia SFSR
- Tajikstan SSR
- Turkmenistan SSR
- Uzbekistan SSR
- Georgia SSR
- Ukraine SSR

The three Baltic States, which were not recognized internationally, were:

- Estonia SSR
- Latvia SSR
- Lithuania SSR

The maximum extent in terms of landmass of the USSR was 22.3 million square kilometres in 1945, a marginally smaller area than the Russian Empire, but still ranking it second (with the Russian Empire) in terms of the world's largest empires. Finland and Poland had both been swallowed up by the Russian Empire, but remained independent after the Russian Revolution.

The dissolution of the Soviet Union occurred on December 26, 1991.

The Beast's kingdom: a divided kingdom

> **And as you saw the feet and toes partly of potter's clay and partly of iron, it shall be a divided kingdom** . . . (Dan. 2:41)

The Beast is a divided kingdom.

Daniel's interpretation of Nebuchadnezzar's dream about the huge Statue informs us that the Fourth Kingdom will be a divided kingdom, just as the feet and toes of the Statue are mixed with iron and clay (Dan. 2:40-43).

Similarly, Daniel also interpreted the word UPHARSIN, written on the wall at Belshazzar's feast, to mean that Belshazzar's kingdom would be divided betwen the Medes and the Persians. The Ram that signified the Medes and Persians was portrayed with two horns in the same way that the Beast of Revelation has a multiple of horns.

In theory, though not so often in practise, the Soviet Union should have been ruled over by all the nations that comprise the Soviet Union. The leaders of the Communist Party did indeed in fact display some variation in nationality: Lenin was a Russian. Stalin was a Georgian. Khrushchev, Brezhnev and Chernenko were all Ukrainian by birth. Gorbachev was born in the USSR, but had both Russian and Ukrainian ancestry. Andropov's true nationality is harder to discern, but he was considered to be of Russian birth.

A **divided kingdom** is a particularly apt description of the USSR. The USSR was not just divided into several Union Republics based on ethnicity, but which was also divided by religion and language. Several of the Union republics were predominantly Muslim, while others were predominantly Orthodox. This same division over religion exists among the nations of the Commonwealth of Independent States. The USSR was made up of many nations and peoples, each with their own language.

Pre-1917 Russia was an imperial state, not a nation. The many non-Russian ethnic groups that inhabited the Russian Empire were classified as aliens. In the early Soviet period, assimilation was actively discouraged, and the promotion of national self-consciousness of the non-Russia population was attempted. Each officially recognized ethnic minority, however small, was granted its own national territory where it enjoyed a certain degree of autonomy, with national schools. A written national language, native-language press, and books written in the native language came with the territory.

After the establishment of the Soviet Union with the boundaries of the former Russian Empire, the Bolshevik government began the process of national delimitation and nation building, a project that attempted to build nations out of the numerous ethnic groups in the Soviet Union. Stalin's work *Marxism and the National Question* became the cornerstone of the Soviet policy toward nationalities, defining a nations as "a historically constituted, stable community of people, formed on the basis of a common language, territory, economic life, and psychological makeup manifested in a common culture." The process relied on the *Declaration of the Rights of the Peoples of Russia*, adopted by the Bolshevik government on 15 November 1917, which recognized the equality and sovereignty of the peoples of Russia.

The Soviet Union was established in 1922 as a federation of nationalities, which eventually came to encompass 15 major national territories, each organized as a Union-level republic.

Russia, the largest republic, was ethnically the most diverse and was constituted as the RSFSR, the Russian Soviet Federative Socialist Republic, a federation within a federation. In the early 1920s the Russian SFSR was divided into some 30 autonomous ethnic territories (Autonomous Soviet Socialist Republics (ASSRs) and autonomous oblasts (AOs), many of which exist to this day as ethnic republics within the Russian Federation. There was also a very large number of lower-level ethnic territories, such as national districts and national village soviets.

The exact number of ASSRs and AOs varied over the years as new entities were created while old entities switched from one form to another, transformed into Union-level republics (e.g. Kazakh and Kyrgyz SSR created in 1936, Moldovan SSR created in 1940,) or were absorbed into larger territories (e.g. Crimean ASSR absorbed into the RSFSR in 1945 and Volga German ASSR absorbed into the RSFSR in 1941).

The first population census of the USSR in 1926 listed 176 distinct nationalities. Eliminating excessive detail (e.g. four ethnic groups for Jews and five ethnic groups for Georgians) and omitting very small ethnic groups, the list was condensed into 69 nationalities, which lived in 45 nationally delimited territories, including 16 Union-level republics (SSRs) for the major nationalities, 23 autonomous regions (18 ASSRs and 5 AOs) for other nationalities within the Russian SFSR, and 6 autonomous regions within other Union-level republics (one in Uzbek SSR, one in Azerbaijan SSR, one in Tajik SSR, and three in Georgian SSR).

The different nations of the USSR might intermarry, but unlike the United States of America with its motto "ex pluribus unum", the Soviet Union was no mixing-pot. The different nationalities within the Soviet Union were deliberately encouraged to retain their own national identity and language. The Union Republics consequently did not mix together to form one strongly united nation. The USSR was not just divided ethnically, but also by language, culture and religion. This division was an intentional part of the process called "national delimitation", the process of creating well-defined national territorial units. It is this division of the Fourth Kingdom (Russia/USSR) into small territorial units based on nationality which is the cause of the "weakness" of this kingdom. These nations will not hold together to form one strong united whole. The result of this weakness was the collapse of the Soviet Union in 1991 and its division into independent nations, most of which became members of the Commonwealth of Independent States.

The division of the USSR by language was manifest in the USSR's State Emblem in which the words "Workers of All Countries, Unite!" are written in the language of each Union Republic.

7

THE BEAST THAT IS NOT (THE C.I.S)

The Ten Kings: currently ten member states of the CIS

> **. . . ten kings who have not yet received royal power, but they are to receive authority as kings for one hour, together with the beast.** (Rev. 17:12)

The Commonwealth of Independent States (CIS) should be perceived as the Beast "**that is not**". It comprises most of the former SSRs of the Soviet Union.

The CIS is an organization that exists in the interim period between the Beast that was and the Beast that is to come.

Before the so-called "collapse" of the Soviet Union, Mikhail Gorbachev had proposed a reorganization of the USSR under the name of "The Union of Sovereign States". The proposal was never implemented in the wake of the August 1991 Coup and the dissolution of the Soviet Union that year. The overall proposal was resurrected as the Commonwealth of Independent States (CIS), as a regional organization, not a confederation.

The Commonwealth of Independent States was founded on 8 December 1991 by the Byelorussia SSR, the Russian SFSR, and the Ukraine SSR, when the leaders of these three republics met in Belarus and signed the "Agreement Establishing the Commonwealth of Independent States", known as the *Creation Agreement*. The Belavezha Accords declared that the Soviet Union was ceasing to exist and proclaimed the CIS in its place.

The Alma-Ata Protocol declared that the Soviet Union was dissolved and that the Russian Federation was to be its successor state. The Baltic States (Estonia, Latvia, and Lithuania), which regard their membership with the Soviet Union as an illegal occupation, chose not to participate in the CIS.

Georgia withdrew it membership of the CIS in 2008, while Ukraine, which participated as an Associate state, announced in 2018 that it would end its participation in CIS statutory bodies.

There are currently nine full members and one Associate Member (Turkmenistan), which makes ten.

- Azerbaijan
- Belarus
- Kazakhstan
- Kyrgyzstan
- Armenia
- Moldova
- Russian Federation
- Tajikstan
- Uzbekistan
- Turkmenistan (Associate Member)

Georgia and Ukraine were former member states:

- Georgia
- Ukraine

Georgia left the organisation in 2009. On 19 May 2018, President Poroshenko signed a decree formally ending Ukraine's participation in the CIS. In Moldova, legislative initiatives to denounce the agreement on the creation of the CIS have been tabled due to Russia's support for the independence of breakaway regions within Moldova, Georgia, and Ukraine, and due to its violation of the Istanbul Agreement.

Moscow's real reason for attacking Georgia was to prevent Georgia joining NATO.

The "bending poles" of the Emblem of the Commonwealth of Independent States resemble toes

The Emblem of the Commonwealth of Independent States (*below*) is a yellow sun on a dark blue field, with eight bending poles holding the sun.

The design allegedly symbolizes the desire for equal partnership, unity, peace and stability.

It is remarkable how similar these "bending poles" look like toes, echoing the dream of the Nebuchadnezzar of the Statue with ten toes. Each "bending pole" gets small the further removed it is from the sun, just as the toes on feet get smaller as they get further from the big toes. Despite the fact that the "bending poles" appear to be cupping the sun like the fingers of a hand, they look more like toes than fingers.

These toes also appear rather like horns because they bend inwards, just like the horns of a bull, particularly the two central ones which resemble big toes. The horn-like appearance of the "poles" remind one of the ten horns of the Fourth Beast.

No doubt the designer of the Emblem did not want the "bending poles" to appear to resemble toes, for he decided to opt for four "bending poles" on either side, with one in the middle, to make nine instead of ten. Yet at its inception the CIS consisted of ten former Soviet Republics: Armenia, Belarus, Kazakhstan, Kyrgyzstan, Moldova, Russia, Tajikstan, Turkmenistan, Ukraine, and Uzbekistan.

There are only eight toes on the Emblem, plus a central "pole" which alone does not form the shape of a toe or horn. Instead the sun seems to rest just above it in place of a toe. This central toe/horn has echoes of the "small horn" which will arise from among the ten horns of Daniel.

The Emblem of the CIS seems to contain allusions to the prophecy of Daniel and Revelation in an uncanny way. Not only is the central "pole" symbolic of the "small horn", but the fact that the other toes/horns surround it suggests the alliance of these horns and their handing over of their sovereignty to the little horn, the Beast. In the CIS Emblem, the little "pole" is equated to the sun, for instead of a toe, the sun is at its end. This would suggest universal worship of the Beast who occupies the place of the sun.

There is an absence of any reference to God, or spiritual things however, and the overall image is materialistic. Mikhail Gorbachev has been recorded saying:

> I believe in the cosmos. All of us are linked to the cosmos. Look at the sun. If there is no sun, then we cannot exist. So nature is my god. To me, nature is sacred. Trees are my temples and forests my cathedrals.

The "bending poles" can also be interpreted as forming the branches of a tree, a tree that like the one in Nebuchadnezzar's dream may grow to dominate the whole earth. The central "pole" is like the central ring of the concentric rings of the section of a tree.

The CIS emblem is clearly meant to be the antithesis of the former Soviet emblem. Where the Soviet Emblem appeared aggressive and domineering, the CIS emblem appears to be a symbol of peace and fraternity, a cup holding light, the sun being warmth for humanity. There are, however, echoes in it of the emblem of Soviet Union with its Hammer and Sickle and Red Star. Where before ears of wheat framed the earth, now "bending poles" frame the sun. In the former Soviet emblem, the sun shed its rays of light on the earth in the former Soviet emblem. (In Hebrew, "ray of light" is *qeren*, whch also means "horn"). In the CIS emblem, the earth is represented by a tree, the "bending poles" resembling the branches of a tree.

It is possible to see the "bending pole" as a synthesis of the Hammer and Sickle. Like horns, these toes bend round to cradle the sun, thus appearing somewhat sickle-like. Instead of tapering off like a sickle to a narrow point, these "bending poles" are more club-like at the end, to make them more like hammers. The straight upright parts of the "bending poles" are the handles. Instead of the single Hammer and Sickle of the former USSR emblem, there are now therefore several Hammer and Sickles in this new emblem.

The toes surround the sun, just as the planets of our solar system rotate around the sun. The central "pole" beneath the sun, which does not bend, may represent the planet Mars, which like the sun, will illuminate the whole world. Here then, may be a reference to Marx, along with the "bending poles" which may also represent Karl Marx through their being a new form of the Hammer and Sickle.

The "bending-poles" resemble snakes to some degree which is apt given that Marduk's sickle was originally a snake.

The Soviet and CIS emblems echo Joseph's dreams

> **. . . my sheaf arose and stood upright, and behold, your sheaves gathered round it, and bowed down to my sheaf.** (Gen. 37:7)

The design of the Soviet and CIS emblems echo Joseph's dreams about his preeminence over his fellow brothers.

The emblems of both the Soviet Union and the CIS echo Joseph's two dreams: one about his brothers' sheaves of wheat bowing down before his sheaf and the other about the stars, sun and moon bowing down before him:

> **" . . . and behold, the sun, the moon, and eleven stars were bowing down to me."** (Gen. 37:9)

The central pole in the CIS emblem would represent Joseph; in the Soviet Emblem the Red Star would represent Joseph, with the sheaves of wheat bowing down before it and the sun beneath it to indicate worship.

8

THE BEAST THAT IS TO COME (USSR REDIVIVUS)

Astonishment at the Beast to come

> **The dwellers on earth . . . will marvel to behold the beast, because it was and is not and is to come.** (Rev. 17:8)

The Beast's ascension from the abyss will inaugurate the kingdom "that is to come", the restoration of the USSR. The Beast's ascension from the abyss associates the Beast with Satan himself.

The restoration of the USSR will be to the amazement of mankind.

The Beast will be invincible in war

> **"Who is like the beast, and who can fight against it?"** (Rev. 13:4).

The Russian Federation already has one of the largest stockpile of nuclear weapons in the world, the second largest fleet of ballistic missile submarines, and the only modern strategic bomber force outside the United States. Russia's tank force is the largest in the world, while its surface navy and air force are among the largest.

Russia, along with China, have a lead over the United States in hypersonic weapons. These missile systems deliver a warhead at speeds greater than five times the speed of sound (faster than 3,800 mph). The United States is yet to deploy such a weapon.

The speed of China's DF-17 missile is such that no defence against this weapon exists.

China's DF-41 intercontinental ballistic missile is the most powerful ICBM in the world, overtaking the Russian SS-18 Satan ICBM in capability. The United States has nothing comparable, at least in terms of ground-launched equivalents.

The Second Soviet Empire will have authority over the whole earth. This universal rule is matched only by that of the Son of Man's kingdom that is to follow (Dan. 7:14).

Russia has around 1550 nuclear warheads, and enough supersonic SS-27 intercontinental missiles to deliver them through the present defenses of the United States, Japan, and Europe. It has the wherewithal to destroy any region in the world.

Russia is currently developing Poseidon 2M39, a nuclear-armed and nuclear-powered 'apocalypse mega-torpedo', the biggest torpedo ever built. Virtually undetectable, the torpedo's explosion could produce a giant tsunami offshore which would swamp cities with radioactive waves.

The Fourth Beast's crushing conquests are prophesied in Daniel with these words:

> . . . . **it shall devour the whole earth, and trample it down, and break it to pieces** (Dan. 7:23).

The Beast will kill the Two Lampstands (the two prophets)

> **"And I will grant my two witnesses power to prophesy for one thousand two hundred and sixty days, clothed in sackcloth." (Rev. 11:3)**

The Beast makes war on the two Lampstands, conquers them and kills them. (Rev. 11:7). As elsewhere in Revelation, these two Lampstands do not only signify one thing. The Lampstands represent the two prophets, but they also represent two churches. This interpretation is consistent with Rev. 1:20, where the seven Lampstands are interpreted as the seven churches in Asia.

The making war and conquest of the two churches in Rev. 11:7 is consistent again with Daniel:

> **As I looked, this horn made war with the saints, and prevailed over them . . .** (Dan. 7:21).

The two Lampstands also signify therefore the **saints** against whom the Beast makes war.

This period of persecution of the saints is given as **time, times and half a time** (Dan. 7:25) and corresponds to the **wonders** of Dan. 12:6 which endures for the same period of time. When this **shattering of the power of the holy people** comes to an end, all will be accomplished (Dan. 12:7).

The Beast: possible agent of the last two Woes

> **"Woe, woe, woe to those who dwell on the earth, at the blasts of the other trumpets . . . "** (Rev 8:13).

The fifth, six, and seventh trumpet blows bring forth the three Woes.

The fact that the Beast arises from the bottomless pit (Rev. 17:8, Rev. 11:7)) in the same way that the smoke did from which the **locusts** of the First Woe emerged (Rev. 9:2). However, there are similarities between Abaddon, the king of these locusts, and the destroying angel of Exodus who killed the firstborn throughout the land of Egypt. The destroying angel left the firstborn of the Hebrews in Egypt untouched, just as in Revelation those who are sealed are not harmed by the locusts that arise from the abyss.

Perhaps though it is possible that the locusts that come forth out of the smoke might be helicopters, with some kind of nerve agent that afflicts mankind with intense suffering for five months. The **crowns of gold** (Rev. 9:7) may be the rotors of these helicopters.

The result of the sixth trumpet blow is the death of a third of mankind at the hands of a vast multitude of troops of cavalry of the Beast:

> **By these three plagues a third of mankind was killed, by the fire and smoke and sulphur issuing from their mouths.** (Rev. 9:18)

The description of the **troops of cavalry** of the Second Woe is one of tanks. Two hundred million of them (Rev. 9:16). Their colour, the colour of fire, smoke and sulphur, is camouflage, enabling these tanks to hide amidst the fire and smoke that they create. The heads of the **horses** were like lions' heads. These lions' heads represent the turrets of a tank, and the breastplates are the armour of the tank itself. Their **tales** have **heads** from which is issued fire, smoke and sulphur (Rev. 9:19). This is a description of the main gun of a tank with its muzzle brake. A muzzle brake is a device connected to the barrel of a firearm or cannon that is intended to redirect a portion of propellant gases to counter recoil and unwanted muzzle rise. The muzzle brake redirects and controls the burst of combustion gases that follows the departure of a projectile. The power of the horses' mouths are machine guns that a placed in the cupola of tanks.

The description of the locusts of the First Woe and the cavalry of the Second Woe are in similar terms which further casts doubt on whether the locusts of the First Woe should be seen as demonic beings but the cavalry as actual military forces. Both are like horses; both have breastplates; one has lions' teeth, the other the heads of a lion.

The utter destruction wrought by these troops of cavalry tallies with the description of the Fourth Beast in Daniel (the Beast of Revelation):

> **. . . and behold, a fourth beast, terrible and dreadful and exceedingly strong; and it had great iron teeth; it devoured and broke in pieces, and stamped the residue with its feet.** (Dan. 7:7)

It can be inferred that these troops of cavalry are the Beast's because the Second Woe is not said to have passed until the Beast that ascends from the bottomless pit has made war on the two Lampstands which symbolize the two prophets (Rev. 11:14). The Beast is not introduced properly until chapter 13 of Revelation, and yet features in chapter 11.

The fall of Babylon the Great brings forth the cry "Woe, woe" three times from kings, merchants, and shipmasters respectively (Rev. 18:10,16,19). This triple cry of woe suggests that the Third Woe may well be this destruction of Babylon the Great at the hands of the Beast and the Ten Kings.

That the Beast may be the agent is also suggested in Rev. 12:12: **woe to you, O earth and sea**, words uttered because the devil has been thrown down to earth. Since the seven-headed Dragon is embodied in the Beast to whom Satan has given his power, throne, and authority (Rev. 13:2), the Beast could well be the cause of all this woe.

The seven bowls of wrath are poured out during the reign of the Beast himself

The first of the seven bowls of wrath causes foul and evil sores to break out on those men who bore the mark of the Beast. This limits the period during which the seven bowls are poured out to the reign of the Beast, for the command to be receive the mark is issued during the reign of the Beast himself by the False Prophet and not before.

It is clear that the days of the bowls cannot refer to any period prior to the reign of the Beast, for reference is even made to the **throne** of the Beast and his **kingdom** with the pouring out of the fifth bowl (Rev. 16:10).

The bowls are retribution for shedding the blood of the saints and prophets, killed presumably for not being marked with the number of the Beast and failing to conform in the worship of the Beast and his image.

Part Two

LENIN IS THE BEAST

9

LENIN IS THE BEAST

ην και ουκ εστιν= איננה, (*einenah:* "is not") =Lenin

. . . .the beast that was and is not . . . . (Rev. 17:11)

The Beast is consistently referred to as the Beast "**that was and is not.** The phrase is repeated three times to describe the Beast in chapter 17 of Revelation from which one can infer that that the name of the Beast might be derived from this phrase.

The Greek word ην ("was") sounds like the Hebrew word *ein* אין which means "not". The Hebrew word for "is not" (with a suffix that agrees with the feminine noun *cheivah*) is based on the same word: איננה (*einenah).* The phrase και ουκ εστιν may therefore be a pointer to the name "Lenin" given that the Aramaic word for "eyes" (*ayneen*) seem also to refer to "Lenin.

The following table illustrates the pattern found in chapter 17 regarding this phrase.

Rev. 17:8	ην και ουκ εστιν	και μελλει αναβαινειν
Rev. 17:8	ην και ουκ εστιν	και παρεσται
Rev. 17:11	ην και ουκ εστιν	και αυτος ογδοος εστιν

It is reasonable to perceive an allusion to a name in the the phrase "**was and is not**" because it echoes the passage in Exodus where God's personal name is explained as being based upon the verb "to be":

> **God said to Moses, "I AM WHO I AM." And he said to Moses, "Say this to the people of Israel, 'I AM has sent me to you.'" God also said to Moses, "Say this to the people of Israel, 'The LORD** (YHWH), **the god of your fathers. . .'** (Ex. 3:14-15)

In the Septuagint, , **"I AM WHO I AM"** (Ex. 3:14) is translated as simply 'o Ων "The BEING". The word Ων (*on*)sounds like ην ("was"), and both words are derived from the Greek verb that means "to be". The irony is that the wordplay based on Lenin's name signifies "unbeing", the antithesis of what God's personal name means. This point is all the more manifest in the Hebrew translation of the phrase "**is not**": אינגה, *(einenah),* a word which may also be an allusion to the name "Lenin".

As mentioned above, theAramaic word "eyes" עינין (*aynin*), found in Dan. 7:8, is alluded to in the Greek of Revelation, when the Beast is described as the Beast "**that was and is not**": ην και ουκ εστιν. The first word in this phrase (ην "was") sound like *aynin* ("eyes") and the Hebrew for "**is not**" (ουκ εστιν) is *einenah* (אינגה), which is also an allusion to the name "Lenin".

If it is correct to identify in the name "Lenin" with the phrase "**was and is not**", then it would suggest that not only will the USSR return, but that Lenin will return too. This reappearance will not be a resurrected Lenin, but a man whose actions resemble those of Lenin will appear. John the Baptist was not a resurrected Elijah, and yet fulfilled the prophecy of Malachi:

> **"Behold, I will send you Elijah the prophet before the great and terrible day of the Lord comes."** (Mal. 4:5)

Lenin did receive a seemingly fatal wound when he was shot by Fania Kaplan. The **sword** (Rev. 13:14) could represent this assassination attempt. The sword also refers figuratively to the Cold War.

The Hammer and Sickle represents Hebrew and Greek letters

> **This calls for wisdom: let him who has understanding reckon the number of the beast, for it is a number of a man, his number is six hundred and sixteen.** (Rev. 13:18) (*Author's translation*)

It is important to realize that the mark of the Beast can only be comprised of those four letters which signify the number 616 in Hebrew (TRTZ). The recognition of any letters in addition to these four obviates the interpretation that the Hammer and Sickle represents the number 616 or any number at all. Any other letters of the Hebrew alphabet that one might be able to perceive in the emblem must be ignored. Failure to do so undermines the whole premise that the Hammer and Sickle represents the number 616. To put it another way: the mark of the Beast can only b comprised of the four Hebrew letters TAV, RESH, TET, and ZAYIN and no others.

As explained later in this book, the Greek letters which represent the number 616 (chi, iota, and digamma) are also represented by the Hammer and Sickle when it faces in the opposite direction to the standard one (i.e. in reverse).

The Hammer and Sickle is a monogram of the number 616 in Hebrew letters:

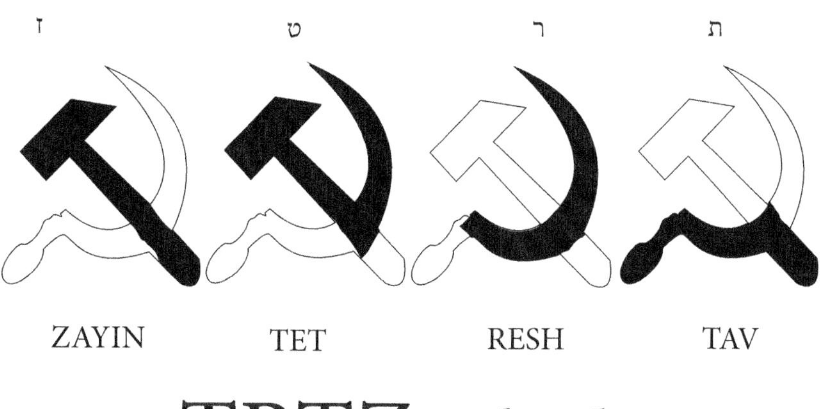

TRTZ=616

In ancient times, the letters of the alphabet represented numbers. The first nine letters of the alphabet represented the units, the next the tens, the next the hundreds.

Out of reverence for the name of God, the numbers 15 and 16 are treated in a peculiar way in the Hebrew alphabetical number system. The letters yod, he, and vav, are the letters that constitute the name of God (YHWH), and so instead of the expected yod/he (10+5) and yod/vav (10+6) to represent the numbers 15 and 16, these numbers are actually represented by the Hebrew letters tet/vav (9+6)and tet/zayin (9+7) respectively. This system is used consistently even beyond the tens and hundreds, even into the thousands and beyond.

Originally this alternative system was only used for religous texts, but today the alternative system is used whenever the Hebrew letters are used to represent numbers. Today numbers are generally written with Arabic numerals, but Hebrew letters still function today as numbers in the same way that others use Roman numerals.

Using this alternative system, in Hebrew letters 616 is rendered תרטז. The number 616 is rendered in Hebrew therefore by the letters tav, resh, tet, and zayin (400+ 200+ 9+ 7).

When the Jews changed their system of numbering between the third and first century BC, they modified the numbers 15 and 16. Instead of using יה (YH: 10+5) and יו (YW: 10+6) to represent these numbers, they used instead טו (TW: 9+6) and טז (TZ: 9+7).

The letters יה are found at the end of the word *Hallelujah* which means "Praise God!" The letters יו are found at the beginning of theophoric names such as *Yonatan* ("Jonathan"). In both these cases, the letters serve as a contraction of the Name (YHWH). As with most Hebrew words, the final syllable of "Jehovah" is stressed when the Name stands on its own. When attached to the end of a word, the stress remains in place, accounting for the contraction "YAH" (יה). When the Name is placed in front of a word (such as in the case of *Yonatan*), the stress falls on the last syllable of the new word to which the Name is attached. The final "yah" sound of the Name is no longer stressed and is consequently swallowed up by the Name's second vowel, hence the contraction "YO" (יו).

The Name was to be avoided during conversation. The Talmud (*Yoma 39b*) indicates that at about the third century BC, at the time of the High Priest Simon the Just, the use of the Tetragram was reserved for the Temple only. Even the divine name stamped on jars was removed to in order to keep it hallowed (*Shabbat 61b*, *'Arakin 6a*).

Alliteration in Rev. 13:18 prompts transliteration into Hebrew

The alliteration in Rev. 13:18 is unmistakeable.

The words αριθμο(ν) (repeated thrice), θηριου, and ανθρωπου, share the letters: θ and ρ in particular. Such alliteration encourages the hearer to expect the number 616 to represent the word *thorion* ("beast") because it incorporates these sounds. Since the Greek letters themselves evidently do not do so, the hearer is encouraged to resort to transliteration of the number 616 from Greek letters into Hebrew letters. Such a strategy is rewarded with resultant letters that do match the sound of those Greek letters (ρ and θ) and the Greek word for "beast": תריו (TRIW=θηριο(ν)).

From here it is only one small step to seek a monogram with the letters תרטז (TRTZ=616). This result encourages the hearer to seek the shape of these Hebrew letters in the mark of the Beast (a criterion which is fulfilled by the Hammer and Sickle).

The Hammer and Sickle is not a monogram of Cyrillic letters

The Cyrillic numeral system is based on, and is extremely similar, to the Greek numeral system. However, the Cyrillic letter that represents the number 6, and which is based on the Greek digamma, is S-shaped rather than Ϛ-shaped and so does not fit the monogram. The Hammer and Sickle does not therefore represent the number 616 in Cyrillic letters XIS.

Explanations for variant readings 666/616 given by others

This section looks at explanations put forward to explain the existence of the two main variant readings of the number of the Beast: 666 and 616.

Bruce Metzger believes that the divergence occurred over Nero. Transliterated into Hebrew letters, NERON CAESAR (the Greek spelling) adds up to 666 provided one spells Caesar in a peculiar way. Treated similarly, NERO CAESAR adds up to 616.

Friedrich Engels shared the same view as Metzger. In 1883 he wrote a work which touched upon the book of Revelation in which he states that a certain Ferdinand Benary discovered that the number 666 referred to Nero and that his name could add up to 666 or 616 depending on how his name was spelt in Hebrew. In this work, Engels concludes that the list of seven emperors started with Augustus; that Nero was the fifth; Galba the sixth and the one in whose reign the book of Revelation was written; (hence Otho is the seventh); and that the prophecy predicts the imminent return of Nero according to the *Nero redivivus* myth. Engels states:

> The mysterious book, then, is now perfectly clear: 'John' predicts the return of Nero for about the year 70, and a reign of terror under him which is to last forty-two months, or 1,260 days. After that term God arises, vanquishes Nero, the antichrist, destroys the great city by fire, and binds the devil for a thousand years. The millennium begins and, so forth.

Showing his contempt for the prophecy, Engels adds:

> All this now has lost all interest, except for ignorant persons who may still try to calculate the day of the last judgment.

A flaw with many of the above arguments is that there is very little evidence, if any at all, that in the first couple of centuries Christians believed that Caligula or Nero was the Beast. According to Irenaeus, the prophet John himself was alive well into the latter half of the first century and never intimated to anyone that he believed that the Beast had already come. Engels is being presumptious when he claims that Irenaeus knew that Nero was the one whose name is contained "in that mysterious number."

In the centuries to follow, commentaries on Revelation were written that did indeed interpret Nero as the Beast. Victorinus of Petovium, Jerome, and Sulpicius Severus all interpret the Beast as Nero, with the mortal wound that healed being a reference to his suicide and *Nero redivivus* myth.

Victorinus of Petovium's commentary is the earliest commentary we have on Revelation, written perhaps as early as AD 258. Victorinus states that the number must be interpreted according to the Greek letters. Victorinus believed that Nero would adopt a new name when he returned as the Antichrist, and that this new name would add up to the correct number. He did not write down which number of the Beast he had in mind.

Some experts in palaeography and textual analysis of the New Testament believe the alternative variant may have come about through deliberate tampering with the text. They see no clear reason for how the mistake could have occurred simply through scribal error.

One possibility that does not appear to have been considered by textual critics regarding the number is that the numerical value of the Greek letter Ξ (with a number value of 60 using the Greek number system), was confused for the numerical value of the Latin letter X, (which has the number value of 10 using the Roman number system). Both letters are pronounced the same way, and so could be mistaken for each other.

The number 616 when translated into Latin is DCXVI. To a Roman mind, there might appear to be a missing letter, namely L (50), in what appears to be the sequence of the letters that the Romans used for numbers. The base numerals were D (500), C (100), L (50), X (10), V (5) and I (1). DCXVI appears to follow this sequence, but with a missing L.

The 666, being the easier reading, symmetrical, and conducive to the DCLXVI Roman numeral system would have had far greater appeal than 616.

A Latin copyist who did not have a Greek manuscript to copy from, who was reliant solely on a Latin copy, may have added the L (50) either out of carelessness, or intentionally, mistakenly thinking that the manuscript he had was faulty. Since we are to "calculate" the number of the Beast, the sequence of Roman letters used for "calculating" may have been unconsciously perceived, when in fact such a sequence was not actually there. Like Irenaeus, who thought that *Lateinos* was the most likely solution because the current rulers were the Latins, a copyist might have drawn similar conclusions and assumed that the Greek number was intended to signify the Roman base numerals.

The Greek letters used to spell the name Jesus, ΙΗΣΟΥΣ, add up to 888 using gematria (Ι=10, Η=8, Σ=200, Ο=70, Υ=400, Σ=200). The fact that Jesus's name added up to a symmetrical number may have inclined people to assume that the number of the Beast must be symmetrical too and so preferred 666. This is the conclusion drawn by Adolf Deissmann, who expresses this view in a footnote in his book *Light from the Ancient East*. He too thought that perhaps the original number was 616. His theory was that perhaps the solution was *kaisar theos* (Caesar god) which, using gematria, adds up to 616.

Irenaeus' work *Against Heresies* reveals the prevalence of people's inclination to use numbers to draw up fictitious systems, particularly within the gnostic system. Chapter 24 of his book entitled "Folly of the Arguments Derived by the Heretics from Numbers, Letters and Syllables" contains the following example of this:

> . . . transferring the name Jesus, which belongs to another language, to the numeration of the Greeks, they sometimes call it "Episemon", as having six letters, and at other times "the Plenitude of the Ogdoads," as containing the number eight hundred and eighty-eight.

The interplay of numbers appears throughout Irenaeus' book. This passage from Chapter 15 is just a small sample:

> But Jesus, he [the gnostic] affirms, has the following unspeakable origin. From the mother of all things, that is the first Tetrad; there came forth the second Tetrad, after the manner of a daughter; and thus an Ogdoad was formed, from which, again, a Decad proceeded: thus was produced a Decad and an Ogdoad. The Decad, then, being joined with the Ogdoad, and multiplying ten times, gave rise to the number eighty; and, again, multiplying eighty ten times, produced the number eight hundred. Thus, then, the whole number of the letters proceeding from the Ogdoad [multiplied] into the Decad, is eight hundred and eighty-eight. This is the name of Jesus; for this name, if you reckon up the numerical value of the letters, amounts to eight hundred and eighty-eight. Thus, then, you have a clear statement of their opinion as to the origin of the supercelestial Jesus.

It is not hard to see that in a climate where such strange systems abounded, some might contrive 666 to be the correct number of the beast, given its symmetry and the fact it is a triangular number.

χις (616) represents חיו the first three letters of cheyvah (Aramaic for "beast": חֵיוָה)

The transliterated Greek letters χις (616) equate to חיו, the core letters of the Aramaic word for "beast". This fact lends enormous weight to the contention of this book that the number of the Beast is indeed 616.

The Aramaic for "beast" is חֵיוָה (*cheyvah*). The word *cheyvah* is used many times in chapter 7 of the Book of Daniel, the chapter which prophesies the advent of the Beast. Despite the many changes of suffix to this word, the letters always form the core of the word, whether in the singular or plural.

The Old Testament is written mainly in Hebrew, but parts of Daniel (Dan. 2:4b-7:28) and parts of Ezra are written in Aramaic. The Aramaic word *cheyvah* points to Chapter 7 of Daniel, written in Aramaic, which records Daniel's visions of the four beasts which rise from the sea. These beasts equate to the Beast which is also seen rising out of the sea (Revelation 13:1).

The Greek number for 666, which is χξς, does not easily transliterate into Hebrew/Aramaic letters as there is no equivalent Hebrew letter to the Greek letter ξ. The letter wouldusually be rendered through the use of two Hebrew letters: either kaf and sigma, or qof and sigma. The resultant letters do not have any meaning or significance. The number 666 in the Hebrew alphabetical number system is תרסו. This does not equate to any word in Hebrew either. Nor do the letters חסו, obtained by transliterating the Greek letters into Hebrew letters, but substituting קס (*ks*) with the numerical equivalent of ξ which is ס. These observations suggest that if the transliteration from Greek to Hebrew, or vice versa, plays any role at all with regard to the correct interpretation of the number of the Beast, then the number 666 is not the correct number of the Beast.

The correct step is to transliterate the Greek letters which represent 616 into Hebrew letters to reveal the number's connection with the word in Aramaic for "beast", *cheyvah*. The Greek letters χις (chi, iota, and digamma: 616) should be transliterated into Aramaic letters (which are the same as Hebrew letters). This reveals that the enigmatic and seemingly random letters chi, iota and digamma, actually represent the root letters of the Aramaic word for "beast". It is perhaps for this reason that the prophecy states: "**let him who has understanding reckon the number of the beast**", for not only should one be able to discern the Greek letters of the number of the

Beast in the emblem of the USSR, but one should also perceive that the root letters of the Aramaic word for "beast" adds up to 616 when transliterated into the Greek letters chi, iota, and digamma.

Any Hebrew word which contains more than three letters will contain surplus letters upon transliteration because the number 616 can only be represented by three Greek letters. To rule out the connection between the word *cheyvah* (Aramaic: "beast") and the Greek letters χις (616) simply because *cheyvah* is spelt with four letters and not just three, is to restrict the interpretation of the number of the Beast to three letter words. (Four, in the case of transliteration of a Greek word into Hebrew.) Surplus letters must be chopped off, rather like the bed of Procrustes. Such action is justified on the grounds that endings of words are not usually important in terms of their core meaning.

The fact that the Greek word for "beast" also adds up to 616 when transliterated into Hebrew, (provided one drops the final letter (nu)), also supports this interpretation.

To be able to interpret correctly the mysteries contained in Revelation requires the knowledge of Greek and Hebrew/Aramaic alone. The Latin word for "beast", *bestia*, does not appear to have any numerical significance. The word *bestia* originally had a stem of *fe*-, whence words like *ferus* ("wild") and *ferox* ("courage"). The Greek word for "beast", *therion*, originated from this same *fe*- stem, the Aeolic for "beast" being φηρ.

Even omission of the archaic digamma produces the word "beast" in Hebrew (χι =chay(ah)) through transliteration

Since the Greek letter digamma (waw) is an archaic letter of the Greek alphabet, some might question the validity of transliterating this letter into Aramaic to obtain *cheyvah* ("beast"). Obsolete by the time the Septuagint was written, the letter was not used to transliterate the Hebrew/Aramaic letter vav. (Names like David are translated with an upsilon: Δαυιδ.)

However, even if one omits the digamma/waw when transliterating, the word "beast" is still produced because the remaining letters χι (chi, iota) transliterate into the Hebrew letters חי which are the root letters of the Hebrew word for "beast" (*chayah*): חיה.

Far from undermining the thesis that the number 616 points to the word "beast", the presence of the archaic letter digamma actually adds a further layer of support to the thesis that 616 indicates the word "beast" because this number not only produces the word "beast" in Aramaic and Greek, but in Hebrew too (when the digamma is omitted), through trasliteration. This consistency is like a threefold cord that cannot be easily broken. One can confidently assert therefore that the Hebrew letters that comprise the number 616, namely TRTZ, must also produce a name, the name of a "**man**"(Rev. 13:18), when transliterated.

After 403 Athens and most other cities adopted the so-called Ionic form of the alphabet, which is the one in use today. which did not include digamma.

תריו/TRIW (616) transliterated into Greek also means "beast" (therion)

As noted elsewhere, when the word in Greek for "beast" is translitated into Hebrew, the resulting letters make the number 616 in Hebrew: תריו (TRIW). Likewise, when the Aramaic word for "beast" (cheyvah) is transliterated into Greek letters, the resulting letters make the number 616. Not just a coincidence, this is a sign to enable one to discern the true number of the Beast.

This strange quirk proves that 616 is the correct number of the Beast. However, a further step must be taken in order to identify the Beast. The number 616 must be made to consist of the Hebrew letters that make the number 616 using the system that changes the number 16 from yod/vav to tet/zayin.

The actual number of the name of the Beast is תרטז (TRTZ). As explained elsewhere in this book, this number is an alternative rendering of the number 616 which avoids using the conjuction of the letters yod/vav for 16 (or yod/he for 15), letters which are used by Jews to denote the name of God. Instead the numbers for nine and seven are used to obtain the number 16 (namely tet and zayin).

The fact that the Greek letters χις (616) transliterate to CHET, YOD, and VAV, the root letters of the Aramaic word for *cheyva(h)* ("beast"), and the fact that the "standard" Hebrew number for 616 (TRIW) can be transliterated as *therio(n)* is not just a coincidence. This pattern indicates that the key to determining the name indicated by the number of the name of the Beast is to be determined through transliteration too.

Transliteration of Hebrew-Greek/Greek-Hebrew : past and present

therion

The Greek letter theta (θ) was always transliterated with the Hebrew letter tav. Hence tav/resj/tet/zayin (616) can be legitimately transliterated as *therion*. A tav was always used, despite the fac that in Hebrew a tav actually has a hard t-sound when it apears at the beginning of a word.

cheyvah

The Greek letter chi was usually tranliterated with the Hebrew letter kaf. Only rarely was the letter chi transliterated with a chet, according to *Griechische und Lateinische Lehnwoerter Im Talmud, Midrasch Und Targum, Vol. 1*, by Samuel Krauss. (His book gives examples of those rare occasions where chet was used to transliterate chi.) Since chet is always pronounced with exactly the same pronuncation as chi (whereas kaf is not always) it is not unreaonable to translirate chi/iota/digamma (616) as *cheyv(ah)* ("beast").

The seven heads of the Beast do not represent General Secretaries

The seven heads of the Beast represent kingdoms, not individual kings. The heads represent the sequence of kingdoms that span history from the kingdom of Babylon through to the USSR. It is just a coincidence that there were also seven leaders (or "kings") of the Soviet Union. The seven leaders of the Soviet Union were these:

1. Lenin (1917-1924
2. Joseph Stalin (1922-1953)
3. Nikita Khrushchev (1953-1964)

4. Leonid Brezhnev (1964-1982)
5. Yuri Andropov (1982-1984)
6. Konstantin Chernenko (1984-1985)
7. Mikhail Gorbachev (1985-1991)

It is a mistake to reckon Georgi Malenkov as one of the leaders of the USSR. There were only seven "heads". The title of Dmitri Volkogonov's book *Autopsy For An Empire: The Seven Leaders Who Built the Soviet Empire* makes the issue clear. Upon Stalin's death on March 5 1953 Georgi Malenkov was made Premier. His name was briefly listed at the top of the secretaries of the Secretariat, but on 14 March Khrushchev's name appeared at the top of a revised list. Khrushchev effectively replaced Malenkov as party leader, but was not named as First Secretary of the CPSU until September 1953.

Lenin led the Soviet Union as Premier. There followed six main General Secretaries of the Soviet Union. Nikita Khrushchev renamed the post First Secretary in 1953; the change was reverted in 1966. By the late 1920s the General Secretaries of the Central Committee of the Communist Party of the Soviet Union had evolved into the most powerful of the Central Committee's various secretaries. With a few exceptions the holder of the office was the de facto leader of the Soviet Union, because the post controlled both the CPSU and the Soviet government.

Vladimir Antonovich Ivashko was actually the last General Secretary of the Communist Party, a post he held for only five days, from 24 August 1991 to 29 August 1991, the date the Communist Party was banned.

Communism's legacy of death and suffering

It is estimated that communists have killed around 100 million people in the last century, more than the total number of deaths in World War I and World War II combined.

The use of violence was repeated in every communist revolution. As late as 1976 Mengistu Haile Mariam unleashed a Red Terror in Ethiopia.

An estimate of deaths by country of those who died under Communist regimes from execution, labour camps, famine, ethnic cleansing, and flight, is found in M. White's *Atrocities: The 100 Deadliest Episodes in Human History*:

- China 40,000,000
- Soviet Union 20,000,000
- North Korea 3,000,000
- Ethiopia 2,000,000
- Cambodia 1,700,000
- Vietnam 365,000 (after 1975)
- Yugoslavia 175,000
- East Germany 100,000
- Romania 100,000
- North Vietnam 50,000 (internally 1954-1975)
- Cuba 50,000
- Mongolia 35,000
- Poland 30,000
- Bulgaria 20,000
- Czechoslovakia 11,000
- Albania 5,000
- Hungary 5,000

A further 26 million died in Communist-inspired wars (i.e wars that lead to communist power, or proxy wars in the Cold War).

In Russia, during the period 1918-1921, industry was almost completely nationalized, private trade was banned, and party squads were sent out into the countryside to requisition food from the peasants. The economic system subsequently broke down and countless thousands died of starvation. Ignorant of economic reality, the Bolsheviks had intended this period to last for decades and lead to communism, a planned economy in distribution as well as production. At the time it was not known as "War Communism" but simply as "Communism".

Early claims that 1917 heralded the advent of the Antichrist

Belief that the communist regime was the anti-Christ was common. For example, in his book *Trotsky* [page 206] Robert Service records an instance where an anonymous letter was sent to the Soviet authorities proclaiming that the time of the Antichrist had arrived

William C. Fletcher's book *The Russian Orthodox Church Underground 1917-1970*, makes it is quite apparent that many of the underground churches regarded the communist regime as the Antichrist.

The sect called the Imiaslavtsy claimed that the Soviet regime was the servant of the Antichrist.

The Orthodox population refused to enter renovationist churches from fear of receiving the 'seal of the anti-Christ'.

The Buevtsy organization, a branch of the Josephite movement, utilized apocalyptic imagery in agitation against ration cards and passports, which were called 'seals of the anti-Christ'. The Buevtsy agitated against the forcible collectivization of agriculture with the cry: "Orthodox, thrash the anti-Christ. It will not be a sin for us, the lord will help us deliver ourselves from Satan."

Among the prison population were some whose sect held that they could not even give their names to Antichrist. This meant that some refused the certificate of release when their term was up and were soon returned to the camps.

The Antichrist was held to have assumed power in 1917 by followers of the True Orthodox Church who were to avoid the clutches of the Antichrist through asceticism and prayer. In the 'Visions of John of Kronstadt', participants in the Renovating Church were considered 'servants of the anti-Christ'. Some rejected the legalized Russian Orthodox churches. They believed the earlier Church was true but that now the Antichrist was making an outrage of her. They called the re-opened churches 'heathen temples of the anti-Christ'. Chain letters would state that the coming of the Antichrist into the world had taken place. Crosses were drawn with chalk by True Orthodox Christians to ward off the power of the Antichrist. They believed that the world was 'contaminated' by Antichrist.

Bishop Antony (Khrapovitsky, Metropolitan of Kiev and Galitsky), the founder of ROCA (Russian Orthodox Church Abroad), viewed the revolution in Russia in the light of the struggle between Christ and Satan. He called the Bolsheviks the "Red Antichrist". The following paragraphs are just a few extracts from a speech he made in 1930 in connection with the activities of the Brotherhood of Russian Truth:

Orthodox Christians! For many years the Antichrist's red power tormented our Motherland . . .

From the very beginning of communist domination over Russia, the robber gang did not stop persecuting against the faith . . .

Now in the face of the growing wrath of the people, the Antichrist government has led the last and decisive battle against the faith of Christ.

Orthodox Christians! Stand up against the red antichrist! Do not listen to anyone's calls to come to terms with him, from whomever the calls come! There is no peace between Christ and Satan. The power given to me by God blesses all the weapons that are being brought up against the red Satanic power . . .

10

THE NERO FALLACY

The number of the Beast: 666 or 616?

Aware of the two most authoritative variant readings for the number of the Beast: 666 or 616, Christians need only wait to see how history unfolds to discern which of the two numbers is the correct one. There is no other way of discerning the correct number, no matter how many fragments of ancient manuscripts might be excavated from ancient dumping grounds in Egypt or wherever. However, if one adopts isopsephy as the means of deriving the name of the Beast from the number, there is still an insoluble problem. Using isopsephy, the numbers 616/666 can be matched with an indeterminate number of names. Hence, using this sytem, there is no way of identifying the name of the Beast and thus the Beast himself.

A man who fails to identify the Beast is more likely to be deceived by Satan and to succumb to receiving the mark of the Beast on his forehead or right hand.

Irenaeus' system: too arbitrary and insufficiently restrictive

Irenaeus, Bishop of Lyons, who mistakenly believed that the number of the Beast was 666, used an ingenious "restricting condition" that limited each set of letters that represents the digits, decads and hundreds respectively to add up to no more than six, sixty, and six hundred in each case. Using this system, Irenaeus came up with three names that are quite different in sound and spelling: τειταν, λατεινος, and ευανθας.

In his commentary *A Critical and Exegetical Commentary on the Revelation of St. John* R. H. Charles explains how Professor J.A. Smith of Magdalen College stumbled across Irenaeus' system when he happened to apply the same system himself and obtained the same names. He justified his sytem on the spurious grounds that the word "calculate" seemed to indicate such a restriction.

Clearly, even this system gives far too much latitude as to the supposed name of the Beast. After all, should by some unlikely chance a man called Ευανθας arise who seemed to fit the description of the Beast, why should anyone recognize this name, when the names Τειταν or Λατεινος, or some other combination of letters, would fit just as well?

This "restricting condition" is also too arbitrary. Jesus' name in Greek (ΙΗΣΟΥΣ) fits within the framework created by this system. Aware that the name Jesus adds up to 888 in Greek letters, Irenaeus might have felt justified in applying this "restriction sytem" to the Beast's name with its similarly symmetrical number: 666. However, in Rev. 13:18, the "number of Beast"is clearly in apposition with the "number of a man", not Jesus' name.

Since most commentators are convinced that the number of the Beast must refer to a Roman Emperor, the names engendered from Irenaeus' system are usually roundly ignored anyway, with Nero's name invariably being put forward as the solution.

Commentaries on Revelation: blind guides!

"Let them alone; they a re blind guides. And if a blind man leads a blind man, both will fall into a pit." (Matt.15:14)

The modern Church is convinced that Revelation is about the Roman Empire. Clinging to this unfounded notion, the Church still maintains therefore that the number of the Beast must point to Nero. The city of Rome is usually misidentified as the city of seven hills: Babylon the Great.

Such misinterpretations in turn leads inevitably to the conclusion that both the Books of Daniel and Revelation are either false prophesies, or that they are prophesies that are to be interpreted as typology, with only a vague relationship to actual events that are occurring now. The "Nero interpretation" fatally undermines Christianity in fact by casting doubt upon not only Christian prophesy, but ancient Jewish prophesy too. At best, commentators leave readers with the view that Revelation was only relevant to a bygone age.

This book proves that the Book of Revelation is true and that it has been misinterpretated by legions of commentators who have no justification for their misinterpretations. Like blind men leading blind men, the writers of commentaries on Revelation merely repeat the same misinterpretations found in earlier commentaries. Not only falling into the pit themselves (Luke 6:39), all those who read their commentaries are in danger of doing the same.

Satan intends to deceive the whole world. The identification of the Beast through his number will prevent Christians from believing a lie and being deceived themselves. How important it is therefore that Christians are aware of the correct number of the Beast and through it the identity of the Beast!

A falsehood lies in the heart of Christians' very own Bibles. The number 666 is false. The falsehood that Nero is the Beast is repeated in most commentaries on Revelation. Given that Christians are misled by their own Bibles and by their own commentaries, it is not surprising that they have failed to identify the Beast. Just as the Jews failed to recognize that John the Baptist was Elijah

(Mal. 4:5), or that Jesus was the Messiah, so modern Christians have failed to recognize that the USSR is the Beast.

Christ's return is imminent and the truth is that the prophecy of Revelation is relevant to what is unfolding in history right now! The prophesy is indeed eschatalogical, a prophesy that is concerned about events at the end of history. But we are now approaching the end of history and the fulfilment of the very events prophesied in Revelation! This book proves that the USSR is the Beast (the kingdom represented by the Beast itself), not the Roman Empire! Nero is not the Beast!

The Book of Revelation makes certain matters quite explicit. For example, it makes it perfectly clear that the Roman Empire is the sixth kingdom (Rev. 17:10). Commentators therefore have no justification for identifying Rome as the Fourth Kingdom. There is no excuse for some of the other egregious misinterpretations found in many commentaries on Revelation either.

Perhaps commentators overextend themselves by trying to interpret every verse in Revelation. This book has limited itself to just those verses that relate to the Beast, the Second Beast, and Babylon the Great (primarily chapters 13, 17 and 18 of Revelation).

There are still several verses in Revelation that continue to mystify the author which he is unable to interpret to his satisfaction. The author has resisted the temptation to rehash the same old material found in other commentaries on these other verses in the way that others do in order to give the false impression of a comprehensive understanding of Revelation.

Many commentators correctly identify the seven heads of the Beast with the heads (seven in all) of the four beasts that arise from the sea in Daniel chapter 7. From this point, though, there is a wide and well-trodden path that leads commentators to draw all the wrong conclusions regarding the identity of the Beast and his kingdom. The first wrong turning is to assume that all four of the Javanic kingdoms represented by the four-headed Leopard must be kingdoms of the Diadochs (former Macedonian generals who served under Alexander the Great). In fact, the Roman Empire is the fourth Javanic kingdom. Failure to realize this leads to the crucial error of deducing that the Roman Empire must therefore be the Fourth Kingdom, rather than merely the sixth head of the Beast, the last of the four Javanic kingdoms represented by the Leopard (the Third Kingdom). This misunderstanding is the font of so many other misinterpretations. The error is then compounded by the fact that Nero is then invariably identified as the Beast, for it is assumed that the Beast must be a Roman emperor.

Academics and theologians have too much at stake to risk making interpretations that might later be found wanting. They are disinclined to put at risk their reputations and careers, be they within academia or the Church. The author of this book has benefited from the fact that he is not a professional theologian or academic. He has been able to self-publish several books on Revelation and then, upon later realization that they were flawed, withdraw them from the market without any negative impact upon his career. This recurrent publishing process has been useful, as each book has improved on the last, and sharpened the author's understanding. The author hopes that this book is the definitive book on the true identity of the Beast and its number.

Revelation is primarily concerned with the trials and tribuations that Christians will have to endure at the hands of Satan throughout history. Their endurance will be rewarded with eternal life and the right to enter the New Jerusalem that will descend out of heaven.

The Book of Revelation is of great relevance today. Those commentators on Revelation who relegate Revelation to the past are blind guides. The twin evils of communism and Islam are evident for all to see, their satanic nature evident from their ceaseless persecution of Christians.

Nero is not the Beast

> **For there is nothing hid, except to be made manifest; nor is anything secret, except to come to light.** (Mark 4:22)

The Hammer and Sickle is the mark of the Beast. Unwittingly, the Soviet emblem (the Hammer and Sickle) incorporates in its design the number of the Beast (616) in the form of a monogram. By imposing the mark of the Hammer and Sickle upon people, the False Prophet will fulfil the prophecy without realizing it.

A common misinterpretation found in numerous commentaries is that Nero is denoted by the number of the Beast. Using an incorrect spelling of Caesar, Nero Caesar is misspelt נרון קסר. The name "Caesar" is actually spelt קיסר (with a yod). For some, the fact that the Latin form of the name Nero omits the final N lends credence to this interpretation, for the name spelt this way (omitting the final N) in Hebrew can then explain the existence of the variant reading of 616: נרו קיסר.

In order to divert from himself the suspicion that the conflagration of Rome in AD 64 was his act, Nero (AD 54-68) instigated the persecution of Christians. Some were crucified, others were covered with pitch or oil, nailed to posts and burned as torches for Nero's amusement.

Nero's suicide in AD 68 is interpreted as the mortal wound (Rev. 13:3) by many commentators. His death marked the end of the Julio-Claudian line and many would have welcomed a restoration of the Republic. Rumours that Nero was not really dead were circulating. He had gone into hiding in Parthia and would return at the head of ten Parthian kings and a vast Parthian army to destroy Rome. Three impostors did in fact come forward claiming to be Nero, and two of them were well received in Parthia (Tacitus, *Hist.* i.2; ii. 8; Suetonius *Nero* 57).

Some commentators see in Domitian a revived Nero. Omitting Galba, Otho, and Vitellius, Domitian can be reckoned as the eighth "head" or Caesar.

The emperors of the Roman Empire tend to be the object of the various other attempts at solving the enigma of the number of the Beast. Other suggestions along these lines are קיסר רומים (=666, "Caesar of the Romans") or קיסר רום (=616, "Caesar of Rome"). The Greek Γαιος καισαρ equals 616. So does "Caesar God" (*Kaisar Theos=616).*

Another solution is to add up the numerical value of the initials of the emperors' names from Julius to Vespasian, which comes to 666, provided one allocates the letter K to Julius Caesar. To add up to 666, this dubious system unjustifiably inludes Galba while omitting Otho and Vitellius.

Another proposed solution is that 666 represents the calculation of the abbreviated Greek titles of Domitian that appear on coins (A.KAI.ΔOMET. ΣEB.ΓE). However, no coin actually exists on which all five of these titles appear together.

These attempts at a solution are misguided because they focus on Rome. The Roman Empire is one of the four kingdoms of the Third Kingdom (the four-headed Leopard) and is not the Fourth Kingdom. Russia/USSR is the Fourth Kingdom and a name that matches the number of the Beast is to be sought from that Kingdom, not Rome.

They are also misguided because they forget that the mark of the Beast is not just a number but also a name. The letters which spell the name "Nero" (or any other Roman emperor) do not comprise the number 616/666 in any alphabet (let alone Hebrew or Greek), nor does any abbreviation of the name "Nero" or "Nero Caesar". The same problem exists for all the other aforementioned attempts at a solution.

The fact that no mark was ever imposed on any citizen of the Roman Empire or their subjects, let alone all the inhabitants of the whole world, proves beyond all doubt that the Roman Empire is not the Beast.

Standard isopsephy: an untenable method for identifying the Beast's name

This author advocates the use of transliteration from Greek-Hebrew or Hebrew-Greek, but rejects the standard use of isopsephy. Calculations should be based strictly on the clear division of letters of the alphabet into hundreds, tens, and units. Isopsephy violates this order, permitting the conversion of a random sequence of letters into numbers.

It is possible that the confusion between 666 and 616 arose when people, desirous to interpret the number of the Beast, took the words "**let him who has understanding reckon the number of the beast**" literally and transliterated the Greek word for "beast", *therion*, into Hebrew. The resulting transliteration תריון (TRIWN) gives the number 666, provided one uses gematria, a system which permits the summing of jumbled up letters. The number 666 in Hebrew is actually תרסו.

Like the Greek letters of the alphabet, each Hebrew letter of the alphabet has a numerical equivalent. The transliterated letters number 616, or 666 if one included the nu/nun: 6=ו ,10=י ,200=ר ,400=ת. The number 50=נ, but should not be included in the addition. The transliterated letters תריון (TRIWN) is not actually a number, for the letters/numbers are not in the correct order. Letters which represent hundreds should be followed by the letters which represent the tens, which are then followed by letters representing the units. The letter for N (*nun*=50) should come before the letters I (*yod*=10) and W (*vav*=6), not after. It is only through the highly suspect system of isopsephy (or gematria, a system used by kabbalists and other occultists), that a number can be derived from these letters, as this system permits the mixing up of letters. The prophecy asks us to reckon an actual number, not a mix of letters.

The genitive case of the Greek word for "beast", θηριου, (*theriou*, meaning "of the beast") appears in Rev. 13:18: "**let him who has understanding reckon the number of the beast**". A person may have thought that these words were an invitation to recalculate the number of the Beast based on the nominative case of the word (which is θηριον) transliterated into Hebrew. This would add up to 666, using gematria, and so this too may have been the cause of the alteration from 616 to 666.

Gideon Bohak ('Greek-Hebrew Gematrias in 3 Baruch and in Revelation') provides evidence that Greek-Hebrew gematrias existed in ancient times. Bohak notes how in Baruch 4.7 (the Greek Apocalypse of Baruch) a snake in Hades drinks from an ocean of water that is refilled by 360 rivers. The word snake δρακων (*drakon*) written in Hebrew letters is דרקונ and, using gematria, adds up to 360. Similarly, 409 giants are killed in a flood. Transliterated into Hebrew, the Greek letters in the word "flood" (*kataklusmos*) add up to 409. However, Bohak's examples of so-called gematria in Revelation seem forced and lack credibility.

The word "Shishak" (Jer. 25:26 and 51:41) means Babylon (*bavel*, in Hebrew) The name "Shishak" is derived from a system known as "atbash" (or "ATBaSH"), a kind of gematria, where each letter of the Hebrew alphabet is replaced with the corresponding letter of the alphabet listed in reverse order. In other words, the first letter of the alphabet would be replaced with the last letter of the alphabet, and so on (hence the name "atbash", based on aleph/tau, bet/shin).

Most commentators of Revelation believe that the number of the Beast is to be found by means of isopsephy. This system involves adding up the number value of each letter of a word spelt in a language where the letters of its alphabet have numerical values. Greek and Hebrew have such a number system.

Latin is a poor language in terms of isopsephy, as so few of the letters of its alphabet have numerical values: just M, D, C, L, X, V, I. (The last six letters of which, incidentally, add up to 666.) Since the book of Revelation was written in Greek, and the Old Testament in Hebrew and Aramaic, it is reasonable to conclude that these languages should be the ones used in trying to determine the correct interpretation of the number of the Beast.

The following three letters which are used as numbers in the Greek numbering system ceased to be used as letters by the time of the prophecy of Revelation: 6 (digamma/stigma); 90 (koppa); and 900 (san) were all obsolete. It is worth noting that any letter with a value above 600 is immediately redundant, namely the letters with the values 700 (psi), 800 (omega) and 900 (san). Since the Greek letter ς *(digamma)* was obsolete even by the time of John's revelation and has been redundant for centuries, one can rule out the possibility that the Beast's actual name will be χις. (Similarly, one can rule out the possibility that the letters which make up the number 666 will be the name of the Beast, as none of them are vowels and every vowel is represented by a letter in Greek.) Despite the immediate redundancy of the five letters of the alphabet with the numerical values of 6, 90, 700,800, and 900, there are still literally thousands of possible combinations of letters that could add up to 616. Just as the seven notes of the musical scale can make so many innumerable different tunes, so thousands of different potential names can be derived from the number 616.

In gematria, the lower the number, the more restricted is the range of possible names.

While it is easy to go from words to an individual number using gematria, it is impossible to reverse the process and find a unique name from a number. For this reason, one must conclude that each of the letters which represent 616 are significant in their own right, and not arrived at through the addition of other numbers as one would do with gematria.

It is also important to note that we asked to **"reckon the number of the beast"** not the numbers of the Beast, or the letters of the Beast. If we had been advised to count the letters of the beast, isopsephy would have been clearly indicated as the method to solve the mystery, but we have not been. The number to be counted is singular.

How the false variant reading came about

The true number of the Beast can only be discerned through the fulfilment of prophecy. However, an understanding of how the false variant number (666) arose lends credence to the premise in this book that the true number of the Beast is 616.

The origin of the variant reading 666 self-evidently revolves around the Greek word for "beast" (*therion*) found in Rev. 13:18 and concerns the common practice of applying isopsephy to determine the name of the Beast. The first five letters of the Greek word for "beast" (θηριον) can be represented by the number 616 in Hebrew letters (TRIW). The false variant number, 666, arose because the Greek word for "beast" (θηριον) can add up to 666 when the whole word is transliterated into Hebrew letters (TRIWN).

It is quite possible that Irenaeus' testimony that 666 was the true reading is the primary reason why all Bibles have 666 in the main text, yet Irenaeus claimed that he could not see how the variant readings arose. Latter-day commentators who argue that the different ways of spelling Nero esplain the variant number are also missing the obvious: *therion* is the key. The number 616 was deliberately replaced with 666 to reflect the fact that the Greek word for "beast"(*therion*) adds up to 666 when transliterated into Hebrew.

Many factors would have also inclined a man to prefer the number 666 to the number 616, not least the fact that the number 666 is both a symmetrical and triangular number. The 666 pattern also mirrors the fact that the name Jesus in Greek (ΙΗΣΟΥΣ) equals 888 when all the letters are added together. Since the Beast is often compared to the Lamb in several ways in Revelation, someone may have felt that the number 666 was more appropriate. Similarly, the final base numbers of the Latin number system also add up to 666: DCLXVI. The number 616 appears to lack all these qualities and thus appears to fall short.

Hubris, a belief in spurious gnostic theories regarding the meaning of numbers, and a presumption that the most familiar form of isopsephy was at play, led someone with little deference for the holy word of God to change the number from 616 to 666. Whoever made the change must have been convinced that the number 616 was meaningless. The number 666, on the other hand, was pregnant with significance and meaning. The falsifier may have deceived himself into believing that the adjustment was justified on the grounds that he was merely changing the numerical value of the word *therion* from its genitive *theriou* (TRIW=616) to its nominative *therion* (TRIWN=666).

It would have been only natural for the false variant to arise, as the fact that the phrase "**number of a the beast**" and "**number of a man**" are in apposition in Rev. 13:18 and appear to employ isopsephy through transliteration.

The exhortation to "calculate" (*psephisato*) the number of the Beast (Rev. 13:18) aparently suggests "isopsephy", a word based on this very same verb. The word "isopsephy" means "equal" and "pebble". Isopsephy was the practice, common in ancient times, of associating words or phrases, usually of the same language, that shared the same numerical value. The order in which the letters of these words appeared was not important. In other words, the letters did not have to appear in the order expected of a number: hundreds first, then tens, and finally units.

In ancient times, letters of the alphabet served as numbers. The first nine letters represented the first nine units, the next nine letters represented the tens, and the final letters represented the hundreds. The letters representing the larger number was written first, followed by the smaller numbers in their respective order.

It would not have taken long for the early Christians, many of whom were Jews, to realize that the the number of the Beast in Hebrew points to the Greek word for "beast" through transliteration.

There is no explanation for why someone would be motivated to change the number from 666 to 616, a seemingly insignificant number. The number 666 equals the sum of all the Hebrew letters that transliterate *therion*. It is therefore consistent with standard isopsephy and its less stringent demands. Therefore there would be no motive to reduce the Hebrew letters that make up the word *therion* from TRIWN (=666) to TRIW (=616), as there would be no indication that such a stringent step was required. Even less so given the absence of any connection between the number 666 (χξϛ) and the Aramaic word *cheyvah*. This connection is only evident with the number 616 through transliteration from the Greek letters for 616 into the corresponding letters in Aramaic.

The two systems for writing 616 in Hebrew

There were two ways of writing 616 in Hebrew: TRIW and TRTZ. The latter is now the standard way of writing this number, whereas in ancient times the latter was only used for primarily works of a theological nature. Today, Hebrew letters are used as numerals in the same way as someone writing in English might use Roman numerals.

The alternative system arose to avoid using the contracted forms of the name of God found in names such as Jonathan, Jonas, or Joel, or words such as Hallelujah.

The letters that made up the numbers 15 and 16 respectively (YH and YW) were replaced with the letters TW (9+6) and TZ (9+7).

Evolution of the author's interpretation of Revelation

The purchase of *The Perestroika Deception* (by Anatoliy Golitsyn) triggered an interest in communism that had hitherto lain dormant. Increasingly aware of the evil nature of communism, the author purchased Richard Wurmbrand's book *Marx & Satan*. The thought occurred to the author that perhaps the Hammer and Sickle could be the number of the Beast. The author was first struck by how the digamma looked like a sickle and how the Hammer and Sickle could be construed as a monogram of the number 616 (in Greek letters). The author was already aware of the variant reading of 616 at Rev. 13:18 thanks to a footnote in the author's RSV Bible.

The author initially interpreted the Beast's seven heads as purely the seven leaders of the Soviet Union. After many months, the author had the nagging feeling that the number should be "**of a man**" (Rev. 13:18). The hunch that the sickle might represent Marduk was immediately confirmed through research on the internet, and the author was convinced for a few years right up until very recently that Karl Marx was the "**man**" of Rev. 13:18 given that the Hammer and Sickle (and Red Star), evidently symbolized the evolution of his family's surname: Mordechai, Markus, Marx.

At one point, fairly early on, the author misinterpreted the seven kingdoms of the Beast as seven caliphates of Islam. The author belatedly realized that the Beast's composition (lion, bear, leopard, ten horns) clearly pointed to the kingdoms represented by the four beasts of Daniel (chapter 7) and that consequently its heads must represent those very same kingdoms.

The conviction that Mecca was a perfect fit for Babylon the Great grew slowly but surely over time, displacing the author's iniital perception that perhaps Moscow was the great city. Joel Richardson and Walid Shoebat's interpretation (in *God's War on Terror*) of the seven mountains with regards to Islam was influential.

For a period the Author interpreted the Beast's head wound and its healing as a reference to the continuation of the Roman Empire in the form of the Ottoman Empire. Both empires would comprise the sixth kingdom. Such an interpretation ignores the Russian Empire and requires the former USSR to be the seventh kingdom, the eighth upon its restoration.

That the Soviet emblem might also represent the name "Satan" (in Hebrew letters) was a later inspiration, a hunch which could only be confirmed once the author had checked how "Satan" was spelt in Hebrew.

At this point the author believed that "Satan" was the name of the Beast, and that Marx was the "**man**" represented by the number of the Beast. In Autumn 2019, the author wrote to almost all the Anglican bishops of England, Wales, Scotland, and Ireland, enclosing a sheet of paper with the diagrams of the "Satan" and "616" (in Greek letters) monograms and a brief cover letter explaining how the Hammer and Sickle also represented Karl Marx. Only two dioceses replied. One merely acknowledged receipt, the other (from the Chaplain to the Bishop of Portsmouth) helpfully gave feedback on my theories. The main gist of his letter (and his follow-up letter) was that "Satan" was not likely to be the name of the Beast as the Beast and Satan are not one and the same; he felt the chi should be straight, and that the final nun looked more like a zayin; my theory involved no calculation; the variant readings of 666 and 616 can be explained by the different ways Nero can be spelt; the correct interpretation of Revelation must have been possible in John's time because he is told not to seal up the words of the prophecy. More pertinently, he pointed out that the number is the number of the Beast's name. The author is grateful for his candid feedback.

Until fairly recently, the author was inclined to believe that an apostate Christian Church was the likely candidate for the Second Beast. Eventually, however, the conviction grew that the likening of this beast to a lamb meant that this Second Beast must also denote a nation in the same way that all the other beasts in Daniel chapters 7 and 8 always referred to nations. Modern Israel was a sure fit in every respect.

Perusal of the Chaplain's letters a year later led to the belated realization that the alternative rendering of 616 in Hebrew (TRTZ, rather than TRIW) might indicate "Trotzky". (The author had previously dismissed the alternative system for writing 15 and 16 (9+6, 9+7) and had therefore neglected to give the number 616 generated by this system (TRTZ) any serious attention. He was unaware that this system had now become the standard way of writing the numbers 15 and 16 in Hebrew letters. He was also ignorant of the fact that the system applied to numbers beyond the tens, into the hundreds and thousands, and so on.) Then came the conviction that the Hammer and Sickle can also be perceived as a monogram of the number 616 in Hebrew letters (TRTZ).

The Hammer and Sickle, given a large degree of latitude, can be perceived as many different letters and consequently many different names and numbers. The concept that the emblem also represented monograms of "Satan", "Trotzky" or "TRIW" (616) in Hebrew was discarded on the grounds that the recognition of any letters in addition to tav, resh, tet, and zayin (TRTZ) renders the whole theory about the Hammer and Sickle being a monogram of 616 obsolete. With other letters, other numbers other than 616 can be construed. It would therefore be untenable to argue that the emblem represented 616 alone.

Then the Hammer and Sickle was construed as a monogram of Cyrillic letters too and that the words in Rev. 13:18 were a play on words based on the meaning of the Hebrew name Joseph and the monogram pointed to the first three consonants of the name Stalin (СТЛ). Finally even this was rejected, mainly because the letters СТЛ do not add up to 616.

The realization dawned that the Hammer and Sickle merely points to the word "Beast" through the number 616 (through transliteration). The monogram does not signify any name other than "Beast" in the same way that the Chi Rho symbol does not signify any name other than "Christ", the only difference being that whereas the Greek letters XP point overtly to the name "Christ", the monogram of the Hammer and Sickle only points to the name "Beast" in a cryptic manner that is comparable to the use of AtBash in Jeremiah.

11

THE CORRECT NUMBER OF THE BEAST: 616

Irenaeus' questionable testimony against 616

Irenaeus (c.130-c.200) was Bishop of Lyons from around AD 178. In his book, *Adversus Omnes Haereses (Against Heresies)* which attacks Gnosticism, he claims that the reading of 616 is a mistake:

> I do not know how it is that some have erred following the ordinary mode of speech, and have vitiated the middle number in the name, deducting the amount of fifty from it so that instead of six decads they will have it that there is but one.

While Irenaeus' refutation of the 616 alternative at first sounds convincing, his testimony must be questioned. His testimony is unique and not supported by any other contemporary witnesses. Later sources who attest to the number 666, such as Hippolytus, are merely relying upon Irenaeus' testimony.

It is likely that through the influence of Irenaeus the text was altered to 666 in most manuscripts.

Irenaeus states that the number 666 is found in "all the most approved and ancient copies". This phrase does not rule out the possibility that the number 616 was found in some of the "ancient copies" but were "not approved", or that some of the "most approved" copies contained the number 616 but were not "ancient". In any case, the error may have been made very early on so that it *would* appear even in these ancient copies. The newness of a copy is irrelevant. Its source and accuracy are what is important. Irenaeus does not clarify on what grounds or by whom these ancient copies were approved. Irenaeus has not seen the original autograph, merely copies, and therefore he cannot confirm that copies he has seen match the original autograph.

Irenaeus cannot explain how the discrepancy over the number of the Beast came about. He suggests that perhaps a copyist elongated the xi so that it ended up looking like an iota, but this theory is not very plausible given the huge difference between the shape of xi (60) (made up essentially of three horizontal lines) and iota (10) (made of one single vertical line). The two letters could scarcely look more different. His theory that the tired hand of a scribe could be responsible for the error might explain his conviction that 666 is the correct number, since the tired hand of a scribe might make the xi look like an iota, but is unlikely to make an iota look like a xi as it would require more effort.

Irenaeus does not name those men who "saw John face to face" and who bear their testimony to 666 as being the correct number; he does not even say that he himself met any of these men who saw John face to face (although Irenaeus is said to have been a disciple of Polycarp, allegedly a disciple of John, and so maybe Polycarp is one of these men); nor does he clarify to whom these men bore their testimony. Irenaeus is not one of those who saw John face to face and so he is not a witness, but at best a witness of a witness.

Irenaeus writes:

> reason also leads us to conclude that the number of the name of the beast will amount to six hundred and sixty six; that is the number of tens shall be equal to the number of hundreds, and the number of hundreds equal to that of the units (for that number which expresses) the digit six being adhered to throughout, indicates the recapitulations of that apostasy, taken in its full extent, which occurred at the beginning, during the intermediate periods, and which shall take place at the end.[1]

---

1 *Against Heresies*, Irenaeus

Irenaeus also deduces that the number of the Beast must be 666 because the statue that Nebuchadnezzar built in the plain of Dura was 60 cubits in height and 6 cubits in breadth. While Irenaeus is surely right to perceive in this statue a type for the image of the Beast, he should not make such deductions. In any case, these dimensions have no connection with the number 666. Whether added or multiplied together, they do not equal 666. The numbers 60 and 6 may be accounted for, but where is the 600?

Irenaeus is surely mistaken to make any deductions about the number of the Beast based on numerical patterns, or based on his theory regarding the recapitulations of the apostasy. Such spurious assertions leads one to question his judgment regarding the other aforementioned areas as well. The true number of the beast cannot be discerned through "reason alone". Spiritual discernment is required too. If his testimony about the authenticity of the number 666 was true, what further need was there for him to draw such inferences about the number of the Beast?

Irenaeus applies similar reasoning to conclude that there could only be four gospels:

> It is not possible that the Gospels can be either more or fewer in number than they are. For, since there are four zones of the world in which we live, and four principle winds ... For the cherubim too were four-faced ... For the living creatures are quadriform, and the Gospels quadriform ... For this reason were four principal covenants given to the human race: one, prior to the deluge, under Adam; the second, that after the deluge, under Noah; the third, the giving of the law, under Moses; the fourth, that which renovates man, and sums up all things in itself by means of the Gospel.

These passages indicate that despite Irenaeus' rejection of the more outlandish teachings of the gnostics regarding numbers, he himself uses numbers to make unjustified assertions.

His testimony regarding the existence of the variant reading of 616 is very important, because it proves that the number 616 was widespread by the end of the second century. In fact his testimony is the earliest known witness to the number 616. P115, the earliest extant manuscript with the reading 616, is dated on palaeographical grounds to the late third/early fourth century. The other main witness to the reading 616, Codex C (one of the four great uncials), is dated to the fifth century.

Josef Schmid, the expert on Revelation, concluded that the history of the Apocalypse text can only be traced back to about AD 200 and that most of the textual variants occurred in the first one hundred years of the transmission of the text. The text of Revelation can be recovered as far back as the middle of the second century, but the gap between this stage and the original text cannot be bridged. The original autograph does not appear to have survived as a witness to the correct number of the Beast. Without this original autograph or proof of the provenance of some ancient manuscript, it would appear impossible to be able to say for sure what the correct number is. For all we know, the variant reading may have appeared within a generation of John's death.

Irenaeus was convinced that the key to the solution to the number of the Beast was in the use of isopsephy. The overwhelming number of potential names appears to have led Irenaeus to the conclusion that the range of possibilities must be limited. He used a system in which all the letters of the alphabet with a numerical value within the range of 100-900 must always add up to 600, those within the range 10-90 must always add up to 60, and those within 1-10 must always add up to 6. Thus he tried to avoid using any letters from the range 70-90, or 7-9, or multiples of letters which would have added up to numbers beyond the units or tens to which Irenaeus restricted them. It can be seen that his proposed solutions, such as *Lateinos* or *Teitan*, fit into this system. The fact that the name of Jesus in Greek fits into this pattern may have encouraged Irenaeus to adopt this system.

Using this method, the potential choice of letters in the 10-90 range is entirely restricted to just the letter iota, with its value of 10. Such a constraint may have led Irenaeus to prefer the number 666 with its wider scope for possible names.

No doubt Irenaeus did not intend to mislead others, else he would not have endeavoured to solve the mystery based on the number 666, but events have proven that his testimony was not true. It is now possible to sort the wheat from the tares. The correct number of the Beast can be discerned because the Beast (the USSR) has now arisen. To wait until people are physically marked with the number of the Beast on their hand or their forehead before drawing the right conclusion regarding 666 or 616 is too late. People need to be warned now about the Hammer and Sickle.

Not only did Irenaeus mislead over the number, but by proposing that the number might refer to the Latins (Λατεῖνος), he promoted the baleful idea that the mark related to the Roman Empire.

Irenaeus' unreliability as a historian

Only two of Irenaeus' works have survived: *Against Heresies* and *The Demonstration of Apostolic Teaching.* In Demonstration 74 of *The Demonstration of Apostolic Teaching*, Irenaeus wrote that Jesus was crucified during the reign of Claudius:

> For Herod the king of the Jews and Pontius Pilate, the governor of Claudius Caesar, came together and condemned Him to be crucified.

In fact Jesus was crucified under Pontius Pilate, the prefect of the Roman province of Judaea from AD 26-36, during the reign of Emperor Tiberius. Caligula was the next emperor, followed by Claudius who ruled from AD 41-54. Irenaeus' testimony is out therefore by two reigns, and by more than at least eleven years (assuming that Jesus was crucified in 30 AD). Irenaeus was clearly capable of making serious factual errors. Bible scholar James Moffatt said: "Irenaeus of course, is no great authority by himself on matters chronological."

Irenaeus may also have been historically inaccurate with his claim that Peter had died before Mark wrote his gospel. This contradicts others, such as Origen and Eusebius, who claim that Peter was alive and approved the work.

Irenaeus' evident desire to employ Polycarp as a living link to the apostolic age has led many scholars to question whether Polycarp was ever in fact associated with the apostle John. Some suggest that the 'John' whom Irenaeus wrote about was a 'John the Elder' – whom Papias mentions – and that Irenaeus was mistaken in making such a connection. It is perhaps significant that Polycarp makes no mention of any connection with the apostle John in his *Letter to the Philippians.* Kenneth Berding in his paper "John or Paul? Who was Polycarp's mentor?" concludes that such matters may remain unresolved unless other ancient documents come to light.

How well did Irenaeus know Polycarp? Irenaeus claims to have seen Polycarp as a child, in "the first age of our life". He did not take notes at this meeting. How reliable was his memory after the three quarters of a century that may have passed before he wrote *Against Heresies*?

Irenaeus describes the church of Rome as:

> [the] greatest, most ancient and known to all, founded and established by the two most glorious apostles, Peter and Paul.

In fact, according to the Catholic scholar F.A. Sullivan, the church of Rome was not as ancient as those of Jerusalem or Antioch, and that it was not actually founded by Peter or Paul.

Irenaeus' statements regarding the date of the prophecy of Revelation are a stumbling-block to those who believe that John received his prophecy during the period between the death of Nero and the fall of Jerusalem in AD 70. Respected scholars such as Hort, Lightfoot and Westcott all rejected the Domitianic date given by Irenaeus in favour of this earlier date.

In *The Early Days of Christianity*, F.W. Farrar writes:

> . . . [we are] obliged to discount the tales and remarks for which Irenaeus refers us to the authority of "the Elders," by whom he seems chiefly to mean Papias and Polycarp. Now Eusebius does not hesitate to say that Papias was a source of error to Irenaeus and others who relied on his "antiquity". When Irenaeus says that the "Pastor of Hermas" is canonical; that the head of the Nicolaitans was the Deacon Nicolas; and that the version of the LXX was written by inspiration; - we know what estimate to put on his appeals to apostolic tradition.

Eusebius, the great chronicler of early church history, clearly did not see in Irenaeus an infallible source of information. Eusebius even disputes the Johannine authorship of the Apocalypse, despite Irenaeus' firm statements on this matter.

Acrophany: further support for 616

The oldest surviving fragment of papyrus with the text bearing 616 as the number in Rev. 13:18 was found in an ancient Egyptian rubbish dump. Codex Ephraemi Rescriptus, one of the four Great Uncials, which also witnesses to 616, is a palimpsest, which is a codex where the original work has been scrubbed out and a new text has been written over the top. In this case the work of the Syrian church father Ephraem the Syrian was written over the top of the text of the Book of Revelation. It requires painstaking work and the use of chemicals to reveal the text of the Revelation hidden beneath the work

It is amazing to think that these rare and precious testimonies to what may be the actual correct number of the Beast should have been found in such a poor state. After all, the activities of the Beast take up a considerable portion of the Revelation, and the Beast and his number is of fundamental importance with regards to the end times and the fate of mankind. You would think there might be a way in which we can reassure ourselves of the correct number. There may be one (in addition to *cheyvah/therion*).

The number 616 may itself contain a hidden clue as to its veracity. Just as Karl Marx's name points to the fact that he is allluded to in the mark of the Beast – (the name Karl Marx can be construed as meaning "man of mark") - so too the number 616 itself may point to its correctness.

The letters of the Hebrew and Greek alphabet are related to each other. For example, the names of the first three letters of the Greek alphabet: *alpha, beta, gamma* are similar to the first three letters of the Hebrew alphabet: *aleph, beit,* and *gimmel.* Many letters of these two alphabets share similarities because most of their letters are derived from the same source. According to the *Cambridge Encylopedia of Language* by David Crystal, the Old Hebrew, Aramaic and Phoenician alphabets were based on the oldest-known alphabet which was the North Semitic alphabet which was developed around 1700 BC in the Palestine area. The Phoenician alphabet in turn was then used as a model by the Greeks around 1000 BC, who also added letters for vowels.

The letters of the alphabet were named after things whose names began with that particular letter of the alphabet. This system is called acrophany. For example, the Hebrew letter *beit* means "house". The Greek letter *beta* therefore is derived from a word that means "house". The fourth letter of the Hebrew alphabet, *dalet*, for example, means "door". The fourth Greek letter *delta* originated too therefore from the word for "door".

The names of the Greek letters of the alphabet do not accurately reflect their original pronunciation and meaning. Only the names of the letters of the Hebrew alphabet retain their original meaning and enable us to discern the ancient meaning of their letters. Hellenistic Judaism adopted the Greek number system around the 5th Century BC. The integrity of the Hebrew alphabet is probably due to the reverence the Jews hold the Torah. The Jews would not have wanted to violate their alphabet with additional letters, given that the original letters of their alphabet held a sacred value for them given their connection with the Torah.

The North Semitic alphabet consisted of 22 consonant letters. The Early Greek alphabet was based on these consonants and did not include the letter *chi*. This letter appeared later in the development of the Greek language and may not bear any meaning at all as do the original letters of the Greek alphabet, just as the additional Greek vowels have no deeper meaning other than simply "big O" (*o-mega*) or "little O" (*o-micron*), for example. The addition of vowels partly accounts for the discrepancies between the Hebrew number system and the Greek number system, which share so many other similarities. It also explains why it is so difficult to find names spelt in Greek that will add up to 616 using gematria as often even short names will stray well over this limit.

The Greek letter which represents the number 6, *waw*, or *digamma*, came to be called *stigma*, which also means "mark" in Greek (See Gal. 6:17: **. . . for I bear on my body the marks** (stigmata) **of Christ**). During the Byzantine era the letter of the alphabet for number 6 was known as *episemon*, a word which literally means "a distinguishing mark" or "a badge". The Hebrew letter *tav* also means ("mark"). The Greek letter χ (chi) may also be a reference to "mark" as its shape represents the archetypal crossed sticks shape which represents the letter T, which means "mark". Also, the Greek for "mark" begins with χ: χαραγμα (*charagma*). The recurrence of these meaning of "mark" in these letters suggest that the actual letters themselves may be significant in determining the true number of the beast.

The name s*tigma* arose because the letter *digamma* which originally looked like a letter F evolved and eventually looked very similar to the ST-ligature and this ligature was known as *stigma*. *Stigma* was co-opted as a name for the ST-sign because of the acrophonic value of its initial *st-* and because of the analogy with *sigma*. The ST-ligature (*sigma-tau* ligature) was one of many ligature forms that came into widespread use as part of the minuscule writing style of Greek from the 9th and 10th centuries onward. It is based on the lunate form of the letter sigma. The ST-ligature was among the last to go out of use, around the middle of the 19th century.

Similar to the Hebrew *vav*, the Greek letter for 6 (which is ς), used to be called *waw*, but when the use of this letter of the alphabet fell out of use in Greek, a new name had to be given this letter since it could no longer be pronounced. The new name was *digamma*, so named because its shape looked like our letter F, which can be perceived as two *gammas*, one on top of the other. The fact that this letter represented the number 6 which is twice 3, the number of gamma, must also have been a factor in the choice of its name.

In Hebrew, the number 616 is formed with the four Hebrew letters *tav* (400), *resh* (200), *yod* (10) and *vav* (6).

The letters *tav* and *resh* mean "mark" and "head" respectively in their related Hebrew words.

Yad means "hand", and can also mean "handle". The Hebrew equivalent of *iota* is *yod*. Although *yad* in Hebrew means "hand", (from which the word "handle" is derived in English, Hebrew, Russian, and numerous other languages), it originally meant "arm" in the original Phoenician alphabet. The word "arm" is defined as "branch" in some dictionaries, and of course the handle of a hammer is made from a branch. In the Bible, the handle of an axe is translated by the word "wood", and it is not far-fetched to argue that "arm/branch" is an extremely apt way of describing the handle of a large hammer.

The Hebrew letter *vav* means "hook". The word *vav* means "hook" or "crook" in Hebrew. According to the *Chambers 20th Century Dictionary* a hook can be defined as "an object of bent form, such as would catch or hold anything: a curved instrument for cutting grain". From this definition, it can be seen that the *vav* can actually mean "a sickle". In the same dictionary, the word "sickle" is defined as "a reaping-hook".

Hence the number 616 using Hebrew letters is made of letters which mean can "mark", "head", "handle" and "hook". The Hammer and Sickle is the "mark" (*tav*), the "head" (*resh*) and "handle" (*yod*) make up the hammer, and the "hook" (*vav*) represents the sickle.

The significance of the words "mark," "head" and "hand," (*tav, resh* and *yad*) are clear in Revelation and could point the importance of these letters in terms of acrophany too:

> **And it causes all, both small and great, both rich and poor, both free and slave, to be marked on the right hand or the forehead, so that no one can buy or sell unless he has the mark, that is, the name of the beast or the number of its name.** (Rev. 13:16,17)

The number of the beast contains letters whose original meanings are mentioned in the very same sentence in which the beast's mark is first mentioned, namely: **mark**, **head** and **hand**. I have underlined "**name of the beast**" and "**number of the beast**" too, since these too are incorporated in the Greek/Cyrillic letters represented in the Hammer and Sickle.

The letter *xi* (ξ) is the Greek letter which represents the number 60. The equivalent Hebrew letter is *samekh*, which means "to trust", "depend upon" and "support". These meanings do not bear any relation to the content of the verse in Revelation under investigation. It would therefore seem reasonable to conclude that if the number of the Beast contains within itself any hidden indication as to the true identity of the number – and, admittedly, it may be presumptuous to maintain such a thing - then 616 would be the reasonable choice, given that *samekh* does not have any relationship to the context of the biblical passage.

The Hammer and Sickle cannot be construed to represent xi, the letter which represents the number 60, whether in its lower case or capital form: ξ/Ξ.

Incidentally, an earlier Greek number system had used an acrophonic system using the letters Π,Δ,H,X,M to represent *pente, deka, hekaton, khilioi, and murioi* (5, 10, 100, 1000, 10000 respectively.

Other commentators who support the reading 616

Many writers of commentaries on Revelation state that 616 is probably the correct number because it is the least obvious and the least symmetrical. The 1950 edition of the *Encyclopaedia Britannica*, for example, subscribes to the view that 616 is probably the original number, because it is the more difficult reading. This conclusion however is obviously not entirely satisfactory, because the correct number of the Beast might well just happen to be a symmetrical number with interesting mathematical qualities, such as being a triangular number.

Philip Comfort argues that 616 is not heretical, on the basis that P115 and Codex C (Ephraemi Rescriptus) are also "good and ancient copies" (Irenaeus' words).

Dr Paul Lewes writes that 616 is probably the original number. He believes that the number 666 has been substituted for 616 either by analogy with 888, the Greek number of Jesus, or because it is a triangular number, the sum of the first 36 numbers. The number 36 is significant here, because it is made up of the square of 6 (6x6=36).

Professor David Parker, Professor of New Testament Textual Criticism and Palaeography at the University of Birmingham, also thinks that 616 is probably the original number. He thinks the number may have originated from the name GAIOS CAESAR which adds up to 616 using Greek letters. He also thinks it is significant that 02 (Codex Alexandrinus), 04 (Codex Ephraemi Rescriptus), and P115, have the better readings in those ten instances where their readings agree with each other but differ from those of P45 and Codex Sinaiticus, (the other ancient text type which Schmid considered slightly inferior to the 02-04 text type). Such analysis shows that Josef Schmid was correct to consider the 02-04 text type the more superior in terms of faithfulness to the original text. That two of the three manuscripts of this text type (if one includes P115) should have the 616 reading is a cogent argument in favour of 616.

As already noted above, A. Deissmann also favoured 616.

J. N. Birdsall also considers 616 to be the likely original reading, as it is the harder reading. He wrote that 616 symbolised Gaius Caesar. Using Greek letters, GAIOS KAISAR adds up to 616. [he notes how the Codex Ephraemi Rescriptus is one of the members of the text–type which is closest to the original text of the Revelation, according to J. Schmid's exhaustive analysis. The Oxyrhinchus papyrus P115 is also a member of that type. The traces which remain show that 616 was once far more widespread than it is given credit for. It would have been in Asia, and perhaps from surviving there passed by way of Constantinople to the Armenian Church. The 616 version is known to have been in Egypt. J.N. Birdsall concludes that the number 616 should be given far more weight than hitherto:

> We have here the traces of a very ancient reading, namely, early Greek manuscript attestation together with evidence of survival on either wing of the ancient world.[2]

2 J.N. Birdsall, 'Irenaeus and the Number of the Beast'

Early widespread use of 616

Here is a list of the manuscripts that contain the number 616 rather than 666:

- the Oxyrhinchus Papyrus 4499 – dated on palaeographical grounds as from the late third or early fourth century (P115).
- The Codex Ephraimi Rescriptus (C,04).
- The editor of the Oxyrhinchus Papyrus following Tischendorf gives two indications of minuscule manuscripts, specifying them by the numbers 11 and 5. These cannot be identified today. 5 was amongst manuscripts used by the Italian humanist Lorenzo della Valle in his Adnotationes (1505). 11 was owned by the seventeenth century patristic scholar Paul Petau.
- The commentary of the Donatist Tyconius. We find it by perusal of later commentators who made use of Tyconius, such as Apringius, Caesarius of Arles, and Beatus of Liebana. Caesarius, Primasius and Beatus all preserve Tyconian material for Revelation 13:18, but Caesarius alone retains the form 616, the others having succumbed to assimilation.
- *Liber Genealogus*, of which at least one form emanates from a Donatist source in Africa.
- Armenian manuscript of fifth or sixth century.
- *Against Heresies*, Irenaeus, Book 5,30,1. He attests the existence of copies which contain 616, although he himself maintains that 666 is the correct number.
- *Excerpta de Monogramma*, by unknown author.
- eighth century Irish *Reference Bible* (or *De Enigmatibus*)
- *The Cambridge Gloss*, the anonymous commentary found in Cambridge, University Library, Dd. X.16, written between 750 and 900.

The scarcity of ancient manuscripts of the first millennium

The key Greek manuscripts which support the reading 616 are Codex C and the Oxyrhinchus papyrus, P115. The number is written down in full as *hexakosioi deka hex* in Codex C. P115 has the number written down as simply χις.

While there are thousands of extant Greek manuscripts of the Gospels, there are only 287 extant Greek manuscripts of Revelation. Of these, only 16 are from before the 10th century. And of these, only five manuscripts contain the passage concerning the number of the Beast (Rev. 13:18). These are:

1. Codex Sinaiticus (01)
2. Codex A: Codex Alexandrinus (02)
3. Codex C: Codex Ephraemi Rescriptus (04)
4. Papyrus P47
5. Papyrus P115

Of these, P115 and Codex C have 616 as the number of the Beast, the others have 666. (Codex B (Vaticanus) does not contain Revelation.)

Codex C - the Codex Ephraemi Rescriptus - is a fifth century Greek manuscript of the Bible, and sometimes referred to as one of the four great uncials, It was possibly written in Egypt. After the fall of Constantinople in 1453, the codex was brought to Florence. Catherine de Medici then brought it to France as part of her dowry, and from the Bourbon royal library it came to rest in the Biblioteque national de France, Paris. Being a palimpsest, potassium ferricyanide was used to bring out the ink of the original work. Tischendorf was the first to read it completely, working by eye alone. According to Edward Miller, Codex C was produced "in the light of the most intellectual period of the early Church."

According to Josef Schmid whose textual criticism on Revelation has advanced the research on Revelation more than any other person, the A and C form (to which P115 has been added) is a superior form to that of P47 and 01. It can be seen therefore that when one looks at only the earliest manuscripts which contain the superior form, the ratio is now in favour of the number 616 by a ratio of 2:1; (04, P115:02)

The number 666, however, became the accepted text throughout the Byzantine Empire, and so consequently there are far more extant manuscripts containing the number 666 than there of those which contain the number 616 if one includes all extant manuscripts without limiting the numbers to the first millennium. A large proportion of these later manuscripts are classified as the Byzantine text-form, which according to most textual critics, is the least likely text-form to resemble the original text. It was from this Byzantine form of the text that the earliest translations of the Bible into English were made by people such as Erasmus. However it must be conceded that some of these later manuscripts do contain texts of

Revelation which may well contain a very early version, in particular the text used in Oecumenius' commentary on Revelation.

Early commentators who used 616 in their writings

The book of Revelation was canonized first by the Latin Church. It is among the books listed as canonical scripture by the third Council of Carthage in AD 397. While Greek fathers in the 4th Century such as Chrysostom and Gregory of Nazianzus were still hesitant to canonize Revelation, Christians ministering in the Latin West in the 2nd Century such as Justin Martyr, Irenaeus, and Tertullian, recognized its canonicity early on. The Muratorian Canon, the oldest known canon that includes Revelation, is a Latin canon. Codex Vaticanus, a Greek codex, does not even have Revelation. Latin commentaries on Revelation by Victorinus and Tyconius existed by the fourth century, but the earliest known Greek commentaries on Revelation by Oecumenius and Andreas of Caesarea date from the sixth century.

Victorinus

Victorinus' commentary is the earliest known commentary on Revelation and was perhaps written during the reign of Gallienus (AD 258-260).

In his original work he did not give any number for the Beast. Jerome added the number 666 in his recension of Victorinus's commentary. That Jerome considered the number of the beast to be 666 is not in doubt, but what Victorinus considered to be the correct number of the beast is indeed in doubt. Caesarius of Arles, who worked with an original version of Victorinus's commentary, does not seem to have been aware of any number other than 616. The name "Nero Caesar", transliterated into Greek, does not add up to either 666 or 616 when using the Greek number system.

In AD 398 a certain Anatolius sent a copy of his commentary to Jerome requesting an assessment of it. Jerome returned it with a letter explaining that he had made corrections. This edition of Jerome gradually replaced Victorinus's original so that by the sixth or seventh century the original was no longer known. Steinhauser claims that Caesarius of Arles still knew and used the original of Victorinus.

The extensive agreement between Caesarius and Victorinus would indicate that Caesarius had access to the original commentary of Victorinus but not to Jerome-Victorinus. Beatus on the other hand had access to Jerome-Victorinus but not to Victorinus.

The original of Victorinus remained unknown until 1916 when Johannes Hausleiter discovered the original in *Codex Ottobonian latinus* 3288A (fifteenth century). In his commentary, Victorinus claims that Nero is the Beast and that Nero will return, with the number of the Beast signifying his new name. Victorinus was martyred during the persecutions of Domitian's reign. It would appear that textual critics are incorrect in asserting that he provides testimony to the 666 reading. In William Weinreich's translation of Victorinus's commentary, a footnote on page 18, Note 9 states:

> MS A [Johannes Hausleiter's 15th Century version of the original, which is published in Commentarii in Apocalypsin Editio Victorini (CSEL 49)] does not have the number [of the beast]. Both Hausleiter and Dulaey adopt it from the Jerome's recension. Victorinus makes no attempt to give a name to the number 666. The later recensions of Jerome, however, include certain traditional guesses: Teitan, Anteimos, Diclux.[3]

From the above it can be seen that New Testament textual critics are quite wrong to include Victorinus as a witness of the 666 version, when in fact it is not him but Jerome and his recension. As mentioned above, Victorinus believed that Nero would return as the Beast under a new name which will be represented by the number of the Beast. Since he did not believe that Nero had returned yet in his new guise, he could not make any conjectures as to his new name.

Tyconius

The Donatist theologian Tyconius (who died around AD 400) wrote a commentary in Latin which used the number 616, written as DCXVI. His chief work, *Liber Regularum*, propounded seven rules for interpreting scripture and these were incorporated by St Augustine in his *De Doctrina Christiana*.

Tyconius argued that the number of the Beast would be a monogram in Greek letters. Tyconius's monogram looked like this:

---

3 *Ancient Christian Tests: Latin Commentaries on Revelation*

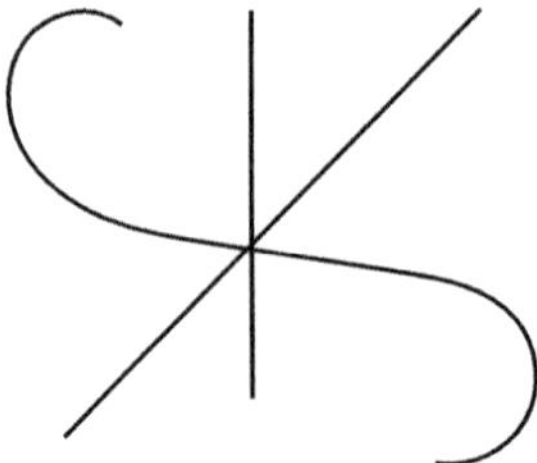

Tyconius saw in this monogram a symbol of Christ whom the Beast would try and resemble. It would appear that Tyconius recognized in the letters χιϛ (chi, iota, digamma) the first and last letters of the words "Jesus Christ" in Greek: Ι(ΗΣΟΥ)Σ Χ(ΡΙΣΤΟΥ)Σ. Rather unpersuasively, Tyconius uses the fact that a digamma can resemble a sigma in his theory.

Caesarius of Arles

Caesarius used the number 616 in his commentary on Revelation. In Homily 11, he writes:

> In Greek letters the number 616 becomes chi, iota, digamma. When these marks are given a value, it is a number. However, when they are rendered as a monogram, they are a symbol and a name and a number.

What is important about Caesarius and his witness to the number 616 is that not only is his life very well attested to, but that he held an extremely important and influential position within the Church in southern Gaul during the sixth century over a significant period of time. Primary biographical information about him comes from the *Vita Caesarii* by Cyprian of Toulon and other associates of Caesarius. Caesarius was perhaps the greatest popular preacher of the early middle ages.

He was born in AD 470 and ordained bishop of Arles in AD 502, a position he held until his own death in AD 542. He was bishop of the most important church in south Gaul.

On a visit to Rome around AD 513, Caesarius became the first bishop outside Italy to receive the *pallium*, a symbol that Caesarius was given responsibility to represent the Bishop of Rome's interests in Gaul. At the same time Pope Symmachus (AD 498-514) decided in favour of Arles over the church of Vienne, making Caesarius the metropolitan bishop of southern Gaul. Caesarius presided over no fewer than six synods: Agde (AD 506), Arles (AD 524), Carperntras (AD 527), Orange (AD 529), Vaison (AD 529) and Marseilles (AD 533).

Caesarius held this important post within the Church during the following pontificates:

- Symmachus (468-514)
- Lawrence (anti-pope 498-488)
- Hormisdas (514-516), John I (523-526)
- Felix IV (III) (526-530)
- Dioscoris (anti-pope 530)
- Boniface II (530-532)
- John II (533-535)
- Agapitus I (535-536)
- Silverius (536-537)
- Vigilius (537-555)

The fact that Caesarius held such an important position within the Church and for such a long time lends enormous credence to the number 616. The Popes listed above may also have considered 616 to be the correct number of the Beast at this time in the Church's history.

Caesarius gives no indication that he was aware of any alternative reading to the number 616, despite being very well read in religious literature, especially the works of Augustine. Traditionally the nineteen homilies of Caesarius were attributed in most manuscripts to Augustine, and the homilies are sometimes even referred to as the "pseudo-Augustinian homilies". Given Caesarius's knowledge of Augustine's works and given Augustine's respect for the works of Tyconius, who also believed that the number of the Beast was 616, it is not unreasonable to suggest that Augustine himself may also have believed that the number of the Beast was 616. No extant work of Augustine's suggest to the contrary.

Caesarius quotes no one explicitly, but the principal sources for his commentary on Revelation are the lost commentary of Tyconius and the original edition of Victorinus's commentary which he sometimes uses verbatim.

Caesarius would have had a manuscript of Revelation that contained the number 616. It is clear therefore that despite Irenaeus' rejection of the reading of 616, even senior members of the church in Southern Gaul continued to read manuscripts which had 616 as the number of the Beast at Rev. 13:18 in their main text for several more centuries.

Friedrich Engels on 666

The Bolsheviks would have been aware of the two variant readings for the number of the Beast in Revelation, because the matter is discussed by Friedrich Engels himself.

Engels concluded that the prophecy was false, unfulfilled because the Antichrist failed to appear around the year 70 AD, arguing that the number of the Beast referred to Nero.

The belief that the Beast refers to one of the early Roman emperors persists to this day and Engels is not alone in thinking that Revelation is referring to the *Nero redivivus* myth.

No revolutionary would have wanted the USSR associated with Nero, the head of a system that was based upon the exploitation of slaves, a system that socialists saw as a forerunner to the capitalist system. Given this association with Nero, it can be taken for granted that the designers had no intention to make the Hammer and Sickle signify the number of the Beast.

616 true number despite the prolific use of 666 among Satanists

The abundant use of the number 666 by many satanic groups and organizations does not undermine this book's claim that 616 is in fact the true number of the Beast. Satan is the **father of lies** and it is not in his interests to advertise the correct number of the Beast. While no doubt satanists sincerely believe that 666 is the correct number, they are no less mistaken than the majority of Christians who also presume that 666 is the correct number of the Beast.

The means of identifying the Beast through its number is a gift from God, and of a spiritual nature. It would be a mistake to suppose that devil-worshippers would be better at identifying the correct number of the Beast than Christians, or at identifying the Beast itself.

The "time is near" (Rev. 22:10): the fall of Jerusalem

> **And he said to me, "Do not seal up the words of the prophecy of this book, for the time is near."** (Rev: 22:10)

Those people are mistaken who assume that Christ's command to John not to seal up the words of the prophecy (Rev. 22:10) indicates that the Apocalypse was only of relevance to the generation alive in John's day. The Apocalypse concerns events that span across time, from events that were to occur in John's day to events that would occur thousands of years later.

However, it is possible that the above verse (Rev. 22:10) points to the imminent fall of Jerusalem. The verse clearly echoes these verses in Daniel:

> **But you, Daniel, shut up the words, and seal the book, until the time of the end.** (Dan. 12:4)

In Daniel, the phrase "time of the end" (see Dan. 11:40, for example) appears to refer to the fall of Jerusalem at the hands of the Romans in 70 AD. The time of trouble "**such as never has been since there was a nation until that time**" (Dan, 12:1) seems to be a distinct reference to the fall of Jerusalem. Only three verses later Daniel is told to seal up the book **until the time of the end** (Dan. 12:4).

The fall of Jerusalem and the its being trampled upon during the first half-week of the seventieth week is alluded to in Rev. 11:2.

The fact that, by any reckoning, John received his prophecy around the time of the fall of Jerusalem supports the deduction that the "time" that was "near" (Rev. 22:10) is the "time of the end" of Daniel. The "time of the end" signifies the end of the "seven weeks and sixty-two weeks" (Dan. 9:25) and the beginning of the final week, the seventieth week of Daniel.

Daniel was told to seal the book because the fall of Jerusalem was some time off. John is commanded not to seal up the words of the prophecy because the fall of Jerusalem was imminent and the beginning of the seventieth week was at hand.

Part Three

THE HAMMER AND SICKLE: THE NUMBER OF THE NAME OF THE BEAST

12

THE HAMMER AND SICKLE IS THE NUMBER OF THE NAME OF THE BEAST

The Hammer and Sickle is the number of the Beast: 616

The Hammer and Sickle is a monogram of the number 616 in Greek letters (ChIV) and Hebrew letters (TRTZ) in obverse.

The author believes he was misguided to see a monogram of the name "Satan" in the emblem. The number 616 does not point to "Satan" in either Greek or Hebrew. Besides, the prophecy specifically states that the number 616 is the number of a man (Rev. 13:18).

The variant reading (616) is not yet found in the main text of any modern versions of the Bible, but is acknowledged in a footnote in over half of the most important editions of the Bible. The most important witness to the number 616 is found in the Codex Ephraemi Rescriptus, where the number 616 is written out in full (Greek: *hexakosiai deka hex*).

The word "monogram" means "one letter", a misnomer, since a monogram must actually contain more than one letter to be a monogram. Since Greek and Hebrew letters represent numbers, as well as letters, a monogram is in effect "one number".

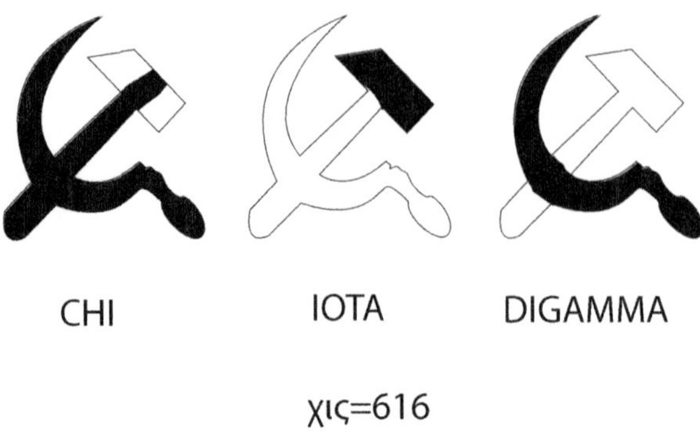

How the Greek letters fit the Hammer and Sickle

The Hammer and Sickle is the number of the Beast, a monogram of the Hebrew letters TRTZ (in obverse) and the three Greek letters which number 616 (in reverse).

The Greek letters χις serve as numbers in the Greek number system and total 616, because χ (*chi*) =600, ι (*iota*)=10, and ς (*digamma*)=6. (*See Appendix 2 for table of the number systems).*

The Hammer and Sickle can be seen therefore as a number, the number of the Beast (Rev. 13:18). The Hammer and Sickle represents these three Greek letters χ,ι, and ς , which serve as numbers in the Greek number system, in the form of a monogram. When these three letters χ,ι, and ς are superimposed they can be made to form the shape of the Hammer and Sickle.

The apocalypse of John was written down in ancient Greek and the ancient Greek number system was based on the alphabet. According to the Greek number system χ=600, ι=10, and ς=6.

The number ς, called *digamma*, was originally the 6th letter of the ancient Greek alphabet but was already in disuse by the time of the Revelation. It originally looked like the letter F but its original shape changed over time until it looked remarkably like a sickle. Sometimes it was written like a C. Originally called a *waw,* the sixth letter of the alphabet was called a *digamma*, because it looked like two gammas one on top of the other and had the numerical value of two gammas (2x3=6).

The Hammer and Sickle represents these three Greek letters: χ,ι, and ϛ. When these three letters are superimposed upon each other to form a monogram, they can be made to form the shape of the Hammer and Sickle.

The Greek word for "letter" is derived from the Greek word for "line". The Hammer and Sickle can be drawn with three strokes of the pen, each stroke representing a letter of the Greek or Hebrew alphabet. For this reason, the Hammer and Sickle should be known as the Trigrammaton.

The head of the hammer represents the *iota* (ι). The *iota* is the smallest letter of the Greek alphabet when written cursively. The word *iota* is derived from the Semitic word *yod*, and the *yod* looks just like an apostrophe when written in Hebrew. The representation of such a small letter by the head of the hammer is quite appropriate.

The crossed shape of the Hammer and Sickle represents the *chi* (χ).

The sickle shape represents the *digamma* (ϛ) which evolved over time from a letter that looked like our English capital letter F until it looked more like a C-shape, even the shape of a sickle. In Papyrus 115, the oldest surviving text which contains 616 as the number of the beast, the *digamma* looks like a lunate C.

Admittedly the hammer could be perceived as *tau* (τ). Unfortunately it is in the nature of monograms that letters can be perceived other than those intended. The book of Revelation is a guide as to which letters should be perceived in the mark of the Beast and which should be ignored.

The handle of the hammer cannot serve as the iota itself. Without the third stroke, representing the hammer-head, it would be impossible to distinguish between the numberChIV (616) and ChV (606).

This theory that the Hammer and Sickle is a monogram is similar to the theory presented in Ceasarius of Arles's commentary on the Book of Revelation, which was probably based on Tyconius's commentary. The theory was that the number of the Beast might be a monogram that imitated the *nomen sacrum* of Jesus Christ based on the three Greek letters which make up 616. In Tyconius's work the number 616 is written using the Latin letters DCXVI.

The Encyclopaedia Britannica [1950 Edition, under "Apocalypse"] reckons 616 as probably the correct number, and suggests that the number was based on Gaius Caesar's (Caligula's) name in Greek. The entry theorizes that the mark of the Beast might be a variation upon the Chi Rho symbol, with a digamma in place of the rho.

No number in Cyrillic numerals fit the monogram

The Beast is "king" of the Fourth Kingdom, whic his Russia. It is reasonable tht the name of the Beast shoudl be found in Cyrillic letters in the monogram, the mark of the Beast. he 33 letters of the Cyrillic alphabet are derived from the letters of the Greek and Hebrew alphabets.

Cyrillic numerals, the number system derived from the Cyrillic script, was used in Russia until early 18th century when Peter the Great replaced it with Arabic numerals. Cyrillic numerals may still be found in books written in the Church Slavonic language to this day.Cyril was a Greek monk who, with Methodius, brought written language to Christian converts in the mid-9th century (c.860) in what is now Russia.

Despite the fact that the Cyrillic numbera system is equivalent to the Ionian numeral system and written with the corresponding graphemes of the Cyrillic script, no number can be made with these letters that fits the monogram.

Although based upon the Greek digamma, the Cyrillic numeral for the number 6 looks like an S and does not fit the Hammer and Sickle.

Although the Hammer and Sickle can be perceived as letters of the Cyrillic alphabet, no number can be made with thse letters that fts the Hammer and Sickele in the form of a monogram. There are four Cyrillic letters that might fit the monogram. These are Л (30), C (2XIS00), T(300) and X (600). (The letter П has been excluded, because, though it is similar to the Л, its downtrokes should be parallel). No combination of these these four letters can be made to form a number because they cannot be separated into hundreds and tens (none of the lettes are in the 0-9 range) in a way that will fit the monogram without leaving surplus lines .

The sickle-shape can only be matched by the letter Es (C) and so the other letters in the hundreds range have to be discarded immediately. (Up until the 14th century the Cyrillic koppa (which resembled a Greek digamma) was sickle-shaped, but was replaced long ago bythe letter Che (Ц) to represent the number 90.)

The Cyrillic letter Es (C) is absed on the lunate form oof the Greek letter sigma. During the Hellenistic period (4th-3rd century BC) the epigrammatic form of sigma was simplified into a C-like shape which has also been found on coins from that period. This became the universal standard form during late Antiquity and the Middle Ages. Today it is known as lunate sigma and is used in typefaces particularly in religious contexts.

The Greek lamda (Λ) is different from the Cyrillic El (Л), and would not fit the Hammer and Sickle as a monogram.

The letters XIϹ of the Greek alphabetand תרטז of the Hebrew alphabet) which one can perceive in the same monogram, represent the number 616.

616 (χις) transliterated into Hebrew form the root letters of חֵיוָה (cheyvah, "beast" in Aramaic)

Confirmation that 616 is the true number of the Beast can be found in the fact that when the Greek letters which represent 616 (χις) are transliterated into Hebrew it results in חיו , the three root letters of the word חֵיוָה (*cheyvah*), the Aramaic for "beast".

The early Aramaic/Hebrew-speaking Christians would have perceived the connection of the three Greek letters with the Aramaic word for "beast". However, the Greek-speaking Christians, who were probably unfamiliar with Aramaic or Hebrew, may have become confused. Aware from their connections with Aramaic-speaking Christians that there was a connection with Aramaic through transliteration, they may have transliterated *therion* (the Greek for "beast") into Hebrew letters (which adds up to 666, using gematria) instead of transliterating χις into Hebrew letters.

The word *cheyvah* appears many times in Daniel, Chapter 7, in several declensions. In this chapter, Daniel has a vision of four great beasts rising up from the sea. The Beast in Revelation also rises up out of the sea and represents the same kingdoms:

> **And I saw a beast rising out of the sea** . . . (Rev. 13:1).

A monogram of 616 in Hebrew letters (TRTZ)

As already discussed, the Hammer and Sickle can be perceived as a monogram of the number 616 in Hebrew letters: TRTZ.

Like a normal tav, the "legs" (downstrokes) of the tav in the monogram are perpendicular to the "roof" (the horizontal stroke) of the tav, but as this horizontal stroke forms part of the curved sickle, the downstrokes appear as though stretched apart and are not parallel.

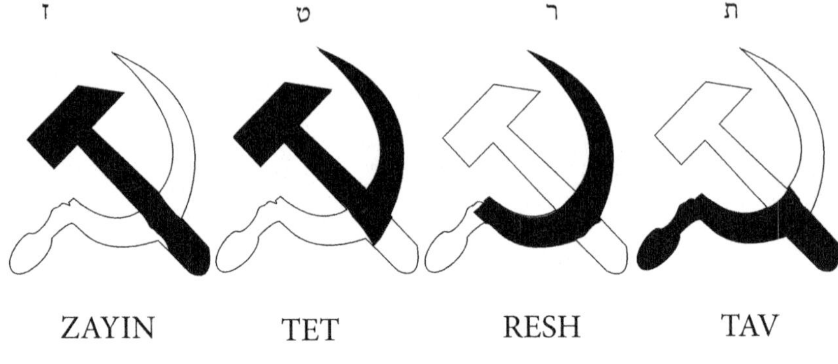

TRTZ=616

In this TRTZ monogram, the resh is more like a resh in Modern Script, completely rounded unlike the standard form where both the “roof” and “leg” are straight except for a slight bend where they join. It is perhaps harder to perceive this particular letter in the monogram than any of the other letters.

The following points support the interpretation that the blade of the sickle does indeed represent a resh:

- The curve of the “roof” is longer than the curve of the “leg” which is consistent with a resh.
- The curvature of the resh’s “roof” had to be rounded to accommodate the curvature of the right side of the tet. Such flexibility is perfectly consistent with how monograms are formed.
- Since the “roof” had to be rounded (to accommodate the tet), the “leg” also had to be rounded to be consistent with the “roof”.
- The “leg” of the resh also had to be rounded to accommodate the curvature of the right side of the tet.
- Unlike a simple monogram, each letter not only have to fit into the shape of the other letters but also the shape of a hammer and/or sickle.

Generally, the blade of a sickle is a good match for the Hebrew letter resh. The blade of the sickle of the Soviet Emblem however is more rounded than is commonly found, and this roundness reduces its likeness to a resh and increases its likeness to a kaf. This deviation from the usual shape of a sickle can be illustrated in the diagram below:

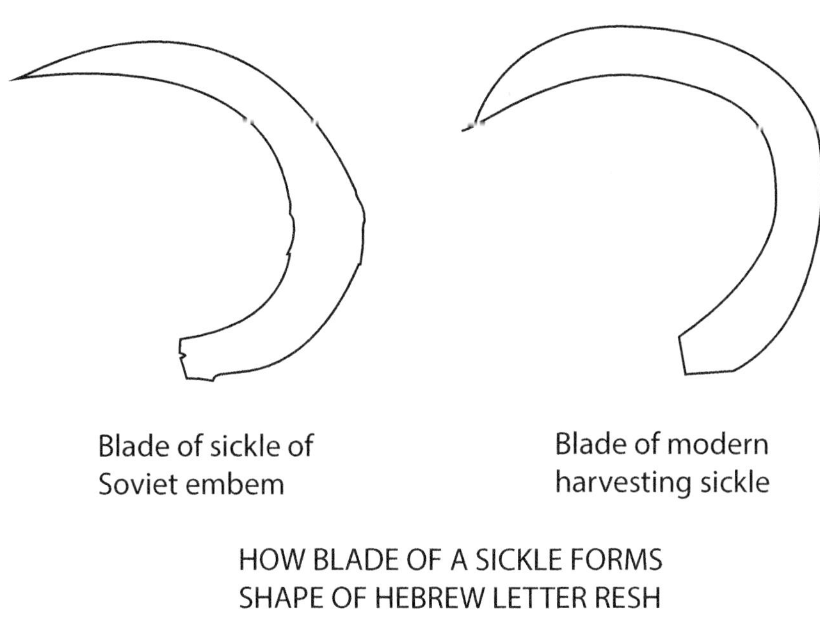

HOW BLADE OF A SICKLE FORMS
SHAPE OF HEBREW LETTER RESH

ר

The blade of the sickle found on the emblem is not symmetrical like a kaf. The blade's lower half is rounded and closely adheres to the shape of a a circle, but its upper half straightens off by following a circular path with a wider radius.

The blade of the modern harvesting on the right of the diagram above is flatter on the top and less rounded at the bottom, giving it a greater likeness to a resh. However, there is still a great likeness between the two blades.

The practice of stretching certain letters in Hebrew

Certain Hebrew letters are stretched in order to ensure that Torah columns are fully justfied, the text extending to each side of the column. (An example of this can be found on the cover of Sarah Nicholson's *Biblical Hebrew* of the Teach Yourself series, 2006).

Dalet, he, resh, and tav are all good candidates for stretching. The form of these letters are not deemed changed by the stretch. These letters are not thought of as having a "roof" of about the same length as their "leg", else they would not be able to be stretched.

The letter tav perceived in the Hammer and Sickle is clearly stretched. It should still be counted as a tav for its form likewise is not changed by the stretch.

The shape of the Hammer and Sickle carved on Trotzky's tomb in Mexico City requires less stretching of tav than the standard shape.

Leg height of letters that can be stretched is limited by the line height, but the "roof" height is not limited. The "roof" height does not have to remain proportional to the "leg" height.

Letters which would morph into the appearance of another letter are not good candidates.

Zayin is conceived as having a head approximately one-third the length of its height, so it is not extended. Given that a zayin cannot be stretched, it would be inappropriate to envisage the resh in the left half of the zayin.

Chet is conceived as being formed from two zayins. Consequently, chet cannot be extended either, except by placing a "peaked roof" (like an upward-pointing angle bracket in appearance) between the two zayins to extend its length (which must be kept short anyway or the "peaked roof" would become flattened and cease looking like a peaked roof). This point is extremely significant because it shows that the base of the Hammer and Sickle cannot be interpreted as a chet instead of a tav. Chet cannot be stretched. Being able to rule out chet is important because a chet looks so similar to a tav.

The mark of the Beast must also be an antonym to name on the saints' foreheads

Paul S. Minear observes in *I Saw A New Earth* that the mark of the Beast must be an antonym to the name of God:

> The figure [i.e. the mark] must represent both the name of the beast and his brand (*charagma*) as they were inscribed on the heads and hands of the earth-dwellers (vss. 12-16). The same name and brand must apply to all who are thus described in the whole book. The name and brand must be intelligible as antonyms to the name and brand worn by those who refused to worship the beast. The name must therefore be integral to the syndrome of deception, idolatry, blasphemy, adultery - in fact, to all the sins which were believed to exclude men from the holy city.

The Hammer and Sickle represents the word "beast" through its numerical association with the words *cheyvah* and *therion*. This name does indeed fulfil the criteria above, and serves as a perfect antonym to the name of the Lamb.

Just as the righteous therefore have the name of God and of the Lamb on their foreheads (Rev. 14:1, plus the name of the new Jerusalem (Rev. 3:12), so the worshippers of the Beast have the name of the "Beast" on their foreheads or right hand.

The number 616 refers to the name "Beast"

> **. . .the mark of its name, or the number of its name.** (Rev. 13:17)

Eusebius describes Constantine's Labarum thus:

> Now it was made in the following manner. A long spear overlaid with gold, formed the figure of the cross by means of a transverse bar laid over it. On the top of the whole was fixed a wreath of gold and precious stones; and within this, the symbol of the Saviour's name, two letters indicating the

name of Christ by means of its intial characters, the letter P being intersected by X in its centre . . .

Eusebius clearly considered the title ΧΡΙΣΤΟΣ (Christ) to be "the Saviour's name". So likewise the appellation "Beast" is to be counted as the Beast's name. Since, through transliteration, the number 616 spells "beast" in Greek and Aramaic, the number 616 may be considered the number of the name of the Beast. The number dos not represent the personal name of any individual man at all.

The Beast's mouth identifies it with the Little Horn"

. . . its mouth was like a lion's mouth. (Rev. 13:2)

. . . a mouth uttering haughty and blasphemous words. . . (Rev. 13:5)

In Daniel the Little Horn is described as having the "eyes of a man" and a "mouth":

. . . and behold, in this horn were eyes like the eyes of a man, and a mouth speaking great things. (Dan. 7:8)

Here in Revelation, there is no mention of any eyes (*aynin* in Aramaic), despite the fact that the Little Horn of Dan. 7:8 and the Beast are one and the same. Instead, allusion is made to the name "Lenin" by the phrase "**is not**" *(einenah* in Hebrew).

The mouth is the only common factor between the description of the Beast here in Revelation and the description of the Little Horn in Daniel. The Dragon also operates by means of its mouth, and tries to wash away the Woman with a flood that is poured out of its mouth (Rev. 12:15).

Since the names "Satan" and "Devil" are derived from verbs which mean "to slander", it is appropriate thatf the Beast should have a mouth that also implies slander. The Beast is said to have a blasphemous name upon its heads (Rev. 13:1). Peter describes the devil as "**a roaring lion, seeeking someone to devour**" (1 Peter

5:8) Given the connection between the Beast and the Devil, it is appropiate that it should have the mouth of a lion. The Second Beast spoke **like a dragon** (Rev. 13:11, and so does the First Beast, hence its name ("mouth of a lion").

The Little Horn/the Beast is identified by a mouth. The Little Horn's mouth is a man's mouth (Dan. 7:8), as are its eyes. The Beast's mouth is alluded to three times in chapter 13 of Revelation. The Little Horn's (Dan. 7:20)/the Beast's (Rev. 13:5) mouth speaks boastful things:

> **. . . [the fourth beast] had great** (*ravrevan)* **iron teeth . . .** (Dan. 7:7)

> **. . . in this horn were eyes of a man, and a mouth speaking great things** (*ravrevan)***.** (Dan.7:8)

The use of the Aramaic word רברבן (*ravrevan*), meaning "great", in the two verses above identifies the mouth of the Little Horn with the mouth of the Fourth Beast with its iron teeth.

USSR: Satan's throne

Satan gives the Beast **his power and his throne and great authority.** (Rev. 13:2). It is for this reason that men worship Satan, **for he had given his authority to the beast** (Rev. 13:4). It is fitting therefore that those who worship Satan should receive a mark on their right hand or forehead which means "Satan".

The **throne** signifies a kingdom. The USSR is Satan's kingdom.

"A name of blasphemy" (Rev. 13:1) indicates the name Devil (διαβολος=-blasphemer, slanderer)

> **And I saw a beast rising out of the sea, with . . . a name of blasphemy upon its heads.** (Rev. 13: 1, *author's translation*).

Both the Greek words διαβολη and βλασφημια mean "slander". The Greek for "devil" (διαβολος) is based upon the word διαβολη and is therefore "a name of blasphemy" (The name Satan is derived from the Hebrew verb *satan*, a verb with similar connotations meaning "to accuse, persecute, act as adversary".)

The fact that this name of blasphemy is on all seven heads indicates that the name of the Beast certainly applies to the seven-headed Beast, and not just to the eighth kingdom or to the Beast himself. The seven-headed Beast is clearly identifiable with the seven-headed Dragon, and hence with Satan (the Devil).

The Beast is Satan because his throne is Satan's throne

> **I know where you dwell, where Satan's throne is . . . where Satan dwells. (Rev. 2:13)**

The throne referred to as Satan's throne in the verse above is surely none other than Caesar's, the king that "**is**" (Rev. 17:10). Pergamum was not alone in this of course, as all seven churches of Asia were situated within the Roman Empire.

The fact that Caesar's throne is referred to as Satan's throne in Rev. 2:13 is extremely significant when it comes to discerning the name of the Beast, for it indicates that Caesar's throne is Satan's throne and thus equates Caesar with Satan.

Satan has handed over his power and his throne to the Beast (Rev. 13:2), and yet Satan clearly retains his sovereignty. If Satan had renounced his sovereignty, the seven heads of the Dragon would not bear seven diadems upon them (Rev. 12:3). Instead these seven heads would be bereft of any crowns to indicate that all of Satan's sovereignty had been transferred over to the kings represented by the seven heads of the Beast.

By handing over his throne and power to the Beast, Satan is merely extending his kingdom into the sphere of men. Far from emptying out his own kingdom, or dividing his kingdom, he is merely transferring power from himself to himself, handing power and authority from Satan to Satan, from Satan to the Beast (Matt. 12:24-26).

Satan can be divided. This is implicit in Jesus' response to the accusation that he was casting out demons by Beelzebub when he explains the implications of Satan being divided against Satan. Like a kingdom or city that is divided, Satan's kingdom would not stand if Satan was casting out Satan.

Satan has been cast out of heaven and now exercises his power and authority on earth through all those kingdoms that are represented by the seven heads of the Beast, not just the eighth kingdom (the Beast itself). This is evident from the fact that all seven heads of the Dragon are crowned and that these heads of the Dragon match the seven heads of the Beast.

Since Rev. 2:13 makes it clear that Satan is seated on the throne of the sixth kingdom (Rome), there can be no doubt that Satan is also to be reckoned as the future occupant of the Beast's throne, the king of the the eighth kingdom. In fact, Satan is seated on the throne of all seven kingdoms.

The Beast himself, by commiting sin, is of the devil, a child of the devil. (1 John 3: 8,10). The children of the devil can be called devils, as Jesus alludes to Judas Iscariot as a devil (John 6:70). How much more so can the Beast himself, the one to whom Satan has given his power and authority, be called a devil. Since "devil" is another name for Satan (Rev. 12:9), one is effectively calling somebody Satan when calling them a devil.

The Ten Kings hand over their power and authority and royal power to the Beast (Rev. 17:13, 17) in the same manner that Satan hands over his power to the Beast. Despite this transfer of power, the Ten Kings are still represented by the Ten Horns of the Beast and are still reckoned to make war on the Lamb.

Both Satan himself and the agents through whom he works can both be designated as Satan. Although it is perfectly well understood that the agents are acting through the influence of Satan, and are themselves distinct from Satan, they too can be referred to as Satan. An example of this can be seen in the incident where Christ rebukes Peter saying **"Get behind me, Satan"** (Mark 8:33).

The agents of Satan can be referred to as "Satan". Jesus warns the church in Smyrna that the devil is about to throw some of them into prison (Rev. 2:10), thereby associating the human agents who will throw these Christians into prison with the devil.

The Beast represents those kings and kingdoms that oppose the Lamb. and which persecute the seed of the Woman in the same manner that the Dragon does. The satanic acts of persecution which are undertaken by the Dragon (chapter 12 of Revelation) are continued by the Beast (chapter 13). The reader is informed that the Dragon went off to make war on the rest of the Woman's offspring (Rev. 12:17), and in the very next verse the Beast is described rising up from the sea. Here the Beast to all intents and purposes is the Dragon, but in a form that identifies which kingdoms are represented by the seven heads of the Dragon.

The persecutions that the Beast commits are the devil's work, and so the

Beast and Satan can be considered as one in the same manner that Christ claimed that he was one with the Father

The seven-headed Beast is surely none other than the Red Dragon but in another form. Both are red, both have seven heads and ten horns. The Dragon represents Satan, a spirit that has no actual physical form. Likewise the seven-headed Beast represents an entity that has no actual physical counterpart. Each individual kingdom can be named, but what name can be given to the seven kingdoms collectively other than the name "Satan", or possibly "Leviathan"?

Just as those who can enter the New Jerusalem shall have the name of God on their foreheads (Rev. 22:3), so the worshippers of the devil shall have the number of the Beast on their foreheads which represents the word "Beast" through the number 616.

The worshippers of the Beast are marked with a symbol in the same manner that the 144,000 have the Lamb's name and his Father's name written on their foreheads (Rev. 14:1).

Lunacharsky, the man entrusted with the design of the Soviet emblem, wrote in his book *Religion and Socialism* that Marx set aside all contact with God and instead put Satan in front of marching proletarian columns. The banner of the Hammer and Sickle was carried in marching proletarian columns, Satan in front.

Many Bolsheviks were Satanists. Lunacharsky was probably a Satanist, as were other high-ranking communists. He was a Nietzschean Marxist and a Theosophist. Both Nietzsche's philosophy and Theosophy denigrate Christianity and encourage Satanism.

The combination of Greek and Hebrew is a constant feature of Revelation and its interpretation. The name of the angel who is king over the locusts is likewise given in both Hebrew and Greek: Abaddon and Apollyon (Rev. 9:11).

It is almost certain that the Bolsheviks did not realize that the Hammer and Sickle forms 616, the number of the Beast.

The three letters of the Hebrew alphabet which spell SATAN actually add up to 359: 300+50+9 in Hebrew (see *Appendix 2* for numerical value of Hebrew (and Greek) letters of the alphabet).

Consecration to Satan

Those who join the Chinese Communist Party swear the following before the party flag, a Hammer and Sickle:

> I wish to join the Chinese Communist Party, to support the Party's constitution, follow the Party's regulations, fulfil the member's obligations, execute the Party's decisions, strictly follow the Party's disciplines, keep the Party's secrets, be loyal to the Party work diligently, dedicate my whole life to Communism, stand ready to sacrifice everything for the Party and the people, and never betray the Party.[4]

This spirit of cult-like devotion to the Party is termed the "sense of Party nature". If the party wants you be kind, then you should be kind; if the Party wants you to do evil, then you should do evil.

There are many similarities between a communist's oath of allegiance to the Party and a consecration to Satan. The Communist promises to "dedicate his whole life to the Party" and to "stand ready to sacrifice everything for the Party". The acolyte of Satan gives his "body and soul" to Satan.

In both cases, the acolytes swear to obey the Party or Satan respectively. The communist acolyte swears before a flag of the Hammer and Sickle.

Three out of the five ruling communist parties use the Hammer and Sickle as their party symbol: China, Vietnam, and Laos. Most other communist parties around the world have also adopted it. Each respective Hammer and Sickle is slightly different in design.

Just as the Satanist renounces all bonds with the Christian church, so the communist is discouraged from having any ties with the Church.

A man usually becomes a Satanist through a consecration to Satan. This normally involves an agreement written in blood, often with a black mass, which sounds like more or less like this:

> Satan, from now on I belong to you, in life, in death, and after death. Accept me as your acolyte. I give you my body and soul, and I shall do what you wish and command, but give me pleasures, success, sex, and riches.

Danyal Hussein made a similar pact with the devil, signing a pact in his

---

4 CCP Constitution, Chapter One, Article Six

own blood promising to sacrifice six women every six months and to build a temple in exchange for a lottery win, wealth and power. In June 2020 he murdered the two daughters of the first black woman to be made a Church of England archdeacon. The pact was addressed to "king" Lucifuge Rofocale. Some speculate that Rofocale may just be the name Lucifer in reverse. Lucifuge means "[he who] flees the light", the opposite meaning of Lucifer. Christ is the bright morning star (Rev. 22:16).

An example of a time dependent pact can be found in Richard Cavendish's book, *The Black Arts,* published in 1967:

> My lord and master Lucifer, I acknowledge you as my god and prince, and promise to serve and obey you while I live. And I renounce the other God and Jesus Christ, the saints, the church of Rome and all its sacraments, and all prayers that the faithful may offer me; and I promise to do as much evil as I can and to draw all others to evil; and I renounce chrism, baptism, and all the merits of Jesus Christ and his saints; and if I fail to serve and adore you, paying you homage three times a day, I give you my life as your own. Made this year and day. Signed, Urbain Grandier.

The seven-headed Beast can be identified with Leviathan

> **Thou didst crush the heads of Leviathan, thou didst give him as food for the creatures of the wilderness.** (Ps. 74:14)

Like Leviathan, the Beast has many heads. The Beast rises from the sea, thus identifying it with this dragon. The Second Beast can similarly be identified with Behemoth.

The hordes of the Beast are given to the birds for food at the battle of Armageddon (Rev. 19:21) in the same way that Leviathan is given as food in theverse above (Ps. 74:14).

It may be the battle of Armageddon that is alluded to in the following verse:

> **In that day the Lord with his hard and great and strong sword will pun-**

ish Leviathan the fleeing serpent, Leviathan the twisting serpent, and he will slay the dragon that is in the sea. (Isa. 27:1)

In this verse, Leviathan is identified with Satan, the serpent.

In *The Satanic Bible*, an inverted pentagram with the five Hebrew letters that spell Leviathan at each point is called the Sigil of Baphomet.

The number 616 signifies the word "beast"

The Hebrew number for 616, is תריו (TRIW) and TRTZ. (TRIW, but not TRTZ) are the same letters as the transliterated Greek letters of the Greek word for "beast", *therion.*

The Greek word for "beast", θηριον, when transliterated into Hebrew is תֵרִיוֹן.

Commentators are incorrect when they state that all five Hebrew letters of the transliterated Greek word *therion*, תֵרִיוֹן, add up to 666 because these five letters are not a number. The last letter is not in the right order.

The Hebrew letter נ (nun) can represent both the number 50 and, in an alternative number system, the number 700 when in its final ("sofit") form, the form it takes when it is as the end of a word. When the letter nun is found at the end of the word, it changes its shape to ן, by lengthening its tail.

The alternative number system avoids the necessity of having to repeat the letter tav (ת) to form numbers above 400. Instead, this alternative system uses the five letters of the Hebrew alphabet which have different final forms. (These are kaf, mem, nun, pe, and tsade: 500, 600, 700, 800, and 900 respectively – *see Appendix 2*).

The Hebrew number for 666 is תרסו. It is definitely not תריונ.

From the above, it can be seen that God did not leave readers of the prophecy without any means of discerning the true number of the Beast. In his omniscience, he knew that the number would be tampered with, and provided a way of alerting the wise to the correct number of the Beast: 616.

The name and number in the Beast's mark will be concealed

The False Prophet is either unaware that the mark can be perceived as a name and a number, or conceals the fact. If the False Prophet was willing to make it publicly known that the mark was a monogram of the Beast's name and number, he would be equally willing to inform mankind what that name was. No wisdom would be required to discern the name of the Beast, as the False Prophet would make it abundantly clear to even the most ignorant in society what that name was.

The mark is comprised of the four Hebrew letters that comprise the number 616. If the name of the Beast was an anagram of these four letters, these letters can only be arranged in 24 different anagrams (4!=4x3x2x1=24), assuming no letter is repeated. Consequently, there would only be a pool of 24 anagrams from which to select the correct name and thus identify the name of the Beast. H

Either the False Prophet intends to deceive, or is himself unaware that he is fulfilling the prophecy. Either way, it follows that the mark cannot overtly have the appearance of a monogram made up of Hebrew letters. Clearly the mark of the Beast will not have all the ornamental curls that usually form Hebrew letters and which help identify one letter apart from another. Without these "jots" and "tittles" (see Matt. 5:18) it is nigh impossible to tell some Hebrew letters apart from each other. Tav looks very similar to he and chet, resh looks like dalet, vav like zayin, tet like samekh, and kaf like bet. It is because the Hammer and Sickle lacks these "tittles" that it is impossible to prove that a particular stroke resembles any one particular letter or that the emblem should even be perceived as a monogram at all.

Those who expect to find a mark composed of perfectly formed letters, with every jot and tittle in place and with every stroke and every letter in perfect proportion to each other, are fooling themselves. Satan intends to deceive, and is not going to lay everything out on a plate so that even the foolish and unwary would fail to be deceived.

Due to the nature of Hebrew, and in the absence of these ornamental curls, other letters in addition to the four letters that comprise the number 616 in Hebrew are perceptible. Monograms can often be interpreted in many different ways as it is. As the number of potential letters increase, the number of possible arrangements of these letters rises exponentially. Eight letters can be arranged in 40,320 different ways (8!=8x7x6x5x4x3x2x1=40,320).

Clearly, one cannot allow the inclusion of letters over and above the original four letters that comprise 616.

Some of the letters in the Hammer and Sickle monogram only loosely resemble the actual letters of the Hebrew/Greek alphabet. The shape of the letters that comprise monograms are determined to a large extent by the shape of the other letters that form the monogram. Even so, tasked with forming a monogram out of the Hebrew letters TRTZ, many might struggle to improve upon the Hammer and Sickle. Likewise, if tasked to create a monogram of the Greek letters chi, iota, and digamma (ChIV) on the reverse of the Hammer and Sickle at the same time, who could improve upon the Hammer and Sickle?

Given the wide variety of ways in which letters of both the Greek and Hebrew alphabet can be formed, a certain degree of latitude should be allowed in this matter. It is in the nature of monograms that not every letter will be perfectly formed and that the sizes of the letters are not always in the correct proportion in terms of size to each other. One only has to look at the modified letters of a Hebrew newspaper to see how these letters differ in shape from those that one finds in hand-written Jewish scrolls. The letters are still recognizable despite such modifications, and the same can be said about the letters in the Hammer and Sickle monograms.

Given too much latitude, many other letters of the alphabet can be construed in the Hammer and Sickle and consequently many other names too. Consequently it seems right to restrict the letters that can be perceived in the Hammer and Sickle to just the Hebrew letters that number 616 in both Hebrew and Greek letters.

Unlike Hebrew letters, few additional Greek letters can be made to fit the Hammer and Sickle, whether it is in obverse or reverse. The same is true of Cyrillic letters .

Just as the Greek and Hebrew letters that comprise the number 616 confirm that 616 is the correct number of the "beast" through transliteration into the other respective language, so the fact that the Hammer and Sickle can be perceived as a monogram of 616 in obverse and reverse in both Greek and Hebrew confirms that the Hammer and Sickle is the mark of the Beast.

Rehabilitation of Stalin and the return of Stalinism in Russia

President Putin is rehabilitating Stalin's image to deflect criticism away from his own leadership.

A Stalin Centre has been built recently in Bor, Nizhny Novgorod, and statues of him have been erected around Russia. Stalin is celebrated as a national hero who defeated the Nazis and who oversaw an era of modernization.

Despite the fact that approximately 107 million Soviet citizens were evicted from their homes and taken to forced labor camps and a further 690,000 were executed during his term in power, approximately 70 per cent of Russians approve of Stalin and his policies.

13

FURTHER OBSERVATIONS ON THE HAMMER AND SICKLE

Constantine the Great's *Chi Rho* monogram

The Chi Rho symbol is also a monogram, and shares similarities with the Hammer and Sickle. Despite being called the Chi Rho, the Chi Rho symbol of Constantine the Great should actually be called the Chi Rho Iota as it in fact represent XPI, the first three letters of the Greek word for Christ: XPI(ΣΤΟΣ).
le

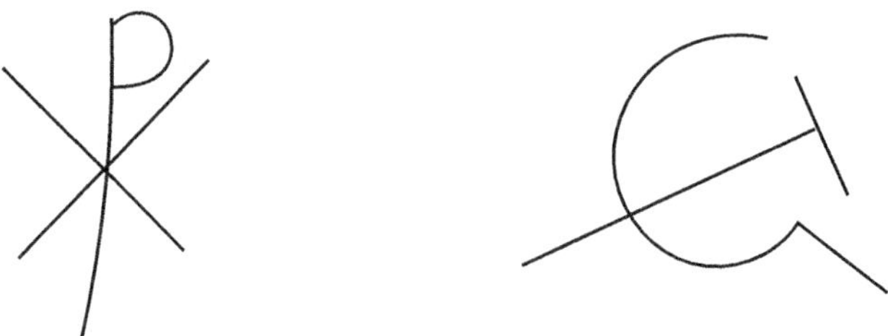

A true monogram is such that if the individual letters in a monogram were separated, they would not be readable as the letters they represent when intertwined. This differentiates the monogram from a cipher. In a cipher the individual letters do not have to connect or even touch. The Hammer and Sickle has elements of a true monogram as demonstrated by the fact that if one separated the down stroke of the chi from the digamma this grapheme would, on its own, not resemble the letter chi. The same holds true for the *Chi Rho* symbol. Remove the downstroke which represents the iota, and there ceases to be any rho.

Monograms first appeared on coins, as early as 350 BC. The earliest known examples are of the names of Greek cities which issued the coins, often the first two letters of the city's name. For example, the monogram of Achaea consisted of the letters alpha and chi joined together.

The Hammer and Sickle can face both directions

As the official emblem of the Soviet Union (adopted on the flag of the USSR on 13 November 1923) the Hammer and Sickle has the open side of the sickle facing left. However, the Hammer and Sickle was employed liberally in either direction. It is therefore appropriate that the emblem should reprsent the number 616 in either direction, in Greek letters in reverse, in Hebrew letters in obverse.

Testifying to this dual use of the Hammer and Sickle, there are multitudes of photographs of flags and banners from the Soviet era showing the Hammer and Sickle facing in either direction.

The famous photograph of the Hammer and Sickle being held aloft the Reichstag after the capture of Berlin by the Soviets in World War II shows the flag with the Hammer and Sickle facing in the direction of the Greek letters for 616.

Similarly, the last flag of the Hammer and Sickle to be flown above the Kremlin, a copy of which is on display at at the Checkpoint Charlie museum in Berlin, has the sickle facing in the direction of the Greek letters for the number 616. (The original flag was displayed at the museum from October 1992-May 1994.)

It was common to see the flag in reverse formation. Flags bearing the Hammer and Sickle had the Hammer and Sickle facing in one direction on one side, and in the other direction on the other side, the outline of the Hammer and Sickle having been printed through and through. The

Hammer and Sickle was removed from the reverse side of the flag in 1980, but many flag makers continued to print the flag through and through to save costs.

If a flag was hung in length, the Hammer and Sickle was reversed 90 degrees.

Many Soviet posters are illustrated with Hammer and Sickles facing in either direction and many statues of the Hammer and Sickle were built, where the direction of the sickle is entirely dependent upon which side of the statue one is standing.

A 1923 logo of the Young Communist League has the sickle facing in the same direction as the Greek letters for 616.

Trotzky's Fourth International adopted a Hammer and Sickle as its emblem with the sickle facing in the same direction as the Greek letters for 616, with an Arabic number 4 placed within.

The Hammer and Sickle is recognized by all as the emblem of the Soviet Union and of communism in general regardless of whichever direction it faces. As Jesus said: "**Do not judge by appearances, but judge with right judgment.**" (John 7:24)

Hammer and Sickle on Chilean currency

The Chilean government produced currency (the peso) with the symbol of a hammer and sickle on it in the decades leading up to the Second World War (1895-1940). This symbol was genuinely intended to represent the workers and the peasants.

The handle of the hammer on the Chilean currency is upright, almost touching the handle of the sickle. Consequently, the tools have been crossed in such a way that they cannot be construed as the Greek letter chi (600).

The head of the hammer on the Chilean pesos is much bigger and more barrel-shaped than the Soviet version.

It is possible that the design of the Chilean currency was an influence in the design of the Hammer and Sickle. Luis Recabarren, who transformed the Socialist Workers Party into the Communist Party of Chile in 1922, travelled to the USSR as the only Chilean delegate to the Union Congress of the Third International that took place in Moscow that same year. The

Hammer and Sickle was formally adopted as the Soviet emblem within a year of his visit to Moscow.

It is possible that the Beast will adopt the Hammer and Sickle as the symbol of his new currency. This new currency might then be called the Mark in honour of Karl Marx whose family names (Mordechai/Markus/Marx) is symbolized by the Hammer and Sickle.

Hammer and Sickle and Red Star banned in Eastern Europe

Bans on the use and display of communist symbols have existed to varying degrees in Georgia, Latvia, Lithuania, Moldova, Estonia, Hungary, Poland, Bulgaria, and Ukraine, where laws have defined the Hammer and Sickle as the symbol of a "totalitarian and criminal ideology". In 2013 courts in both Hungary and Moldova annulled the ban.

In Indonesia, the display of communist symbols of the country's Communist party was banned by decree of Suharto, following the 1965–1966 killings of communists in which over 500,000 people were killed.

Ukraine made it a criminal offence to be a member of the Communist Party of Ukraine, despite the fact it won 2.6 million votes in 2012, the third highest in electoral support, and had over 100,000 members. It also became a criminal offence to promote Marxism or to sell anything written by Marx.

However, there is still widespread use of the Hammer and Sickle in the Russian Federation, and the emblem is still ubiquitous. Aeroflot still uses the symbol.

Soviets unaware that the Hammer and Sickle could be construed as monograms

There are strong grounds for suspecting that the Soviet Emblem is based on occult symbolism with strong connections with Satanism. However, the Hammer and Sickle was not consciously designed to represent the number of the Beast. Had the Bolsheviks deliberately chosen the number of the Beast, they would have chosen the more widely accepted 666.

After the revolution, the Codex Sinaiticus, which had been gifted to the Tsar of Russia, fell into the hands of the Bolsheviks. In need of money, they sold the codex to the trustees of the British Museum for around half a million pounds in today's money. Since this codex has 666 as the number of the Beast, there is every reason to believe that the Bolsheviks would have considered 666 to be the authentic number.

It is no mystery why the Bolsheviks have hidden the true meaning of the symbolism of the Hammer and Sickle from the world. The pagan symbolism alone of Mars and Marduk would surely have outraged the large Christian, Jewish and Moslem populations within the Soviet Union and the Bolsheviks were unwilling to provoke these people.

Likewise, the Soviets did not perceive that the Hammer and Sickle can be construed as a monogram of the name "Trotz(ky)" in Hebrew. This is evident from the fact that the emblem appears universally. It appears above Lenin's body on the ceiling of his Mausoleum. This would not have happened if the symbol was associated with the name "Trotzky".

Definition of communism

In his book *The Red Devil of Communism*, E.J. Daniels uses the definition of communism used in House Report No. 2 of the Seventy-sixth Congress, First Session, under the heading, "Investigation of Un-American Activities and Propaganda", which states:

> Communism may be defined as an organised movement which works for the overthrow by force or violence of the government of countries which are not yet under the control of the Communists, and establishment in place thereof (a) a regime termed proletarian dictatorship, and (b) an economic system based upon the substitution of communal ownership of property for private ownership.
>
> Communism is a world-wide political organization advocating: (1) the abolition of all forms of religion; (2) the destruction of private property and the abolition of inheritance; (3) absolute social and racial equality; (4) revolution under the leadership of the Communist International; (5) engaging in activities in foreign countries in order to cause strikes, riots, sabotage, bloodshed, and civil war; (6) destruction of all forms of representative

or democratic government, including civil liberties, such as freedom of speech, of the press, and of assemblage; (7) the ultimate objective of world revolution is to establish the dictatorship of the so-called proletariat into a universal union of Soviet socialist republics with its capital at Moscow; (8) the achievement of these ends through extreme appeals to hatred.

Each Soviet Republic had its own emblem based on the Hammer and Sickle

Every constituent republic of the Union of Soviet Socialist Republics had its own emblem featuring the Hammer and Sickle and the Red Star in a predominant way.

The USSR State motto, *Workers of the world, unite!*, in both the republic's language and Russian was also placed on each one of the emblems. In addition to a rising sun and a frame of wheat, emblems of many Soviet republics also included features that were characteristic of their local landscapes, economies or cultures.

Most Asian post-Soviet republics use arms based on or reminiscent of the Soviet-era emblems. Most European republics, on the other hand, have reverted to their traditional pre-Soviet heraldic arms.

Eternal damnation for whoever receives the mark

> **"And the smoke of their torment goes up for ever and ever; and they have no rest, day or night, these worshipers of the beast and its image, and whoever receives the mark of its name."** (Rev. 14:11)

Those who do not worship the image of the Beast will be slain (Rev. 13:15) and no one can buy or sell who does not have the mark (Rev. 13:17).

Those who do not worship the Beast or its image and who do not receive the mark will come to life in the first resurrection and reign with Christ for a thousand years (Rev. 20:4).

All those whose names are not written in the Lamb's book of life will worship the Beast (Rev. 13:8) and be thrown into the lake of fire (Rev. 20:15).

The Red Star symbolizes Satan's war on the saints

> **Then the dragon was angry with the woman, and went off to make war on the rest of her offspring . . .**(Rev. 12:17)

The Red Star represents Mars, a synonym for war. The Dragon and the Beast both make war on the saints (Rev. 12:17; Rev. 13:7). The Little Horn of Daniel (which represents the Beast) is also envisaged making war on the saints and prevailing over them (Dan. 7:21). Clearly, a symbol of war is apt for the devil.

In the scriptures, stars represent the angels in heaven and the saints. God is the "Lord of hosts". The word "hosts" can refer to the angels in heaven, the stars in heaven, or the armies of Israel. The Red Star represents an angel, the fallen angel Satan who makes war against the saints. The fact that the Red Star represents Satan is confirmed by the fact that the Hammer and Sickle also represents Satan, being a monogram of his name. The Red Star and Hammer and Sickle are placed in juxtaposition because they both represent Satan.

On Baphomet's forehead is found the Tetragrammaton Pentagram. Such a position on the Devil's forehead indicates that this symbol is the equivalent of the mark of the Beast which is also found on the forehead (or right hand). Both the Tetragrammaton Pentagram, Baphomet, and the mark of the Beast, represent Satan. The Red Star is the Soviet equivalent of the Tetragrammaton Pentagram.

Both the Dragon and the Beast are red. A red flag has been a symbol of revolution since the French Revolution (1789-1799). Socialists displayed the Red Flag during the revolution of 1848.

The Red Flag became a symbol of communism as a result of its use by the Paris Commune of 1871. In 1921, members of the French Communist Party presented the Soviet government with one of the original Communard banners. This banner has been placed in the tomb of Vladimir Lenin, next to his open coffin.

Part Four

SOVIET LONG-RANGE DECEPTION STRATEGY

14

SOVIET LONG-RANGE DECEPTION STRATEGY

Anatoliy Golitsyn: the man who shed light upon Soviet long-range deception strategy

Born in the Ukraine in 1926, Anatolity Golitsyn served as a senior analyst in the NATO section of the Information Department of the Soviet intelligence service (1959 to 1960) at a time when Soviet long-range strategy was being formulated. He defected to the United States in December 1961.

The accuracy of Golitsyn's predictions regarding events in the Soviet Union was noted in *Wedge* by Mark Riebling. The chapter entitled "The Final Phase" in Golitsyn's *New Lies for Old* is quoted extensively by Pat Robertson in his best-selling book *The New World Order.*

Golitsyn revealed that the Soviets adopted a long-term political strategy during period 1957-1960.

The purpose of the long-range deception strategy is to convert the regimes in the Soviet Union and other Communist countries into states of 'mature socialism with a human face' to promote the strategy of convergence. It aims at the 'reform' of Western attitudes, and ultimately at the peaceful conquest of the United States and Western Europe from within.

The essence of the special manoeuvre is the creation of secretly controlled opposition movements and the use and manipulation of these into a spectrum of 'democratic' and 'non-Communist' and 'nationalist' power structures which will remain Communist-controlled in practice. The aim is to stimulate changes in the Western system to facilitate the convergence of the two systems with a view to the eventual absorption of the Western democracies within a World Government.

The long-range strategy of the communist movement is to broaden its political base in non-communist countries by forming a united front with socialist and nationalist parties. When a parliamentary majority has been won, the communists will seek through the development of extra-parliamentary mass action, to bring about fundamental changes in the democratic system.

In a Memorandum to the CIA dated 30 April 1993, written well after the alleged collapse of communism in 1991, Golitsyn warns that the Clinton administration's policy of partnership with "Russian reformers" led by Boris Yeltsin spells disaster. Both Europe and America are the targets of a political offensive that seeks to embrace them only to strangle them later.

The contemporary Russian reformers have adopted the guise of "reformers", "democrats", "non-Communists", and even "anti-Communists". Western governments and public opinion have concluded that there has been a genuine revolution in Russia when in fact the same government elite is in power as in 1984. Golitsyn observes:

> The 65 million or more former Communist Party and Komsomol members did not disappear or change their views overnight.

The Memorandum states that the soviets are projecting an image of moderation and avoiding revolutionary phraseology in line with Lenin's tactics laid down in his work *Left-wing Communism: an Infantile Disorder.*

The Soviets have manufactured political "crises" and manipulated the Western media through Russian experts and agents of influence like Georgi Arbatov.

Andrei Sakharov, under the guise of a 'dissident', was used as an unofficial mouthpiece of the former Soviet regime. In the late sixties Sakharov revealed the essence of Soviet strategy, predicting that around 1968-80 there would be "a growing ideological struggle"; Sakharov foresaw World Government by 2000.

Golitsyn predicts that Russia may be on the road to a technological revolution, even surpassing China's "economic miracle", without any loss of political control by the communists.

The US policy of partnership with Russia will be exposed as bankrupt. The US President will find himself with armed services that have been cut down in size due to mistaken assessments of long-term threats, equipped for regional conflicts but not global confrontation:

> Too late it will be realised that there have been no equivalent reductions in the power and effectiveness of the Russian and Chinese armed forces or their intelligence and security services. A real swing in the balance of power in favour of the Sino-Soviet alliance in relation to the free world will have taken place giving the Russians and the Chinese a preponderant share in setting up the new World Government system, with the West having little choice but to compete with them in designing the New World Social Order.[5]

Fragmentation of Soviet Empire only fictional

The West has been deceived by the Soviet strategists into believing that the USSR collapsed in 1991.

Anatoliy Golitsyn warned in his book *The Perestroika Deception* that the fragmentation of Soviet Empire is only fictional. The states of the former USSR are still acting as one unit despite their so-called independence within the CIS:

> The strategists are concealing the secret coordination that exists and will continue to exist between Moscow and the 'nationalist' leaders of these independent Republics. There has been ample time and every opportunity to prepare this coordination in advance. Because of its existence, the fragmentation of the Soviet Empire will not be real but only fictional. **This is not true self-determination but the use of 'national' forms in the execution of a common Communist strategy.**

The Soviet strategists themselves have created the so-called 'independ-

5 *The Perestroika Deception*, A. Golitzyn

ent' states of the CIS, repeating on a broader scale the tactics used by Lenin with the Far Eastern and Georgian Republics. The strategy also resembles Stalin's dissolution of the Comintern in 1943.

The six interlocking strategies of the Soviets

Golitsyn identified six interlocking strategies aimed at the advance of communism.

The first strategy related to the activities of communist parties in the advanced industrial countries, such as the use of Eurocommunism, with the aim of establishing unity of action with social democrats and Catholics in Europe and to create a neutral socialist Europe tilted toward the communist side.

The second strategy includes the support of national liberation movements by the USSR to establish unity of action with developing countries of Asia, Africa and Latin America.

The third was an effort to reverse the military balance of power in the USSR's favour, such as antimilitary campaigns in Western Europe.

The fourth was the undermining of ideological resistance of the non-communist world to the advance of communism.

The fifth was the disinformation programme. Much of Golitsyn's book *New Lies For Old* is concerned with the identification of Soviet disinformation programs. The book analyses the outcomes these programs and their purpose. Golitsyn identified these Disinformation Programs:

- The Soviet-Yugoslav "Dispute" of 1958-60
- The "Evolution" of the Soviet Regime (such as the "Dissident" Movement)
- The Soviet-Albanian "Dispute" and "Split"
- The Sino-Soviet "Split"
- Romanian "Independence"
- The alleged recurrence of power struggles in the Soviet, Chinese, and other Parties
- "Democratization" in Czechoslovakia in 1968
- The continuing Eurocommunist contacts with the Soviets

Generally, the purpose of the Disinformation Programs was to give the West the impression that the Soviet Empire was fragmenting and that Marxist ideology was weakening. False splits and disputes between countries within the communist bloc were to create this impression. (The most important of these was the Sino-Soviet split, with China becoming a tactical friend of the US, but its strategic enemy.) A deluded West would cease to unite against a common foe, would drop their guard, weaken their defences, and form false alliances with members of the Communist bloc under the delusion that foe had become friend.

The sixth major strategy, the grand strategy, involves the use of false opposition during the introduction of controlled democratization in the communist regimes, for the purpose of creating a favourable condition for unity of action with the social democrats, the free trade unions, and with Catholics, against NATO and the United States' Military Industrial Complex. This use of false opposition and false democracy is analysed thoroughly in Golitsyn's memoranda, many of which were published in his book *The Perestroika Deception*.

Golitsyn saw in Gorbachev's *perestroika* the fulfilment of all his predictions of a false liberalisation throughout the Soviet bloc. The existence of a common pattern in the communist world shows that the introduction of 'democratic' and 'non-Communist' structures is deceptive.

According to Golitsyn, *perestroika* was based on the New Economic Policy of the 1920s when forms of capitalism were introduced. These concessions induced the West into thinking that communism was being abandoned for ever. However Lenin had made it clear to the Party (in a statement that was only revealed to the public in 1965) that the duration of capitalism in Russia would be limited. Lenin said:

> [the New Economic Policy] will be carried out seriously and for a long time – five to ten years.

The general secretary of the Communist Party of Britain wrote that China's use of private capital to drive the economy, under licence by the state, could be compared to Lenin's New Economic Policy, "but on a vast scale and over decades rather than years". This statement hints that at some point China's cooperation with capitalism will end too and the socialist system will be enforced rigorously and without compromise.

Convergence

According to Anatoliy Golitsyn, the Soviet's present grand strategy is the application of the following Hegelian dialectical triad:

> Thesis: Stalinist regime;
>
> Antithesis: criticism and rejection of Stalinist regime.
>
> Synthesis: "convergence", the joining of two opposites: the merging of Communist substance (content) with democratic format. The democratic format is deceptive, and is the *essence* of the strategic manoeuvre.[6]

The communist strategists aim to achieve world dominance through the strategy of "convergence":

> The purpose of these actions will be to achieve political systems in the West approaching closer to the communist model. The changes planned for the communist system will be deceptive and fictitious; those planned for the West will be real and actual. That is the meaning of convergence in communist language.

Their adoption of some forms of capitalism and Western-style democracy is an illusion, according to Anatoliy Golitstyn, which will be exploited to further their policy of convergence:

> [the communists] are not introducing true capitalism but creating an illusion to tempt Western European social democrats into new forms of popular front and eventual alliance with the Soviet Union. They intend to exploit the same illusion to induce the Americans to adopt their own restructuring and convergence of the Soviet and American systems using to this end the fear of nuclear conflict.

---

6 *The Perestroika Deception*, A. Golitsyn

'Cuckoo-egg' democracy

The Communsits intend to exploit their pseudo-social democratic mixed-economy image.

The Western democracies have been acutely vulnerable to the entry of the polical and security potential of so-called 'non-communist' governments, new political parties, members of new parliaments, renewed trade unions, prominent churchmen and intellectuals, and so forth. Their democracy is 'cuckoo-egg democracy'. The Communists intend to dominate the nest. They aim to converge the 'former' communist and non-Communist systems on communist terms

The West has been fooled into such ideas as 'collective security' and the enlargement of the EU through the entry of Eastern European and CIS states. Having successfully abolished the 'image' of the enemy, the Soviets inveigled the West into signing bilateral treaties and into supporting broad inter-bloc 'collective security' arrangements.

The entry of Eastern European and CIS states into the EU is a device intended to establish irreversible Soviet hegemony through convergence with the West on communist terms.

The Soviets see three centres of nuclear power: the United States, Western Europe and Israel. They have neutralized Western Europe through the concept of Common European Security and through the membership of so-called "independent" Eastern European states into Western European institutions.

The 'Common European Home'

Soviet strategy has long aimed at creating 'Greater Europe' or a 'Common European Home', a neutral socialist Europe stretching from the Atlantic to the Urals.

In the course of his Noble Peace Prize Lecture, delivered in Oslo in June 1992, Gorbachev said:

> Our vision of the European space from the Atlantic to the Urals is not that of a closed system. Since it includes the Soviet Union, which reaches to the shores of the Pacific, it goes beyond nominal geographical boundaries.

In an interview on Moscow Television on 19 November 1991, Eduard Shevardnadze said:

> I think that the idea of a Common European Home, the building of Great Europe, great, united Europe, from the Atlantic to the Urals, from the Atlantic to Vladivostok, including all our territory, most probably a European-Asian space – this project is inevitable. I am sure that we will come to building a united military space as well. To say more precisely: we will build a united Europe, whose security will be based on the principles of collective security. Precisely, collective security.

With regards to Western Europe, the strategic objective of *perestroika* was to bring about a new political alliance between pseudo-social democratic regimes in the USSR and Eastern Europe and the Euro-Communist parties and genuine social democratic parties in Western Europe.

In the course of his Nobel Peace Prize Lecture (given in Oslo, June 1992), Gorbarchev explained:

> I dare say that the European process has already acquired elemnts of irreversibility . : . Should it now gain the necessary momentum, every nation and every country will have at their disposal in the foreseeable future the potential of a community of unprecedented strength, encompassing the entire upper tier of the globe, provided they make their own contribution, in such a context, in the process of creating a new Europe, in which erstwhile curtains and walls will be forever relegated to the past and borders between states will loe their "divisive" purpose, self-determination of sovereign nations will be realised in a completely different manner . . .

Destruction of NATO intended

One aim of *perestroika* was to weaken NATO with the United States' withdrawal from its commitment to the defence of Europe. The Russians have long had the strategic aim of 'one Europe' without NATO.

Jan Sejna, who was the head of Czechoslovakia's Secretariat of the Defence Council, who defected from Czechoslovakia in 1968, also testified to the existence of a long-range plan aimed at destroying NATO:

> The erosion of NATO begun in Phase Two would be completed by the withdrawal of the United States from its commitment to the defence of Europe, and by European hostility to military expenditure, generated by economic recession and fanned by the efforts of the 'progressive' movements. To this end, we envisaged that it might be necessary to dissolve the Warsaw Pact, in which event we had already prepared a web of bilateral defense arrangements, to be supervised by secret committees of Comecon.

Having failed to destroy NATO, the communists have taken on board the advice of Sun Tzu and have entered the camp of their enemies unopposed. The united Germany acceded in October 1990, the Czech Republic, Hungary, and Poland in 1999. Bulgaria, Estonia, Latvia, Lithuania, Romania, Slovakia and Slovenia signed membership protocols in March 2003 and officially joined NATO in March 2004. Albania and Croatia became official members in April 2009, having signed membership accords in September 2008.

The bombing of Grozny during the Chechen War succeeded in strengthening the argument that former member states of the Warsaw Pact should be admitted membership of NATO.

Given the leverage that Russia still has over the former states of the Eastern bloc, Anatoliy Golitsyn argued that the entry of former Warsaw Pact countries into NATO heralded its doom.

Tony Blair (British Prime Minister from 1997-2007) and both the Clinton and Bush administrations deserve our opprobrium for failing to heed Golitsyn's warnings. Instead they were fooled by the apparent signs of democracy and liberalization that took place throughout the former Soviet bloc. By allowing the former Soviet bloc states into NATO, they may well have sealed the fate of the West.

President Clinton and National Security Adviser Tony Lake apparently believed that NATO enlargement would "enlarge" the democratic and free-market area in the post-Cold War world. When Clinton met several central European leaders, including Lech Walesa and Vaclav Havel, at the opening of the US Holocaust Memorial Museum in Washington D.C. in 1993 every one of them said their number one priority was to get into NATO. These leaders said that they knew that NATO would provide a security umbrella for its members.

NATO may be provoked by Russia to make war against it at a time when NATO is grossly overestimating its own strength. In the misbelief that all the former members of the Warsaw Pact are genuine allies, NATO might make war against Russia only to find that it does not have the support that it took for granted. NATO currently has a false sense of its own strength. Its foe, on the other hand, is much stronger than realized and has entered NATO, the camp of its enemy, unopposed. Such a false sense of security might lead a reckless state to give up its nuclear weapons unilaterally, under the delusion that NATO is unassailable in terms of conventional warfare.

NATO's Secretary-General is living under this false sense of security. Jens Stoltenberg is already talking in terms of "a response from NATO" for Russia's actions in Georgia, Moldova, and Ukraine, and for the recurrent Novichok poisonings. Stoltenberg alleges that all NATO allies are increasing defence spending after years of cuts, but he misunderstands the geopolitical situation. Asked whether he feared another Cold War, Stoltenberg says:

> This is a different situation, particularly because during the Cold War we had two military blocs confronting one another. Europe was divided. Germany was divided . . . It's not the same kind of ideological situation.

Stoltenberg is wrong on all counts. The world is still divided between two blocs, but one of the blocs is concealing its true intentions behind a mask. At the opportune moment, the mask will be dropped:

> Western belief in the collapse of Communism will be shown to be an illusion.[7]

Stoltenberg talks about Russia's attempt to establish a new sphere of influence, but fails to realize that Russia's influence already extends over a dozen members states of NATO in secret alignment.

NATO's future is already being threatened by the failure of some member states to spend 2% of their GDP on defence. The United States may decide that it is no longer prepared to support an organization whose members are not prepared to play their part. The withdrawal of the United States from NATO would be catastrophic for the West.

The following arguments have been employed to question the existence of NATO:

---

7 *The Perestroika Deception*, A. Golitsyn

- NATO is too much of a Cold War institution;
- Global security should be handled by the United Nations, not NATO;
- European security should be managed by the Europeans. The influence of the United States is too great in NATO.

Current attempts within the European Union to form its own collective defence organization, one that is independent of NATO, would result in the weakening of NATO. To question the involvement of the United States in NATO is pure foolishness. As Montgomery of Alamein wrote in 1959 in his study on East-West relations:

> Finally, in all this business one thing is very clear to me – the English-speaking peoples of the world must be solidly united. The preservation of Christian civilisation hangs on such unity.
>
> East and West, north and south, wherever the English tongue is spoken men must clasp hands and forget all else save that they are brothers of blood and speech – eager and ready to unite and to co-operate, and thus save the Free World from being engulfed by the onward march of international Communism.[8]

The time may come when the former-Eastern bloc member states may decide that their interests are no longer served by cooperating with NATO. They may declare themselves neutral, in the hope of influencing Western democracies to follow their example. They may even transfer their allegiance across to the CSTO. This would certainly be the likely outcome if the other member states of NATO failed to take into account their strategic interests, interests which in the long-run are not in the interests of the Western democracies.

Ultimately the former-Eastern bloc member states are only interested in neutralizing NATO through the "Finlandization" of Europe.

"Finlandization" meant that the United States and NATO would be unable to rely upon the support of their Western allies. Although Finland was considered neutral, the Finno-Soviet Treaty of 1948 required Finland to defend the Soviet Union from attacks through its territory, which in practice prevented Finland from joining NATO. Through what was in

---

8 *An Approach to Sanity*

effect a veto in Finnish foreign policy, the Soviet Union was able to exercise "imperial" hegemonic power over a neutral state.

The eventual involvement of Russia itself in NATO is a long-term Russian strategic interest

NATO and the Warsaw Pact

The North Atlantic Treaty (Treaty of Washington) was signed in 1949 by Belgium, Canada, Denmark, France, Iceland, Italy, Luxembourg, the Netherlands, Norway, Portugal, the US and the USA. Greece and Turkey acceded to the treaty in 1952, the Federal Republic of Germany in 1955, and Spain in 1982.

Signed in Warsaw in May 1955, the Warsaw Pact was a collective defense treaty established as a counterweight to NATO.

Along with the USSR, seven of the Soviet satellites in Eastern Europe joined the Warsaw Pact: Albania, Bulgaria, Czechoslovakia, East Germany, Hungary, Poland, and Romania. (Albania withheld support in 1961 because of the Soviet-Albanian split, but did not formally withdraw until 1968.)

The Warsaw Pact's largest military engagement was the invasion of Czechoslovakia in August 1968 (with the participation of all Pact nations except Albania, Romania, and East Germany).

The Pact appeared to unravel with the spread of the Revolutions of 1989 through the Eastern Bloc, beginning with the Solidarity movement in Poland and its electoral success in June 1989. East Germany withdrew from the Pact following the reunification of Germany in 1990. On 25 February 1991, at a meeting in Hungary, the Pact was declared at an end by the defense and foreign ministers of the six remaining member states.

Throughout the following 20 years, the seven Warsaw Pact countries outside the USSR each joined NATO (East Germany through its reunification with West Germany; and the Czech Republic and Slovakia as separate countries), as did the Baltic states which had been part of the Soviet Union.

Sakharov's four stages towards a Marxist World Government

Golitsyn argued that the contents of Sakharov's book *Sakharov Speaks*, published in 1974, were a means of informing Marxist sympathizers in the West of events that were about to unfold in the USSR and Soviet bloc. Sakharov anticipated the liberalization of the Soviet bloc through *perestroika* thus:

> In the first stage . . . the Soviet Union and other socialist countries, this process will lead first to a multiparty system (here and there) . . . (1968-80).[9]

Sakharov alludes to the strategy of convergence:

> In the second stage, persistent demands for social progress and peaceful coexistence in the United State and other capitalist countries, and pressure exerted by the example of the socialist countries and by internal progressive forces (the working class and the intelligentsia), will lead to the victory of the leftist reformist wing of the bourgeoisie, which will begin to implement a programme of rapprochement (convergence) with socialism, i.e. social progress, peaceful coexistence, and collaboration with socialism on a world scale and changes to the structure of ownership . . . (1972-85).

In the third stage, Sakharov predicts the alliance of the United States and the Soviet Union and their use of science to solve the problem of the poorer half of the world through the harnessing of science.

In the fourth stage he predicts world government:

> . . . the socialist convergence will reduce differences in social structure . . . and lead to a world government . . . (1980-2000).

The "dissident" Andrei Sakharov was a key agent of influence. He initiated the International Foundation for Survival and Development of Humanity (IFSDH), a joint Soviet-US collaboration into research on the environment, pollution, human rights, arms control and economic development. All these issues are of enormous relevance to the strategy of convergence. The IFSDH was an especially important element in the soviet

9 *Sakharov Speaks*, A. Sakharov

drive to inject their strategic influence into the US. In Sakharov's inaugural speech at IFSDH he said that the West should engage with the USSR, thereby reducing the risk of war.

Eduard Shevardnadze's International Foreign Policy Association (IFPA) was designed to have a parallel influence, and even shared a common office, with the Gorbachev Foundation, at the Presidio in San Francisco. It is concerned with issues such as economic development. It is an instrument for the mobilisation of the unsuspecting American liberal and policymaking elite in the furtherance of the long-range deception strategy of 'convergence' between East and West on communist terms.

Mikhail Gorbachev is an extremely important agent of influence. Gorbachev is president of the International Green Cross, an organisation which intends to exploit global issues to do with environmentalism with the aim of attacking private property.

East-West partnership is meant to lead to East-West convergence and eventual world government on Communist terms.

> This 'convergence ' is to take place not on the West's terms – as elite Western globalists surely imagine – but rather on the terms intended by the Leninist strategic planners. The resulting 'one world' will be Marxist-Leninist-Gramscian-Communist - hardly what unwitting Western collaborators truly want to see established.[10]

The soviet strategists want to disarm the West and swing the balance of power in their favour thereby increasing the pressure upon Western politicians to restructure the American political and economic system. Golitsyn calls this 'cooperation-blackmail' which means 'cooperate with us or face the prospect of nuclear chaos and conflict'.

"Socialism with a smiling face", with its democratic façade, has succeeded where Stalinism failed. Communists are now in executive positions in the European Union and throughout the West. Agents of influence have been able to dupe the public and governments, blinding them to the danger in which the West and its democratic institutions are in.

Konstantin Preobrazhensky warns that even Angela Merkel may be a Russian agent given her history. It is incompatible that she, the daughter of a priest, was appointed the secretary of the committee of the Union of

---

10 *The Perestroika Deception*, A. Golitsyn

Free German Youth, a position responsible for the communist education of youth. In a socialist country, the children of priests were considered ideologically unreliable. Only the KGB could have brought such a thing about. Despite international pressure, Merkel has insisted that a second pipeline will be built from Russia to North Germany via the Baltic Sea as part of the Nord Stream Project.

The balance of power is shifting in favour of the enemies of democracy. China now equals the United States in economic strength and has the largest standing army in the world with over 2 million soldiers. It will soon have a larger navy than the United States, be it with fewer aircraft carriers. North Korea has the fourth largest army, with one million soldiers and 13,000 artillery pieces on the border with South Korea alone. South Africa has already fallen into the orbit of Russia and China through BRICS and the influence of the South African Communist Party. Many countries in Latin America, such as Nicaragua, Cuba, Brazil, Venezuela, Bolivia, Ecuador, Uruguay, Argentina and Chile are under strong socialist influence. The Russian Federation is confident of stepping into a leadership role with miscreant countries such as Cuba, Iran, and North Korea.

The 120 nations of the Non-Aligned Movement frequently side with these countries against the United States in the United Nations. Some of the former members of the Warsaw Pact who have joined NATO are now looking for ties with Putin's Eurasian Economic Union.

"Neo-communists" in United States

America is becoming more socialist by the day, with the Democratic Party the equivalent of the Social Democratic Party. The vast network of other Marxist allies in the United States is thoroughly investigated by Robert Chandler in his book *The Shadow World.* A large cadre of fifth column Marxists are hidden inside a solar system of radical Left institutions. According to Chandler, the Institute for Policy Studies has been at the centre of this network for many years, but is beginning to be eclipsed by the Campaign for America's Future and the Institute for America's Future. The latter is funded by the Open Society Institute of George Soros, which is headed by Robert Borosage, a former director of the Institute for Policy Studies.

In *Left Illusions* (published 2003) David Horowitz identified the "hard-left", the dedicated enemies of America at that time:

> They are people who support hostile regimes like North Korea, Cuba, and China, or- more commonly- believe the United States to be the imperialist guardian of a world system that radicals must defeat before they can establish "social justice."
>
> Among the intellectual leaders of this left are Noam Chomsky, Howard Zinn, Gore Vidal, Edward Said, and Cornel West; among its figureheads, Angela Davis and Ramsey Clark; among its cultural icons, Tim Robbins, Barbara Kingsolver, Arundhahti Roy, and Michael Moore; among its political leaders, Ralph Nader and the heads of the three major "peace" organizations (Leslie Cagan, Brian Becker, and Clark Kissinger); among its elected officials. Congresswoman Barbara Lee (D-CA) and Congressman Dennis Kucinch (D-OH); among its organizations, the misnamed Center for Constitutional Rights and the National Lawyers Guild; among its publications and media institutions, the *Nation*, *Z Magazine*, the *Progressive*, *Counterpunch*, Pacifica radio, Indymedia.org, and commondreams.org.

Horowitz has been called "red-baiter" and "McCarthyite" for pointing out that the "peace" organizations like International ANSWER and Not In Our Name were fronts for the Workers World Party, a Marxist-Leninst vanguard that identifies with North Korea, and the Revolutionary Communist Party, a Maoist sect .

In his books *Radical Son* and *The Politics of Bad Faith*, Horowitz shows that by the end of the 1960s the "new left" had become virtually indistinguishable from the communist predecessor it claimed to reject.

Marxists in the United Kingdom

In Great Britain, the electorate has largely been deceived into believing that New Labour had become less socialist after its dropping of Clause IV with its demands for the nationalization of the means of production, a pale imitation of the tactics of perestroika.

Ties existed between the Labour Party and the Kremlin over the thirty years leading up to and including Margaret Thatcher's premiership. This was revealed in a diary kept by Anatoly Chernyaev, a deputy in the Soviet International Department. Prominent among those with such ties was Ron Hayward, the Labour Party's general secretary between 1972 and 1982. Moscow's International Department wanted to infiltrate the unions. The TGWU's deputy leader Alec Kitson was a regular visitor to Moscow. In 1981, Michael Foot led a delegation to Moscow to meet Brezhnev.

In 1984 Neil Kinnock went, accompanied by Charles Clarke and Patricia Hewitt, to meet Constantin Chernenko. In 1985 Kinnock returned again to Moscow for advice on how to topple Thatcher. The decision to give Gordon Brown the safe seat of Dunfermline East was made by two TGWU officials, one of whom was Jack Jones, a paid agent for the USSR, the other was Alec Kitson. Neil Kinnock, Tony Blair, Margaret Beckett, Harriet Harman and John Reid, were all sponsored by TGWU. Michael Meacher had similar contact with Moscow as did no doubt others. New Labour cannot be understood unless these communist influences are taken into account.

Tony Blair tried to conceal the fact that he had been a member of the Campaign for Nuclear Disarmament, the pressure group that sought to make the USSR the only nuclear power in Europe. Blair has admitted that he was briefly a Trot during his student days, and that he embraced socialism through Marxism after reading Isaac Deutscher's biography of Trotzky.

Peter Mandelson had been a member of the Young Communist League. He attended a youth conference in Cuba and used to sell copies of the Morning Star outside Kiburn tube station. Mandelson has ties with Russian businessmen through his consultancy Global Counsel, and he has connections with Russia's Sistema Group whose RTI business is a top defence contractor. Like Blair he gives advice to those with communist backgrounds like Nursultan Nazarbayev of Kazakhstan and Ilham Alayev of Azerbaijan.

Blair stood as a candidate for the Presidency of the European Union. Both he and Mandelson spearheaded movements, such as Open Britain, aimed at thwarting the result of the Brexit vote.

Stephen Byers, the future transport secretary, was a supporter of Militant. Alan Milburn too was a Trotzkyist, running a Marxist bookshop called Days of Hope.

Tony McNulty, a Minister of State at the Home Office announced that he and many of his fellow ministers were former Marxists. John Reid, who became Home Secretary and Defence Secretary was a former member of the Communist Party. Charles Clarke was a former President of the National Union of Students at time when it was controlled by a close alliance between Labour Left-wingers and open communists. One of Blair's closest friends, Geoff Gallop, was an active member of the International Marxist Group (IMG). Alistair Darling is also said to have been a supporter of the IMG.

The Blairites were actually even more Left wing than Jeremy Corbyn. Their ideas came from the magazine *Marxism Today* which in turn was inspired by Antonio Gramsci. Gramsci wanted a cultural revolution which meant a Leftist takeover of schools, universities, media, police and courts. The Security Services destroyed files kept during the 1960s on Marxist Left-wingers soon after New Labour came to power in 1997.

Both Donald Dewar's and Robin Cook's funerals ended with the communist anthem 'The Internationale' which was played at Lenin's funeral, the first lines of which are:

> Stand up, ones who are branded by the curse, All the world's starving and enslaved!

The phrase "branded by the curse" takes on a new meaning in the light of the mark of the Beast. The song has strange sentiments to want have sung at one's funeral:

> No one will grant us deliverance, Not god, nor tsar, nor hero.

Many members of the current shadow Labour Party were either present at, or sent tributes to, the funeral of Redmond O'Neill in October 2009 held in Highgate Cemetery, where Karl Marx is buried. O'Neill was one of the key figures of the Trotzkyite group called Socialist Action. Its members seek a communist revolution and believes the collapse of the Soviet Union was a "tragedy for humanity". It fought elections in its own right and was initially known as the International Marxist Group (IMG). Piers Corbyn, Jeremy Corbyn's brother, was a prominent member of IMG. The IMG split in the early 1980s with the majority changing its name to Socialist Action. It resolved to pursue of policy of "deep entryism" which meant secretly infiltrating Labour. Among the mourners at O'Neill's funeral were his wife Kate Hudson, Pat Doherty, Diane Abbott, John Ross, Simon Fletcher, Steve Bell, John McDonnell and Jeremy Corbyn.

Jeremy Corbyn became leader of the Labour Party; Fletcher his chief of staff; Abbott was in the shadow cabinet; Hudson and Bell were part Corbyn's leadership campaign and co-officers of Stop the War; Ross co-signed a letter from economists backing Corbyn's policies. Kate Hudson has also been a leading figure in the CND. Corbyn hired Laura Murray as a political adviser to the shadow cabinet. A former Momentum organiser, she is the daughter of Andrew Murray, chairman of Stop the War from its formation in 2001 until June 2011, and again from September 2015 to 2016.

After forty years in the Communist Party of Great Britain and then the Communist Party of Britain, Andrew Murray joined Labour towards the end of 2016. Former Labour deputy leader Tom Watson recently expressed amazement that a life-long "hardcore Stalinist" such as him could be at the very heart of decision-making in the Labour Party. Watson was also appalled that an avowed Stalinist-Communist such as Seumas Milne could be director of communications for the leader of the Labour party.

Members of Militant Tendency, such as Peter Taaffe and Tony Mulhearn, are expecting to be readmitted to the Labour Party. Members of Militant have reportedly been attending meetings of Momentum, the radical organisation behind the Labour leader. After it was banned from the Labour Party, Militant renamed itself the Socialist Party.

Among others, Peter Mandelson, Tony Blair, John Prescott, Jack Straw., Mchael Prescott, Alex Salmond, and Michael Heseltine, have been identified as members of Britain's 48 Group Club in *The Hidden Hand* by Clive Hamilton and Mareike Ohlberg. This group promotes China's interests wihin the UK. So entrenched are the Communist Party of China's influence networks within the UK, the authors of *The Hidden Hand* conclude that any attempts to extricate Britain from China's orbit is probably futile.

The 'renewal of American democracy'

The winning of elections by the American left will result in military, political, and economic restructuring of the US system. This 'renewal of American democracy' is intended to lead to the convergence of the US system with the Soviet system and eventually to a Communist World Government.

Barack Obama restructured the United States in a socialist direction.

Several books, such as Aaron Klein's *The Manchurian Candidate: Barack Obama's Ties to Communists, Socialists and Other Anti-American Extremists* have explored Obama's ties with the far Left. He was mentored by Communist Party member Frank Marshall Davis and by members of the communist Weather Underground, Bill Ayers and Bernardine Dohrn, and he received backing from the Democratic Socialists of America.

Born in the former Soviet Union and a graduate of the University of Marxism-Leninism, Markovsky accuses Obama of using Bolshevik tactics such as:

> . . . exploiting class warfare, civil disobedience, and riots; reaching out to minorities and intellectuals, dividing the nation along racial lines and income brackets to implement "Change".[11]

He compares the czars that Obama created to the Bolshevik commissars. ("Green Jobs Czar", Van Jones, was in fact subsequently found to have founded a communist organization.)

Markovsky notes how over the past thirty years the Democratic Party has effectively turned into the Social Democratic Party. Former communist and political "convert"

According to Markovsky, there were three main elements to Obama's strategy:

Firstly, Obama aimed to destroy wealth. Through spending, the country would be in such debt that a state of hyper-inflation would result that would destroy the currency. The markets would then be flooded with cheap dollars, devaluating the net worth of productive citizens. The Bolsheviks created hyper-inflation in order to destroy personal wealth and thereby solidify their control over all aspects of people's lives.

Secondly, Obama wanted to replace American self-reliance with government dependency. Already over half of Americans pay no income tax at all. The Soviet system was built on dependency because people who become dependent soon become socialists. Tens of millions of Americans are already living in virtual communism given all the handouts they receive that are "in accordance with their needs". Obama is making American citizens dependent on government handouts. Fully implemented, the Universal Health Care Bill would give the government control over 17% of the US economy. Markovsky writes:

---

11 *Anatomy of a Bolshevik*, A. G. Markovsky

> The Universal Health Care Bill is a "cornerstone" in the President's bid to restructure American society.

Thirdly, Obama tried to replace the capitalist market-oriented economy with a government-controlled political economy. Markovsky stresses the importance of the "theology of Global Warming" for the President's strategy of re-engineering America. He argues:

> Global Warming justifies unlimited expenditure, strangles oil and gas production, practically stops coal mining, and puts power generation under tight government control.

If Obama's plans were to have come to fruition, Markovsky foresaw a tragic future for America:

> . . . high taxation, hyperinflation, depleted savings, and the devaluation of the dollar; prolonged economic stagnation and the destruction of our democracy, all culminating in one party rule for all Americans in a social-democratic Obama era.

An edited version of article that first appeared at peoplesworld.org in the communist newspaper *Morning Star* (31 December 2011) states:

> Obama in the White House gives the people the possibility of changing the political landscape, of moving politics in this country in a profoundly more progressive direction.

The same article argues that you cannot defeat the one per cent without defeating the Republicans in the polls. It also foresees the collapse of the Republican Party in about 30 years when whites become a racial minority and predicts a "tipping point" for working class voters with their rise in "class consciousness".

Konstantin Preobrazhensky believes that Barack Obama may be a Russian agent.[12]

---

12 *Back From The Dead*, Cliff Kincaid

Federal Security Service (FSB) still inwardly communist

According to Konstantin Preobrazhensky, the author of *FSB's New Trojan Horse,* agents of the FSB (Federal Security Service of the Russian Federation) still remain communists in their hearts.

The FSB suffers from a nagging nostalgia for communist days and continues to glorify the Soviet Union. After the collapse of the USSR, the pro-communist orientation of the FSB did not weaken but gathered strength, becoming more communist than it had been during the Soviet years. FSB agents have proved to be the staunchest of communists.

The FSB has not repented of the crimes of its communist predecessor the NKVD, but even celebrates 20th December, the day it was established. There has been no cleansing of the old communists from the ranks of the KGB. All those who were agents during the Soviet era have remained agents today.

The KGB has not fallen, but has control of the entire government. According to a 2003 report in *Novaya Gazeta*, some 6000 former KGB officers were running Russia's federal and local governments.

At FSB intelligence and counter-intelligence headquarters, not a single church has been built. When an old church on Lubyanka Street was re-opened in 2002, no mention was made of the fact that it had been converted to a prison and torture chamber in the 1920s, and that its walls and floor had been soaked in the blood of thousands of martyrs, some tortured to death.

Russia is returning to Stalinism and the former Soviet culture. Russia still supports the Bolsheviks and has still not bestowed equality between the Whites and the Reds. The honorary title of "Participant of the Civil War", with all its privileges, is still only bestowed upon those who fought on the side of the communists. Rallies are forbidden on the Day of Remembrance of the Victims of Political Repression (October 30th). Putin has brought back the Red Star to the cockade of the Russian military caps, removing the double-headed eagle. It is now considered unpatriotic to talk about Stalin's repressions and the record of them has been removed from school books, just as new repressions have already begun in Russia.

Communism in Russia was not condemned and continues to exert its influence. The anti-West and anti-American tendencies in Russian diplomacy are the direct result of communist influence. Now communism is called "stateruledom", an ideology that encompasses the central ideal of communism which is the subjugation of the individual to the state. The new ideology is a new embodiment of Lenin's *The State and Revolution*. Though they actually support Putin, the Communists are in the opposition party, proving that the democracy in Russia is false democracy, "democratism", as predicted by Anatoliy Golitsyn,

Russian laws are written in such a way that any entrepreneur can be criminally charged at any time. In the spring of 2004, Russia began to de-privatize. The Church is called a collective oligarch. Everything is being placed under heel of government, starting with businesses.

A Russian agent cannot risk asking a Western intellectual liberal to fight for Lenin's ideal since the Westerner truly believes that Russia has finished with Communism, therefore the fight against American hegemony is proposed instead.

In a symbolic gesture, in 1996 the Russian Duma voted to abrogate the decision of the Belovezh Agreement of 1991 which declared the Soviet Union officially dissolved. The Duma simultaneously voted to recognize as legally binding the results of the 1991 referendum, in which 70 per cent of Russian voters supported the preservation of the USSR.

The symbol of the Hammer and Sickle is still to be found throughout Moscow and the rest of Russia. The huge Stalinist skyscrapers, the Seven Sisters, still have the Hammer and Sickle prominently displayed upon their towers. The statue of Felix Dzerzhinsky, which had been torn down from its former position in Lubyanka Square is now standing upright again in a different location in Moscow. Lenin's tomb is still in Red Square. The KGB (FSB) has as much power as ever.

The Communist Party has managed to conceal the fact that it still pulls all the strings.

Whether deliberate disinformation or not, the following edited extract taken from a book about the assassinations carried out by Putin is typical of the line blindly accepted by most newspapers as the true state of affairs:

> His [Putin's] aims in taking out such opponents are non-ideological. Unlike the hard-line Communists who preceded them, all Putin and his cronies want is monopoly control over Russia's resources, finances, and economy, for their personal gain.

The truth of the matter is that Putin and the *siloviki* are still activated by the same ideological motives as their communist predecessors.

The China-Russia axis

Golitsyn warned in *The Perestroika Deception*:

> The Russian and Chinese leaders are still committed to their objective of world domination and believe that, disguised as 'democrats', in accordance with Leninist teaching, they will be able to achieve it.

As Shoen and Kaylan observe in *Return to Winter*, the Russia-China Axis is operating against the interests of the United States in every possible area:

> Overseeing massive military build ups of conventional and nuclear forces, on which they collaborate and supply each other, as well as of missile defence – on which they have signed an agreement of partnership
>
> Conducting aggressive and underhanded trade and economic policies – in everything from major gas and oil deals to collaborating with newly developed nations on creating alternative international financial institutions
>
> Taking aggressive action to consolidate and expand territorial claims in their sphere of influence, often in violation of UN norms: Russia in Central Asia and its "near abroad"; China, with its belligerence toward various disputed islands in the East and South China Seas and toward its Asian neighbours
>
> Facilitating rogue regimes, economically and militarily, especially in regard to nuclear weaponry. China has kept the deranged North Korean regime afloat for years with economic aid and enabled Pyongyang's nuclear pursuits by its refusal to endorse UN sanctions. Russia has bankrolled Iran's nuclear program and also acted as Bashar al-Assad's strongest ally, showering the regime with weapon systems, bases, and funding – even as Putin has played a key role in spearheading the diplomatic agreement calling for Assad to turn over his chemical weapons
>
> Using energy resources and other raw materials as weapons in trade wars
>
> Acting as the two leading perpetrators of cyber warfare worldwide aimed almost entirely at US or Western targets
>
> Waging a war of intelligence theft and espionage against the West - an effort that has gone on for years but was epitomized in 2013, when China

temporarily sheltered, and then Russia accepted for asylum, American NSA contractor and intelligence leader Edward Snowden

Facilitating, albeit indirectly, terrorist groups such as Hamas and Hezbollah

Standing together at the UN, as when the Russians vetoed – and the Chinese abstained from voting on – a Security Council resolution declaring the Crimea referendum invalid.

The restoration of the Soviet Empire

The beast that you saw was, and is not, and is to ascend from the bottomless pit ... (Rev. 17:8)

Golitsyn argued that the best outcome for the free world would be public exposure of the full significance of the communist threat. The resultant re-emergence of the communist monolith with China and Russia "reconciled", and with Romania and Yugoslavia openly back in the fold, would inspire the Western democracies to close ranks and face up to reality. He wrote:

> For the West [the re-emergence of the communist monolith] would be the most advantageous of all possible outcomes, for it would mean that the communist bloc had had to retreat; and that the Western miscalculations, which the bloc had striven so long and hard to create, would be left unexploited while the innate strength of the West was still intact. It would, moreover, have a salutary effect on the peoples of the Western nations. A full-strength communist bloc, all illusions of splits and rifts removed, would inspire them to close ranks and to face up to reality . . . [13]

The Book of Revelation indicates that the communist monolith will indeed reemerge, but the Soviet Bloc will surely only reemerge when it reckons that the "innate strength of the West" is no longer "intact".

Golitsyn's desire to see a newly emerged Soviet Bloc may have been

13 *New Lies For Old*, A. Golitsyn

desirable back in 1984, but forty years later such a prospect is not so appealing.

Nearly thirty years have passed since the so-called "collapse" of communism, and even more years since the introduction of *perestroika*. During that time, the communist bloc has not failed to exploit Western miscalculations.

The re-emergence of the communist monolith will not be a retreat, forced upon the communist bloc through public exposure of its duplicity. Golitsyn's warnings fell largely on deaf ears and all his advice on how to resist the hidden threat have been ignored. All the former Warsaw Pact members are now members of NATO (except the Russian Federation), and most of the former Eastern bloc countries are now members of the EU.

The West has shown no comprehension of communist strategy and, apart from reservations about the Russian Federation itself, considers all former member states of the Warsaw Pact to be friends. Through their entry into NATO, the European Union, and other Western institutions, these crypto-communist states will weaken the Western democracies to such an extent that they will not be able to resist the Communist Monolith when it reemerges. The Beast will be militarily stronger than all before it.

It is possible that the communists will have succeeded in breaking up NATO and in paralysing Western military programmes and commitments. A reemergent Warsaw Pact, no longer counteracted by NATO, could obtain world domination through military might alone. The fact that the British Army is considering mothballing all its tanks, and replacing them with Apache helicopters, indicates how the West has no inkling of the huge threat that it faces. Massive military assaults upon the Western democracies could bring about the desired end, a Marxist world, without all the complications involved in setting up a World Government.

How Golitsyn's advice on how to combat the communist threat has been ignored

Perceiving the danger that the West was faced with back in 1984, Golitsyn counselled that national interests could no longer be protected through national efforts alone. Such nations would be picked off one by one. Golitsyn advised that the allies should submit to some form of supranational authority for policy coordination.

Golitsyn feared that the growing radicalism of the far left of European socialism would inevitably lead to a united front with the communists unless halted by a combination of conservatives and social democrats. Their mutual love of democratic freedom should make them natural allies against communism.

Golitsyn also counselled the following: a cross-party political alliance in defense of democratic institutions should be created; NATO membership should be widened to include Japan, Australia, Brazil, Indonesia, Singapore, Nigeria, Pakistan, Saudi Arabia, and Israel; the security services should be used to neutralize the political damage caused by communist agents of influence; there should be no independent consultation between communist leaders and member nations of the alliance; an economic offensive should be taken against every bloc country, including Yugoslavia, Romania, and Poland. Credit facilities should be denied; socialist and nationalist parties in non-communist countries must not fall into the trap of forming a united front with communist parties; the peoples of the communist bloc should be given accurate information about the situation, but no trust should be put in the pseudo-democratic parties of the communist states.

The West took none of these steps to avert the danger that it was facing. Perhaps it is already too late to reverse the situation, even if the above measures were belatedly put into practice. Which statesman will eject the former member states of the Soviet bloc from the European Union and NATO? It would be argued that such action would simply throw these states back into the arms of the "ex"- Soviet Union and turn them against the West, regardless of their political affiliations. All the West is likely to do is hope that Golitysn was mistaken in his analysis. However, since the Book of Revelation actually supports his analysis, such hope is forlorn.

Recently published books such as Catherine Belton's *Putin's People* show how "black cash" is being used by Putin's regime to buy influence in the West. This is how she concludes her book:

> The reformers who declared to the world with such great promise nearly thirty years ago that the country was on a new market path towards global integration were either soon compromised, or had been working with the KGB on Russia's transition all along. Those who believed they were working to introduce a free market had underestimated the enduring power of

the security men. 'This is the tragedy of twentieth-century Russia,' said Pugachev. 'The revolution ws never complete.' From the beginning, the security men had been laying down roots for revanche. But from the beginning, it seems, they'd been doomed to repeat the mistakes of the past.

The Eurasian alliances that counter NATO: the CSTO and SCO

Together, the members of the CSTO and SCO represent over 40% of the entire population of the world.

The CSTO and SCO complement each other and may indeed merge in the future. Both Eurasian organisations signed a military cooperation agreement in 2007 which effectively makes China a de facto member of the CSTO.

This unified Sino-Russian military bloc is a challenges to the domination of the US and NATO in Eurasia. Collectively the members of the SCO and CSTO could easily overpower NATO, were it not for the presence of the United States. Russia alone could defeat almost all of NATO's members combined should they go to war against it without the United States.

The SCO

The Shanghai Cooperation Organisation Charter, which formally established the SCO, was signed in June 2002 and entered into force on 19 September 2003.

The original five nations, with the exclusion of Uzbekistan, were previously members of the Shanghai Five group. Current members are:

- China [1996]
- Kazakhstan [1996]
- Kyrgyzstan [1996]
- Russia [1996]
- Tajikistan [1996]
- Uzbekistan [2001]
- India [2017]
- Pakistan [2017]

Bahrain and Qatar_have also officially applied to join the SCO.

The following countries have observer status:

- Iran
- Afghanistan
- Mongolia
- Belarus

Iran's observer status within the SCO is to camouflage the nature of the trilateral cooperation between Iran, China, and Russia.

Armenia, Azerbaijan, Bangladesh, East Timor, Nepal, Sri Lanka, Egypt, and Syria applied for observer status.

The following countries are dialogue partners:

- Armenia
- Azerbaijan
- Cambodia
- Nepal

Israel, Maldives, Ukraine, Iraq, and Saudi Arabia have applied for dialogue partner status.

Turkmenistan has declared itself a permanently neutral country.

The United States applied for observer status in the SCO, but was rejected in 2005.

The CSTO

The Collective Security Treaty Organization (CSTO) has evolved from being the military wing of the CIS to being a separate body independent of the CIS.

In 1992, six post-Soviet states belonging to the Commonwealth of Independent States (Russia, Armenia, Kazakhstan, Kyrgyzstan, Tajikistan, and Uzbekistan) signed the Collective Security Treaty. Three other post-Soviet states (Azerbaijan, Belarus, and Georgia) signed the next year and the treaty took effect in 1994.

Five years later, six of the nine (all but Azerbaijan, Georgia, and Uzbekistan) agreed to renew the treaty for five more years, and in 2002 those six agreed to create the Collective Security Treaty Organization as a military alliance.

Full CSTO members:

- Armenia [1994]
- Belarus [1994]
- Kazakhstan [1994]

- Kygyzstan [1994]
- Russia [1994]
- Tajikstan [1994]

Observer status of the CSTO:

- Afghanistan [2013]
- Serbia [2013]

Former member states of the CSTO:

- Azerbaijan [1994-1999]
- Georgia [1994-1999]
- Uzbekistan [1994-1999] [2006-2012]

In May 2007, the CSTO secretary-general Nikolai Bordyuzha suggested Iran could join the CSTO saying:

> The CSTO is an open organization. If Iran applies in accordance with our charter, we will consider the application.

If Iran joined it would be the first state outside the former Soviet Union to become a member of the CSTO. Other potential CSTO candidates are Moldova, Mongolia, Serbia, Turkmenistan, and Ukraine.

Observer status of CSTO:

- Republic of Serbia
- Islamic Republic of Afghanistan

The Second Soviet Empire in waiting

In his anti-NATO book *The Globalization of NATO*, M.D. Nazemroaya draws up a list of countries that he reckons can be counted as part of "The Eurasian Entente and its Global Alliance Network". This network consists of four groups:

- SCO/CSTO nations: Armenia, Belarus, China, Kazakhstan, Kyrgyzstan, Russia, Tajikstan, Uzbekistan.
- Iraq, Iran, Lebanon, Syria.
- Antigua and Barbuda, Bolivia, Cuba, Dominica, Ecuador, Nicaragua, St. Vincent and Grenadines, Venezuela.
- Other allies: Abkhazia, Algeria, Bangladesh, Brazil, Bhutan, Eritrea, India, Korea (DPRK), Nagorno-Karabakh Republic, Nepal, Moldova (including Transnistria), Mongolia, Myanmar, Namibia, Nepal, Republika Srpska, Serbia, Sudan, South Ossetia, Sri Lanka, Turkmenistan, Ukraine, Zimbabwe.

To this list should be added of course the former members of the Eastern Bloc. Of these, the following are now embedded within NATO: Albania, Bulgaria, Croatia, Czech Republic, Estonia, Hungary, Latvia, Lithuania, Poland, Romania, Slovakia, and Slovenia.

Revelation indicates in fact that the Beast will have dominion over the entire world.

Part Five

MARXISM AND SATANISM

15

SATANISM

With the advent of the Beast mankind will worship Satan

> **Men worshiped the dragon, for he had given his authority to the beast . . .** (Rev. 13:4)

When the Devil tempted Jesus (Luke 4:5-6), he offered Jesus **authority** over the kingdoms of the world if he would worship him. The implication of Rev. 13:4 is that the Beast worships Satan, and therefore Satan has rewarded him by giving him power and authority over the kingdoms of the world. To the Beast, **the dragon gave his power and his throne and great authority** (Rev. 13:2).

Soviet power and authority is derived from the Devil.

Traditional and rationalist Satanism

Satanism is the practice of the cult, or worship, of Satan. Satanists explicitly decide to consecrate themselves to Satan and to enter into a sect. They follow the teachings of the Prince of Darkness to the letter.

One distinguishes between a personal Satanism and an impersonal or rationalist Satanism. Traditional Satanism recognizes the personal nature of Satan, and the followers entreat, adore, and honour him as a god. The second, the impersonal or rationalist, does not believe in Satan's personal nature, in the metaphysical sense, rather, they see him as a cosmic energy that is present in each man and in the world, and that, when called upon, will emerge in all his power to carry out the most absurd and atrocious perversions, always connecting them to esoteric rites.

In his book *An Exorcist Explains the Demonic*, the exorcist Gabriele Amorth explains that Satan desires only slaves, whom he buys by promising them a guaranteed and unlimited enjoyment of things with unchecked liberty, which is the foundation of Satanism itself. The promise of liberty is deceitful.

Satanists wish to develop this depraved form of devotion through a diffusion of the theory and practice of three basic principles:

1. **you can do all that you wish**; this first principles intends to confer full liberty to the adherent on everything he wishes to do, without limits; the occultist Aleister Crowley's credo was "Do what thou wilt;"
2. **no one has the right to command you**; the release from the principle of authority, that is from any obligation to obey parents, the Church, the state, and whoever places restrictions in the name of the common good;
3. **you are the god of yourself**; this third principle denies all the truth that comes directly from God: paradise, the inferno, purgatory, judgement, the Ten Commandments, the precepts of the Church, Mary, and so forth.

Modernist Satanists do believe in Satan or his demons, basing their philosophy on atheism. They are more concerned with material wealth than with spiritualism. However, even in the opinion of a traditional Satanists, LaVey's *Satanic Bible* is very effective at teaching people how to break away from the Judeo-Christian moral codes. LaVey taught people that mankind's natural desires are not evil and that it is perfectly natural to indulge in them without guilt. He taught people to think like Satanists.

The philosophy of Traditional Satanism

Much of the following material on Traditional Satanism has been gleaned from *Satanism: A Beginner's Guide to the Religious Worship of Satan and Demons* written by the self-proclaimed Satanist "Brother Nero".

Traditional Satanists believe that Satan, in his Luciferian form, gave mankind knowledge, wisdom, and most importantly, self-awareness and freedom. He and his demons planted the seed for medicine, science, and the modern technologies, thereby giving mankind a true understanding of their own potential. Satan gave man the ability to think for himself, allowing him to develop his intellect. The demons guide man enabling mankind to evolve as a species.

Without Satan and the demons, Traditional Satanists believe that mankind would be nothing but slaves to the Judaeo-Christian god. They believe that God does not like people to have free will or to do anything he does not approve of. Man was only created to be a slave to God and He derives his power to exist through prayer, guilt and the selfless worship of his followers. Satan and his angels departed the heavenly realm because they did not wish to submit to slavery of the Christian god.

Traditional Satanists believe that Satan gets his power from the worship of his followers, and also from sacrificial offerings, sexual activity, and other natural human emotions. Aleister Crowley performed animal sacrifices and combined these with sexual ritual in order to raise magickal energy. White animal are to be sacrificed to Lucifer because he is a solar deity. Black animals are sacrificed for Satan.

Traditional Satanists credit Satan for giving man the ability to think for himself and to realize there were other ways to look at things besides the Christian god's way. This made God angry, which is why God cursed Adam and Eve. Satan gave mankind freewill, freeing man to do whatever he wanted, including things which God considered evil. This made God regret making mankind, as we were no longer solely his creation, but also Satan's.

Traditional Satanists assert that Satan is not constrained by moral concepts such as good and evil. He can adjust his morality to fit any situation. Traditional Satanists believe they should base their moral code on Satan's example and so do not have morals as such. Morals are fixed and unchangeable, like the Ten Commandments. Boundaries are principles that Satanists can adjust based on circumstances.

Traditional Satanists permit themselves multiple sex partners in a relationship, but believe it is not right to marry or procreate with a non-Satanist. Satanists refuse to capitulate to Christian morality and recognize polygamy and homosexual marriage as a legitimate form of marriage.

For Satanists, evil is relative. Satan is only evil if you define him by a Christian moral code.

The relationship between the Demons is like the bond between siblings. They are motivated by the same goals, chief of which is the destruction of the Christian god and his followers. Demons do things that are beneficial to Satan's kingdom. They can reach a person through dreams, mental images, and other day-to-day circumstances.

Traditional Satanists see Satan as both male and female as symbolized by Baphomet, a symbol of all aspects of Satan in one image.

The *Al-Jilwah* is a sacred text in the Yezidi religion, an ancient form of Devil Worship. Sheikh Adi is said to have received it in the 12th century AD. According to this text, believed to be the direct word of Satan, it is Satan's desire for people to unite in a bond of unity.

Satan's primary purpose is to preserve himself, then his Demons, and lastly man. Satan may have interacted on man's behalf out of sympathy, but also his motivation was to have those among mankind who felt a connection with Satan to help him in his war against the Judaeo-Christian god.

According to Satanists, God is afraid of man's united effort to destroy God and his kingdom, for this unity will ensure the victory for Satan, especially if the unification is orchestrated and eventually led by Satan.

Satan is likely to make the world aware of his literal existence by manifesting in one of three ways: corporeal, spiritual, or by possessing a human being with his spirit, which would be the Antichrist or Satanic leader. This must happen before the satanic community can unite. No matter what form he manifests in, it will be obvious to Satanists and non-Satanists alike that he is Satan.

All those who swear allegiance to Satan will help in the process of eliminating all those who oppose his will. Then Satan's eternal reign will begin.

According to Satanists, Hell is a kingdom created by Satan and ruled by him, where Satanists go to be with him and to be rewarded for their service to him when they die. It is totally separate and distinct from the Christian god's Lake of Fire or bottomless pit.

Traditional Satanists believe that when they die they will reside with Satan in his kingdom. Those who die loyal to the Christian god will be with him in his kingdom and will stay there until the final battle. Individuals of different religions will be placed in a state of purgatory until a time just before the final battle, at which time they will be allowed to make a choice as to which side they will fight for.

Some Traditional Satanists believe in reincarnation to some extent.

To be a Satanist you have to be be embraced by and swear allegiance to these forces. There are satanic blessings and a Satanic baptism. Pagan traditions are a part of Satanism. Certain demons are also pagan deities, and so there is no conflict teaching children the pagan origin of certain holidays.

Those with a Satanic mother and father find it easier to connect and communicate with Satan and Demons. Satan honours these who carry a hereditary bloodline. Satanists are a race unto themselves.

If forced to attend Church ("the enemy"), Satanists are advised to anoint themselves, asking Satan and the Demons to protect them against the spirit of the Judeo-Christian god and his angels. If there is no oil, prayer will suffice.

Brief history of Satanism

Satanism is linked to Manicheanism. This can be seen in the dualistic doctrine that "good" and "evil" or light and darkness, are equivalent. This of course contradicts Christian doctrine which teaches: "**God is light and in him is no darkness at all**". (1 John 1:5) This doctrine of equivalence of good and evil permits the immersion of the devotee into the depths of evil in his quest for "salvation".

The Black Mass evolved from Cathar ritual. The use of a naked woman as an altar and the substitution of fecal matter for the consecrated host were expressions of this dualist idea. Catharism is derived from Zoroastrianism, which in later variations became Manicheanism.

In the twelfth and thirteenth centuries, offshoots of the Cathars were called "Luciferians". The Luciferians were infamous for disgusting rituals such as kissing a toad, or the buttocks of a priest, and the veneration of a black cat. They can be traced to certain "invisible colleges" within the Catholic Church itself. Their chief tenet was that Satan had been wronged by God. By bringing down the institutions of Christianity and the political regimes of the day, Lucifer would be restored to his rightful office. The

Luciferians anticipated the Illuminati with their belief that all social injustice was due to influence of Christianity. Social injustice resulted from the great primeval wrong done by God to Satan. The Satanic restoration would coincide with a new era of perfect equality and social justice.

The Satanism of the nineteenth century was a revival of certain heresies, particularly that of Catharism.

16

SOCIALISM AND SATANISM

Ties between Satanism and materialist philosophy of communism

According to the The Nine Satanic Statements found in *The Satanic Bible*, Satan represents indulgence instead of abstinence; vital existence instead of spiritual pipe dreams; undefiled wisdom instead of hypocritical self-deceit; kindness to those who deserve it instead of love wasted on ingrates; vengeance instead of turning the other cheek; responsibility to the responsible instead of concern for the selfish. Man is just another animal, and usually worse than other animals because of his "divine spiritual and intellectual development". Satan represents all sins, as they all lead to physical, mental, or emotional gratification.

These statements pervert the teachings of Jesus Christ and the commandments of God. It is interesting to compare them with the following statements found in *The Fundamentals of Marxism-Leninism* which expound upon the materialist philosophy of communism:

> Materialist philosophy is an effective weapon against the pernicious influence of spiritual reaction.

> For centuries the Church has tried to instil contempt for earthly life and fear of God.

> The Church threatened with the wrath of God and torment in hell those who dared rise against the divinely established rule of exploiters

> The great historic service rendered by materialist philosophy is that it helped man to break free of all superstitions.

> It teaches us not to hope for happiness beyond the grave, but to prize life on earth and to strive to improve it.

> Materialists do not expect aid from supernatural forces. Their faith is in man, in his ability to transform the world by his own efforts and make it worthy of himself.

William Henry Chamberlin notes the theomachism of the USSR:

> There have been many instances in history when one religion cruelly persecuted others; but in Russia the world is witnessing the first effort to destroy completely any belief in supernatural interpretation of life.

Karl Marx and Satan

Karl Marx's name is bound up with that of Satan's on the Hammer and Sickle and so the satanic nature of his philosophy should not be underestimated.

Marx set aside all contact with God and instead put Satan in front of marching proletarian columns, wrote Lunacharsky in his book *Religion and Socialism*. Lunacharsky was involved in the design of the Soviet emblem, so such a statement coming from his pen supports the assertion that the Hammer and Sickle is indeed a monogram of the name "Satan" in Hebrew.

In his book *Marx & Satan*, Richard Wurmbrand purports Karl Marx may well have been a devil-worshipper.

The young Karl Marx expressed Christian convictions, but these changed into strong ungodly ones. For example, in one of his poems Marx writes:

> I wish to avenge myself against the One who rules above.

Wurmbrand believed that for Marx, socialism was a pretence. Marx's diabolical plan was to ruin mankind for eternity. Marx believed in God, but hated him. The ultimate aim of communism in conquering new countries, according to Wurmbrand, is not to establish another social or economic system, but to mock God and praise Satan. Marxism's alleged care for the poor is simply hypocrisy. Its real aim is the total eradication of God and His worship.

Marx said "Communists preach absolutely no morals." Such a moral outlook conforms to the first principle of Satanism, which is that you can do all that you wish.

Marx was a Young Hegelian. The philosopher Georg Hegel's work can be considered blasphemous because, given what his system alleges, a divine position must be claimed. Hegel presents God as thoroughly knowable by human minds and blurs the distinction between humanity and God, construing divine nature in human terms and human nature in divine terms.

Marx refined the atheism of Feuerbach into a critique of the socio-economic conditions responsible for the "invention" of religion. Marx claims that religion originated as a psychological solace for the exploited workers, the wage slaves of an industrial society. Despite the working-class origin of organised religion, the clergy allowed the ruling class to control this religious sentiment. With Christian slaves hoping for a reward in the after-life, the ruling classes could control the whole of society.

Such a cynical outlook denies the authority of the Church and adheres to the second Satanic principle that no one has the right to command you. Seeing in the Church only a willing tool of the exploiters, the Marxist does not acknowledge the authority of the Church. A Marxist is not obliged to obey parents either, for such observance is the teaching of the Church, the lackey of the exploiting classes.

Marx said that it was important to defend "the freedom of conscience from religious superstition". This adheres to the third principle of Satanism which states that you are god of yourself. This principle denies the existence of hell, the day of judgement, the Ten Commandments, the precepts of the Church, and so forth. The satanist and founder of the Temple of Set in 1975, voiced similar ambitions to Marx. Michael Aquino said:

> [we want to] destroy the influence of conventional religion in human affairs . . . not so much that we want everyone to be converted to Satanism as an institutional religion, but that we want to unravel the web of fear and superstition that has perpetuated all formal beliefs. Satanism should not be just another religion. It should be an unreligion.

To Marx, religious beliefs are mere "illusions". Marx calls religion the "opium of the people." Religion was an "illusory happiness" and merely a palliative for the oppressed classes. He advocated the abolition of religion on the grounds that it would bring forth better conditions for the exploited:

> The abolition of religion, as the illusory happiness of the people, is the demand for their real happiness. To call on them to give up their illusions about their condition is to call on them to give up a condition that requires illusions. The criticism of religion is, therefore, in embryo, the criticism of that vale of tears of which religion is the halo.

Marxist theory posits that organised religion is a human product derived from the objective material conditions. Therefore, with the advent of communism and the abolition of unequal systems of political economy and of stratified social classes, the State and the official religion would wither away. Such a philosophy resulted in the wholesale killing of priests, the removal of children from their parents, and the near destruction of religion throughout the USSR and the Eastern bloc.

Marxism is a satanic philosophy, dressed up in the sheep's clothing of concern for the exploited masses. David Aikman, in *The Role of Atheism in the Marxist Tradition*, traces Marx's anti-theism to the young Marx's preoccupation with the Promethean cult of 'Satan as a destroyer . . . emphasis on destruction for its own sake [is present] in so much of the Marxist tradition'.

Paul Kengor has written an excellent book on the evils of communism and its "long march of death, deception, and infiltration" called T*he Devil and Karl Marx*. It is a must-read for all those interested in such matters.

The satanic influence of Friedrich Nietzsche (1844-1900)

Nietzsche's satanic outlook needs to be explored in order to see how his views may have inspired these Bolsheviks to become Satanists themselves. For instance, the first Soviet Commissar of Education and Culture (1917-1929), Anatoliy Lunacharsky, was a Nietzchean Marxist.

Friedrich Nietzsche's anti-Christian philosophy has had a marked influence on modern Satanists. It greatly influenced Anton LaVey, the founder of the Church of Satan, who lifted the categorization of Christianity as a "slave morality" from Nietzsche and adapted the Ubermensch as the ideal Satanist.

Aleister Crowley also recognized Nietzsche as a Satanist, writing:

> The Book of the Law announces a new dichotomy in human society; there is the master and there is the slave; the noble and the serf; the 'lone wolf' and the herd. Nietzsche may be regarded as one of our prophets.

Nietzsche's philosophy is directed towards the breaking of old moral codes and the erecting of new ones, enabling the emergence of the 'Higher Man", the superior individual who stands above the mass. He is a transitional type between mass-man and the 'Over Man' (Ubermensch), the latter being still a higher form of existence.

Pity preserves that which should naturally be destroyed. Nietzsche despised Christian notions of pity:

> Christianity has taken the side of everything weak, base, ill-constituted, it has made an ideal out of opposition to the preservative instincts of strong life.

Many of Nietzsche's criticisms of Christianity can be found in his books *Thus Spoke Zarathustra* and *The Antichrist* in which he attacks Christian values of good and evil and its belief in an afterlife. Nietzsche claimed that the Christian religion and its morality are based on imaginary fictions. It thus squanders our earthly lives in pursuit of a perfect afterlife that does not exist. Nietzsche blasphemes God, claiming:

> [God is a] formula for every slander against 'this world,' for every lie about the 'beyond'.

Christianity has contempt for every good and honest instinct, according to Nietzsche. Man is debased only so that God can be exalted. Nietzsche wrote:

> Christianity's lies are not holy. They serve . . . *bad* ends: the poisoning, slandering, denying of life, contempt for the body, the denigration and self-violation of man through the concept of sin . . .

Like all Satanists, Nietzsche hated priests. The priest is a "denier, slanderer, and poisoner of life" who stands truth upside down on its head. Church doctrine is merely lies invented to keep the priests in power:

> The 'Law,' the 'will of God,' the 'sacred book,' 'inspiration' — all merely words for the conditions *under* which the priest comes to power, *by* which he maintains his power . . .

Only a sick people, whose will to power has declined, worship a God who is purely good, according to Nietzsche. Nietzsche criticized the Nordic races for having failed to create their own god.

Nietzsche denigrates Christianity, but exalts Rome. He argues that Christianity lied about guilt, punishment, and immortality in order to destroy Imperial Rome, an organization that was designed to promote life.

Nietzsche considered Christianity to be a curse and a corruption, a conspiracy against life itself. He therefore suggested that time be calculated from the date of his book *The Antichrist*, instead of from the date of Christ's birth, with Year One beginning on September 30, 1888.

Nietzsche's "Decree against Christianity" consists of seven propositions, one of which was that sacred (earthly) things which Christianity has deified should be eradicated (e.g. sacred sites and rituals). Another proposition was the transvaluation of values in which the divine becomes criminal, etc. The seventh proposition was that the Christian religion (rather than Christian philosophy) is the ultimate evil.

Immersed in such satanic philosphy, Lunacharsky promulgated his education decree of 26th October 1917 by which schools were immediately secularized, religious teaching being forbidden, (This was followed by a second decree (on 3rd January 1922), which banned the teaching of religion to children, even singly, in churches, church buildings, or private homes.)

The satanic influence of Theosophy

The satanic element in theosophy must also have influenced many Bolsheviks. Anatoliy Lunacharsky, for example, was not only a Nietzshean Marxist, but also a theosophist. Such influences might account for the Bolsheviks' incorporation of Satan's name into the emblem of the Soviet Union.

Lunacharsky and Maxim Gorky were interested in Theosophy, partly because it was compatible with socialism and opposed acquisitiveness. In 1912 Gorky requested all Helena Blavatksy's writings to be published in Russian. Lunacharsky was also interested at one time in Anthroposophy and read Rudolf Steiner.

Lunacharsky's familiarity with a broad spectrum of occult ideas, from the folkloric occult to Anthroposophy, can be seen in his early poetry, his plays, and his two-volume *Religion and Socialism* (1908,1911), which discusses such topics as "the destruction of harmony," Pythagoras, Gnosticism, the Logos and cults. He had a detailed knowledge of demonology, and even wrote about white magic. There are even references to the Astral Spirit in some of his work.

The *Theosophical Society* was founded by Helena Blavatsky (1831-1891), a Russian medium, with Henry Olcott in New York in 1875. The Theosophical Society's journal was named *Lucifer.*

The Russian Theosophical Society was opened in 1908. In Theosophy, Satan is a symbol of occult wisdom on earth. Lenin's tomb was shaped like a cube because the cube represented the fourth dimension of life, which according to Theosophists, survived the body's disintegration.

Blavatsky fought for the Carbonari whose aim was the complete annihilation of Catholicism and ultimately of Christianity. Throughout her book *The Secret Doctrine,* Blavatsky praises the devil and belittles God:

> [Lucifer] was transformed by the Church into Lucifer or Satan, because he is higher and older than Jehovah, and had to be sacrificed to the new dogma.

Blavatsky defends Satan's rebellion against God:

> For, instead of remaining a mere blind, functioning medium, impelled and guided by fathomless LAW, the 'rebellious' Angel claimed and enforced his

right of independent judgment and his will, his right of free-agency and responsibility . . .

"Much-slandered" Satan is in her opinion "the highest divine Spirit." The Church is fighting againt divine Truth in its repudiation of the "Dragon of esoteric Wisdom." She hails Satan as man's Saviour:

> [it is but natural] to view *Satan*, the Serpent of Genesis, as the real creator and benefactor, the Father of Spiritual mankind. For it is he who was the 'Harbinger of Light,' bright radiant Lucifer, who opened the eyes of the automaton *created* by Jehovah . . . who conferred on us spiritual, instead of physical immortality – the latter a kind of static immortality that would have transformed man into an undying 'Wandering Jew.'

Adolf Hitler kept a copy of *The Secret Doctrine* by his bed. His choice of the swastika as the symbol for his party was based upon material on the swastika found in that book. Blavatsky calls the swastika the "Worker's Hammer" and "Thor's Hammer". It is clear from what she writes that she considers the Swastika to have the same mystical properties as Eliphas Levi's Pentagram and Baphomet.

In her attempts to denigrate God, and rehabilitate Satan, Blavatsky displays the same philosophy as a Satanist.

The satanic ferment of the Russian Symbolists and Decadents

The period leading up to the Russian Revolution was a period of Satanist ferment. The Symbolists and the post-Symbolist avant-garde were important disseminators of occult doctrines in Russia, as were the Nietzschean Marxists Gorky and Luncharsky.

In Russia, Nietzsche influenced Russian Symbolism. Figures such as Dmitry Merezhkovsky, Andrei Bely, Vyacheslav Ivanov and Alexander Scriabin incorporated or discussed parts of Nietzsche philosophy in their works. Scriabin (1871-1915) was also an adherent of Theosophy and practiced Black Masses. His Piano Sonata No. 9, Op. 68 is commonly known as the *Black Mass Sonata*.

Occult themes and symbols permeated early Soviet literature. Eleven of the many works of Papus (Gerard Encausse) on Kabbala, alchemy, spiritualism, Rosicrucianism, Freemasonry and the tarot were translated into Russian. Like Eliphas Levi, Mystical Freemasons hold the mythical Egyptian Hermes Trismegistus in great esteem.

Astrological, Masonic, and Theosophical symbols decorate the journals in which the Symbolists published.

The rise of French Symbolist and Decadent Satanism in the late 19th century aroused an interest in the Satanic and Satanism, demonism, and anti-Christian views form the basis of Russian Decadence. The Russian Decadents were influenced by Eliphas Levi's works, especially his *Histoire de la magie (1860)*. So too were French Symbolist writers, such as Rimbaud, Verlaine and Villiers de l'Isle-Adam; and Huysmans, whose book *Là-bas* (1891) portrays a Black Mass; and Charles Baudelaire, for whom God and the Devil were the same.

Fedor Sologub (1863-1927), Symbolist poet and novelist, was deeply influenced by Victor Hugo, Charles Baudelaire, Joris-Karl Huysmans, and other French Satanists. Sologub held the view that the world was more evil than good and that the underworld was controlled by Satan. He wrote: "My father is the Devil".

Though many of his fellow Symbolists fled Russia after the Russian Revolution of 1917, Valery Bryusov remained until his death in 1924. He became a member of the Communist Party in 1920 and received a position in the cultural ministry of the new Soviet state working under Lunacharsky. Briusov wrote: "I will glorify equally the Lord and the Devil". Both he and the Symbolist poet Aleksandr Dobroliubov repeatedly experimented with black magic and drugs.

As head of the Commissariat of Enlightenment, Anatoliy Lunacharsky invited artists to collaborate with the Soviet government. The Symbolists and the Futurists worked in early Soviet cultural agencies and taught in Proletkult schools and studios, as did many Theosophists and Anthroposophists.

Lunacharsky, a freemason of the highest degree, wrote a Symbolist fairy-tale play called *Vasilisa the Wise* (1919). The play employs archetypes and obscure references to ancient pagan divinities and occult principles and practices, in particular Freemasonry. In the play are depictions of clairvoyance and fortune-telling. Mitra, the son of Vasilisa and her divine husband Merodakh (Marduk), will usher in the end of history and the Marxist workers' paradise. The play is an example of God-building, the propagandist use of occult, pagan and Christian symbols to popularize the secular religion of Marxism.

The satanic philosophy of Proudhon (1809-1865)

Pierre-Joseph Proudhon referred to his ideal of an ordered society as 'anarchy'. He argued that the abolition of exploitation of man by man and the abolition of government was one and the same thing.

Karl Marx praised Proudhon's work *What is Property?* but lascerated Proudhon's *The Poverty of Philosophy.*

Proudhon praised Satan in some of his works:

> And for my part I say: The first duty of man, on becoming intelligent and free, is to continually hunt the idea of God out of his mind and conscience. For God, if he exists, is essentially hostile to our nature, and we do not depend at all upon his authority. We arrive at knowledge in spite of him, at comfort in spite of him, at society in spite of him; every step we take in advance is a victory in which we crush Divinity. I shall purify myself, idealize my being, and become the chief of creation, the equal of God. By what right should God still say to me: Be holy, for I am holy? Lying spirit, I will answer him, imbecile God, your reign is over; look to the beasts for other victims. For God is stupidity and cowardice; God is hypocrisy and falsehood; God is tyranny and misery; God is evil.

Proudhon adored Satan:

> Come, Satan, come, thou the calumniated of priests and of kings! What would man be without thee? A beast.

Proudhon also blasphemed God:

> God is stupidity and cowardice; God is hypocrisy, and falsehood; God is tyranny and poverty; God is evil . . . God is essentially anticivilized, antiliberal, antihuman.

These utterances are so aligned with the philosophy of Traditional Satanism that one cannot deny that Proudhon was a Satanist.

Leon Trotzky admired Proudhon's "capacity for despising official public opinion". Despite his declaration that Proudhon's views and world outlook were alien to him, Trotzky ends his autobiography with a quotation from one of Proudhon's letters which expresses Trotzky's own views about destiny.

Mikhail Bakunin (1814-1876) and his satanic philosophy

Mikhail Bakunin, a friend and associate of Karl Marx, expresses the philosophic outlook of a Satanist in his book *God And The State.*

Bakunin first met Karl Marx in Paris in the early 1844. Bakunin joined the socialist International Working Men's Association in 1868, in which he was very active until he was expelled by Karl Marx at the Hague Congress in 1872. Between 1869 and 1870 Bakunin became involved with the Russian revolutionary Sergey Nechayev who wrote *Catechism of the Revolutionist,* a work that justifies all means to achieve revolutionary aims. Bakunin was a strong supporter of the Paris Commune of 1871.

Bakunin wrote that socialists greeted each other with virtually the same words that Luciferians greeted each other:

> The Evil One is the satanic revolt against divine authority, revolt in which we see the fecund germ of all human emancipation, the revolution. Socialists recognize each other by the words, "In the name of the one to whom a great wrong has been done".

Such a greeting imitates the practice of the Luciferians, who would greet each other with the words: "Lucifer, who has been wronged, greets thee."[14] The Luciferians claimed that God unjustly cast Lucifer into hell, but that eventually the devil would be restored to his former glory and happiness.

Like Traditional Satanists, Bakunin stated that God only created man to be his slave:

---

14 *The Secret Societies Of All Ages and Countries*, C. Heckethorn

> He wished, therefore, that man, destitute of all understanding himself, should remain an eternal beast, even on all-fours before the eternal God, his creator and master.

> Slaves of God, men must also be slaves of Church and State, in so far as the State is consecrated by the Church.

> If God is, man is a slave; now, man can and must be free; then God does not exist.

> [God's] existence necessarily implies the slavey of all that is beneath him. Therefore if God existed, only in one way could he serve human liberty – by ceasing to exist.

In agreement with Satanists, Bakunin sees Satan as an emancipator:

> But here steps in Satan, the eternal rebel, the first freethinker and the emancipator of worlds. He makes man ashamed of his bestial ignorance and obedience; he emancipates him, stamps upon his brow the seal of liberty and humanity, in urging him to disobey and eat of the fruit of knowledge.

Bakunin sees materialism, as Lenin did, as the foundation of socialism and identifies himself as a materialist and Revolutionary Socialist. The Bolsheviks shared his philosophy on virtually all matters. However, they were more cunning, and did not make war on God openly for dialectical reasons.

Like the Bolsheviks such as Lenin and Trotzky, Bakunin believed that religion was used to exploit the poor:

> The people, unfortunately, are still very ignorant, and are kept in ignorance by the systematic efforts of all the governments, who consider this ignorance, not without good reason, as one of the essential conditions of their own power.

Like Lenin, he believed that only the "social revolution" would sound the death knell for religion and end the abuse of alcohol. Only the "social revolution" will have the power to close the "dram-shops" and churches, whose priests "poison" the innocent and are numbered among the "exploiters of humanity".

Like Marx, and his disciple Lenin, he sees religion as the opium of the people:

> [Religious beliefs] do not signify in man so much an aberration of mind as a deep discontent of Heart. They are the instinctive and passionate protest of the human being against the narrowness, the platitudes, the sorrows, and the shame of a wretched existence. For this malady, I have already said, there is but one remedy – Social Revolution.

Bakunin also promotes the desecration of churches and their replacement with atheist schooling, acts that eventually came to be enacted by the Bolsheviks themselves. Bakunin writes:

> Instruction must be spread among the masses without stint, transforming all the churches, all those temples dedicated to the glory of God and to the slavery of men, into so many schools of human emancipation.

Bakunin, like Marx again, was influenced by Ludwig Feuerbach. In his book *The Essence of Christianity* (1841), Ludwig Feuerbach wrote that humanity created deities as reflections of the human Self. Feuerbach said that religion exercised socio-political power upon the human mind through the promotion of fear of the mystical forces of the heavens, and concluded that churches should be destroyed and religion eradicated through education. Expressing similar sentiments, Bakunin writes:

> Consequently, the religious heaven is nothing but a mirage in which man, exalted by ignorance and faith, discovers his own image, but enlarged and reversed – that is, divinized.
>
> To proclaim as divine all that is grand, just, noble, and beautiful in humanity is to tacitly admit that humanity of itself would have been unable to produce it – that is, that, abandoned to itself, its own nature is miserable, iniquitous, base and ugly. Thus we come back to the essence of all religion

– in other words, to the disparagement of humanity for the greater glory of divinity.

Lenin wrote:

> We must combat religion – that is the ABC of *all* materialism, and consequently of Marxism.

Lenin also wrote:

> Marxism is materialism. As such, it is relentlessly hostile to religion as was the materialism of the eighteenth century Encyclopaedists or the materialism of Feuerbach.

The undercurrents of Satanism that run through Bakunin's philosophy are evident for all to see. The fact that the Bolsheviks shared in Bakunin's "materialist" philosophy cannot be doubted, for their actions speak for themselves. Bakunin was openly anarchic and anti-God. The Bolsheviks played a cleverer game, endeavouring to destroy religion in a more subtle and occult manner – not openly through "materialism" but through the more subtle "dialectical materialism." However, it is self-evident that Karl Marx and the Bolsheviks shared the same anti-God and satanic philosophy as Bakunin.

Just as in Soviet days the League of the Godless took pains to blaspheme God and denigrate the saints and all heavenly beings, so Bakunin blasphemes God, describing him a "very brutal, cruel and selfish person". In *God and the State*, Bakunin describes God as:

> . . . the most jealous, the most vain, the most ferocious, the most unjust, the most bloodthirsty, the most despotic, and the most hostile to human dignity and liberty.

Communist hatred of God: in their own words

Karl Marx:

The idea of God is the keynote of a perverted civilization. It must be destroyed.

Lenin:

Religion is a kind of spiritual gin in which the slaves of capitalism drown their human shape and their claim to any decent human life.

Religion is the opium of the people – this dictum by Marx is the corner-stone of the whole Marxist outlook on religion. Marxism has always regarded all modern religions and churches, and each and every religious organisation, as instruments of bourgeois reaction that serve to defend exploitation and to befuddle the working class.

All oppressing classes of every description need two social functions to safeguard their domination: the function of a hangman and the function of a priest. The hangman is to quell the protest . . . the priest reconciles them to class domination, weans them away from revolutionary actions.

We must be engineers of souls.

The only idol we permit and maintain is godlessness.

Among other purposes, we created our party specifically for the fight against any religious deceiving of the people.

To talk about God-seeking, not in order to declare against *all* devils and gods, against every ideological necrophily (all worship of a divinity is necrophily – be it the cleanest, most ideal, not sought-out but built-up divinity, it's all the same), but to prefer a blue devil to a yellow one is a hundred times worse than not saying anything about it at all.

Stalin:

America is like a healthy body and its resistance is threefold: its patriotism, its morality, and its spiritual life. If we can undermine these three areas, America will collapse from within.

Anatoliy Lunacharsky:

Why should we believe in God? – We hate Christianity and Christians. Even the best of them must be regarded as our worst enemies. They preach love of one's neighbour, and pity, which is contrary to our principles. Christian love is a hindrance to the revolution. Down with love of one's neighbour; what we want is hatred. We must know how to hate, for only at this price can we conquer the universe. We have done with the kings of the earth; let us now deal with the kings of the skies. The anti-religious campaign must not be restricted to Soviet Russia: it should be carried on throughout the entire world. The fight should also be developed in the Musselman and Catholic countries, with the same ends in view and by the same means.

Christians teach love and compassion, which is contrary to our convictions; down with "love our neighbours;" what we preach is a gospel of hate!

[God is the one] who has in truth throughout the whole course of history inflicted diabolical evil on mankind.

Grigory Zinoviev:

> We shall vanquish Him from the highest heaven and wherever He seeks refuge, we shall subdue Him forever.

Yemelyan Yaroslavsky

Yaroslavsky was President of the Society of Militant Atheists and editor of Bezbozhnik (The Godless). He wrote:

> Remember the struggle against religion is a struggle for socialism.

George Lukacs:

Lukacs was a Commissar for Culture and Education in Bela Kun's short-lived Hungarian Soviet Republic is said to have advised a comrade the following:

> Communist ethics make it the highest duty to accept the necessity of acting wickedly. This is the greatest sacrifice the revolution asks from us. The conviction of the true Communist is that evil transforms itself into good through the dialectics of historical evolution.

> Any political movement capable of bringing Bolshevism to the West would have to be "Demonic".

> The abandonment of the soul's uniqueness solves the problem of 'unleashing' the diabolic forces lurking in all the violence which are needed to create a revolution.

Mikhail Gorbachev:

A footnote in *The Perestroika Deception* quotes Gorbachev:

> There must be no let-up in the war against religion because as long as reli-

> gion exists Communism cannot prevail. We must intensify the obliteration of all religions where they are being practised or taught.

This statement was made by Mikhail Gorbachev on 15 December 1987 to a group of Communist Party officials, cadres and Soviet military personnel in Uzbekistan.

Chairman Mao:

> Communism is not love. Communism is a hammer, which we use to crush the enemy.

Kim Philby:

> Early rejection of Christianity probably had something to do with my early rejection of the bourgeois state.

Satanism and socialism

Saul Alinsky's acknowledgement of Satan in his book *Rules for Radicals* fits a socialist pattern that goes back centuries:

> Lest we forget at least an over-the-shoulder acknowledgement to the very first radical: from all our legends, mythology, and history, the first radical known to man who rebelled against the establishment and did it so effectively that he at least won his own kingdom – Lucifer.

John Milton's *Paradise Lost* pioneered the use of Satan as a symbol of heroic defiance of God, and, consequently, of the existing social order. William Godwin follows on with his *Enquiry Concerning Political Justice*, as does Shelley, Godwin's son-in-law, who makes Satan a positive political role model. The English Romantics are well-known for celebrating Lucifer, including such writers as Blake and Byron.

Per Faxneld reveals the celebration of Satan by socialists in his work *The Devil is Red: Socialist Satanism in the Nineteenth Century.*

The figure of Lucifer and the notion of his redemption of Satan was a topic essential to those radical socialist writers who moved in romantic circles during the 1830s and 1840s. Balzac, Hugo, Lamartine, Michelet, Alexandre Soumet, and George Sand wrote about Lucifer and Satan as revolutionary and tragic figures, symbolizing the human quest for freedom and redemption. The occultist and socialist Eliphas Lévi was personally acquainted with some of these authors, including other *romantiques* such as Théophile Gautier and Gérard de Nerval, who were friends and collaborators of Esquiros.

A view of God as protector of the strong and rich can logically lead to the conclusion that Satan must be the god of the oppressed and poor. In Charles Baudelaire's *Les Fleurs Du Mal*, the devil is portrayed as a saviour, especially for the downtrodden and despised. In George Sand's, *Consuelo*, Consuelo has a vision of Satan where he tells her:

> I am not the demon, I am the archangel of legitimate rebellion and the patron of the grand struggles. Like Christ, I am the god of the poor, of the weak, and of the oppressed.

Many socialist writers come dangerously close to producing actual religious writings in praise of Satan. In this they were acting like Anton LaVey, the founder of the Church of Satan, who claims to be an atheist and yet often writes as if he is praising Satan as an existing and conscious entity.

"Blasphemous chapels" existed in London in the 1810s, where agitators attacked the authority of Christianity with burlesque parody and diatribes.

Torch symbols on socialist banners were often a reference to Lucifer. Lucifer journals portrayed a hand grasping a burning torch. The etymological content of word Lucifer is "light-bearer". Star decorations on banners could also be tied to Lucifer, being the morning star.

In some socialist circles, Christianity was perceived as yet another capitalist tool for domination. Consequently, Christian hymns were appropriated and socialist weddings and baptisms were held in lieu of the usual Christian ones. This may have been an attempt to eradicate Christianity by replacing it with new rituals and symbols. All these kinds of practices of course were put into full use by the USSR.

Since the Bible makes it explicit that God has appointed the existing order (Rom. 13:1-2), socialist revolutionaries who wish to oppose this order oppose God, and praise the Adversary, Satan.

In his book *The Socialist Phenomenon*, Igor Shafarevich examines socialism from its earliest origins to the present day. The constant elements running through socialism are the abolition of private property; of the family; of hierarchies; the hostility towards religion; the suppression of individuality and the creation of an anonymous society. He observes that socialism is hostile to religion in all contemporary socialist states, though the abolition of religion is rarely legislated as it was in Albania. Calls to assassinate the Pope and to annihilate all monks and priests run like a red thread through the history of the heretical movements in which socialist tendencies were particularly pronounced:

> Their hatred for the basic symbols of Christianity – the cross and the church - is very striking. We encounter the burning of crosses and the profanation of churches from the first centuries of Christianity up to the present day.

Shafarevich draws the conclusion that the death of mankind constitutes the goal of socialism. He also thinks that socialism is a manifestation of the allure of death:

> Understanding socialism as one of the manifestations of the allure of death explains its hostility toward individuality, its desire to destroy those forces which support and strengthen human personality: religion, culture, family, individual property. It is consistent with the tendency to reduce man to the level of a cog in the state mechanism.

Éliphas Lévi: socialist and exponent of magick and satanism

The famous drawing of Baphomet was created by the socialist Eliphas Levi Zahed (born Alphonse Louis Constant, 1810–1875). In 1848, he and his friend Henri-François-Alphonse Esquiros founded the the extreme-left Club de la Montagne in 1848.

In his first socialist writings, Constant (Éliphas Lévi) openly identified as a pantheist. He reflected the Romantic tendencies of July Monarchy socialism, which led critics to identify the socialist reformers as "modern pantheists." "pantheism" was a term widely used to decry recent philosophical and religious tendencies, including the contemporary socialist currents to which Lévi adhered.

Every French study of socialism that appeared between the 1830s and early 1850s depicted the socialists as the heirs of a heretical tradition that included the theosophists of the eighteenth century, medieval groups such as the Templars and the Cathars, and protagonists of the School of Alexandria, most notably the Gnostics.

Constant (Lévi) envisioned the rehabilitation of Lucifer after the second coming of Jesus. In his *Bible de la liberté*, Éliphas Lévi described Lucifer as the "angel of liberty" who stood for the emancipation of human intelligence. Far from being an evil entity, he would eventually be rehabilitated and unified with God through his revolutionary striving for freedom and science. Constant was given a prison sentence for publishing this notorious book.

Constant was inspired by the writings of Félicité de Lamennais, who propagated a Christian socialism. Constant described his ideology as *communisme néo-catholique* and published a number of socialist books and pamphlets. He propagated his socialism as "true Christianity" and denounced the Church as a corruptor of the teachings of Christ. Constant developed his "occultism" as a direct consequence of his socialist and neo-catholic ideas and continued to propagate the realization of "true socialism" throughout his entire life in distinct opposition to "false" socialism and "false" Catholicism.

In the 1840s, Constant developed close ties to the Fourierist movement. He published in Fourierist publications and praised Fourierism as the "true Christianity". Charles Fourier (1772-1837) preached sexual freedom and the abolition of marriage and the family. There are clear occult elements in Fourier's fantastic cosmology.

Constant (Éliphas Lévi) was romantically involved with the feminist Flora Tristan for a short period. Five years before the political slogan "Workers of the world, unite!" appeared in *The Communist Manifesto*, the phrase appeared in her book *The Workers' Union* (1843). A Utopian Socialist, Tristan knew Charles Fourier personally, and studied the works of the Saint Simonians.

The debates in the *Revue philosophique et religieuse* demonstrate how natural it was for a socialist writer like Constant to discuss topics like magick or the Kabbalah in a socialist journal.

Constant (Éliphas Lévi) was the first to incorporate Tarot cards into his magical system.

Constant developed his ideas about magick in a milieu marked by the confluence of socialist and magnetistic ideas. Henri Delaage and Jean du Potet de Sennevoy propagated magnetistic, magical, and kabbalistic ideas as the foundation of a superior form of socialism. The spiritualistic magnetists were socialist veterans who were pursuing their old dream of a synthesis of religion, science, and politics, seeking to establish a perfect social order. Du Potet had an openly revolutionary past and concealed his socialist tendencies only because of the unfavorable atmosphere of the 1850s.

Constant resumed the use of openly socialist language after the government had loosened the restrictions against socialist doctrines in 1859. He continued to develop his idea of an élite of initiates that would lead the people to its final emancipation.

The satanic nature of communism

Friedrich Engels wrote:

> . . . communism abolishes eternal truths, it abolishes all religion, and all morality.

Blasphemous versions of the Lord's Prayer are common in Marxist organisations.

The communist cannot be a Christian. Communists are fond of emphasising that they are opponents of Christian evangelical morality based upon love, pity, and sympathy. Such sentiments are found in such works as Yaroslavsky's *Against Religion and the Church*.

The Communard Flourens said "Our enemy is God. Hatred of God is the beginning of wisdom". On the first day of the Commune the communards hanged the Archbishop of Paris.

One of Engel's influential friends, Bruno Bauer, said: "My spirit of blasphemy will be satisfied only if I am authorized to preach openly as professor of the atheistic system".

Nikolai Bukharin was convinced he was the Antichrist when he was young.

The communist revolutionaries often used pseudonyms to do with the devil.

Richard Wurmbrand witnessed how the communist regime turned even Christians into murderers and denouncers of innocent victims. It can therefore only be abhorred by the children of God. The communists imprisoned and tortured family members of those found guilty. In this Wurmbrand sees the hand of Satan:

> Marxism is not an ordinary sinful human ideology. It is Satanic in its manner of sinning, as it is Satanic in the teachings it purveys.

For belief in God, children were separated from families and kept in atheist boarding schools.

Wurmbrand argues that in a few extreme cases Marxism has lifted its atheistic mask to reveal its true face, the face of Satanism. Christians in Romanian Communist prison of Piteshti were tortured in order to make them blaspheme. Prisoners were forced to say Mass over excrement and urine. Prisoners had to sit on Bibles with naked bottoms. In Romania, nuns were raped anally and Baptist girls had oral sex forced on them. Using Luciferian techniques, the communists made martyrs die blaspheming, because of the delirium provoked by torture.

In Piteshti, Romania, the communists perfected the practice of torture. They tortured Christians to such an extent that they in turn became torturers. At first they would pretend to be fellow Christian prisoners to the new Christian inmates, praying with them and so forth, but then they would turn on them and torture them day and night. There was no relief from this kind of torture, unlike the usual kind that might only last an hour or two in a day. Only one in a thousand could bear this new refined system of torture without breaking.

The Marxist ideology is not, in fact, atheism, but fervent hatred for God.

A communist paper let slip the comment: "We fight against God to snatch believers from Him".

Wurmbrand writes:

> The ultimate aim of communism in conquering new countries is not to establish another social or economic system. It is to mock God and praise Satan.

In his book *Tortured for Christ*, Wurmbrand makes several perceptive observations:

> Our highest goal is to become Christ-like. To prevent this is the main aim of communists. They are primarily anti-religious.

> We saw that communism is not from people but from the devil. It is a spiritual force – a force of evil – and can only be countered by a greater spiritual force, the spirit of God.

> The secret police recognised, as only the devil can, an immediate threat to them. They knew if a man believed in Christ, he would never be a mindless, willing subject.

> Religion is incompatible with communism. It is hostile to it. The content of the program of the Communist Party is a death blow to religion. It is a program for the creation of an atheistic society in which people will be rid forever of the religious bondage.

> Communism is a tremendous foe of Christianity and most dangerous. Against it, we must unite.

A proto-Communist organisation was called "Hell": a super-secret circle within the "Organization".

The crimes of communism are unequalled. No other political system has killed so many. According to the Russian statistician Professor Ivan Kurganov's analysis, from 1917 to 1959 socialism cost the Soviet Union 110 million lives. Socialism then cost another 60 million in China. These sins surpass the ordinary and are Satanic indeed.

Marxism is a materialistic philosophy that blinds followers to spiritual realities. If people do not adhere to a God-fearing religion, they will worship Satan and persecute those who do not worship their "god".

The doctrine of dialectical materialism effectively renders void every word uttered from the mouth of God. There is no room for the idea of God;

there is no difference between matter and spirit, between soul and body; there is neither survival of the soul after death nor any hope in a future life.

In answer to a party questionnaire, Lenin stated that he stopped being religious at the age of sixteen. Anna Yelizarova-Ulyanova (1864-1935), Lenin's elder sister, had noticed that around this time:

> [Lenin's] mood was one of strong opposition to high-school authorities, high-school studies, and also to religion . . .

In his biography of Lenin, Trotzky questions whether the reports of him throwing his cross away in a sacrilegious manner were based in fact. However, Trotzky records the testimony of three people who claimed that that he did, one of whom was Nadezhda Krupskaya, Lenin's own wife.

Communists were well aware of the incompatibility of religion with communism. Lenin expresses this incompatibility thus:

> If a priest comes to us to take part in our common political work and conscientiously performs Party duties, without opposing the programme of the Party, he may be allowed to join the ranks of the Social-Democrats; for the contradiction between the spirit and principles of our programme and the religious convictions of the priest would in such circumstances be something that concerned him alone . . . [but] if, for example, a priest joined the Social-Democratic Party and made it his chief and almost sole work actively to propagate religious views in the Party, it would unquestionably have to expel him from its ranks.

Lenin's observations concur with those in *The ABC of Communism* which states that one cannot be a believer and a communist, as a communist has to "reject the commandments of religion":

> Communism is not compatible with religion. The tactics of the communist party require of its members a certain kind of action. The morality of all religion also requires of believers a certain species of conduct. Between the directives of communist tactics and the commandments of religion there are, more often than not, irreconcilable contradictions. A communist who rejects the commandments of religion and acts according to the directions of the party, ceases to be a believer. On the other hand, a believer who

pretends to be a communist, but who infringes the directions of the party in the name of the commandments of religion, ceases to be a communist.

In *Alexander Solzhenitsyn Speaks to the West* Solzhenitsyn writes:

Communism has never concealed the fact that it rejects all absolute concepts of morality. It scoffs at any consideration of 'good' and 'evil' as indisputable categories. Communism considers morality to be relative, to be a class matter. Depending upon circumstances and the political situation, any act, including murder, even the killing of hundreds of thousands, could be good or could be bad. It all depends upon class ideology.

Ex-communist Bob Darke writes in *The Communist Technique in Britain*:

If the moment of revolutionary change is hastened by acts that are illegal, unjust and inhuman, the end, to him, makes them right.

The Communist is a man who lives on hatred.

Too readily I accepted the Party's declaration that my conscience was a vestige of capitalist society . . . But they liberate my soul and allow me to look my fellow-man in the face without shame. We face a conspiracy against such intangible values.

In his book *Socialism*, Ludwig von Mises writes:

[Lenin] was the brutal superman for whose coming the pseudo-philosophers had yearned. He was the counterfeit saviour whom history had elected to bring salvation through bloodshed.

Now the majority of quasi-civilized men bowed to the dictator who was prepared to shed much more blood than Bismarck ever did.

This was the true meaning of the Lenin revolution. All the traditional ideas of right and legality were overthrown. The rule of unrestrained violence and usurpation was substituted for the rule of law. The "narrow horizon of bourgeois legality," as Marx had dubbed it, was abandoned. Henceforth no laws could any longer limit the power of the elect. They were free to kill *ad libitum*.

In his essay *"Left" and "Right": The False Dichotomy*, Tibor Szamuely wrote in a similar vein:

Today the entire structure has been swept away. To be more precise, it was irrevocably destroyed on the 7th November 1917, when Lenin announced the seizure of power in Russia by the Bolsheviks. On that day a whole new dimension was added to the nature of politics. Totalitarianism, the system created by the Russian Revolution, is implacably opposed to every basic principle held in common by the traditional Left and Right - whatever their respective differences. Totalitarianism is a theory and a system operating on an entirely different plane from that of politics as practised in Europe since the dawn of the modern age. Its fundamental principle, its be-all and end-all, is the concept of total, unlimited State power, of dictatorship - which according to Lenin himself, "means neither more nor less than unlimited power, resting directly on force, not limited by anything, not restricted by any laws or any absolute rules. Nothing else but that".

In *Liberalism*, von Mises writes:

The Third International seeks to exterminate its adversaries and their ideas in the same way that the hygienist strives to exterminate a pestilential bacillus; it considers itself in no way bound by the terms of any compact that it may conclude with opponents, and it deems any crime, any lie, and any calumny permissible in carrying on its struggle.

To reject inhuman Communist ideology is simply to be a human being, a "protest of our souls against those who would have us forget the concepts of good and evil". Alexander Solzhenitsyn declares:

those people who have lived in the most terrible conditions, on the frontier between life and death, be it people from the West or from the East – they

> all understand that between good and evil there is an irreconcilable contradiction, that good and evil are not one and the same thing, that one cannot build one's life without regard to this distinction.

In *Warning to the Western World*, Alexander Solzhenitsyn states that communism is anti-humanity:

> Humanity acts as if it does not understand what Communism is, as if it does not want to understand, is not capable of understanding . . . I think it is not only a question of the disguises that Communism has assumed in the last decades. It is rather that the essence of Communism is quite beyond the limits of human understanding. It is hard to believe that people could actually plan such things and carry them out. And it is precisely because its essence is beyond comprehension, perhaps, that Communism is so difficult to understand.

He notes how even socialists from countries neighbouring Russia do not understand it. He warns:

> The Communist ideology is to destroy your social order. It is a concentration of hatred, a continued repetition of the oath to destroy the Western world.

Solzhenitsyn chastises the West for not even noticing the fifteen-million-strong Gulag Archipelago. He explains that there can be no reconciliation with communism. He writes:

> . . . the failure to understand the radical hostility of communism to mankind as a whole – the failure to realize that communism is irredeemable, that there exist no "better" variants of communism; that it is incapable of growing "kinder," that it cannot survive as an ideology without using terror, and that, consequently, to coexist with communism on the same planet is impossible. Either it will spread, cancer-like, to destroy mankind, or else mankind will have to rid itself of communism.
>
> Never has the Politburo numbered a humane or peace-loving man among

its members. The communist bureaucracy is not constituted to allow men of that calibre to rise to the top – they would instantly suffocate there.

> A Russia of peace and national integrity is inimical to the communist madness. A Russian national awakening and liberation would mark the downfall of Soviet and with it of world communism. And Soviet communism is well aware that it is being abrogated by the Russian national consciousness. For those who genuinely love Russia no reconciliation with communism has ever been possible or ever will be. That is why communism has always been most ruthless of all in its treatment of Christians and advocates of national re-birth. In the early years this meant wholesale execution; later the victims were left to rot in the camps. But to this very day the persecution continues inexorably . . .

The Communist Party fears the spiritual strength of nations whose traditional and Christian morality is practiced both in private and public life. The communists therefore endeavours to break down the moral integrity of free nations of the world. Lenin stated the necessity for undermining morals and for encouraging heterosexual and homosexual looseness. Once people are unable to say No to themselves, they will be unable to say No to communism.

Lenin found Sergei Nechayev before Karl Marx. It was this confluence of Nechayev and Marx that was so truly diabolical. Nechayev writes in *Catechism of a Revolutionist*:

> . . . for [the revolutionist] everything is moral which assists the triumph of revolution. Immoral and criminal is everything which stands in its way.

> . . . tender and effeminate emotions of kinship, friendship, love, gratitude and even honour must be stifled in him by a cold and single-minded passion for the revolutionary cause.

> He is not a revolutionary if he feels pity for anything in this world.

> . . . this foul society must be split up into several categories: the first category comprises those to be condemned immediately to death.

> Our task is terrible, total, universal, merciless destruction.

Nechayev's fanaticism is reflected in Lenin's dictum:

> Everything is moral that serves the communist party.

Such a philosophy approves of the depraving of the young, the destruction of the family, the desecration of religion, lying, torture, and murder, provided they serve the ends of communism.

The renowned exorcist Gabriele Amorth states his belief that Stalin and communism were under the influence of the devil:

> It is possible for the demon to use one person to strike even a very large group – these groups can even take over or influence one or more nations. In our times, I believe that this was the case of men such as Karl Marx, Hitler, and Stalin. The atrocities perpetrated by the Nazis, the horrors of communism, the slaughters of Stalin, for example, reached diabolic proportions.[15]

Amorth also sees Marxism's influence as reason for the increase in evil influence:

> I believe a good portion of the blame [for the increase of evil influence] is to be attributed to socialism and communism, especially in Italy, where Marxist doctrine has dominated the media and the culture in the past few years.

During an exorcism, Amorth asked an unclean spirit why he had so much hatred toward John Paul II. He replied: "Because he has ruined our plans." Amorth imagined that he was referring to the fall of communism.[16]

---

15 *An Exorcist Tells His Story*, G. Amorth

16 *An Exorcist Explains the Demonic*, G. Amorth

The Ukrainian Metropolitan of the Catholic Church, Andrew Count Sheptytsky requested there to be an exorcism of the communists on the grounds that the "regime cannot be explained except by a massive possession of the Devil".

Konstantin Preobrazhensky, a former KGB officer who publicly repented and became the KGB's harshest critic, claims its ideology is satanic:

> The FSB exhibits the chief characteristics of anti-Christian behaviour – persistence in sin, and refusal to repent.

> I appealed to my former colleagues, KGB officers . . .to renounce the devil's ideology of Communism.

> Hatred toward Christianity is what characterizes the worldview of today's Russian counter-intelligence officers . . . It is an entity with an insatiable sense of having been insulted, a stronghold of Communist revenge. The FSB is a political power. Leading a spiritual war against it I am fulfilling my Christian duty of fighting the Devil.

Aleister Crowley visited Russia in 1898 and in 1913. Some allege he may have masterminded an international conspiracy rooted in Satanism and may have helped the Communists in Russia. Walter Duranty, the New York Times correspondent, allegedly indulged in satanic orgies with him, according to S.J. Taylor in *Stalin's Apologist.*

Stalin was rumoured to have employed the services of Natalya Lvova, "a third-generation witch". Shake-ups in the Communist Party, which often resulted in exile to the Gulag, may have been the result of Stalin and Lvova's black magic sessions in the Kremlin.

In modern Russia today, people are heavily involved in the occult. In 2010, a psychologist with the Russian Academy of Sciences cited World Health Organisation data that indicated there were 800,000 occultists/faith healers in Russia. In 2013, Russian citizens spent almost £20 billion every year on magical and paranormal services. Russia's Academy of Sciences estimates that two thirds of all Russian women have at some time sought help from a psychic or sorcerer. The figure for Russian men is one in four.

Communism's atheism

Atheism is the keynote of communism. The ex-communist Whittaker Chambers reiterates this point several times in *Letter to My Grandchildren* found in his book *Witness*:

> Communism restores man to his sovereignty by the simple method of denying God.

> The communist vision is the vision of Man without God.

> Its [communism's] promise was whispered in the first days of creation under the Tree of the Knowledge of Good and Evil: "Ye shall be as gods." It is the great alternative faith of mankind.

> The crux of the matter is the question whether God exists. If God exists, man cannot be a Communist, which begins with the rejection of God.

The Jesuit Vincent Miceli confronts the phenomenon of communism in his books *The Antichrist* and *The Gods of Atheism* and declares that atheistic humanists revel in destroying the faith of others. Atheists want to create a community of haters of God. Atheists beget atheists. The satanic nature of atheism is its blasphemous joy at hating God and the thrilling decision to unite men in a community of enduring hate for the purpose of banishing God from the hearts of men. For atheists, God is the enemy of man. Miceli writes:

> [the] most satanic project of the fifty years of the Revolution is its program to extinguish Christian hope and the hope of any transcendent life hereafter in the hearts of all men

Anatoliy Lunacharsky recounted the story that when he was playing in the workshop of a silversmith as a young boy, he intentionally smashed a religious icon on the table to see if God would punish him. His mother refused to stand in for God's wrath when no punishment came forth.

In 1923 Lunacharsky and Trotzky held mock trials of God in public.

Trotzky's morality akin to the morality of Satanists

In 1918, while Ukraine was under German occupation, the rabbis of Odessa pronounced *herem* against Trotzky, Zinoviev, and other Bolshevik leaders in the synagogue. Such anathematization can be likened to being excommunicated by the Roman Catholic Churc

In his two pamphlets *Their Morality and Ours* and *The Moralists and Sycophants against Marxism*, Leon Trotzky addresses the accusations made against Marxists that they were lacking moral scruples, allowing the ends to justify the means.

Trotzky admits that the Bolsheviks maintain the "dialectical consideration" that morals serve merely an "ideological function" in class struggle.

Satanists believe that since Satan is not constrained by moral concepts such as good and evil, so they too can adjust their morality to fit any situation. Like Trotzky, they do not believe that morals are fixed and unchangeable.

Satanists slander God by stating that he only wanted men to be mindless obedient automatons. Similarly, Trotzky argues that the exploiters use morality to turn men into obedient sheep who will patiently endure their exploitation:

> The ruling class forces *its* ends upon society and habituates it to considering all those means which contradict its ends as immoral.

Trotzky does not attack God directly. His war against God is couched in terms of class warfare, it being more expedient dialectically to attack God's agents than God himself. In place of "God" or "God's laws" or "the morality of God," Trotzky uses phrases such as "the ruling class," "official morality," "the bourgeoisie and their morality." "exploiters," "idealist morality," "transcendental morality," and "petty-bourgeouis theoreticians and moralists." If one replaces such phrases with words such as "God" or "God's commandments," it becomes apparent how his philosophy is so similar to that of a Satanist.

Satanists believe that mankind would be nothing but slaves to the

Judaeo-Christian god, were it not for Satan and his demons. They believe that God does not want people to have free will. Mankind was only created to be a slave to God. Trotzky's view are not so distant from this satanic philosophy. He writes:

> ... petty-bourgeouis theoreticians and moralists (i.e. *those who preach the commandments of God*) radiate all the colors of the rainbow but in the final analysis remain apostles of slavery and submission.

Trotzky cannot envisage a successful revolutionary party of the proletariat which does not have complete independence from God and his commandments, for he sees this morality as "counter-revolutionary". He writes:

> From the point of view of "eternal truths" revolution is of course "anti-moral." But this merely means that idealist morality (i.e. *God's law*) is counterrevolutionary, that is, in the service of the exploiters (i.e. *God*).

The workers need to be ruthless to prevail, and recognition of any moral boundaries would weaken their resolve. These morals, in fact, were created by the exploiters only to serve as chains:

> To accomplish the overturn, the proletariat needs all its strength, all its resolution, all its audacity, passion, and ruthlessness. Above all, it must be completely free from the fictions of religion, "democracy," and transcendental morality (i.e. *God's laws*) – the spiritual chains forged by the enemy (i.e. *God*) to tame and enslave it. Only that which prepares the complete and final overthrow of imperialist bestiality (i.e. *God*) is moral and nothing else. The welfare of the revolution – that is the supreme law!

Rejecting all religion as mere fiction, the only commandment Trotzky recognizes is the welfare of the revolution. In his opinion, the end does indeed justify the means.

Like Satan, who masquerades as an angel of light, Bolsheviks were able to appear righteous, rather than evil, through the doctrine of the class struggle. Class warfare is set forth as a battle between Marxists and "exploiters" rather than a battle between Marxists and God. This sleight of hand is a "dialectical" ploy, for to admit open warfare with God would invite opposition. Lenin advised against playing into the hands of the clergy with open declarations of war against religion. Lenin takes it as given that a Marxist is an "enemy of religion", but he advocates a covert war against God. Lenin wrote:

> [To preach atheism] would only be playing into the hands of the priest and the priests, who desire nothing more better than that the division of the workers according to their participation in the strike movement should be replaced by their division according to their belief in God. An anarchist who preached war against God at all costs would in effect be helping the priests and the bourgeoisie . . . A Marxist must be a materialist, i.e. an enemy of religion, but a dialectical materialist . . .

The class struggle is a war against God, for the Bolsheviks see God as the enemy. The chains that the workers are being exhorted to throw off are not just the chains of exploitation, but spiritual chains too. The "rupture of the Bolsheviks from conservative moral philosophy," as Trotzky puts it, is a rupture with God and should be equated to Satan's war against God.

In his address at the mass meeting held in New York on October 28 1938 to celebrate the founding of the Fourth International, Trotzky's unwavering war against God is clear. Trotzky talks not only of the full material liberation of the toilers and exploited through the socialist revolution, but also of their "spiritual liberation". Like a prophet, he predicts not "one stone upon another" being left of the other internationals. Only by giving oneself wholly to the Party does one find oneself. Such language reminds one of Jesus' words that a man will only save himself by losing his life for Jesus' sake (Matt. 10:39). In the speech, Trotzky talks of eliminating unworthy elements from the Party, in the same manner that Paul speaks of ejecting the immoral from Christian assemblies (1 Cor. 5:11). Trotzky speaks of the Trotzkyist victims of Stalin as Christians might speak of martyrs. The "spirits" of these dead continue to fight in the ranks. He predicts that the program of the Fourth International will be a guide for millions and these millions will know how to "storm earth and heaven".

In this revealing address, which Trotzky delivers in English (a recording of which can be easily found on the internet), the pseudo-religious nature of Trotzky's philosophy is laid bare. Membership of the Party is akin to being a member of the true Church. Heaven must be stormed.

Trotzky's words confirm Leszek Kolakowski's thesis that Marxism is the messianic faith of a post-religious world.

Aleksandr Dugin's occult ties

Aleksandr Dugin founded the Eurasian Party.

An adherent of Traditionalism (or "Perennialism"), Dugin believes that all 'traditions' convey a "Primordial Tradition". A pivotal moment for Traditionalists was when Marsilio Ficino, an Italian scholar and Catholic priest, translated the *Corpus Hermeticum*, a work brought to Florence in 1460. Before then, the early Church had only been aware of Hermes Trismegistus' work *Asclepius*. St Augustine condemned Hermes for his "impious art" of summoning demons into statues. With the discovery of the Vedas, Traditionalism took off again in the West. Traditionalists such as Julius Evola and Rene Guenon rejected Christian values and embraced Nietzsche's ubermensch. Evola is particularly favoured by those who reject Christianity.

The black flag of the Eurasian Movement is a modified "Star of Chaos" and presumed to refer to Chaos Magic. The Eurasian flag comprises eight white or yellow thunderbolts (or arrows) shaped in a radial pattern and set behind a black background. The eight-arrow star had first appeared on the cover of *Osnovy geopolitiki*, placed in the centre of an outline map of Eurasia.

Chaos Magick is an occult doctrine based on the writing of Aleister Crowley, Austin Osman Spare, and Peter Carroll.

In the 1980s Dugin is reported to have been a member of the Moscow-based "Black Order of the SS", a group of intellectuals fascinated with both mysticism and Nazism. Members of the group also experimented with drugs and sex magick.

Dugin has open sympathy for Eastern religions, and Western Satanism. Dugin turned to occult when young.

Dugin offers the world in Eurasianism both a geopolitial ideology and an occult, political religion with its roots in Traditionalist teaching. His movement Arctogaia, both a think-tank and publishing house, launched its "New University" to spread occultism and Traditionalism, hermeticism, and mysticism.

In the early 1990s, Dugin became editor of the Eurasian magazine *Elementy*. The front cover of the magazine's second issue (1992) featured a portrait of Baphomet, the symbol of the Church of Satan. Dugin frequently wrote about the occult within the pages of *Elementy* and praised the "spiritual and transcendental side of fascism".

In 1995, during an unsuccessful attempt to get elected to parliament, Dugin took part in a pre-election concert which was described as a "black mass" by participants. It was held in memory of the British occultist Aleister Crowley. During the performance, Dugin's supporters read aloud from Crowley's *Book of the Law.*

Crowley, notorious for his sex "magick", proclaimed himself *To Mega Therion* ("the Great Beast") and is considered one of the most important exponents of modern Satanism.

Dugin is also reported to have met with figures from the Ordo Templi Orientis, a worldwide occult organisation that once boasted Crowley among its ranks.

Dugin wrote two essays on Crowley and tried to explain why his ideas are significant to the builders of the 'New Eurasian Order'. In these essays, Crowley was presented as a 'conservative revolutionary' who promoted ideas of renewal of the modern world. Despite his approval of Crowley's legacy, Dugin claims to be an Orthodox Christian (an Old Believer).

17

THE INFLUENCE OF FREEMASONRY ON BOLSHEVISM

Illuminism and Freemasonry: precursors of Bolshevism

Freemasonry and Illuminism played their part in the revolutionary movements which sprang up in Europe after the French Revolution. The Bolsheviks saw themselves as heirs of the French Revolution and often compared the Russian Revolution to the French Revolution. The design of the Hammer and Sickle may well have been influenced by the masonic symbol of the Square and Compass.

Revolutionaries used masonry in the early nineteenth century as a model and recruiting ground for their conspiratorial experiments. Nicholas Bonneville was the decisive channel of Illuminist influence. His book developed Adam Weishaupt's idea that freemasonry had been infiltrated by Jesuits and that they had to be driven out by some new order opposed to tyrants and priests:

> If Freemasonry provided a general milieu and symbolic vocabulary for revolutionary organization, it was Illuminism that provided its basic structural model.
>
> There seems good reason to believe that Illuminist influence was not

so much a "legend" as an imperfectly perceived reality. Illuminist ideas influenced revolutionaries not just through left-wing proponents, but also through right-wing opponents.[17]

Buonarroti published *History of the Babeuf Conspiracy* in 1828, thereafter becoming the patriarch to a new generation of revolutionaries until his death in 1837. Buonarroti had been fascinated with Illuminism even before the revolution and that he may even have been committed to Illuminism. His organizational plan was lifted straight from the Bavarian Order of Illuminists.

Billington writes:

> The Illuminists' vision of the world was of a dualistic struggle between the forces of darkness and of light. The name Illuminist was chosen from the image of a sun radiating illumination to outer circles. At the very centre within the inner circle burned a candle symbolizing the solar source of all illumination. The Zoroastrian-Manichaean cult of fire was central to the otherwise eclectic symbolism of the Illuminists. Their calendar was based on Persian rather than classical or Christian models.

Billington sees in Illuminism the core of the revolutionary spirit:

> The Illuminist strain represented the hard, ideological core of the revolutionary faith as it developed from Bonneville through Babeuf to Buonarroti.

The Illuminist Knigge had described the Illuminist program as one using Jesuit methods to combat Jesuit objectives, a "counter-conspiracy of progressive, enlightened forces." Illuminist propaganda contended that there was a secret Jesuit conspiracy and that the nominally abolished order had established underground links between Bavarian Jesuits and Berlin Rosicrucians. The Illuminists became more revolutionary in the course of the 1780s in the process of winning converts from conservative Masonic lodges of Strict Observance.

During the early days of the Russian Revolution, the revolutionaries called themselves Spartacists after Adam Weishaupt's Illuminati pseudo-

---

17 *Fire In The Minds of Men*, James Billington

nym. Winston Churchill alluded to this in London's Illustrated Herald (8 February 1920):

> From the days of Spartacus-Weishaupt, to those of Karl Marx, to those of Trotsky . . . this worldwide conspiracy for the overthrow of civilization and for the reconstitution of society on the basis of arrested development and envious malevolence, and impossible equality has been growing.

Adam Weishaupt developed a system of three successive "classes", the first two of which incorporated the three traditional grades and the higher symbolic grades of Masonry. It was the third class, the Areopagites, where all the ultimately irrelevant symbols were discarded for the pure reign of natural liberty and equality, where man was freed from all authority to live in egalitarian harmony. This final grade was secret from all the others. Could it be that communism retains a similar inner circle, where the true symbolism of the Hammer and Sickle is finally revealed?

The satanic character of Illuminism is clear from accounts of its ceremonies which clearly included black magic. Candidates were conducted through a long tunnel into a room adorned with black drapings and real corpses wrapped in shrouds. There was an altar made of human skeletons. Two men would tie a pink ribbon, which had been dipped in blood and bore the image of Our Lady of Loretto, around the initiate's forehead. A crucifix was placed in the candidate's hand and his clothes burned. Crosses of blood were painted on his body. The initiate was to swear to sever all bonds with parents, brothers, and wives, and all other familial ties. A candelabra with seven black tapers was set down in front of a chalice of human blood. The initiate washed himself with the blood and drank some of it.

Illuminism was Masonic magic with a worldly program. The "magical" objective of the Illuminati was the abolition of a millennium of feudalism together with the creation of a universal, utopian society that knitted all mankind together. In this they share a similar vision with communism. They believed that only the reign of the violent and repressed would be sufficient to "liberate" humanity from the tyranny of religion, law, and the class domination:

> The notion was to become the turnkey of revolutionary doctrine from Marx to Mao, and it also highlights not just the close connection between Nazism and Satanism but also the ongoing affinity throughout the nine-

teenth and twentieth centuries between occultism, social anarchism and organized criminality.[18]

Raschke writes that the basic theology of Satanism is undying hatred of Christians. This hatred of Christianity is shared with communists who believe that Christians are an impediment to their building of communism.

In the 1884 Encyclical on Freemasonry, *Humanum Genus (On Freemasonry and Naturalism)*, Leo XIII makes it clear how he believes that freemasonry promotes secularism. The actions listed here seem to foreshadow the actions taken by the Bolsheviks against the Church:

> By a long and persevering labor, they endeavour to bring about this result – namely, that the teaching office and authority of the Church may become of no account in the civil State; and for this reason they declare to the people and contend that Church and State ought to be altogether disunited.
>
> The least possible liberty to manage affairs is left to the Church; and this is done by laws not apparently very hostile, but in reality framed and fitted to hinder freedom of action. Moreover, We see exceptional and onerous laws imposed upon the clergy, to the end that they may be continually diminished in number and in necessary means. We see also the remnants of the possessions of the Church fettered by the strictest conditions, and subjected to the power and arbitrary will of the administrators of the State, and religious orders rooted up and scattered
>
> In the education and instruction of children they allow no share, either of teaching or of discipline, to the ministers of the Church; and in many places they have procured that the education of youth shall be exclusively in the hands of laymen. In this insane and wicked endeavour we may almost see the implacable hatred and spirit of revenge with which Satan himself is inflamed against Jesus Christ.
>
> Ingratiating themselves with rulers under a pretence of friendship, the Freemasons have endeavoured to make them their allies and powerful helpers for the destruction of the Christian name.
>
> Proclaiming with a loud voice liberty and public prosperity, and saying that it was the owing to the Church and to sovereigns that the multitude were not drawn out of their unjust servitude and poverty, they have

18 *Painted Black*, Carl A. Raschke

imposed upon the people and, exciting them by a thirst for novelty, they have urged them to assail both the Church and the civil power.

The Pope sees in Freemasonry a supporter of communism:

> The fear of God and reverence for divine laws being taken away, the authority of rulers despised, sedition permitted and approved and the popular passions urged on to lawlessness, with no restraint save that of punishment, a change and overthrow of all things will necessarily follow. Yea, this change and overthrow is deliberately planned and put forward by many associations of Communists and Socialists; and to their undertakings the sect of Freemasons is not hostile, but greatly favours their designs, and holds in common with them their chief opinions.
>
> They prepare the way for not a few bolder men who are hurrying on even to worse things, in their endeavour to obtain equality and community of all goods by the destruction of every distinction of rank and property.
>
> To wish to destroy the religion and the Church which God Himself has established, and to bring back after a lapse of eighteen centuries the manners and customs of the pagans, is signal folly and audacious impiety.

A decree of July 28, 1949, of the Holy Office of the Roman Catholic Church, declared that anyone who had anything to do with communism should be excommunicated.

In 1983, the Church issued a new Code of Canon Law. Unlike its predecessor, it did not explicitly name Masonic orders among the secret societies. The matter was clarified, however, in November 1983 when the Vatican's Congregation for the Doctrine of the Faith issued a Declaration on Masonic Associations, which states:

> . . . the Church's negative judgment in regard to Masonic association remains unchanged since their principles have always been considered irreconcilable with the doctrine of the Church and therefore membership in them remains forbidden. The faithful who enroll in Masonic associations are in a state of grave sin and may not receive Holy Communion.

At some point there was a transformation of Freemasonry. It ceased being an association of believers, due in great part to scientific discoveries, and due to the new thinkers such as La Mettrie, Diderot, D'Alembert,

Montesquieu, Helvetius, Voltaire, and Baron d'Holbach, The Freemasons branded Roman Catholicism, the Pope and the Society of Jesus as the three big obstacles to Enlightenment. Clement XII condemned Freemasonry as incompatible with Catholic belief and excommunicated those in Lodges.

The Jesuits were the sworn enemy of Freemasonry and in turn the Freemasons were the sworn enemies of papal centralized jurisdiction and of Roman Catholic dogmatic teaching. Freemasons' beliefs were unacceptable to Catholics, such as their denial of heaven and hell, and of the Trinity. Freemasonry's enmity towards the Roman papacy can be gleaned from the contents of the *Permanent Instruction* drawn up shortly after the Congress of Vienna by the French, Austrian, German and Italian Grand Masters of the Lodges which, apart from expressing a hatred of the Roman papacy and the calling for the total annihilation of Catholicism and even Christianity, advises on the infiltration of the Church so as to influence the selection of a Pope of their own choice. Malachi Martin observes that such tactics foreshadowed Antonio Gramsci's.

There is no proof that Lenin was a Freemason, despite claims that he was a member of the Grand Orient of Russian Peoples. However, many of the Bolsheviks were freemasons: Boris Solovyov, Vikenti Veresayev, Grigori Zinoviev (Grand Orient), Maxim Litvinov, Nikolai Bukharin, Christian Rakovsky, Yakov Sverdlov, Anatoli Lunacharsky, Mechislav Kozlovsky (Polish freemason), Karl Radek (Grand Orient), Mikhail Borodin, Leonid Krasin, and Vladimir Dzhunkovsky.

In his autobiography *My Life*, Trotzky informs us that he studied Freemasonry. Presumably his interest lay in the revolutionary aspects of Freemasonry. He associates the Illuminati ("the forerunners of the revolution") and the Carbonari with Freemasonry and notes how Freemasonry in southern Germany was "openly revolutionary":

> It was during that period that I became interested in freemasonry . . . In the eighteenth century freemasonry became expressive of a militant policy of enlightenment, as in the case of the Illuminati, who were the forerunners of the revolution; on its left it culminated in the Carbonari. Freemasons counted among their members both Louis XVI and the Dr. Guillotin who invented the guillotine. In southern Germany freemasonry assumed an openly revolutionary character, whereas at the court of Catherine the Great it was a masquerade reflecting the aristocratic and bureaucratic hierarchy. A freemason Novikov was exiled to Siberia by a freemason Empress . . .

> I discontinued my work on freemasonry to take up the study of Marxian economics . . .The work on freemasonry acted as a sort of test for these hypotheses . . .I think this influenced the whole course of my intellectual development.

The eminent Freemason, Colonel Pike wrote in his book *Morals and Dogma of the Ancient and Accepted Scottish Rite of Freemasonry* (1871):

> All Masonic associations owe their secrets and symbols to the Kabbalah . . . the Kabbalah is the key of the occult sciences.

The Carbonari

The Papal bull *Ecclesiam a Jesu Christo*, promulgated by Pius VII in 1821, linked Freemasonry with the Carbonari, an anti-clerical revolutionary group active in Italy.

The Papal bull accused the Carbonari of affecting a love of the Catholic religion while its true goals were disestablishment of the church and total religious freedom. Profaning Jesus Christ through their ceremonies, they aimed to replace the sacraments of the church and plotted against Papal primacy. All members of the Carbonari were excommunicated as were those connected with them. Freemasons were excommunicated too because of their oath bound secrecy and because of their conspiracies against church and state.

The Carbonari ("charcoal makers") was an informal network of secret revolutionary societies active in Italy from about 1800 to 1831 which aimed at the creation of a liberal, unified Italy. The controversial document Alta Vendita, which called for a liberal or modernist takeover of the Catholic Church, was attributed to the Sicilian Carbonari.

In 1830, Carbonari took part in the July Revolution in France. A subsequent bid in Modena failed outright, but in February 1831, several cities in the Papal States rose up and flew the Carbonari tricolour. A volunteer force marched on Rome but was destroyed by Austrian troops who had intervened at the request of Pope Gregory XVI. After the failed uprisings of 1831, the governments of the various Italian states cracked down on the Carbonari, who now virtually ceased to exist.

The more astute Carbonari realised they could never take on the Austrian army in open battle and joined a new movement, Giovane Italia ("Young Italy"), which was led by the nationalist Giuseppe Mazzini (1805 –1872). Giuseppe Garibaldi (1807-1882) was one of his followers.

Mazzini was vigorously opposed to Marxism and Communism, and in 1871 he condemned the socialist revolt in France that led to the creation of the short-lived Paris Commune. This caused Karl Marx to refer to Mazzini as a "reactionary" and an "old ass". Mazzini, in turn, described Marx as "a destructive spirit whose heart was filled with hatred rather than love of mankind". Mazzini observed this about Marx:

> Despite the communist egalitarianism which [Marx] preaches he is the absolute ruler of his party, admittedly he does everything himself but he is also the only one to give orders and he tolerates no opposition.

18

COMMUNIST PERSECUTION OF CHRISTIANS

Communism sets itself up as an alternative religion to Christianity

Nicolas Berdyaev argues that the passionate tone of anti-religious propaganda and persecution in Soviet Russia can be understood if one realises that Communism is a religion that is striving to take the place of Christianity. Communism persecutes all religions because it sees itself as the one true religion and can therefore cannot suffer others. Berdyaev writes:

> Communism is in actual fact the foe of every form of religion and especially Christianity, not as a social system, but as itself a religion. It wants to be a religion itself, to take the place of Christianity.[19]

In Berdyaev's view, communism is "a dictatorship which is not only political [it is] a dictatorship over spirit, conscience and thought".

The communist government, states Berdyaev, is unlimited government, which finds its motive power in hatred of Christianity, in which it sees the

19 *Origin of Russian Communism*, N. Berdyaev

cause of slavery, exploitation and darkness of mind. Berdyaev sees that there is a domain in which communism is "changeless, pitiless, fanatical and in which it will grant no concessions whatever", namely its world outlook, of philosophy and consequently of religion. The communists hate Christianity and religion in general.

In *The Russian Revolution* Berdyaev writes:

> . . . [communism] is the kingdom of this world, the last and final denial of the other world, of every kind of spirituality.

> [The Communist state] is a sacred, "theocratic" State, which takes over the functions that belong to the Church. It forms men's souls . . . demands their whole soul, exacts from them not only "what is Caesar's", but even "what is God's"

> [communism is] a system of extreme social monism, . . . no distinction between State, society and the Church

> The only thing to pit against integral Communism, is integral Christianity

> If there is not a Christian revival in the world . . . atheistic Communism will conquer over the whole earth . . . In the name of God and of Christ . . . or in the name of Antichrist . . .

Nicolas Berdyaev sees in the Communist Party something in the nature of a religious atheist sect. In *The Russian Revolution* he devotes his second chapter to "The Religion of Communism". On its spiritual nature, he writes: "Its spirituality is a dark, Godless spirituality".

The Jesuit Vincent Miceli describes communism as anti-Church Church, as anti-catholic catholicity; as anti-Messiah Messianism. Its humanism is a deliberate transposition of Christian revelation into secularised, pseudo-scientific doctrines. Private property is seen as the "original sin" of mankind. Communism sees the Church as the ultimate enemy that must be destroyed. Miceli thinks that communism is so intensely anti-Christian, that the best weapon to defeat it is the sword of Christ's truth and love as incarnated in His Church. He writes:

> The Catholic Church sees in Communism that latest, most organized, most pernicious incarnation of antihuman, anti-God diabolism.

Richard Wurmbrand also sees Marxism akin to a religion, with its own Bible, namely *Capital* by Karl Marx, with Satan as its god.

To the Bolsheviks, Marxism is not just another political and economic theory but "the supreme gospel, an infallible truth that prophesies universal social justice".

The desire of communists to imitate the religious rites and practices of the Church is illustrated by Louis Richard Patmont in *The Mystery of Iniquity*:

> Late rules of the communist party prescribe specific ceremonies for "star baptisms" and "red funeral services. That this is a mere absurd imitation of the requirements of religion is obvious. These red baptismal rituals are now called "Star Festivals". Each new-born child of a communist must be brought to the executive committee of the local party unit. This is to take place on a red holiday if possible. The secretary names the child and places upon it the emblem of bolshevism, together with that of the children Pioneers, after which the child is wrapped in a red flag. The "service" usually ends by ridiculing religion. There are godfathers and god mothers (kumy) who are called "star fathers" and "star mothers", and these have to sign an obligation pledging themselves to the raising of the children in the fear and admonition of communism.

Louis Richard Patmont sees in the vetting of applicants for Party membership an imitation of the discipline within the Church:

> Acquisition of membership in the red party is more difficult than was ever the act of becoming affiliated with even the most conservative of religious bodies. Those still eligible must be of proletarian or peasant stock and even then their family records are diligently searched. The least trace of bourgeois heredity, the most insignificant action arousing suspicion of opposition to the existing order, faith in God and the divine origin of the Bible, and a multitude of other reasons are sufficient cause for debarring

> the applicant from membership. The whole is an aping of the most puritanical church discipline.

For those on the left, Lenin is regarded as a demigod. Political cults deify leader figures, dead or alive: Marx, Hitler, Pol Pot, Stalin, Mao, Trotzky.

The concept of Armageddon, an end-world scenario, has its paralled among political cults:

> Left political cults with a Marxist -Leninist ideology have transformed this religious belief [Armageddon] into a theory of the collapse of the capitalist system. A world crisis of capitalism is predicted, creating conditions for revolutionary upheavals. The revolutionary party led by the political guru who heads the political cult, will triumph and a new communist utopia will emerge. The vision of a communal society based on equality and plenty for all, is similar to religious concepts of a post-apocalyptic society. Both respond to the ancient dream of humanity for a world free of hunger and strife.[20]

Trotzky's involvement in the early USSR anti-religious campaigns (1917-1924)

A myth has grown up around Trotzky that somehow he was more humane than Stalin, and that had he not been sidelined by Stalin's political manoevres, the USSR might have turned out to be a shining beacon for the world. The truth is that Trotzky shared the same anti-Christian viewpoint as all the other communist leaders. He was, as Pospielovsky puts it, "one of the most violent enemies of the Church in the 1920s".

As Commissar of War, Trotzky is heavily implicated in the persecution of saints during the Russian Civil War. Soviet authors would eventually admit central responsibility for the thousands of clergy and faithful laymen who were murdered or persecuted during the Civil War period. Yaroslavsky justified these killings by the fraudulent charge that Patriarch Tikhon had given his blessing to the anti-Bolshevik forces.

In his autobiography, Trotzky states that it was Charles Darwin's theory

20 *On The Edge*, Tourish and Wohlforth

on evolution that extinguished any last remaining religious belief he held. In his mind, belief in the theory of natural selection ruled out any belief in God.

In *An Appeal by the Church of Ekaterinodar to the Christian Churches of the Whole Word, April 5, 1919* [found in Appendix 2, D. Pospielovsky, *The Russian Church*], the priest G. Loshako writes about the crimes against the Church committed by the Bolsheviks whom he refers to as "the power usurpers, Russian tyrants with Ulyanov-Lenin and Bronstein-Trotsky at their head". The priest writes:

> Many temples have either been desecrated and ruined by the Red Army or sealed by the Soviet authorities - or converted by them into fun houses, jails or even refuse dumps. Fourteen bishops and hundreds of priests - especially preachers of the word of God - were shot by firing squads, hanged, drowned or burned alive. Executions of clergy are often accompanied by the cruelest of tortures . . .They [the dark masses, all the unfortunate and the unhappy] become easy prey to any promises of paradise on earth, which are generously disseminated by the Bolsheviks. It is in this that the danger threatening Christianity and all world civilization is hidden . . . This is why we appeal to you in the name of the Lord Jesus Christ . . . to rise in defense of Christianity against its modern persecutors, and thus to become the merciful Samaritan, for the Russian people and the timely defender of the rest of humanity against Bolshevism - the cruelest enemy of our Savour Jesus Christ and of all Christianity

Metropolitan Sergei (of Vilnius) begins his letter written for the Germans in 1944 during their occupation of the Baltic territories, thus:

> The self-appointed goal of the Bolsheviks was to obliterate Christianity. Renunciation of this task would have been tantamount to self-destruction for Bolshevism. Such a renunciation was inconceivable. This is clear to everyone who realized the satanic essence of Bolshevism. [21]

In his memoirs, Trotzky writes that in 1922 Lenin had entrusted the leadership of Soviet church policies to him.

---

21 Appendix 1, D. Pospielovsky, *A History of Soviet Athiesm in Theory and Practicr, and the Believer,* Vol II,

Trotzky saw Orthodoxy as merely a series of rituals and shared Yaroslavsky's view that religion was nothing more than a base supersition exploited by the ruling class. He believed religion would be eradicated over time by education and new diversions such as cinema. He stressed the advance of applied science in workers' lives as the panacea against religion. In his letter to Comrade Burnham of January 7, 1940, Trotzky writes:

> Religion diverts attention away from the struggle for a better life to false hopes for reward in the Hereafter. Religion is the opium of the people. Whoever fails to struggle against religion is unworthy of bearing the name of revolutionist . . . We revolutionists never "stop" bothering ourselves about religious questions, inasmuch as our task consists in emancipating from the influence of religion, not only ourselves, but also the masses.

In common with Satanists, Trotzky saw religion as some kind of bondage from which one must be emancipated. His views on religion are so closely aligned with those of Lenin (and Marx) that they are virtually identical. No wonder Lenin and Trotzky worked so harmoniously together when it came to trying to destroy the Church.

Trotzky influenced many of today's secular movements that war against Christianity. Evidently Trotzky has been largely successful in trying to "emancipate" the masses from the "opium" of religion.

Biographies on Trotzky often overlook the significant part he played in the anti-religious campaigns of the Bolsheviks. In his autobiography, *My Life*, Trotzky only mentions in passing that among his part-time jobs ("privately and unofficially") was "antireligious propaganda, in which Lenin was very interested". Richard Pipes' book *Russia Under the Bolshevik Regime 1919-1924* reveals the significant part that Trotzky in fact played in antireligious work (in the chapter entitled "The Assault on Religion").

Lenin placed Trotzky in charge of the antireligious campaign (he was chairman of the Society of the Godless). Being Jewish, Trotzky had to keep a low profile. Now that the civil war was over, the Bolsheviks no longer feared antagonizing the church with its one hundred million followers. On January 30 1922 Trotzky advised Lenin to use the famine as an excuse to demand the Church turn over its consecrated vessels for sale to aid victims of the famine, knowing that the Church could not comply with such a demand. The direction of this campaign to remove from churches all object made of gold, silver, and precious stones, was entrusted to a commission of the Politburo, chaired by Trotzky. As anticipated, Patriarch Tikhon refused to hand over those vessels which had been consecrated, and he was placed under house arrest.

The Church was to be crushed under the spurious pretext that it refused to aid the hungry. Efforts by the faithful to protect sacred vessels from seizure were depicted as an antistate conspiracy.

Lenin wrote a letter demanding that many should be sentenced to death even before being charged with any crime. Acting on this letter, the Politburo (composed of Trotzky, Stalin, and Kamenev, along wiith Molotov as secretary) resolved to carry out Lenin's isntructions. A precedent was set here for the quota system of executions that Stalin would introduce in the late 1930s. On March 22 the Commission for the Realization of Valuables, meeting under Trotzky's chairmanship, voted to proceed with the recquisitions and to dispose of the acquired valuables on foreign markets. As was noted at the time, the Communists already had in their possession the Russian crown jewels, the value of which greatly exceeded that of the church vessels. These could have been sold for famine relief instead.

Trials began almost immediately and predetermined sentences were passed down. Lenin demanded to be informed on a daily basis of the number of priests who had been shot. These were the original show trials.

An English journalist learned that the anti-Church campaign cost the lives of 28 bishops and 1,215 priests. Subsequent evidence indicates that over 8,000 persons were executed or killed in the course of 1922 in the conflict over church valuables.

Traditional religious holidays became ordinary working days. They were replaced by secular celebrations of which there were six: New Year, the anniversaries of Bloody Sunday (January 22) and of the February Revolution (March 12), the day of the Paris Commune (March 10), International Labour Day (May 1) and the anniverary of the October coup (November 7).

1922 saw the appearance of the daily *Bezbozhnik* ("the Godless"), edited by Yaroslavsky, which marked the years from the year of the Russian Revolution instead of the birth of Christ.

Trotzky proposed to split the Church over the issue of consecrated vessels by enrolling the pro-Soviet priests to assist in their confiscation. The Living Church was brought into being in March 1922, first to incriminate the church hierarchy and then to dislodge it from authority.

Trotzky had wanted Patriarch Tikhon killed after the excommunication in 1918, but Lenin would not allow it for fear that he might become another

Germogen (a patriotic Russian patriarch martyred by the Polish occupying forces in 1612). Trotzky continued to attack Tikhon until he was released from prison in 1923 and made his declaration of loyalty to the Soviest state.

Trotzky advocated an 'atheistic substitute' for religion such as the use of theatre for antireligious propaganda. He also promoted Communist rituals of 'red' baptisms, 'red' weddings, 'red' Easters, and so on.

In 1922 Trotzky wanted to unleash a mad persecution of the Church. It was Trotzky who in 1922 presided over the strategy of pitting the Renovationists against the Patriarch and the regular Orthodox Church. The Renovationist *putsch* was synchronized with the GPU's arrest of the Patriarch. Under house arrest, Patriarch Tikhon was pressured to give up his authority. The patriarchate was replaced with the "Higher Church Administration" which claimed that the Soviet government was trying to create "the ideal Kingdom of God". In December 1922 Tikhon anathematized the Higher Church Administration and those connected with it as doing the "work of the Antichrist" and exhorted Christians to brave death in defense of the true Church.

Trotzky's involvement in anti-religious matters was short-lived. In 1922 the Central Committee unified the numerous commissions and subcommittees concerned with religion into one standing commission, dubbed the Antireligious Commission. Trotzky was not appointed to this new commission. Instead, Yemelyan Yaroslavsky was appointed chairman in early 1923, effectively ending Trotzky's direct influence on antireligious matters.

Trotzky considered himself an Internationalist, rather than a Jew. When a Jewish delegation appealed to him to help his fellow Jews, he raged, "I am not a Jew but an internationalist."

Trotzky appeared not to even notice when thousands of Jews were being killed in pogroms. Trotzky was in Ukraine in August 1919, the scene of the worst massacres, yet Soviet archives prove that despite the fact that he had received hundreds of reports about his own soldiers' violence and looting of Jewish settlements, he made no reference to them in either public pronouncements or confidential dispatches to Moscow. During that year of slaughters Trotzky never once intervened by either word or deed on behalf of the Jews.

Trotzky believed that the proletariat had no fatherland and so believed that Zionism was reactionary. In his autobiography Dr Chaim Weitzmann writes:

> My resentment of Lenin and Plekhanov and the arrogant Trotsky was provoked by the contempt with which they treated any Jew who was moved by the fate of his people and animated by a love of its history and its tradition.

Trotzky refused to give his even his own father any special treatment despite the fact that the Revolution had ruined him. Trotzky buried his father in his garden, despite his father's request to be buried in the grounds of the synagogue.

Trotzky was indifferent to the actions of the *Evseksia*, the "Jewish section" of the Communit Party whose task it was to eliminate the Jewish private trader and to bring the cultural Yiddish life in line with the communist party line. The *Evseksia* wrought havoc on observant Jews and tried to eradicate the Jewish religion, yet Trotzky never once interceded on the behalf of any Jew.

Communist persecution of Christians

> **Then the dragon was angry with the woman, and went off to make war on the rest of her offspring, on those who keep the commandments of God and bear testimony to Jesus.** (Rev. 12:17)

Communism's persecution of Christianity betrays the motivation it shares with the devil, symbolised by the red Dragon in Revelation. Enmity towards Christianity is a sure sign of satanic work. In fact failure to care for Christians in distress, let alone their persecution, is seen as warranting eternal damnation according to Jesus' teaching (Matt. 25:41-46). Those who fail to care for the Christians in need, or visit them in prison, share the same fate as the devil and his angels. Conversely, those who receive Christians are blessed and will receive the reward of the righteous (Matt. 10:40-42).

Persecution of Christians in USSR

In the Preface to his book *The Mystery of Iniquity: An Expose of the Spirit and Nature of International Communism* (1933) about Christian persecution in the USSR, L.R. Patmont states that his book exposes "the unmistakable earmarks of the "Mystery of Iniquity"" and that his book may serve to warn the Christian World against the great apostasy. Many of his chapters begin with quotes from the book of Revelation. He states that Leninism opposes all idealism of Christianity:

> It is the mystery of iniquity in that it opposes all claims of religion and has determined to exterminate it at all costs. International communism fits into the apocalyptic picture. It restricts the commercial activity of those who do not bear its mark.

Since 1721, the Russian Orthodox Church had been the established church of the Russian Empire. In 1914 there were 55,173 Russian Orthodox churches and 29,593 chapels, 112,629 priests and deacons, 550 monasteries and 475 convents with a total of 95,259 monks and nuns in Russia. By 1987 the number of churches in the Soviet Union had fallen to 6,893 and the number of functioning monasteries to just 18.

One of the first major decrees of the new regime was the Decree of the Soviet of People's Commissars, 12 January 1918, the Separation of the Church from the State and the Schools from the Church. This decree deprived the church of its status of legal person, the right to own property or to teach religion in both state and private schools or to any group of minors. The Declaration of the People's Commissar of Education, 17 February 1918, dismissed all teachers of religious education.

There were numerous incidents of torture and murder of the clergy, such as the crucifixion of a priest in the Kherson province. A letter written by a priest (Priest G. Loshako) of a Church in Ekaterinodar in 1919 reads:

> Fourteen bishops and hundreds of priests – especially preachers of the word of God – were shot by firing squads, hanged, drowned or burned alive. Executions of clergy are often accompanied by the cruelest of tortures. For instance, they gouged out the eyes of Andronik, Bishop of Perm, cut out his cheeks, and then he was led around the town, bleeding while they mocked him.[22]

In this same letter, the priest writes about local decrees by the Bolsheviks that reduced the status of women to sex objects. In *The Naked Communist*, W. Cleon Skousen records how some Bolsheviks attempted to

---

22 *The Black Book*, A. A. Valentinov

replace marriage with complete promiscuity. A decree issued in the Soviet of Saralof, which came into effect on March 1 1919, abolished the right to possess women between the ages of 17 and 32. Women were no longer to be considered private property but instead the property of the nation. Men who wished to make use of a "nationalized" woman need only obtain a certificate attesting that they belonged to the working class and contribute a small percentage of their income to a fund to support these "natonalized" women. As Skousen observes, the underlying rationale for such decrees was the understanding that Judeo-Christian ethics were based on a "class" morality created to protect private property and the property class. Laws forbidding adultery only merely served to ensure that women remained the private property of their husbands.

The "Laws on Religious Associations" of 8 April 1929 curtailed the church's public presence and mostly limited religious activities to services conducted within religious buildings only. The 1929 Legislation on Religious Associations is found in the Appendix to Dimitry Pospielovsky's book *The Russian Church under the Soviet Regime 1917-1982* together with the corresponding 1975 Amendments to this legislation. Much persecution was based upon the alleged failure of the churches to comply with these rules.

Those under 18 years of age could not be part of a religion. Churches were banned from being used for activities beyond worship, thereby outlawing parish libraries, organized religious education, prayer meetings for women and young people, religious study groups and sewing circles. The Legislation passed in 1929 also forbade clergy or monastics from wearing religious garb in public. Islamic courts in Central Asia that interpreted Shariah were fully eliminated after this legislation in 1929.

The Bolsheviks barbarically murdered massive numbers of priests. Some were picked off by snipers as they carried crosses during religious processions.

In the 1920s, the Varsonofyev Monastery stood near Lubyanka. It served as one of the first Soviet Concentration camps where the VCHK (the Cheka) murdered all of Tsarist Russia's social classes. It was subsequently demolished.

The *lishensy* ("disenfranchised") could not send their children to school. Red ration cards, granting to the holder the privilege of buying bread and other necessities, were not issued to them. They were doomed to starvation unless they possessed illegal means of support:

> Priests and ministers have been placed in the eighth class affected by the food ordinance, and therefore can anticipate only starvation. Offerings of bread, eggs, and fowl are not allowed them, yet many people share all they have with their religious leaders. The Godless Society of Moscow, in its desperate effort to break up the passive resistance of the Russian people, has organised anti-religious schools to turn out "educated helpers" who can professionally and officially conduct anti-religious propaganda among the masses. Many anti-God "seminaries" have been Established, and there are already more than six thousand students in these institutions.

All Sunday schools were closed. The reading aloud of the Holy Scriptures to children has at times been punished by death. No new churches could be acquired since the state claimed ownership of them and diverting them to purposes other than worship. The second Five-Year Plan includes the closing of all churches. In 1929 alone, 1,370 church properties were either confiscated or destroyed.

Only atheists could obtain work and procure food cards. The meagre food supplies sold by small private venders of food can only be purchased at exorbitant prices. L.R. Patmont records the acts of war on Christianity:

> All literature is carefully censored in order to root out any reference to religious and spiritual terms. The name of God can be used only in connection with anti-religious propaganda and blasphemous designs. The Bible is a forbidden book; it may be neither printed or sold in the USSR.
>
> Christians, who are not given the right to work in government factories, usually are not permitted to buy food in the regular stores; they must secure it elsewhere. One can buy secretly bootlegged food articles, but at an excessive price.
>
> A leading Christian worker was sent to the lumber camp for eight years. He was sentenced for three years because he carried a Bible, and for five additional years because he dared to preach the Gospel.
>
> It is difficult to describe the degree of misery in which true Christian believers find themselves in Russia at present. Truly, the Beast is making war with the saints, but the Church will not be crushed.[23]

On June 13, 1921, the Soviet Government decreed the prohibition of

---

23 *The Mystery of Iniquity*, L.R. Patmont

teaching of religion to any person under 18. In a decree of April 8, 1929, the Constitution was changed so that religion could no longer be propagated.

Patmont's testimony is supported by F.A. Mackenzie in *The Russian Crucifixion*:

> . . . in these [government] schools religion is systematically ridiculed and attacked. There is no "conscience clause" allowing children, whose parents do not agree, to abstain from attending.
>
> The child of religious parents finds it difficult, and in many cases impossible, to obtain facilities for higher education. He or she is largely excluded from the Universities and higher technical schools.
>
> Religious people are denied the right of class teaching for their children in religion under the age of eighteen. This prohibition goes so far that many priests fear to visit the families of their flock, lest they should be charges with propaganda among the children.
>
> The Russian Government is guilty of persecution of the rank and file of religious worshippers. No member of the Communist party, the governing party of the State, is allowed to take part in any religious ceremony and the Communist who is married in Church is expelled from the party. People who are prominent in religious work run a very great danger of expulsion from their employment, even in its humblest forms. The Government is guilty of persecution in depriving priests, rabbis, ministers of religion and, in many cases, lay preachers, of citizenship. It has robbed churches of their legitimate rights. Organized religion is as far as possible fettered and bound. A church or religious group is not allowed to have any central fund for collecting voluntary donations or for making a levy. Its members must not form mutual aid societies or co-operative institutions or workshops. It must not give any material aid to its members and it is equally forbidden to exercise charity to those outside its ranks. Bible study circles and even sewing circles are forbidden. Prayer meetings for young women, adolescents and children are a crime. A religious society must not open lending libraries or reading rooms, maintain sanatoria, or give medical advice or

> aid. It cannot invite preachers from the outside to come to it, for preachers are restricted to the local congregations.

> The Government runs a department of state, whose sole purpose is to control with a view to destroy religion, and this department has caused and is causing the arrest and imprisonment of many thousands of religious leaders and active workers, sending them into exile under conditions inhuman in their severity. Many have died and many and still more have had their lives completely ruined.

> It has deliberately evicted from their homes and driven to beggary multitudes whose only offence was their belief in God. It has shot many because of their faith. It is today holding multitudes of religious men and women in captivity or exile, for no other reason than that they refuse to renounce God.

The League of the Militant Godless' weekly *Bezbozhnik (The Godless)* magazine produced blasphemies of God, Christ and the Saints.

A five-day working week was enacted which made it impossible to have regular Sunday church attendance. The celebration of holidays such as Christmas or Easter was also hampered by mandatory work on those days.

Most of the bishops arrested between 1928–1932 were arrested for reasons surrounding opposition to Metropolitan Sergey and his notorious declaration of loyalty; opposition to Sergey was used as a pretext to close many churches and sending clergy to exile.

The pursuit of pastoral duties by clergymen became punishable by law; laws forbade Christian charity efforts, the participation of children in religious activities; priests were not to be invited to private homes; donations to churches were to discontinue; clergy were deprived of any social security rights; a lack of housing forced many priests to leave their vocation and take civilian jobs; priests' wives could nominally divorce their husbands in order to get jobs to support their families; priests could be seen in rags in front of churches begging for alms and reportedly it could occur where priests had to mount the pulpit wearing their underclothes.

Paul Voronaeff witnessed the suffering of members of the Church in the USSR and writes about the "diabolical" character of the principles behind the Soviet system. His parents were persecuted because "they steadfastly refused to renounce God". In his book *Under the Hammer and Sickle*, Voronaeff explains how the inability to get bread cards meant that priests could literally starve:

> Preachers and others who profess belief in God and the Bible are denied bread cards. This means starvation.

Voronaeff saw "saints of God" chewing dirt, and eating such things as grass and weed roots. He goes on to say that priests are not allowed to live in houses. Life under the False Prophet will be similar, where man will not be able to buy or sell without the mark of the Beast.

"Parental care, home discipline, motherly love and fatherly responsibility are things of the past in Russia", writes Voronaeff. Such things are considered "counter-revolutionary". He tells how young people were taught to hate God according to Lenin's dictum:

> Religion must be abolished. The best country is a godless country.

Stalin called for an "atheist five year plan" from 1932–1937, to completely eliminate all religious expression in the USSR; it was declared that the concept of God would disappear from the Soviet Union.

During Stalin's Great Terror from 1937 to 1938, mass executions took place at Butovo Polygon, a firing range near Moscow, of Orthodox priests who were later canonized as the New Martyrs. Between 1917 and 1935, 130,000 Orthodox priests were arrested and most of these were put to death.

The 22nd CPSU congress in 1961 re-affirmed the need to eliminate religion in order to build true communism and the need for true anti-religious education; it was declared that freedom of conscience did not apply to children and that parents should not cripple children spiritually; parents of children who openly demonstrated their faith at school or of children who did not join the Pioneers or wear their kerchiefs for religious reasons were prosecuted by the courts which resulted in the deprival of parental rights and their children being sent to boarding schools; parents who tried to raise their children in their faith could be also prosecuted and have their children removed from them.

Around 50,000 clergy had been executed by the end of the Nikita Khrushchev era since 1917.

Educated people who became religious believers were diagnosed as suffering from a psychotic disorder. Popular monks and nuns, and other believers, were sent to psychiatric facilities. They were given immediate release if they renounced their faith in God; those convicted of religious crimes in the Soviet Union were classed as "especially dangerous state criminals", which disqualified them from amnesty or leniency. Religious crimes such as circulating a petition or organizing religious classes for children could be punished with strict terms in concentration camps; openly religious people could not join the Communist Party of the Soviet Union, which meant that they could not hold any political office.

Arrests and persecution of clergy continued under Gorbachev.

For a thorough insight into the persecution of the Church in the USSR, the author recommends Volumes I and II of Dimitry V. Pospielovsky's *A History of Soviet Atheism In Theory and Practice, and the Believer.*

Persecution in Albania

Albania declared itself to be the first atheistic state in the world. It had closed down all the churches and shot the clergy. Christmas was abolished: the feasts were to be New Year's Day and Labour Day. In 1976 the government abolished Christian names, and ordered everyone who had one to change it. The penal code of 1977 imposed prison sentences of three to ten years for "religious propaganda and the production, distribution, or storage of religious literature". All placed of worship, including mosques, were seized. Stephen Kurti, was sentenced to death for baptizing one child.

Persecution in North Korea

North Korea is officially the worst place in the world to be a Christian, according to the annual Watch List compiled by Open Doors. The previous year Open Doors held the fundamental requirement for 'leader reverence' responsible for fuelling a rise in persecution in both North Korea and Turkmenistan. The latter was listed the nineteenth most dangerous place to be a Christian.

Christian Solidarity Worldwide have called for the implementation of a UN Commission of Inquiry recommendation that the North Korean regime be referred to the International Criminal Court. So far China and

Russia on the Security Council have blocked this. The UN Commission found evidence of:

> extermination, murder, enslavement, torture, imprisonment, rape, forced abortions and other sexual violence, persecution on political, religious, racial and gender grounds, the forcible transfer of populations, the enforced disappearance of persons and the inhumane act of knowing causing prolonged starvation.

Kim Il-Sung made no secret of his extermination of Christians. These are his own words:

> Through court trials, we have executed all Protestant and Catholic Church cadre members and sentenced all other vicious religious elements to heavy punishment. The repentants have been given work, but non-repentants have been sent to concentration camps . . .

> We cannot carry such religiously active people along our march toward a Communist society. Therefore, we tried and executed all religious leaders higher than deacon in the Protestant and Catholic churches. Among other religious active people, those deemed malignant were all put to trial. Among ordinary religious believers, those who recanted were given jobs while those who did not were held at concentration camps . . . There in 1958 we completely and thoroughly apprehended that group of people and had them executed. That is how we found out that the only way to fix the bad habit of religious believers is for them to be killed . . .

> The guidelines for dealing with religious believers are clearly set out in our Party's public security policy. You need only to follow it. Silly old religionists need to die in order for their bad habits to be corrected. In which case, we must mercilessly eradicate them . . .[24]

A leading academic authority on religion in North Korea reckons that around 400,000 religiously active people and their families have been

---

24 *Dear Leader*, Jang Jin-Sung

either executed or banished to political prison camps. There are now no longer any religiously active people in North Korea.

Visitors to North Korea are sometimes invited to attend Sunday services at a Christian church, which leads them to believe there is a degree of freedom of religion in the country, while their guides dutifully explain that it is promised in the North Korean constitution. But the reality is that there are three government-controlled churches (two Protestant, one Catholic) in the country for foreigners. The government bans any other form of organized worship as counter-revolutionary and grounds for charges of treason against the state. Buddhism, widespread, in Asia, is accepted in the North, within limits, as a philosophy, but not as a religion. The existence of deep underground Christian movements in the North is a telling sign of the absence whatsoever of any freedom to worship anything but Kim Il-sung.

Religious institutions are controlled by the United Front Department (UFD). All of North Korea's religious institutions are staffed by UFD operatives, including the Chosun Buddhist Association, the Chosun Christian Association, the Chosun Catholic Association and the Chosun Catholic Central Committee:

> In practice North Korean is a one-religion state, where only the worship of the Leader is allowed. Although a cadre might be a monk or a priest as far as the outside world was concerned, in the UFD they were all faithful followers of the Kim cult.

Jang Jin-Sung warns that although you might see crosses on churches, and hear authentic Christian hymns sung, they are composed exclusively of UFD operatives and members of their families.

The North Korean regime practises inter-generational punishment. The offender's parents and children are incarcerated too, often for their entire lives, in the camps which house 200,000 people. Kim Il Sung said:

> The seed of factionalists or enemies of class, whoever they are, must be eliminated through three generations.

The most notorious camp is the one at Haengyong. Chemical experiments have been carried out on families, and there have been reports of entire families being gassed.

Persecution in China

China forced its Catholic church to cut ties with the Vatican in 1951.

Christians were brutally persecuted in the early years. Some were burnt to death. In his testimony to the US House of Representatives in 1967, Richard Wurmbrand said:

> In Red China thousands of Christians are killed now. The Red Guards, who frog-marched diplomats on the street, where everybody sees, have cut, in Chinese jails, the ears and tongues and the legs of Christian prisoners, if they did not deny Christ.

More recently, in the past two years the provincial government of Zhejiang, on the east coast, has removed over 1,500 crosses from churches. At least 400 churches in the eastern province of Zhejiang have been demolished since 2014.

In China there is a widespread "underground" church loyal to Rome. Across China, about six million Catholics have refused to join churches sanctioned by the Communist Party and chosen instead to worship in "house churches". In 2007 Pope Benedict XVI told Chinese Catholics not to shun the state-controlled church.

Another six million people are members of the Catholic Patriotic Association, a Communist-Party-controlled body which does not display images of Pope Francis.

In November 2010, for the first time since 2006, the government-backed church ordained a bishop, Guo Jincai, without agreement from the Vatican. The Vatican called the event a grave violation of church law and of religious freedom.

Catholics are concerned about the possibility of a deal where bishops will be formally agreed by both sides, but where the Vatican will be able to veto candidates proposed by Beijing. They fear any agreement along these lines would compromise the independence of the Church. Mr Fu, director of ChinaAid says: "the move will legitimise the Communist Party's persecution, past, present and perhaps future." (*Daily Telegraph, 4/6/2016*)

Cosmas Shi Enxiang, a bishop who had spent half of his life in prison or labour camps died in 2015 after 14 years in jail. Bishop James Su Zhimin is still in secret detention, having been held since October 1997.

Church authorities recently demolished the Golden Lampstand Church in Linfen northern Shanxi province, a church built with £2 million raised by local worshippers. A Catholic church in the neighbouring province of Shaanxi was demolished the previous month, twenty years after it opened (*Daily Telegraph, 12/1/2018*).

European Parliament resolution 2013/2981 expressed disapproval of China's harvesting of organs of non-consenting prisoners of conscience, including from large numbers of Falun Gong practitioners imprisoned for their religious beliefs, as well as from members of other religious and ethnic minority groups. 90% of the 10,000 organs used in transplants performed per year in China come from prisoners executed in China. Prisoners of conscience are killed on demand and their organs sold for a large profit. (UN reports state that 66% of torture cases in China were of Falun Gong practitioners.) The Independent Tribunal into Forced Organ Harvesting from Prisoners of Conscience in China concluded that China is "a criminal state" which, "beyond reasonable" has committed crimes against humanity, acts of torture, and that enemies of the state continue to be killed for their organs *["UK 'ignored' China's harvesting of organs", Daily Tel., 18.6.19].*

There are around two million Chinese citizens encarcerated in more than 300 "Re-education Through Labor" camps. Many of these have been punished for being an "unregistered" Christian or a member of Falun Gong. Falun Gong comprises around 20% of the Laogai system.

One million Muslims, mostly from the Uighur community, are being held in secret prison camps for indoctrination aimed at breaking their roots and origins. Former detainees have described being tortured, forced to drop their Islamic beliefs and having their children placed in orphanages.

The Epoch Times has put together a superb book entitled *Nine Commentaries On The Communist Party* which is essential reading for an understanding of the evil nature of communism. It traces the history of the Chinese Communist Party and explains how the Party relies upon brutality and cruelty to cower the Chinese population into submission. It details the wicked deeds perpetrated by the Communist Party of China and is comprehensive in its scope.

19

PAPAL DENUNCIATION OF COMMUNISM AS SATANIC

Papal denunciation of Communism as satanic

The encyclical *Qui pluribus* (subtitled "On Faith And Religion") contains the first mention of Communism.

It was promulgated by Pope Pius IX on November 9 1846, at a time when there was widespread civil unrest across Italy as nationalists sought the unification of Italy.

The encyclical is particularly directed against socialists and communists:

> [who through] their outlandish errors and their many harmful methods, plots and contrivances . . . which they use to set in motion their plans to quench peoples' zeal for piety, justice and virtue, to corrupt morals, to cast all divine and human laws into confusion, and to weaken and even possibly overthrow the Catholic religion and civil society.

Pius described Communism as:

> . . . a doctrine most opposed to the very natural law. For if this doctrine

> were accepted, the complete destruction of everyone's laws, government, property, and even of human society itself would follow.

Leo XIII called communism:

> the fatal plague which insinuates itself into the very marrow of human society only to bring about its ruin.

In *Divini Redemptoris* (1937), Pius XI states how the Papacy has called public attention to the perils of Communism more frequently than any other public authority on earth. He describes communism as the "the satanic scourge" and talks of "the communist plague". He notes how dialectical materialism permits no room for the concept of God. He observes how the communists' belief in the principle of absolute equality results in the rejection of all "divinely-constituted authority", including the authority of parents.

He attributes the rapid diffusion of communism to "a propaganda so truly diabolical that the world has perhaps never witnessed its like before" and to a conspiracy of silence favoured by "various occult forces which for a long time have been working for the overthrow of the Christian Social Order."

His encyclical condemns communism for striving to destroy the Christian religion whenever it comes into power and for its persecution of not only the clergy but even laymen who were simply suspected of defending their religion. He also addresses the persecution of religion in Spain. In the Spanish Civil War, the Communists killed 4000 Catholic priests. He writes:

> as far as possible every church and every monastery was destroyed. Every vestige of the Christian religion was eradicated . . . The fury of Communism has not confined itself to the indiscriminate slaughter of Bishops, of thousands of priests and religious of both sexes; it searches out above all those who have been devoting their lives to the welfare of the working classes and the poor. But the majority of its victims have been laymen of all conditions and classes . . . masses of them are slain almost daily for no other offense than the fact that they are good Christians or at least opposed to atheistic Communism.

The Pope observes how men can do barbarous things when the very idea of God has been removed from their hearts. Perhaps the Pope had in mind acts such as the destruction of church property. During the Spanish Civil War, communists raided convents and raped the women. Then their bodies were piled up and torched in public places.

Pope Pius XI hints that one can see in communism signs of the coming of the 'man of lawlessness' through his quote of a small section of 2 Thessalonians 4:

> For the first time in history we are witnessing a struggle, cold-blooded in purpose between man and 'all that is called God.

Pope Pius XI warns how communism seeks to mask its true nature through trickery. He explains how communists establish organisations and periodicals under names that do not suggest Communism, for the purpose of transmitting their ideas into otherwise inaccessible areas, endeavouring thereby to attract even men of faith with "insidious deceits". He notes how they use hypocrisy to deceive people into thinking that communism will assume a milder form in countries where faith is more entrenched.

Pope Pius XI compares the curse of communism with that of the possession of an evil spirit and concludes that "the evil which today torments humanity can be conquered only by a world-wide crusade of prayer and penance." He says that:

> . . . the evil we must combat is at its origin primarily an evil of the spiritual order. From this polluted source the monstrous emanations of the communist system flow with satanic logic.

He reveals the danger of banishing religion from the school and from public life. Such acts, he argues, foster the materialism which is the fertile soil of Communism.

He hopes that the zeal with which "the sons of darkness" work day and night may be surpassed by the "the sons of light".

Anatoliy Golitsyn confirms this assessment of communism:

> The statement by the late Pope [Pius XI] concerning **the incompatibility and irreconcilability of Communism and religion** is as correct as ever. The Vatican should reaffirm this dictum and should use its influence and

its 'divisions' to defend Western values from the new, deadly but 'hidden' Communist assault.

Pius XI added a particular intention for the conversion of Russia in an allocution of June 30, 1930. After reminding all to pray for Russia, and of the religious persecution in Russia, he proposed the proclamation of the prayers that Pope Leo XIII had directed all to pray at the end of the Mass for the particular intention of the conversion of Russia. This prayer has been written by Pope Leo XIII in 1886 after he had apparently seen a fearful vision during celebration of Mass. This is the prayer:

> Saint Michael the Archangel, defend us in battle, be our protector against the wickedness and snares of the devil; may God rebuke him, we humbly pray; and do thou, O Prince of the heavenly host, by the power of God, thrust into hell Satan and all the evil spirits who wander through the world for the ruin of souls. Amen.

The further testimony of Miceli, Vornoaeff, and Wurmbrand against communism

Vincent Miceli calls the Communists "godless shadows of the Antichrist":

> Since 1917 the Communists, godless shadows of the Antichrist, have kept the earth in continuous bloody turmoil for the purpose of creating a mankind without God, a mankind hating God, a humanity united, under the shadows of the Antichrist, in its fight against Christ and His Mystical Body.

Paul Voronaeff writes in *Christians under the Hammer and Sickle*:

> What the cause of Christ has been passing through these eighteen years in Soviet Russia surpasses the persecution of the Church during the first and second centuries of its existence.
>
> Russian saints believe they are already passing through the Great Tribulation prophesied in the Bible.

> The words of John the revelatory recorded in Revelation 7:14 seem particularly appropriate for Russian Christians: "These are they which came out of great tribulation, and have washed their robes, and made them white in the blood of the Lamb."

Richard Wurmbrand (1909-2001) was an evangelical minister who endured a total of fourteen years of Communist imprisonment and torture in his homeland of Romania. Many of Wurmbrand's books intimate that the USSR is the Beast. In *Soviet Saints* he asks if Communism will mellow, and concludes that it will not because:

> . . . in the book of Revelation, chapter thirteen, we read that the beast will have power to overcome the saints. In the twelfth chapter of Daniel we read that the 'power of the holy people will be scattered.'

In a chapter about latter day prophecies in *The Answer to the Atheist's Handbook* he writes:

> In a general sense, communism itself is a fulfilment of prophecy. It is like the great Antichrist predicted in the Scriptures: "It was granted to him to make war with the saints and to overcome them. And authority was given him over every tribe, tongue, and nation" (Revelation 13:7)

In his book *If that were Christ, would you give him your blanket?* Wurmbrand states that Christians should have been on the side of the Underground Church in Communist countries, not on the side of the official church leaders, who were stooges of the "anti-man" Communists. Wurmbrand asks:

> If anybody makes friendship with them [the Communists] and obeys them now, what will be his attitude when the Anti-Christ will appear?

In *Tortured for Christ* he records how Russian soldiers professed that the Hammer and Sickle was a symbol of the Antichrist:

> These Russian Christians had such beautiful souls! They said, "We know that the star with the hammer and sickle, which we wear on our caps, is

> the star of the anti-Christ." They said this with great sorrow. They helped us greatly to spread the gospel among other Russian soldiers.

The convictions of these Russian soldiers were well founded, for the Hammer and Sickle is the mark of the Beast.

Patriarch Tikhon anathematized the Bolsheviks in 1918

In a pastoral letter, dated 1 February 1918, Patriarch Tikhon anathematized the Bolsheviks, and beseeched the faithful of the Orthodox Church to have nothing to do with them. A part of this letter reads:

> The open and concealed enemies of the truth of Christ have started to persecute that truth and are aiming a mortal blow at the cause of Christ. In place of Christian love they are sowing seeds of malice, envy, and fratricidal war
>
> Christ's precept to love is forgotten and trampled under foot. Every day we learn that innocent people, not excluding those lying sick in bed, are being frightully and brutally murdered for the sole offense that they have honestly discharged their duty to the country and have devoted all their energies to serve the welfare of the people. These crimes are committed . . . in broad daylight with unprecedented effrontery and outrageous brutality . . . in almost every city of our native land . . .
>
> Think what you are doing, you madmen! Stop your bloody reprisals. Your acts are not merely cruel, they are the works of Satan for which you will burn in Hell fire in the life hereafter and be cursed by future generations in this life.
>
> By the authority given me by God I forbid you to partake of the Christian Mysteries. I anathematize you if you still bear a Christian name and belong by birth to the Orthodox Church . . .

20

RUSSIA AND THE FATIMA PROPHECIES

In Fatima, Portugal, Francisco and Jacinta Marto, nine and seven years old, and their 10 year old cousin, Lucia dos Santos, claimed that on the thirteenth day of each month, beginning on May 13, 1917, Mary the Mother of Jesus had appeared to them at a spot called Cova de Iria. She told them she had an important message for all nations and that on October 13 she would perform a miracle to substantiate her message.

On that day, thousands witnessed the sun as a fast-spinning plate of brightly shining silver, a giant pinwheel turning on its own axis, casting off beams of coloured lights of the rainbow that tinted the faces and all surrounding objects. No one damaged their eyes. This lasted a couple of minutes. Then the sun seemed to tremble and pulsate within itself. Next it hurtled in zigzag fashion towards the earth and the thousands of observers. Following these wonders, everyone noticed that they were bone dry despite the downpours that had preceded this spectacle.

The first two messages put the Church and all men on notice that the world as a whole society was following a path of sin along which a multitude of men and women were being led to the eternal punishment of Hell.

The second message was a prediction about the outbreak of World War II. Mary spoke about Russia and asked the Pope and all bishops of the Church to consecrate it in an especially solemn manner to her. If this was not done, Russia would spread error and evil throughout the world; many human beings would suffer and die as a consequence.

Lucia was adamant the third message should remain a secret until whoever was Pope in 1960 should open her letter containing the third message.

It did remain largely secret until the Pontificate of John Paul II. Lucia's single-page written formulation of the "Third Secret" covers three main topics. A physical chastisement of the nations, involving catastrophes, man-made or natural. A spiritual chastisement, especially for Roman Catholics - the disappearance of religious belief, a period of widespread unfaith in many countries. A central function of Russia in the two preceding series of events. Russia is the ratchet.

The chastisements were to punish the nations for their ungodliness. The process could be averted if the Pope in 1960 (John XXIII) should publish the text of the "Third Secret" and if he, with all bishops acting collegially, should consecrate Russia to Mary. Russia was the regulator of the timetable. If these requests were denied, Russia would spread its errors throughout all nations. Millions would die. Widespread corruption would infect the Church's clergy and laity.

Part Six

MARXIST PERVERSION OF CHRISTIANITY

21

MARXIST PERVERSION OF CHRISTIANITY

Patriarch Sergius and "adaptation"

The Moscow Patriarchate (MP) works hand in hands with the Soviet regime. It was created by Stalin and is a mouthpiece for communism.

Archbishop Ilarion saw in Patriarch Sergius' "adaptation" (or "Sergianism") an indication of "Satan's counsel" upon the Church. In a letter addressed probably to Pavel Florensky he writes:

> Hasn't Sergeii's declaration, which has caused varied and fully justified negative reactions, thrown the church organization, headed by him, into the loathsome, adulterous embraces of the atheistic, blasphemous and Christomachistic power, and hasn't it introduced a frightening profanity into the bosom of our Church? Please note that this declaration appeared not from the hands of the schismatic Renovationists . . . [it came] from a canonical, lawful, apparently Orthodox hierarch.
>
> This symphony between the theomachistic power and the regular Orthodox hierarchy has already produced some "blessings" . . .
>
> Everybody with ears to hear and eyes to see knows that contrary to the decree on the separation of Church and state, the Orthodox Church has entered into a close alliance with the state. And what a state? . . . a state whose government aims at the destruction of any religion on the face of the

> earth, and the Orthodox Church before all the others, because it justly sees in her a basic world foundation of religious faith and a first-class fortress in the struggle against materialism, atheism, theomachism and Satanism (practiced, according to hearsay, by some members of the contemporary powers that be) . . .

[Quotations from Revelation (17:3,5,6; 12:6; 18:2) are cited and followed by a comparison of the current church situation with the apocalyptic scenario of the whore sitting on a red beast. The situation is particularly tragic, he says, because:]

> It is not a lawless, schismatic woman who saddles a beast with profane names, but a faithful woman having an image of genuine piety . . .
>
> . . . the forces of Hades are attacking [the Church] with unprecedented power . . . How should we behave in these terrible moments of the new threat, advancing by Satan's counsel upon our mother, the holy Orthodox Church?[25]

Metropolitan Sergey's accommodation with the atheistic regime of the USSR was called an "adaptation" by Y. Yaroslavsky. This "Adaptation" was seen by atheists as one of the paths to the dying out of religion. Sergey's betrayal of the Church was revealed in his Appeal to the faithful of August 19, 1927. Bishops who condemned the Appeal were soon banished to concentration camps where they died.

Boris Talantov, who died in prison in the Soviet Union in 1971 for his writings, wrote about this betrayal of Patriarch Sergey (Sergius):

> Any accusation against the actions of the civil authorities or any doubt of the correctness of the official ideology was considered a deviation from purer religious activity and counter-revolution. The Church Administration headed by Metropolitan Sergius not only did not defend the believers and clergy who went to concentration camps for accusing the arbitrariness and violence of the civil authorities but even spoke out itself, with slave-like servility, for the condemnation of such people as counter-revolutionaries.
>
> In the Theophany Cathedral in Moscow, with a cross in his hands, he came out with a declaration that there was no persecution at all against believers and their organization in the Soviet Union, and there never had been any. Individual clergymen and believers, according to his assurance,

25 *The Russian Church Under the Soviet Regime*, D. Pospielovsky

were tried, not for faith, but for counter-revolutionary manifestations against the Soviet Regime. *Such a declaration was not only a monstrous lie, but also a base betrayal of the Church and believers. By this declaration Metropolitcan Sergius covered up the monstrous crimes of J. Stalin and became an obedient tool in his hands.*

Adaptation to the atheist regime was clearly and precisely set forth in the book, *The Truth about Religion in Russia,* published under the editorship of Patriarch Sergius in the last years of his life, with the participation of Metropolitan (now Patriarch) Alexis and Metropolitan Nicholas.

In this book Patriarch Sergius and Metropolitan Alexis and Nicholas categorically affirm that there has never been in the USSR any persecution of Christians, that information in the Western press about these persecutions are malicious inventions of the enemies of the Soviet regime, that bishops and priests during the years 1930-41 were sentenced by Soviet courts exclusively for their counter-revolutionary activity, and that the Church Administration itself at that time was in agreement with their being sentenced . . . The most courageous fighters for truth and Christian faith are declared in this book to be schismatics ,"politicians," and practically heretics. This book should be anathematized; it will be an eternal shameful memorial of Patriarch Sergius. And now with full justification we can call Adaptation to the atheistic regime by the name of Patriarch Sergius – Sergianism.

Adaptation is incompatible with true Christianity, because at its foundation there is a lie, servility before the mighty of this world, and a false separation of spiritual needs into the purely religious and the socio-political.

Talantov continues his letter by proving that beginning in 1960, the Moscow Patriarchate and the majority of bishops participated in all actions of the Council for the Affairs of the Russian Orthodox Church, actions directed towards the closing of churches and the limitation of the propagation of the faith.

The unspoken idea of Sergianism is that when the Church is threatened by the danger of annihilation, it is acceptable to submit to any compromise with falsehood, even to the point of joining with the persecutors.

The Moscow Patriarchate and ties with KGB/FSB

Former KGB officer Oleg Kalugin observed:

> Russia's current [political] system is based on the KGB at the head of the government, on the Russian Orthodox Church as a former part of KGB agencies among the clergy, and on Russian business . . .the Russian Orthodox Church always played a significant role in [the KGB's recruitment efforts], and is likely to play an even greater role today.

The Russian Orthodox Church (ROC), legally known as the Moscow Patriarchate, claims exclusive jurisdiction over the Orthodox Christians who reside in the former member republics of the Soviet Union, excluding Georgia and Armenia. This claim is disputed in Estonia, Moldova and Ukraine, where parallel Orthodox jurisdictions exist. The ROC is one of the autocephalous Eastern Orthodox churches and ranks fifth in the Orthodox order of precedence, immediately below the four ancient Patriarchates of the Greek Orthodox Church, those of Constantinople, Alexandria, Antioch and Jerusalem.

According to Konstantin Preobrazhensky, the KGB's infiltration into church affairs is natural, given that the KGB considers itself to be a kind of "church" too, in the business of controlling human souls. It checked people's Communist faith to see if it was sincere or hypocritical which is why officers called themselves "physicians of the soul" as if they were priests (which some of them were and still are).

Founded in 1943 by Stalin, the Moscow Patriarchate was intentionally created to be a liaison with the KGB. It is Stalin's church. Stalin created the Moscow Patriarchate with the hands of the KGB. The Moscow Patriarchate is terrified that this secret will be revealed, for fear that people will question its sanctity. According to Konstantin Preobrazhensky, the KGB became the Moscow Patriarchate's "mother." The genetic ties between the KGB in the Moscow Patriarchate are just as strong as between ROCOR and the White anti-communist movement.

The "Temporary Holy Synod of the Patriarchate" of the Metropolitan Sergey (Stagorodsky) was formed on Lubyanka (KGB headquarters). In 1927 the NKVD offered the New Martyr Archbishop Seraphim of Uglich, who had been ruling the Russian Church for one hundred days, to head this Synod, but he refused, instead putting forth his own Synod, for which he was placed under arrest. Metropolitan Sergey, meanwhile, accepted this gift from the *chekists*. He usurped the church power illegally, with the help of the NKVD, thereby defying the still-living partriarchal *locum tenens* Metropolitan Peter, who was imprisoned.

During the Soviet Period, all the Moscow Patriarchate bishops were KGB agents without exception, and the overwhelming majority of priests collaborated with the KGB. It was first necessary to become a KGB agent, and only then could you become a bishop. Towards the end of Perestroika, Metropolitan Chrysostom publicly declared he was an agent of the KGB, but he was the only one to openly acknowledge his collaboration with the KGB.

Bishops were part of the nomenclature of the Central Committee of the CPSU) and each candidate had to be approved by its Ideological Department. Recommendation for any future bishop would have been prepared by the Fifth Department, which had general responsibility for the Church. (Vladimir Putin worked in the Fifth Department.) After consecration, the bishop had to be registered in the Council of Religious Affairs. Registration was granted after an interview with its chairman, Kuroyedov, a KGB lieutenant general. All those bishops registered by this man still hold their posts and are instrumental in attaching the Church Abroad to the MP.

Those highest up in the church's hierarchy were also members of the Communist Party. The first Communist within the church was Patriarch Pimen. He was a senior officer of the Red Army who joined the CPSU at the front.

Patriarch Aleksey II would not have remained in his exalted position had he expelled *chekists* from his ranks. There definitely were no purges of the KGB within the MP, the most supportive of the Soviet past.

In August 2006 a Moscow Patriarchate church, dedicated to the Holy Trinity, was opened in Pyongyang, despite the fact that religion is forbidden in North Korea, and belief in God is considered a political crime. North Korea is creating an Orthodox Church patterned after Stalin's church, with the hands of the security forces.

The ROC is the pillar of Putin's neoimperialist policy. The Moscow Patriarchate has challenged the principle of canonical territory in Estonia and Ukraine. The UOC-KP is not acknowledged by Moscow, a stance which reflects the struggle between pro-Russian forces and supporters of Ukraine's independence.

Metropolitan Hilarion has compared the trinity of Russia, Belarus and Ukraine with the Holy Trinity.

The capitulation of the Russian Orthodox Church Outside of Russia (ROCOR) to the Moscow Patriarchate

In May 17, 2007, most of the parishes of the Russian Orthodox Church Outside of Russia (ROCOR) in the USA and the rest of the world came under control of the Moscow Patriarchate. The church merger brought the ROCOR's 400 parishes and 400,000 members worldwide within the fold of the Moscow Patriarchate. These ROCOR parishes may well have become outposts of Russian state interests forever, for the ROC and Russian government collaborate closely. In effect the Moscow Patriarchate simply annexed the ROCOR with the signing of the Act of Canonical Communion.

Metropolitan Hilarion became the first in ROCOR's history to be First-Heirarch of ROCOR, approved by the Holy Synod of the Moscow Patriarchate.

Metropolitan Agafangel, a ROCOR bishop suspended for his rejection of the merger, has claimed Russian agents are out to assassinate him for establishing a breakaway church. He announces that if he were ever "accidentally" killed, Patriarch Kirill would likely be responsible.

Putin has launched a new globalized Church as his state's main ideological arm and a vital foreign policy instrument. It all fits in with Putin's "vision for global domination" according to Konstantin Preobrazhensky. New Orthodox churches are being built across the globe in this bid to create a "superchurch" to restore Russia's lost superpower status. They are being built in Africa, Argentina, China, Tokyo, Havana, Thailand, Madrid and Abu Dhabi. Russia has secured permission to build a church next to the Eiffel Tower. This is strange given that the majority of Russians already have a church, the St Alexander Nevsky Cathedral, and are affiliated with the Ecumenical Patriarchate (Constantinople) and do not recognize the MP's jurisdiction.

Reverend Victor Dobroff of New York City declared that in a very short time the FSB would have new spy nests all over the world, absolutely untouchable, working under the cover of the church.

Many thousands of Russian Americans are now nourished in a spirit of loyalty to authoritarian Russia. KGB-backed priests with Russian passports are replacing local clergy. Their churches become insidious fronts for Russian state interests.

The KGB had its agents within ROCOR. "Friend" was the KGB pseudonym for Archpriest Vasili Fonchenkov, a ROCOR priest. In the 1970s he helped the KGB imprison anti-Communist priests. In 1979 he became member of The Christian Committee for the Defense of Believers' Rights, an organisation he only joined so that he could send its members to prison.

A blogger writing about the ROCOR/MP merger states:

> The cold hard truth is that Ecumenism and Sergianism are not gone: they are rather there in full force . . . we are still dealing with the same of Soviet, ecumenist . . . the same of KGB agents with mitres: a communist hierarchy in a capitalist – but still sometimes totalitarian-modern Russia.

Oleg Kalugin wrote that the KGB had "nearly total control" of the Russian Orthodox Church both home and abroad.

In his book *KGB/FSB's New Trojan Horse: Americans of Russian Descent*, Konstantin Preobrazhensky reveals the use of Russian priests to implement Russia's intelligence agenda. The communists plan to use parishioners of the Russian Orthodox Church Outside of Russian (ROCOR) to be a fifth column within the United States. The takeover of a parish starts with the appointment of a nationalistic, "soviet" rector, then the gradual replacement of the old American parish council and warden with mysterious recent Soviet emigres. The next wave of immigrants will come from the Russian Federation with the explicit assignment from the Intelligence Service to infiltrate these parish councils. There are plenty of pseudo-immigrants already in America to corrupt the émigré community from within.

According to Preobrazhensky:

> The whole strategy of the émigré-unifiers is built on that sigh of relief when the Soviet Union collapsed, and on the illusion that "gigantic changes" have taken place in Russia. But the changes are regressing! Putin's Russian today is similar to Brezhnev's; only the prison terms have lengthened.

Those who want to unify ROCOR with the Moscow Patriarchate are forced to deny the sovietization of Russia.

The Patriarch Aleksey II gave communism his ideological support.

When he met a group of youth in Kaluga he quoted from the "Moral Code of the Builder of Communism", which supposedly parallels Christian norms.

Replacing the religious element with the Marxist element

Lenin advised against playing into the hands of the clergy with open declarations of war against religion. Lenin wrote that the practice of dialectics would prevent the communists making such a tactical mistake:

> To preach atheism . . . would only be playing into the hands of the priest and the priests, who desire nothing more better than that the division of the workers according to their participation in the strike movement should be replaced by their division according to their belief in God. An anarchist who preached war against God at all costs would in effect be helping the priests and the bourgeoisie . . . A Marxist must be a materialist, i.e. an enemy of religion, but a dialectical materialist . . .

Lenin advised against giving offence to any religious convictions of workers:

> We must not only admit workers who preserve their belief in God into the Social-Democratic Party, but must deliberately set out to recruit them; we are absolutely opposed to giving the slightest offence to their religious convictions, but we recruit them in order to educate them in the spirit of our programme, and not in order to permit an active struggle against it.

The notorious document written by Li Wei Han of the Central Committee of the Chinese Communist Party in 1959 and addressed to the leaders of the Cuban Communist Party, echoes Lenin's aim of educating believers in the spirit of the communist programme:

> The line of action to follow against the Church is to instruct, to educate, to persuade, to convince, and, gradually, to awaken and fully develop the political conscience of Catholics by getting them to take part in study circles and political activities. By means of these activities, we must under-

take the dialectical struggle within religion. Gradually, we will replace the religious element with the Marxist element, gradually change the false consciousness into a true consciousness, so that the Catholics will eventually destroy of their own accord and on their own account, the divine images which they themselves had created.

Putin's influence over evangelicals in the United States

Franklin Graham, son of the US evangelist Billy Graham, is an outspoken defender of Christian convictions (pro-family values, anti-abortion, traditional sexual identity). In 2014 he applauded Russia's anti-gay law banning the distribution of information on non-traditional sexual orientation.

During his stay in Moscow, Graham met with Patriarch Kirill of the ROC (a former KGB agent) and with Russian politicians sanctioned by the United States for their support of Russia's military attack on Ukraine. Graham told RIA Novosti press that his private meeting with State Duma Speaker Vyacheslav Volodin, a close Putin ally, was wholeheartedly supported by US Vice-President Mike Pence.

American evangelicals have been coopted into helping the ROC expand its sphere of influence.

The international Christian relief organization "Samaritan's Purse" and the Billy Graham Evangelistic Association are working in partnership with the Russian Orthodox Church to finance food and humanitarian supplies sent to Russia, allegedly to aid refugees fleeing Ukraine and living in Rostov.

By presenting itself as the protector of the "Christian family unit" and encouraging a combination of homophobia and Islamophobia, the Kremlin seeks to position itself as the post-communist guardian of Christian values and cultural conservatism. The endorsement of Putin by evangelicals will weaken the resolve to keep anti-Russian sanctions in place. Moscow is deploying religion to exercise spiritual and political control across the US and Europe.

Anti- EU billboards depicting same-sex couples holding hands appeared throughout Ukraine's capital city of Kiev in 2013 with the line: "Association with the EU means same-sex marriage." The group behind the posters was an organization funded by Putin ally, Viktor Medvedchuk.

Franklin Graham is being pressured to hold the next "World Summit in Defense of Persecuted Christians" in Moscow.

Liberation Theology

According to Ion Pacepa, Liberation Theology was an invention of the KGB.

The term "Liberation Theology" was coined in 1971 by the Peruvian priest Gustavo Gutierrez, who wrote *A Theology of Liberation* in which he writes:

> The church must place itself squarely within the process of revolution.

The beginnings of Liberation Theology can be discerned at the 1968 Conference of Catholic Bishops held in Medellin, near Bogota, Colombia, where the delegates determined "to exercise a preferential option for the poor and the oppressed". The delegates highlighted the plight of the poor.

Fidel Castro had stressed the importance of "Marxists and honest Christians working together" on Radio Havana in 1977. A "strategic alliance" must be formed between Marxists and Christians, he said, "so that the Latin American revolution can move forward". Progressive priests played a leading role in guerrilla movements in Central America.

Base communities were formed which were composed of lay Catholics and riddled with liberation theology and openly Marxist hatred of the United States. By 1987, there were 600,000 Base Communities in Latin America. The Peace and Justice Commissions were allies of Liberation Theology. The Maryknoll Congregation started Orbis Books, an important publisher of books on Liberation Theology.

Liberal Theologians proclaim an earthly paradise. Communism is this paradise, capitalism its foe. The triumph of communism is equated with His coming. Ernesto Cardenal writes in his book *The Zero Hour*:

> A world of perfect Communism is the kingdom of God on earth. They are the same thing for me.

In Liberation Theology Christ has been converted into the John the Baptist of Marx.

Raimundo Garcia Franco writes in *Christian-Marxist Unity: A Miraculous Explosive Prescription*:

> Christian faith and Marxism-Leninism do share almost complete overlapping of common objectives in the building of socialism. We cannot look backward, since the path ahead is that of creative transformation to communism and to the Kingdom of God on this earth.

Lewis Sperry Chafer's *Satan: His Motives and Methods* seem almost prophetic with regards to Liberation Theology. His book was published during the First World War. Liberation Theology fits his description of a counterfeit system of doctrine.

Chafer draws attention to how false prophets will deny the purchase or redeeming work of Christ, rather than His Person or character. Liberation Theology also uses every phrase and dogma of the Church and twists them to give them a different Marxist meaning. According to Chafer, "these Satanic agents" seem to be teachers in the true faith, yet they bring in heresies "crystallizing in a denial of the redemption that is in Christ."

Describing the tenets of liberation theology in his *Instruction on Certain Aspects of the "Theology of Liberation" for the Congregation for the Doctrine of Faith,* Cardinal Ratzinger notes:

> An exclusively political interpretation is thus given to the death of Christ. In this way, its value for salvation and the whole economy of redemption is denied. This new interpretation thus touches the whole of the Christian mystery. In a general way, this brings about what can be an inversion of symbols . . .

How truly it can be said of the teachers of Liberation Theology that, to use Chafer's words, they "fortify their lies and hypocrisies by contending for almost every phases of revealed truth, grounding their authority so positively in the scriptures of Truth" and yet fail to teach the true importance of the blood redemption of the Cross.

Chafer explains how the scriptures abound in statements that the transforming work of redemption is accomplished on the ground of the sacrificial blood of the cross, such as:

> **Even as the Son of man came not to be served but to serve, and to give his life as a ransom for many** (Matt. 20:28).

Chafer explains that since the blood redemption of the cross is the central truth, a counterfeit system of doctrine would have to force some secondary truth into the place of prominence. Liberation Theology does this by emphasising the importance of the class war and general human welfare.

The promoters of this false system, writes Chafer, might use biblical language and scriptural texts, but still be of a satanic nature:

> . . . if the curtain could be lifted, their "angel of light" would be found to be Satan, working through them to resist the purpose of God, and themselves the ministers of Satan, speaking lies in hypocrisy, having their conscience seared as with a hot iron, daring in their exalted position to devitalize the Gospel of its power unto salvation.

Chafer predicted a false system where "humanitarian appeals for the betterment of the world" would be made in place of the preaching of the gospel of the cross and noted the appeal of the leader who "announces that he is not concerned with the doctrines of the Bible, because the helping of humanity is his one passion and care."

He saw in various contemporary counterfeit systems evidence that the "last days" are drawing near and that the "man of lawlessness", in other words the Beast, may be the power behind these systems.

Throughout the 1990s, Ratzinger, as prefect of the Congregation for the Doctrine of Faith, continued to condemn aspects of Liberation Theology, and prohibited dissident priests from teaching such doctrines in the Catholic Church's name. Leonardo Boff was suspended and others were censured. Tissa Balasuriya, in Sri Lanka, was excommunicated. Sebastian Kappen, an Indian theologian, was also censured for his book *Jesus and Freedom*. Under Cardinal Ratzinger's influence, theological formation schools were forbidden from using the Catholic Church's organization and grounds to teach Liberation Theology in the sense of theology using unacceptable Marxist ideas, not in the broader sense.

In March 1983, Cardinal Ratzinger accused Gustavo Gutierrez of interpreting the Bible in a political sense and of supporting temporal messianism, the predominance of orthopraxis over orthodoxy in his thought proving a Marxist influence. Cardinal Ratzinger objected to the spiritual concept of the Church as "People of God" being transformed into a "Marxist myth" where:

> . . . 'people' is the antithesis of the hierarchy, the antithesis of all institutions, which are seen as oppressive powers. Ultimately anyone who participates in the class struggle is a member of the 'people'; the 'Church of the people' becomes the antagonist of the hierarchical Church.

Cardinal Ratzinger wrote *Instruction On Certain Aspects of the "Theology of Liberation"*, for the Congregation for the Doctrine of the Faith in which he calls the system of Liberal Theology "a perversion of the Christian message as God intrusted it to His Church". Cardinal Ratzinger mentions the millions deprived of liberty by totalitarian and atheistic regimes which came to power by revolutionary means, precisely in the name of the liberation of the people. Cardinal Ratzinger warns that atheism and the denial of the human person, his liberty and rights are at the core of the Marxist theory. He argues that it is the transcendent character of the distinction between good and evil, the principle of morality, which is implicitly denied in the perspective of the class struggle. In Liberation Theology there is a tendency to identify the kingdom of God and its growth with the human liberation movement. Faith, hope, and charity are given new content: "fidelity to history", "confidence in the future" and "option for the poor", thus emptying them of their theological reality. In this new theology, the desire to love everyone here and now, despite his class, and to go out to meet him with the non-violent means of dialogue and persuasion, is denounced as counterproductive and opposed to love. The participation of Christians who belong to opposing classes at the same Eucharist Table is questioned. There is denunciation of members of the hierarchy and the magisterium as objective representatives of the ruling class which has to be opposed. Jesus becomes a kind of symbol who sums up in Himself the requirement of the struggle of the oppressed.

An exclusively political interpretation is given to the death of Christ. Its value for salvation and the whole economy of redemption is denied. This new interpretation touches the whole of the Christian mystery. The Eucharist becomes a celebration of the people in their struggle.

Cardinal Ratzinger advises that one should keep in mind the true meaning of ethics in which the distinction between good and evil is not relativized, the real meaning of sin, the necessity for conversion, and the universality of the law of fraternal love. He warns against the politicization of existence, the sacralisation of politics, betraying the religion of the people in favour of the projects of the revolution.

In *The Ratzinger Report*, Cardinal Ratzinger is recorded saying that of the many atheisms of our time, the most deadly is Marxism:

> It seems to me that, in its philosophy and its moral goals, marxism represents a more insidious temptation than many practical atheisms which are consequently less ambitious intellectually. For the Marxist ideology actually uses the Jewish-Christian tradition and turns it into a godless prophetic movement; man's religious energies are used as a tool for political ends and directed to a merely earthly hope, which is equivalent to standing on its head the Christian yearning for eternal life. This perversion of the biblical tradition deludes many believers who are convinced in good faith that the cause of Christ is the same as that proclaimed by the heralds of political revolution.

Many of Malachi Martin's books deal with the threat of Liberation Theology and Marxism in general, such as *The Keys of This Blood, The Jesuits,* and his novel *The Final Conclave.* Martin sees the hidden influence of Modernism as the precursor to the Jesuits' willing adoption of Liberation Theology. So-called "Liberators" such as George Tyrrell and Pierre Teilhard de Chardin undermined orthodox Roman Catholic principles. Jacques Maritain was also influential. In his book *Integral Humanism*, Maritain describes the French Revolution as "the eruption of Christian thought in the political order". Montini, the future Paul VI, even wrote the preface to this book. Liberation Theology was the answer to Maritain's summons to the Church to identify itself with the masses. It was Paul VI who did away with the rule that imposed on all theologians an oath to combat Modernism.

As Martin puts it, Liberation Theology masquerades as Catholicism and the Vatican has not successfully convinced people that it is an impostor siphoning off the Church's manpower, credibility and good name.

In *The Jesuits*, Martin reveals how the Jesuits came to adopt the tenets of Liberation Theology and to use them for the cause of the Marxist revolution in Latin America. He tells how the Pope was humiliated by the Marxist leadership of Nicaragua in 1983.

Martin describes how the diehard opposition of Pius XII to Marxism was undone by John XXIII's agreement with Khrushchev. Khrushchev permitted two Soviet clerics to attend Vatican II as observers provided that there was no condemnation of Marxism. This was a huge papal concession which Martin sees as the opening of the first breach in the Catholic bulwark against Communism. A proposal to condemn Marxism was quashed by Vatican authorities.

Martin blames Pope Pius VI for his farewell address. In this speech the Pope opts for man; to serve man. Martin sees it as a script for the secularization of Roman Catholicism, the de-Catholization of Roman Catholic hierarchy. The speech was subsequently used as an umbrella for secularisation and by the heirs of Gramsci. Martin sees Liberation Theology as the perfect vehicle for Gramsci's theories.

Pope Francis is willing to accommodate Liberation Theology. He lifted the suspension of Mighel d'Escoto in August 2014, a Maryknoll priest from Nicaragua, who had been sanctioned with an *a divinis* suspension from his public functions in 1984 by Pope John Paul II, for political activity in the leftist Sandinista government in Nicaragua. D'Escoto had joined the Sandinista regime in Nicaragua as foreign minister. He was an advocate of liberation theology and served as President of the General Assembly of the United Nations from September 2008 until September 2009. He received the Lenin Peace Prize from the old Soviet Union.

Pope Francis recently said "I can only say the communists have stolen our flag" because the Marxists claim to be concerned about the poor. Before he became Pope Francis, Bergoglio said:

> The option for the poor comes from the first centuries of Christianity. It's the Gospel itself. If you were to read one of the sermons of the first fathers of the Church, from the second or third centuries, about how you should treat the poor, you'd say it was Maoist or Trotskyist. The Church has always had the honour of this preferential option for the poor . . . At the Second Vatican Council the Church was redefined as the People of God and this idea really took off at the Second Conference of the Latin-American bishops in Medellin.

On Sept 11, 2013 Pope Francis hosted Father Gutierrez in his residence, leading some to comment that this was a sign of warming relations between the hierarchy and liberation theologians. The same month *L'Osservatore Romano* published an article praising Gutierrez by the prefect of the Congregation for the Doctrine of the Faith, Archbishop Gerhard Muller.

On January 18, 2014, Pope Francis met with Fr Arturo Paoli, an Italian priest whom the Pope knew from Paoli's long service in Argentina. Paoli is recognized as an exponent of liberation theology and the meeting was seen as a sign of "reconciliation" between the Vatican and liberationists.

Konstantin Preobrazensky has stated his belief that the current Pope has been influenced by the KGB:

> This Pope has been infected by Russia many years ago. He was head of Church in Argentina, where a huge KGB-ruled Russian Church exists too. They made the future Pope their constant guest at beautiful receptions. KGB has always had great achievements in the Vatican. On the contrary, the Vatican has never managed to win Russia in almost 1000 years.[26]

In July 2015 Evo Morales, President of Bolivia, presented Pope Francis with a wooden Hammer and Sickle to which was affixed the effigy of the crucified Christ when he arrived in La Paz. It had belonged to Father Luis Espinal who was tortured and murdered in 1980.

Infiltration of the Church by communists

> **For such men are false apostles, deceitful workmen, disguising themselves as apostles of Christ. And no wonder, for even Satan disguises himself as an angel of light. So it is not strange if his servants also disguise themselves as servants of righteousness.** (2 Cor. 11:14)

The Li Wei Han document shows the great importance that communist regimes attach to having their own men placed within the Church:

> The separation of Church and Vatican having been consummated, we can proceed to consecrating the leaders of the Church chosen by us.
>
> Then the masses will be protected against all pressure and all obligation to put in an appearance in the church, to practice religion, or to organize associations of whatever religious group. We know full well that when the

26 Back From The Dead, *Cliff Kincaid*

practice of religion becomes no more than an individual responsibility, it is slowly forgotten.

In his testimony at the 1966 hearing before the Committee of the Judiciary United States Senate (recorded in *Communist Exploitation of Religion*) Richard Wurmbrand testified:

> We live in the times of the abomination of the desolation of the holy places . . . the leadership of churches is dominated by the central committee of an avowed atheistic power.

Wurmbrand also testified:

> . . . you could hear in our theological seminary in Bucharest the theology that God has given three revelations – once through Moses, second through Jesus, the third through Karl Marx, and so on. Religion is corrupted from within.

In *From Torture to Triumph*, Richard Wurmbrand warns that *glasnost* and *perestroika* is another Communist manoeuvre, a deceit:

> 'Let the Christians believe,' the argument runs. 'Communists will infiltrate the Christian ranks, will befriend them, disguising themselves as having similar ideals on many points. They will attract Christians to common social actions and will influence them to keep only an external form of religion, while becoming basically as godless as ourselves.'

Wurmbrand believes that these are the wolves in sheep's clothing alluded to by Jesus.

Bella Dodd, a leader of the CPUSA in the 1930s and 1940s before she returned to the Catholic Church, personally helped hundreds of young communists enter the seminaries. She testified before the US House of Un-American Activities Committee:

> In the 1930s, we put 1100 men into the priesthood in order to destroy the Church from within. The idea was for these men to be ordained, and then climb the ladder of influence and authority as Monsignors and Bishops.

Dodd maintained that such men had reached the highest places within the church dozens of years before Vatican II, weakening the Church's effectiveness against communism. She told a friend that when she was an active party member, she had dealt with no fewer than four cardinals within the Vatican who were working for the CPUSA. In a public affidavit she testified thus:

> In the late 1920s and 1930s, directives were sent from Moscow to all CP organizations. In order to destroy the Roman Catholic Church from within, party members were to be planted in seminaries, and within diocesan organizations. I, myself, put some 1200 men in Catholic seminaries.

Anatoliy Golitsyn warned that the apparent tolerance of religion within the Soviet Union was accompanied by a secret drive to increase the Party and KGB penetration of the Catholic Church. Part of the program was to destroy religion from within. He warned that many communists entered seminaries in the late 50s in order to promote communist strategy from within the church. Once the goal of world communism has been achieved, there would be a mass exodus of agents from the Church which will destroy the church. He wrote in *The Perestroika Deception*:

> Never in its history since Nero has Christianity faced such a threat to possible destruction.

This infiltration reminds one of the verses in Paul's letter to the Corinthians:

> **For such men are false apostles, deceitful workmen, disguising themselves as apostles of Christ. And no wonder, for even Satan disguises himself as an angel of light. So it is not strange if his servants also disguise themselves as servants of righteousness.** (2 Cor. 11:13-15)

Antonio Grasmsci (1891-1937) theorized that the Church had to be silenced as a rival hegemon in society because it created an "apolitical fatalism" among the oppressed which undermined the influence of Marxism. Gramsci proposed replacing Christianity's ethics with Marxist ones. He promoted the idea of corrupting the West's Christian cultural basis, to reduce all men's expectations of any salvation from on high. In order to

"Marxize the inner man", a subversive program of "counter-hegemony" must be created.

In his book *Living in the Shadow of the Cross* Paul Kivel sets out a program that aims at destroying Christianity from within. The title of this book appears to be based on the pledge that "name-parents" made at communist-style baptisms when they signed the registry book:

> We accept the duty of protecting him, so that the mouldy fingers of outworn relics of the past do not touch him and the shadow of the cross does not darken his bright life's dawn. We will guide his first steps carefully, so that he does not stray from the single path that leads to Communism.[27]

Some Gramscian-Marxists are probably putting Kivel's program into practice right now while pretending to be sincere members of the congregation of the Church.

Kivel uses terms which have an inverted meaning:

- "Christian allies" – those who will join him in confronting Christian hegemony;
- "Collaborators" - those who follow the rules "set up to benefit white Christians";
- "Agents" – those complicit in perpetuating the system that benefits them being themselves "white Christians". These people might be "servants of the ruling class (the 1%)" who are not "working for changes in the system". However these people could become allies provided they "subvert the hierarchical system".

Kivel is interested in the "allies" and gives them guidelines on how they can subvert this the "system of oppression". These "allies" should be on their guard against any policies that might support misogyny, homophobia or racism. Jesus's "Arab" roots have been whitewashed. These allies should "search for the truth and validity of other religious and cultural traditions". In so doing they will realize that "people who are not Christian do not need saving". His final observation is that their congregations "may even want to work to preserve or defend indigenous sacred sites, mosques or temples or make reparations for historical wrongs". These "allies" are recommended

---

27 *Land Of Crosses*, Michael Bourdeaux

to support the separation of church and state, and to challenge missionary programs.

Kivel declares that a Christian hegemony dominates all aspects of American society and examines ways in which "Christian hegemony" can be undermined. He blames Christianity for black and white thinking and for differentiating between good and evil. He leaves no stone unturned in his search for Christian influences and lifts the lid on even the most insignificant "parachurch" Christian organisations and their ties to American organizations, ties which he wants to sever. He winkles out an impressive and lengthy list of situations and events where Christian words, holidays, symbols, and references occur in everyday American life.

This "Christian hegemony" is accused in his book of acts of aggression against the LGBTTQ community and all non-Christians: Jews, Muslims, women, heretics, homosexuals, pagans, and the disabled. It is blamed for creating a system of patriarchy that oppresses women; for creating a sense of guilt over our bodies and sexuality; for destroying the environment; for harbouring known child molesters; for fighting abortion; for islamophobia; for its war on drugs; for domestic violence; for the destruction of Native Americans; and for fomenting war, and so on. He blames Christianity for confusing love with hierarchy and obedience, and disagrees with smacking. Kivel states that Christians do not care about the environment because they believe that the Earth is going to be destroyed in the apocalypse anyway.

Kivel totally misrepresents the story of the gospel, arguing that the early Christians were committed to Jesus's life - "not his death". The primary goal of Christians, he argues, was to create "paradise on Earth, in the here and now, not waiting for salvation in some future time or place." In this early church of his imagination, homosexuality was accepted, war was condemned, and women had leadership positions.

Belief in a devil, he argues, leads to paranoia.

Humanitarian work merely prolongs the dependency of those in need, he argues. His book promotes the socialist economic model, and blames capitalism for environmental destruction, poor health and short lifespans. He attributes Christian benevolence to an unjust economic system:

> The privileges allowing the middle-class and wealthy to be generous were materially dependent on the unpaid or low-paid labour of the very population they were helping.

Kivel argues that current social justice movements would be so much more powerful if:

> they understood Christian dominance as a core part of the roots of the accumulation of wealth and power by a few.

In order to destroy "Christian hegemony", he would remove all tax breaks afforded to religious movements; abolish proselytizing in prisons; and prevent the distribution of Bibles at schools. In fact he would oppose any and every act, however small, that might promote Christian ethics and teaching.

Kivel approves of Christian dissidents and liberation theologians who continue to build "alternative Christianities" and feminist, black, Native American, Latin/a, gay and social justice-focused churches.

The Ecumenical Movement

In 1971 the KGB sent Kirill, who is the current Patriarch, to Geneva as emissary of the Russian Orthodox Church to the World Council of Churches, the largest international religious organisation after the Vatican, which represents some 550 million Christians in 120 countries. Kirill's job was to involve the World Council of Churches in spreading the new liberation theology throughout Latin America. In 1975 the KGB was able to infiltrate him into the Central Committee of the World Council of Churches, a position he held until he was "elected" patriarch of Russia in 2009. The ROC's Department for External Church Relations granted Kirill the privilege of duty-free importation of cigarettes as a reward for loyalty to KGB. In 2006 his personal wealth was estimated at $4bn by *Moscow News*.

Russia still remains in the World Council of Churches. The Moscow Patriarchate's involvement in the ecumenical movement is a smoke screen for Russian intelligence which needs to influence Western politicians through recruited clergy.

In the late 1960s the World Council of Churches had a powerful Central Committee in which representatives of the Third World and Marxist countries outnumbered those of the West. At its Uppsala General Assembly in 1968 it endorsed violence in revolutions against colonial institutions.

It gave a large to the Rhodesian Patriotic Front guerrillas and to militant Black Power Marxist organisations in England. At the 5th Assembly of the World Council of Churches, Jesus was described as a "Liberator". Liberal bishops described themselves as "Christian Humanists." In mid 1970s proof was found that showed that Metropolitan Aleksii Ridiger of Tallinn was a KGB agent, codenamed DROZDOV. Despite this, he became Aleksi II, the 15th Patriarch of the Russian Orthodox Church. Metropolitan Nikolay Krutitskiy was an old KGB agent, codenamed ADAMANT.

The thought of convergence between Communism and Christianity was first introduced through the growing ecumenism of the National and World Council of Churches. Dr W S McBirnie opposes the ecumenical movement on the grounds that it appeases communism:

> Every prophetic Bible student in America opposes the ecumenical movement of the National and World Council of Churches because of the trend in the direction of a superchurch, headed by the "False Prophet". Bible believing Christians are not against a united effort of churches, per se, but this movement is often anti-Christian. It is moving people away from the historic truth of the Gospel of Christ and encouraging the preaching of a substitute gospel which is no gospel. The ecumenical movement is permeated with socialism and espouses the appeasement of communism; which is not surprising if the ecumenical movement is the first stage in the progression toward the one-world-religion mentioned in the Bible.[28]

The symbol of the World Council of Churches is of a boat with a mast like a cross on a wave. Above is the word *oikumenia*, a word which means "the whole world" indicating the organisation's aim to unite all the branches of Christianity throughout the whole world. The prophecy in Revelation shows that this aim will be achieved.

In another of his pamphlets, *The Coming convergence of communism and the Apostate Churches*, Dr McBirnie examines how communists started to reach out to Christians. He highlights the dangers:

> Biblically minded Christians are aware of the ancient predictions of a coming world (apostate) "church" which would link itself to a tyrannical world

---

28 *The Real Power Behind Communism*, Dr W. S. McBirnie

dictatorship, and become its partner. As never before, this trend is now observable (see Rev.12:13-17).

The book *Christians and Communism* by the Red Dean of Canterbury is a prime example of an attempt to show that Christianity and Communism are compatible.

Western churchmen had been among the USSR's strongest supporters. The anti-nuclear position of the National Conference of Catholic Bishops in their Pastoral Letter reflected this.

The World Peace Council (WPC) was the oldest organisation used by the Soviets. The WPC mobilised public opinion against the UN forces in Korea. Exposed as an arm of the USSR, the WPC was expelled in 1955 from Vienna once Austria had regained its independence.

In 1975 the WPC made a tour of ten cities in the United States after which it was able to become a front-line organ of Soviet propaganda. During its period of decline, the Soviets concentrated on the Prague Christian Peace Council (CPC) and the World Council of Churches (WCC).

The CPC emphasised peace and Christian pacifism and provided positions that churches adopted against the war in Vietnam.

The Christians Associated for Relationships with Eastern Europe (CAREE) had gained some credibility among liberal church leaders in the United States. The National Council of Churches (NCC) gave it subcommittee status and the NCC president joined the board of CAREE. It provided a conduit for propaganda to reach US religious leaders.

Appeals from protest movements triggered by Khruschev's antireligious campaign in the late 1950s to the Baptist World Alliance and the World Council of Churches fell on deaf ears.

According to Golitsyn, the Christian Peace Conference played an active part in influencing Western churches in the interests of the long range policy.

The Pontifical Commission for Justice and Peace (PCJP), though still nominally Roman Catholic, has been taken over by converts to Marxism. It consistently endorses the main themes of Soviet Marxist policy – the evils of capitalism in Western democracies, the call for unilateral disarmament by the Western powers, the absolute need to establish a one-world economic system based on the distribution of wealth. The PCJP cooperated with the World Council of Churches to establish a joint Committee on Society, Development and Peace (SODEPAX) in 1968. Condemning the Pope's claim to head the Church, it promotes the World Council of Church's Mega-Religionist brief for the equivalence of all religions. It also maintained that the new ecumenism was not confined to the "church of the Christian faith" but included people of any faith. Hence the World Council of Churches and SODEPAX enlarged their "interfaith" meetings to promote their adopted anti-capitalist and anti-Western themes of Soviet foreign policy.

Pope Francis promotes communist strategy of convergence through environmentalism

Pope Francis is the first Jesuit to become a Pope. In his book *The Jesuits*, Malachi Martin analyses how the Jesuits adopted Liberal Theology and spread it throughout Latin America. This development may have originated with the neo-Modernists. The Jesuit Vincent Miceli declared that the apostasy of Catholic modernists must be unmasked as shadows of the Antichrist within the Church:

> The Christ of neo-Modernists is a non-historical fiction, tailored to push socialist and Marxist ideology through the means of propaganda.

Pope Francis's encyclical *Laudato Si'* received plaudits from groups and individuals on the Left such as Joe Biden, Barack Obama, and the General Secretary of the UN. Leonardo Boff helped Pope Francis write the encyclical *Laudato Si'*, (as did Jeffrey Sachs, an atheist). Boff is a notorious proponent of Liberation Theology and was twice silenced by the Congress for the Doctrine of the Faith under John Paul II before he declared his abandonment of the Catholic faith. Boff is an important link between the Marxist Liberation Theology movement and the ecological movement.

Pope Francis promotes the Earth Charter in his Encyclical *Laudato Si'*, revealing a close alignment with Gorbachev. Like Gorbachev, Pope Francis wants to restructure the world and to:

> bring about significant change in society . . . profound changes in lifestyles, models of production and consumption, and the established structures of power.

Gorbachev is the main architect behind the Earth Charter, the principles of which are expanded in the book *The Earth Charter In Action*. The principles are divided up across the book and printed on paper coloured the colours of the rainbow. Hence a Marxist movement is wrapped up in the most innocuous and welcoming colours one can imagine. To the religious, the rainbow is reminiscent of Noah's Ark and of God's covenant to man that he would never destroy the earth again with a flood. Gone are the hammer and sickles, and the blood red flag of communism. Photographs of young children from around the world populate the book, as each chapter is introduced by a full-page colour painting drawn by a child. What is in fact a drive towards the abolition of capitalism and Christianity is wrapped up in the most innocent garb, like a wolf in sheep's clothing.

Mikhail Gorbachev's introductory essay promotes the idea that the Earth Charter should be the third pillar in global governance, along with the Charter of the United Nations and the Universal Declaration of Human Rights. His essay concludes by noting that UNESCO, the United Nations Educational, Scientific and Cultural Organisation, and many NGOs, have endorsed the Earth Charter.

Liberal Theologian, Leonardo Boff, author of *Introducing Liberation Theology*, is another contributor to *The Earth Charter in Action*. He is a member of the Earth Charter Commission. It was he who also helped Pope Francis write his *Laudato Si'* encyclical which promoted the environmental agenda. The introduction to his contribution does not shy away from his past and reveals that:

> . . . in 1984, as a result of his book *Church: Charisma and Power* he faced a doctrinal process imposed by the Congregation for the Doctrine of Faith in Rome. An "obsequious silence" was imposed on him and he was prohibited from writing and teaching.

The introduction lists some of his many books, amongst which are *Jesus Christ Liberator*, *The Maternal Face of God*, and *Ecology: Earth's Scream, the Poor's Scream*.

In this essay, Boff draws attention to paragraph four of the Preamble to the Earth Charter which states that: "fundamental changes are needed in our values, institutions, and ways of living". This restructuring is of course the entire purpose of Perestroika and the Ecological Movement. The restructuring is to make the West more similar to the former Soviet system so that it can be absorbed into the structure of a worldwide government. However the ecological movement coats itself with a sugary surface that conceals the hardnosed Marxist reality beneath. Goff adds that these 'fundamental changes' "derive from a new ethics, derived from a new point of view: the ethics of love, care, caution, solidarity, responsibility, and compassion". A stark change from the brutality and repression of Stalin and Dzerzhinsky.

Adding to the rainbow imagery used throughout, Boff quotes words from Mikhail Gorbachev's *Perestroika* in which Gorbachev writes:

> This time there will no Noah's Ark to save some few and allow all others to perish: we save ourselves together or together we all perish.

Saved humanity will see the birth of a civilisation "unified in the same common house", in other words, a world government.

Gorbachev's Green Cross International also plays an influential role in restructuring. A document called *The Earth Charter: The Green Cross Philosophy* reveals the hidden agenda behind the environmental movement. This document was prepared by Gorbachev's Green Cross International. It starts with a call for "fundamental economic, social, and cultural changes" and in content bears a similarity to Pope Francis's *Laudato Si'*. *Principle 14: Global Sovereignty* calls for a supranational body with absolute power:

> The protection of the Biosphere, as the Common Interest of Humanity, must not be subservient to the rules of state sovereignty, demands of the free market or individual rights. The idea of Global Sovereignty must be supported by a shift in values which recognize this Common Interest.

The section entitled "Implementation" demands among other things:

> The creation of an international body for the Sustainability of Human Life on the Earth. This body must have the independence and power to facilitate agreement between all societal actors to support the protection of the Biosphere as the Common Interest of Humanity.

> To accelerate the implementation of a new social and economic system

> based on the respect of the existing limits of the Biosphere, priority must be given to Education and in particular, environmental education.

Mikhail Gorbachev makes it clear in *Prophet of Change* that the United Nations must assume aspects of a world government:

> The emerging 'environmentalisation' of our civilisation and the need for vigorous action in the interest of the entire global community will inevitably have multiple political consequences. Perhaps the most important one of them will be a gradual change in the status of the United Nations. Inevitably, it must assume some aspects of a world government. Indeed, such a process has already begun. One day, however, the entire structure of the organisation will have to be reconsidered.

James Delingpole addresses the open conspiracy to build a World Government through the fear of environmental destruction in his book *Watermelons.* He explains how he was reluctant to address this issue, as it had been his intention to focus solely on the fraudulent use of science to promote the climate scare. In the chapter entitled "Welcome to the New World Order", Delingpole looks at how the Club of Rome promoted the climate scare and reveals Gorbachev's influence through the Gorbachev Foundation, Green Cross International and the *Earth Charter*, which he helped write. Delingpole also examines the scope of works such as *Our Common Future* and charters such as *Agenda 21*, the significance of the Earth Summit in Rio held in May 1992, and the role played by Dr Robert Muller, who called for a United States of the World.

It is no coincidence that Earth Day, first celebrated in 1970, falls on the same day as the birthday of Lenin, 22 April. The honouring of Lenin on his birthday was part of the Lenin cult that continued throughout the days of the Soviet Union. Those promoting the ecological agenda are Marxists who are using fears of an ecological catastrophe to restructure the West and its institutions to be in line with Soviet practices.

Maurice Strong was extremely influential and promoted environmentalism so that the United Nations could make itself a world government. He became founding director of the UN Environment Programme (UNEP) which sponsored the UN's Intergovernmental Panel on Climate Change (IPCC). Strong also set up the UN Framework Convention on Climate Change (UNFCCC) which staged the "Earth Summit" and the conferences such as those at Kyoto, Copenhagen, and Paris. Strong wrote a section for *The Earth Charter In Action*. According to the climate agenda expert Christopher Booker, Strong had been close to China's communist leaders all the way back to Mao. (*Sunday Telegraph*, 6/12/15)

Hans Modrow, the former prime minister of the German Democratic Republic, is also playing a role in the environment agenda:

> If humanity wishes to continue living on this planet and to survive, then it needs to address today's realities. Wealth and power are concentrated in still fewer hands and the basis for the wellbeing and means of survival for humanity are being sacrificed on the altar of the market. (*Morning Star*, 26-27 July 2014).

Modrow was honorary chairman of Die Linke (The Left Party) which wins up to 25 per cent of the votes in the East of Germany. He wants to bring change in Europe:

> Only when a broad movement develops throughout the countries of the EU can we begin to build the necessary strength for a progressive alternative.

Throughout both the Catholic and Protestant churches, the meaning of all the Sacraments are being subtly transformed so that they become instead celebrations, even "Earth festivals".

Pope Francis is promoting the communist strategy of convergence through environmentalism as is evidenced by his encyclical *Laudato Si'*. He states he wants religion to play its part in promoting environmentalism with all its socialist trappings and writes: "all Christian communities have a role to play in ecological education" and talks of "ecological citizenship".

His Encyclical has nothing to do with Catholicism as such. Even the quotation of St Francis's "Canticle of Brother Sun" is emasculated, erasing the lines about the apocalyptic second death found in the original Canticle.

In his Encyclical, Pope Francis uses the term: "our common home" with all its Marxist overtones. He calls for "sustainable development".

He states that "enforceable international agreements are needed" as well as "global regulatory norms". What is needed he says is "an agreement on systems of governance of the whole range of "global commons." He sees the "common good" from the global perspective and sees the need for institutions that will govern on a world basis to "ensure that solutions are proposed from a global perspective, and not simply to defend the interests of a few countries" and to ensure that "countries place their national interest above the common good." These global institutions should be: "empowered to impose penalties for damage inflicted on the environment." The Pope is promoting a world government.

He believes that good will only come "when the economic and social costs of using up shared environmental resources are recognised with transparency." As Charles Derber observes in his book, *The Ghost of Karl Marx*, such moves could totally destroy capitalism.

Pope Francis takes global deterioration for granted. Denial of global warming stem from "obstructionist attitudes".

He claims that creation is harmed "when everything is simply our property." Like *Agenda 21*, this is a subtle attack on private property. The Christian tradition, he believes, has stressed the social purpose of all forms of private property. There is a social mortgage on all private property, he claims. The natural environment is a collective good.

In *Laudato Si'* he appears to attack profit making and consumerism when he writes: "profit cannot be the sole criterion to be taken into account". He criticizes the power of the financial system and wants speculation regulated. He mouths the usual Marxist economics about the overproduction of some commodities and states that: "the environment cannot be adequately safeguarded by market forces" and that the "time has come to accept decreased growth in some parts of the world". He blames the market for promoting "extreme consumerism." He does not concern himself with freedom from sin but says: "those really free are the minority who wield economic and financial power" and talks of their increasing greed, and their mental and social conditioning. All this can be dealt with if we can overcome "individualism."

The Pope calls for universal "solidarity". The communists have been trying for years to create solidarity and united fronts with Catholics. That was one of the purposes of Perestroika.

Pope Francis repeats the premise of the Club of Rome's *Beyond the Limits* by refuting unlimited growth. It is a lie that there is an infinite supply of goods, he states, and this leads to the planet being squeezed dry beyond every limit.

Pope Francis talks of the weakness of democracies. His call for "public pressure" reminds one of the communist tactic of pressure from above and pressure from below that was used to such effect in the communist takeover of Czechoslovakia in 1948, the use of this tactic being fully exposed in *And Not A Shot Is Fired* by Jan Kozak. The Pope states that: "unless citizens control political power it will not be possible to control damage to environment." He calls for pressure from below as politicians will be weak and will not take the required action. His use of phrases such as "the quickening of the struggle for justice and peace" with its overtones of the class struggle also resound of Liberation Theology.

He calls for the abandonment of fossil fuels.

He mentions the 1992 Earth Summit in Rio de Janeiro and the 1972 Stockholm Declaration with its call for the "obligation of those who cause pollution to assume its costs". He also mentions the Basel Convention, Vienna Convention and Montreal Protocol. He approves of the Rio Declaration 1992's precautionary principle.

He recalls John Paul II's call for a "global ecological conversion" and quotes from Pope Benedict XVI's *Caritas in Veritate (2009)* with its call to manage the global economy; revive economies; bring about disarmament, food security and peace; protection of the environment and to regulate migration; and its claim that there is an urgent need for a true world political authority.

His disapproval of capitalism was laid bare when he said:

> We discard a whole generation to maintain an economic system that no longer endures, a system that to survive has to make war. But since we cannot wage the third world war, we make regional wars. And that does that mean? That we make and sell arms. And with that, the balance sheets of the idolatrous economies – the big world economies that sacrifice man at the feet of the idol of money – are obviously cleaned up. I think we are in a global economic system that is not good. (*Morning Star*, 14 June 2014)

This Pope is so socialist that Raul Castro said recently: "I will resume praying and return to the Church again if the Pope continues in this vein". Pope Francis recently condemned as "true blood suckers" those bosses who exploited their staff:

> This is starving the people with their work for profit. Living on the blood of the people. And this is a mortal sin." *(Daily Mail, 20 May 2016).*

The present Ecumenical Patriarch, Bartholomew, Archbishop of Constantinople and New Rome, has earned the title 'the Green Patriarch'. This title suggests that he too is promoting a doctrine that is designed to restructure the West so that it becomes more socialist.

The Anglican Church has also adopted the socialist agenda. At its General Synod in 2015, the Anglican Church adopted a green agenda, saying it was 'called to protect the earth now and for the future' and voted to 'encourage prayer and fasting for climate justice' on the first day of the month. The Bishop of Sheffield has called for an 'ecological conversion of individuals and communities'.

Charles Derber explains in his book *Greed to Green* how socialists hold capitalism responsible for the damage of the environment. He even entitles one of his chapters "How Climate Change and Environmental Destruction are the DNA of capitalism".

Derber explains how a legal environment with the power to crack down on any form of "externality" would destroy capitalism. He defines an "externality" as "a social cost, a benefit that corporations do not have to put on their balance sheet". A World Environmental Court, with full legal powers, could place so many legal restrictions upon companies that they are unable to function as normal competitive businesses. Laws would be made to create socialism out of capitalism.

In *Marx's Ghost*, Derber explains:

> [if] you eliminate externalities, you end capitalism because capitalism is based on exploitation for profit – of the worker and the environment.

In *Socialism with a Human Face*, Michael Meacher devotes a chapter to the environment, entitled "An Ecological Crisis?" In that chapter he calls for a "world environmental agency" with the remit of world planning. He recommends the establishment of "a UN-type environmental agency equipped with full powers. Such a body would oversee the totality of remaining supplies of particular raw materials and would be responsible for worldwide planning of resources."

Meacher promotes this idea of a World Environment Court again in his later book *The State We Need* in which he again used the environment as an excuse to push for socialism:

> . . . the need now is for a much tighter regulatory framework – whatever the biosphere requires for its viability – and allowing market mechanisms

> to operate strictly and exclusively within those boundaries. That may well require a World Environmental Court to ensure the new rules are implemented.

Meacher promotes the idea of a "a new world order" which will have its own World Central Bank, a World Environment Court, a World Finance Authority, and a World Investment Organisation, amongst other world bodies.

In an attempt to capitalize on the publicity from the worldwide Occupy movement, Ross Jackson, the chairman of Gaia Trust, in his book *Occupy World Street*, proposes a new world order in which there is a Gaian Trade Organization; a Gaian Clearing Union: using Keynes' model will not use any national currencies; a Gaian Development Bank; funded by freed-up foreign exchange reserves; a Gaian Congress; the legislative body; a Gaian Commission: the executive organ; a Gaian Court of Justice: interprets Gaian law; a Gaian Resource Board; charged with administering use of both non-renewable and renewable resources; control of carbon dioxide emissions; a Gaian Council made up of 'wide elders' with power to overrule any Congress resolution.

Impossible to be a true socialist and a good Christian

In *Christ and Revolution*, Marcel Clement agrees with Pius XI's assertion that one cannot be a true socialist and a good Christian:

> Socialism is not restricted to a purely economic plane. It is a philosophy of happiness, and unfolds itself in the spiritual domain . . . In practice, both [Christianity and socialism] claim, on a certain level, to bring *redemption*. It is here that their mutual antagonism is manifest.
>
> Socialism opposes established disorders, social injustices, and, in short, *the sins of this world*. It claims that its cause is rooted in private economic activity, in free enterprise, and the resulting exchange, in the dictatorship of monopolies which allegedly accompanies it. The social redemption which derives from socialism consists in changing the form of society in establishing a collective control of economy, and thereby guaranteeing both social justice and the participation of workers.

> Christianity, in its turn, teaches us that Christ came *to take on and to expiate the sins of the world*. The cause of this sin lies in the inherent frailty of fallen man . . . Christ's redemption is not for the purpose of changing the form of society, but of renewing the hearts of men and, through them, the face of the earth.
>
> Thus, at this point, we are facing *two interpretations* of sin. One of them basically ascribes sin to structures which allow man the freedom to exploit workers. The other attributes it to the basic frailty of the human will. We face *two plans of redemption*. One of them comes about through the reform of economic structures, the other through the renewal of persons and societies regenerated in Christ. And we face *two hopes*, The one in the merits of a collectivistic system which should realize the material aims of life according to an ideal of justice, the other in the virtue of each individual man, enlightened and strengthened through grace, and living interiorly according to the demands of justice and charity in order to fulfil God's will, on earth as in heaven. . .
>
> The temptation to impose justice on earth is subtle and seductive. It engages simultaneously generosity, virtuous pride, wrath against the rich, and stoical renunciation. It can mislead great and noble souls.

The vast majority of trainee vicars at Church of England theological colleges would describe themselves as socialists. Only 5% of ordinands in full-time training might describe themselves as Conservatives. A sizeable minority are Marxists. Within the Church, the holding of even mild centre-right views is strongly disapproved of. *The Spectator* published the account of one ordinand (under the pseudonym Harry Pinker) who witnessed that he was fed nothing but left-wing views in preaching and a constant diet of propaganda that assumes all Tories are evil. Should a bishop find out you supported Ukip, you might struggle to find a post after ordination. It was generally considered right that clergy should convert the laity to socialism.

Only 6 per cent of Church of England clergy admitted voting Tory at the last election.

Part Seven

CONTEMPORARY WAR ON CHRISTIANITY IN WEST

22

WAR ON CHRISTIANITY IN THE WEST

Contemporary Marxist war on Christianity in the United States and Great Britain

Mary Eberstadt wonders why secularists work so hard to "exorcise Christianity from the public square," to close Christian charities that help the poor, and to undo hundreds of years of good that religious organisations have built up. She concludes that the culture war is due to the fact that these secularist-progressives are like a rival faith to Christianity:

> [the secularist-progressives] believe they are in possession of a higher truth, and they fight to universalize it – to proselytize just as anyone else who believes himself charged with guardianship of the Truth seeks to do.[29]

Eberstadt's book reveals the resignation of some Catholic priests about having to go to jail in the future "because they see a day coming when they're accused of "hate crimes" just for being Catholic priests, in other words, for refusing to recant and succumb to whatever militant secularism now demands." Her book is a catalogue of unprecedented legal attacks

29 *It's Dangerous To Believe*, Mary Eberstadt

on Christian colleges, Christian associations and clubs on campuses, on Christian home-schooling, and on Christian charities.

The drive to eliminate Christianity from the public square has perhaps gone even further in America than in the United Kingdom. In *Shadow World*, Robert Chandler pinpoints four organizations that lead the anti-Christian secularization of American culture:

- American Civil Liberties Union
- American United for Separation of Church and State
- People for the American Way
- Freedom From Religion Foundation

Each of these organizations use the "Establishment Clause" to justify their actions. This clause in the First Amendment to the Constitution states that "Congress shall make no law respecting an establishment of religion." These "progressive-socialist-marxist anti-Christian crusaders", as Chandler designates them, leave no stone unturned as they endeavour to remove the slightest reference to Christianity from public life. Their war on the celebration of Christmas and Easter and all associated activities is, according to Chandler, because "Gramsci's blueprint cannot be satisfied until Christianity's back is broken and erased from American culture."

The elimination of prayer or any phrase of religious expression in schools on the grounds that it violates the principle of "separation of church and state" is listed as one of the 45 Goals of Communism published in *The Naked Communist.*

David Limbaugh examines individual cases of discrimination against Christianity in his book *Persecution* as do George and Andrew Carey in *We Don't Do God.* Dr Richard Scott examines of discrimination against Christians in *Christians in the Firing Line.*

David Horowitz argues in *Dark Agenda* that neo-communists no longer refer to their earthly redemption as "communism" but as "social justice". They see Christianity as counter-revolutionary. In *Big Agenda*, Horowitz explains that progressives are "intoxicated with their own virtue" :

> [progressives] are zealots of what can only be described as a crypto-religion modeled on the Christian narrative of the Fall and Redemption-the difference being that they see themselves as the redeemers instead of the divinity. To progressives, the world is a fallen place - beset by racism, sexism, homophobia, and the rest-that must be transformed and made right.

> This redemption was once called communism and is now called socialism, or "social justice".
>
> Progressives dream of a world of political correctness and politically enforced equality, where everybody is taken care of by taxing the rich until there are no more rich, universities and schools admit no ideas that are hurtful or offending, environments have no pollution, countries have no borders, and nations have no armies. Progressives are so enthralled by their dreams of heaven on earth that they see those who oppose their dreams as evil, which is why they hate them . . . They see themselves as saving the vulnerable and saving the planet. Consequently, they regard themselves as the army of saints and those who oppose them as the party of the damned.

It is worth comparing actions taken against Christians today with those that were taken against the Church in the USSR. The current use of laws to diminish the role of the Church within Great Britain is reminiscent of Soviet tactics and some recent British law-making can be compared to some of the Soviet laws. (Soviet decrees are quoted in *italics* where appropriate in the next few paragraphs which follow.)

A campaign at Bideford Town Council to ban prayers at council meetings, which was backed by the National Secular Society echoes the USSR law:

> *The actions of the government or other organizations of public law may not be accompanied by any religious rites or ceremonies.*

The following events should be compared with the USSR's law:

> *No one may refuse to carry out his citizen's duties on the grounds of his religious views.*

Eunice and Owen Johns were denied the opportunity to foster children because they are unwilling to promote a homosexual lifestyle to a child; Peter and Hazelmary Bull were sued for refusing to let a gay couple share a room; Lord Neuberger, Master of the Rolls, ruled that Lillian Ladele, a registrar, had broken the law by refusing to conduct civil partnership ceremonies because they were against her Christian beliefs. Gary McFarlane, working for Relate, was sacked for refusing to give sex therapy to homosexual couples.

A Christian school is facing closure for failing to invite other religious leaders from other faiths to speak to pupils. It was downgraded by Ofsted inspectors for breaching the Independent School Standards which aim to promote 'British values' such as tolerance and individual liberty. The Department of Education said:

> We make no apology for demanding high standards and the promotion of tolerance and respect of all faiths and cultures.

Traditionalists fear vicars could be taken to court for discrimination if they reject requests to hold civil partnership ceremonies on religious premises over fears that same-sex couples could use the Equality Bill or the Human Rights Act to take action.

An electrician faces the sack for displaying a small palm cross on the dashboard of his company van from Wakefield and District Housing in West Yorkshire.

Nurse Shirley Chaplin was barred from work for wearing a cross. She was moved to a desk job; Duke Amachree, a Homelessness Prevention Officer, was dismissed from his job for encouraging a client with an incurable medical condition to believe in God; a nurse was suspended for offering to pray for a patient's recovery; a Christian magistrate was disciplined for expressing his belief that a child should be raised by both a mother and a father, rather than a gay couple.

The Home Office has proposed a scheme where religious figures must enrol on a "national register of faith leaders". This would be compulsory for faith leaders who work with public sector. This would be a significant deepening of the state's involvement in religion. Extremism was defined as "the vocal or active opposition to fundamental British values, including democracy, the rule of law, individual liberty and the mutual respect and tolerance of different faiths and beliefs".

Mike Overd, a Christian street preacher, was fined £200 for quoting from Leviticus 20. He was supported by Paul Diamond, the Christian rights lawyer, and the Christian Legal Centre. He was convicted of breaching Section 5 of the Public Order Act which deals with threatening words or behaviour. The judge said the fact the passage called for gay men to be put to death meant his remarks could be seen as a threat. Overd said:

> I am amazed that the judge sees it as his role to dictate which parts of the Bible can and can't be preached. This is not free speech but censorship.

Even the National Secular Society appeared to disapprove of this ruling, saying that the ruling appeared to make the quoting of certain passages of the Bible illegal.

The Equality and Human Rights Commission (ECHR) wanted the Department for Education to reconsider the School Standards Act, which allows a school to dismiss staff if their behavior is incompatible with its religious ethos.

Such intrusion is reminiscent of the Soviet law:

> *Religious organizations are prohibited from ... disciplining any of its members in any way.*

The EHCR imposes the creed of the hard Left on Britain and is the chosen instrument for implementing the 'new social order' of Harriet Harman's Equality Bill. At one point not a single Conservative was among the fifteen ECHR Commissioners and more than half of them were active members of the Labour Party.

Anti-church laws often originate from Brussels. The European Union is being used as a vehicle to impose Marxist values on its member states, a body which refused to mention Christianity in its proposed constitution. Anatoliy Golitsyn foresaw that the EU would be used as a vehicle to create a socialist Europe. Its humanist values are reminiscent of the Soviet Union.

Regarding the freezing official intolerance of Christianity in the state sector, the columnist Peter Hitchens predicts that this campaign will spread to the private sector through cunning regulations and rules over the awarding of contracts. Many trades and professions already have binding codes of conduct and practice which insist that you must promote equality and support diversity. These are code words for political correctness. Hitchens also predicts increasing attacks on Christian state schools and on the celebration of Christian festivals and claims that "politically correct revolutionaries" hope to destroy the Christian religion through a thousand regulations. First they plan to rob Christianity of its ancient standing by treating it as equal to other religions.

Founded in 1859, the Catholic Children's Society will no longer assess individuals as prospective adoption or foster parents because it cannot reconcile Church teaching with the demands of the Sexual Orientation Regulations that compel adoption agencies to assess same-sex couples. The Vatican declared it was "gravely immoral" to place children in care of same-sex couples.

Secularists are pushing through legislation such as the Equality Act 2010 that are curtailing the freedom of people to express their religious beliefs in public. The British Humanist Association launched an enquiry, questioning whether The Equality Act's guidance that schools can give preference to religious candidates in 'recruitment, remuneration and promotion' is at odds with EU directive. This is reminiscent of the USSR law:

> *Every citizen may confess any religion or profess none at all. Every legal restriction connected with the profession of no faith is now revoked.*

Christian schools have been under investigation by the European Commission for 'discriminating' against non-religious teachers. According to EU rules, schools must prove a 'genuine occupational requirement' as set out in EU directive. Many complaints arose from bishops and the Pope who argued that the discrimination provision in Harriet Harman's Equality Bill would prevent churches from hiring Christians for key jobs.

The Christian Institute has complained that there is a relentless agenda to secularise religious organisations. The Christian Institute complains that secular organisations are dictating how religious bodies identify who was and who was not religious. Church schools are being robbed of the power to select children on religious grounds. Thirty schools were subjected to investigations by the Admission watchdog, the Office for the Schools Adjudicators, after being accused of breaching the guidelines.

The mandatory daily act of worship does not happen in schools, not even in Church schools. The teaching of Christianity gave way to pagan cults. In 2009 the government announced that pupils would learn about the teachings and rituals of Druids, Moonies and Rastafarians for a new "religious studies" 16-plus exam, along with atheism and humanism.

In 2015 the High Court ruled that it was unlawful to exclude atheism from new Religious Studies GSCE. Schools will have to put non-religious views, such as humanism, on an equal footing with religious ones, like Christianity and Judaism, when teaching religious education. Three families were supported by British Humanist Association. Simon Calvert of the Christian Institute asked:

> Why can't humanists leave RE [Religious Education] alone? It's one of the subjects where students are encouraged to think positively about religion. Children don't have to learn about maths in history lessons, so why do they have to learn about atheism in religious education?

The National Secular Society

On its website the National Secular Society claims that:

> The separation of religion and state is the foundation of secularism. It ensures that religious groups don't interfere in affairs of state, and makes sure that state doesn't interfere in religious affairs.

The Soviet Union was a secular state and it was permanently interfering in religious affairs. One of Lenin's most important decrees was to end the establishment of the Russian Orthodox church in 1918.

Charles Bradlaugh established the National Secular Society in 1866. He and Annie Besant, a former leader of the Theosophical Society and Co-Masonic hierarch, were both prosecuted under obscenity laws and convicted for publishing their pamphlet on family planning, *The Fruits of Philosophy.* Annie Besant also had political ties and friendships with the left. Friedrich Engels knew her and was aware of her adoption of theosophical beliefs.

The seeds of secularism go back to Jeremy Bentham and the French Revolution with works such as Thomas Paine's *The Age of Reason*. On his death bed, Paine had declared:

> I would give worlds, if I had them, if *The Age of Reason* had never been published. Oh, Lord, help me. Christ, help me. Stay with me. It is hell to be left alone.

The National Secular Society was involved in the abolition of the blasphemy laws in 2008.

Honorary Associates of the NSS have included Professor Richard Dawkins, Professor A C Grayling, Peter Tatchell, Nick Cohen, Angela Eagle MP, Dr Evan Harris, Baroness Kinnock, Dan Snow, Baroness Tonge, and Polly Toynbee. Past Honorary Associates have included Michael Foot, Christopher Hitchens, and Lord Peston.

Phil Shiner, whose firm Public Interest Lawyers pursued false allegations of torture and murder against British troops who served in Iraq, has ties with the the Haldane Society of Socialist Lawyers. This organisation's masthead features the communist red star. When the president of The Haldane Society of Socialist Lawyers, Michael Mansfield, QC, appeared on *Desert Island Discs* he requested a Bible of vegetarian cooking instead of the customary Bible. When told by the presenter that he had no choice, the National Secular Society made a complaint about this. (The Bible is the most widely read book of all time, followed by *Quotations from the Works of Mao.*)

The National Secular Society spent 140 years campaigning for the abolition of the blasphemy laws. Their efforts were rewarded finally with the Criminal Justice and Immigration Act 2008 which abolished the common law offences of blasphemy and blasphemous libel.

The cause of homosexuality was used as a pretext to fight the blasphemy laws. A poem written by James Kirkup called *The Love That Dare To Speak Its Name*, a euphemism for homosexuality, had been the cause of the legal action *Whitehouse v Lemon* in 1977 after it was published in a 1976 edition of *Gay News*. The editor of *Gay News* was convicted and given a suspended prison sentence. The poem is written from the viewpoint of a Roman centurion who fantasizes about having sex with Jesus after his crucifixion. The poem suggests that Jesus had sex with numerous disciples, guards, and even Pontius Pilate and John the Baptist. The poem was read aloud publicly outside St-Martins-in-the-Field in Trafalgar Square in 2002. This time no action was taken. Peter Tatchell, the human rights activist and member of the National Secular Society, was quoted as saying:

> The blasphemy law gives the Christian religion privileged protection against criticism and dissent. No other institution enjoys such sweeping powers to suppress the expression of opinions and ideas.

Removing blasphemy laws makes Britain more like the USSR, in which God and Christianity were blasphemed with impunity.

Importance of the establishment of the Church of England

It is the aim of every Satanist to separate the Church from the State. They seek to deprive Christian believers of any sort of voice or role in public life.

In the United States, Satanism is a constitutionally protected religion. There is therefore a great benefit of raising a child in the United States from a Satanist's point of view. The Supreme Court has determined a separation between church and the state, meaning teachers and administrators are not allowed to teach children religion in school. However, most private schools are based on Judeo-Christian teachings.

In England, the secularist strategy at the moment is to pretend that the current state of constitutional affairs does not exist.

Secularists might argue that by privileging no religion they safeguard all of them. However, they want to limit faith to the private sphere with the expectation that religious belief will disappear altogether.

The secular society of today is effectively a pagan society that worships false gods.

There is an established Church in England and Scotland. At the great coronation of King Edgar at Bath in 973 the king promised to fulfil the three duties of a Christian monarch: to protect God's Church; to punish malefactors; and to rule with justice and mercy. In return the Archbishops of Canterbury and York anointed him, bestowing God's blessing and setting above all other lords. As former Archbishop George Carey has pointed out, that promise – or covenant – has remained central to royal coronations right up to modern times. The constitutional arrangements in the UK vest sovereignty in the monarch in Parliament under God.

Carey gives a good summary of the views of those who would disestablish the Church:

> [They believe] that Christianity sold itself out under Emperor Constantine in a Faustian pact with temporal power, which resulted in some 1,500 years of spiritual dead-end. The uncoupling of Christianity from the machinery of State, reduction of the Christian message to just another competing voice in a world of ideas of roughly equal validity, is simply a necessary evolution for the Churh. It must be freed from the curse of privilege, prestige, and recognition to follow its true mission as Jesus Christ's community for outcasts, the poor, and dispossessed.[30]

30 *We Don't Do God*, Carey & Carey

How correct Carey is to warn against the disestablishment of the Church:

> The brave new world into which secularists believe the Church may emerge with its integrity intact, may in contrast be a wholly bad thing. The signs point to restriction in religious freedoms and an outcome that actually suppresses rather than releases the true voice of Christianity.[31]

Secular states often conduct its own wars against religion. One of Lenin's first acts was to deprive the Church of state support. In 1918 Lenin separated the Church from the state in his Decree on the Separation of the Church from the State and of the School from the Church, the Decree of 23 January. The ensuing persecution of the Church shocked the world.

We must recognize that the establishment of the Church is a blessing. The two wings of the eagle enabled the Woman - those who bear testimony to Christ and who keep the commandments of God – to flee from persecution inspired by Satan. Constantine's acceptance of Christianity was a tremendous blessing for the Church, enabling the Woman to find the place prepared for her by God (Rev. 12:6).

British Humanist Association

The British Humanist Association (BHA)'s website argues that "religious pictures on the walls may seem inoffensive to those of the religion in question but can create a hostile or offensive environment for others".

The British Humanist Association offers alternative ceremonies for humanists, such as humanist weddings and funerals, where no prayers are said and no religious hymns are sung.

Among the British Humanist Association's official supporters are Nick Brown, Glenys Kinnock and Fiona Millar (the partner of Alastair Campbell who famously said: "We don't do God" while helping Tony Blair handle the Press). According to Peter Hitchens in his section in *The Mail on Sunday (26 February 2017)*, Fiona Millar expressed delight at the singing of the

---

31 *We Don't Do God*, Carey & Carey

Communist anthem, "The Internationale", at the 2001 memorial service for Tony Benn's wife Caroline.

Polly Toynbee was appointed President of the BHA in 2007. Since 2012 she has been its Vice President. An atheist and feminist, she has writes regularly for the *Guardian*. Her father, Philip Toynbee, became the first communist president of the Oxford Union.

An example of the extent to which the BHA will go to eliminate any overt form of religion from work is the City of London Police having to change the name of their 'prayer rooms' to 'quiet rooms'.

Secularists are pushing through legislation such as the Equality Act 2010 that are curtailing the freedom of people to express their religious beliefs in public. The British Humanist Association sparked an enquiry, questioning whether The Equality Act's guidance that schools can give preference to religious candidates in 'recruitment, remuneration and promotion' is at odds with EU directive. This is reminiscent of the USSR law:

> *Every citizen may confess any religion or profess none at all. Every legal restriction connected with the profession of no faith is now revoked.*

Christian schools have been under investigation by the European Commission for 'discriminating' against non-religious teachers. According to EU rules, schools must prove a 'genuine occupational requirement' as set out in EU directive. Many complaints arose from bishops and the Pope who argued that the discrimination provision in Harriet Harman's Equality Bill would prevent churches from hiring Christians for key jobs.

Dr Sentamu said some people wanted to relegate the church to a place only in the private lives of its members.

Alexander Solzhenitsyn connects humanism to the rise of Communism:

> [humanism] did not admit the existence of intrinsic evil in man nor did it see any task higher than the attainment of happiness on earth. It started modern Western civilisation on the dangerous trend of worshipping man and his material needs. Everything beyond physical well-being and the accumulation of material goods, all other human requirements and characteristics of a subtler and higher nature, were left outside the area of attention of state and social systems, as if human life did not have any higher meaning. Thus, gaps were left open for Evil and its draughts blow freely today.

As humanism in its development was becoming more and more materialistic, it also increasingly allowed its concepts to be used first by socialism and then by Communism. So that Karl Marx was able to say, in 1844, 'Communism is naturalised humanism'.

Humanism teaches that people should rely on reason, science, and empathy towards other people and animals to be good and find fulfilment, without the need for a deity or a hope of heaven. The American Humanist Association's motto "Good without a God" contradicts the Bible:[32]

The fool says in his heart, "There is no God." They are corrupt, they do abominable deeds, there is none that does good." (Psalm 14:1)

The motto also contradicts Christian doctrine which teaches that only God is good. Jesus said:

"Why do you call me good? No one is good but God alone." (Luke 18:19)

Despite the fact that no one is good except God, people can still do good. Jesus himself said:

"if you then, who are evil, know how to give good gifts to your children, how much more will your Father who is in heaven give good things to those who ask him!" (Matt. 7:11)

The motto "Good without God" also contradicts the teaching found in the epistle of John in which John writes that those who do good are "**of God**" and that we should love each other because "**love is of God**." He writes further that "**whoever does not do right is not of God**." From this, we may conclude that without God, there is no love and no good.

Written by University of Buffalo philosophy professor Paul Kurtz and published in 1973, the Humanist Manifesto II shares communism's faith in

32 *Alexander Solzhenitsyn Speaks to the West*

the limitless advances of science. Like Richard Dawkins, it has a problem with the teachings of Jesus on heaven and hell:

> Promises of immortal salvation or fear of eternal damnation are both illusory and harmful.

The manifesto promotes the disestablishment of the church. Section 12 calls for some form of world government based upon a transnational federal government, a goal of the communists. Section 14 could have come straight from the mouth of Gorbachev himself in its promotion of environmentalism:

> The world community must engage in cooperative planning concerning the use of rapidly depleting resources . . .

Section 15 promotes a worldwide distribution of wealth. The Marxist nature of this document is further confirmed by the fact that amongst the many who undersigned the manifesto is found the agent of influence, Andrei Sakharov.

According to Malachi Martin, the Pope read and reread the Jan-Feb 1983 issue of *Humanist Magazine* which speaks of "the rotting corpse of Christianity" and "the new faith of Humanism." The first phrase reminds one of Lenin's description of religion as "necrophily":

> To talk about God-seeking, not in order to declare against all devils and gods, against every ideological necrophily (all worship of a divinity is necrophily) . . . (*Lenin, writing to Maxim Gorky about god-building*)

Humanism has made converts even among the highest Church officials. There is a drive to have humanism included in the new religious studies schools curriculum alongside Christianity and Islam.

"Political Correctness": a concept of the Chinese Communist Party

The term "Political Correctness" is actually a term coined by Chairman Mao and meant adherence to the official position of the Communist Party. Those who deviated from the party line were expelled from the Party with the resultant loss of friends and comrades. This fear of loss of friends through shaming is a prime reason why progressives in America today do not break ranks.

Political Correctness is totalitarian in nature. Its roots lie in a version of Marxism which sees culture, rather than the economy, as the site of class struggle. Its practitioners believe that the "ruling class" blind the workers with a "false consciousness".

Conservative commentator Patrick Buchanan wrote that "political correctness is cultural Marxism", and that "its trademark is intolerance".

Political correctness is a form of "collectivism" where people are made to conform under group pressure to the 'common global mind'.

William S. Lind in the online booklet *Political Correctness: A Short History of an Ideology* states:

> Very few Americans realize that Political Correctness in in fact Marxism in a different set of clothes. As that realization spreads, defiance will spread with it. At present, Political Correctness prospers by disguising itself. Through defiance, and through education on our part, we can strip away its camouflage and reveal the Marxism beneath the window-dressing of "sensitivity", "tolerance" and "multiculturalism".

Cultural Marxism

Cultural Marxism is a totalitarian movement that seeks to create a new world order.

Antonio Gramsci and Gyorgy Lukacs were among the group of Marxist scholars who founded the Frankfurt School (the Institute of Social Research) in 1923. Their philosophy, Critical Theory, is aimed at destroying the Christian-based civilization of the West through incessant and unrelenting criticism:

> The West had to be portrayed as evil, corrupt, authoritarian and oppressive. Christianity, capitalism, authority, family, patriotism, patriarchy, morality, and especially traditional sexual morality had to be attacked and brought down. Marxism had cried out against oppression of the workers. Cultural Marxism turned its attention to creating specific victim groups – women, homosexuals, racial and ethnc minorities and portrayed the oppressor as Western Christian civilisation, the traditional nuclear family, parents, the white heterosexual male, the Christian church, the capitalists and all conservative and traditional values.[33]

Karl Marx had attacked the family in *The Communist Manifesto:*

> Abolition of the family! Even the most radical flare up at this infamous proposal of the Communists.

Fleeing from the Nazis, these neo-Marxists fled to America where many gained influence by joining prestigious universities.

Wilhelm Reich's *The Sexual Revolution* and Herbert Marcuse's *Eros and Civilization* (1955) were seminal works which undermined Christian sexual morality, the sanctity of marriage, and parental authority.

In 2017, the Church of England's General Synod passed resolutions in favour of transgenderism and homosexuality. This is just one indication of how the Church of England is becoming an apostate church.

Patrick Sookhdeo sees in Cultural Marxism the roots of Political Correctness. Herbert Marcuse had argued that tolerance of all viewpoints contributed to social oppression and that therefore some viewpoints should not be tolerated.

Sookhdeo sees in Cultural Marxism a major cause of Christian persecution. Christians in the West should be concerned about Christianophobia because the sections in society that are infected with Christianophobia tend to be powerful elites with influence in higher education. They are also prominent in government and the judiciary and so the targeting of Chrisitans is probably systemic and intentional.

Former Bishop of Rochester Dr Michael Nazir-Ali, who recently defected to the Ordinariate in the Catholic Church, accuses the Anglican Church of failing to stand up for Christian values in an article published

---

33 *The Death of Western Christianity*, P. Sookhdeo

in the *Daily Mail (18 September 2021, "The Church I so loved has lost its way. I simply HAD to leave")*:

> The Church councils and synods are permeated by activists who each have a single issue, often faddish agenda, whether it is about cultural correctness, 'climate change', identity politics, multiculturalism (which actually encourages communities to live separately) or critical theory on race, religion and gender - a Marxist theory developed to create conflict by dividing people into victims and villains.

Mega-religions

According to Malachi Martin, Pope John Paul II and his advisers concluded that the World Conference of Religion for Peace (WCRP), World Congress of Faith (WCF), and the Temple of Understanding (TU) were under the control of the Kremlin. Martin sees Humanism, Mega-Religions, and the New Age as forging an alliance with Gramsci's heirs. These mega-religionist groups afford aid to Gorbachev by persuading millions who would never choose Marxism that all the world's ills are due to the capitalist democracy, in particular the United States.

The Temple of Understanding is located near the United Nations at the Cathedral of St John the Divine, a centre of New Age activism, which also houses the Interfaith Center of New York. It was launched in the 1960s as the "spiritual counterpart of the United Nations". It works closely with the UN Secretariat, the World Council of Churches, the World Conference on Religion and Peace, the UN's Society for Enlightenment and Transformation, and other "spiritual leaders" to sponsor conventions for "global spirituality".

The United Religions Initiative (URI) is firmly aligned with the Left:

> The URI's official support for the Earth Charter, and its leaders' support for population control and the SIECUS sex education "declaration," firmly align the URI with political Left.[34]

---

34 *False Dawn*, Lee Penn

In *False Dawn*, Lee Penn gives several reasons why Christians should stay clear of the URI. It is against Christian evangelism; stigmatizes "exclusive religions" as "fundamentalists"; lays the ground for a new religion of "Sacred Earth"; fosters dissent within traditional religions; promotes a "new ethic" for the New World Order (Hans Kung's Global Ethic); suffers from secular millenarianism; has a fanciful view of history which blames religion for most warfare; adopts religious relativism; promotes population control; promotes a worldly utilitarian view of religion; supports a new world order, a form of communism; promotes feminism and the ordination of women; promotes the New Age Movement, Pantheism, and Theosophy.

The primary catalyst for the URI, Bishop William Swing, counts the 1893 meeting of The World's Parliament of Religions as the starting point for the history of the development of the URI. In the chronology laid out in his book *The Coming United Religions*, he notes that a significant milestone was when the Temple of Understanding held Spiritual Summit Conferences to parallel the Summit Conferences of world leaders. In the second chapter of the book, Swing explains how he and his fellow ordinands wrestled with their consciences over the passage in Deuteronomy 13:1-13 which teaches that anyone who tries to draw people away to worship other gods must be stoned to death, even if that person is your own brother. "Is the lesson about killing those who do not have the correct name for God, actually going to end?" he asks, insinuating that all gods are effectively the same.

Swing sees the environment as a cause that will unite people. The Draft Agenda of Action wants to "restructure" the economic system:

> [The United Religions will] take action to meet the dire need to revisit the global economic system from a religious/spiritual perspective in order to make fundamental changes.

The URI and other Mega-religionists want to harness the full authority of religion to create a world government which will control the world's resources and redistribute wealth.

Like Tony Blair's Blair Foundation, which aims to reduce strife between religions, Swing predicts that when there is a URI, "there will be a cadre of reconcilers, conflict management teams made up of various religions, at work throughout the whole world." Presumably these teams will try and prevent any belief in "one god" from getting in the way of this new world order, just as the Soviets sent people into the homes of believers to try and turn them away from religion.

The cover to William Swing's book *The Coming United Nations* features twelve religious symbols, one of which is the symbol of witchcraft, a pentagram within a circle.

Although Mikhail Gorbachev is not affiliated to the United Religions Initiative (URI), there are many philosophical ties between the URI and Gorbachev and the organisations with which he is connected, such as the State of the World Forum.

New Age serves the classic Marxist ideal by corroding those blocs of traditional resistance to the notion of total control of human life by all-powerful leaders. New Agers look to the elimination of existing political systems and national boundaries and are prepared to welcome the subsequent blending of all nations and peoples into one planetary culture:

> [with a] single court of justice, a single police force, a single economic and educational system – all under a single government dominated by a superbureau of "enlightened ones".[35]

New Age doctrine declares that the new age is to be supervised by a "Maitreya", or Messiah, endowed with superhuman wisdom and fantastic psychic abilities, who would establish the global village. These powers may find their fulfilment in the miraculous powers of the false prophet described in Revelation 13 who deceives the whole world into worshiping the Beast and the image of the Beast, by means of his miraculous powers and signs.

Groups such as the New Agers and Mega-religionists are a godsend to Gorbachev because:

> [their] aim is to promote homogeneity and unity between what was once the hermetically sealed Marxist society of the Soviet empire and the cultures of Western countries. Standing in the way of such an aim was organized Christian religion.[36]

---

35 *The Keys of This Blood*, M. Martin

36 *The Keys of This Blood*, M. Martin

For a long period those who want to create a World Government have foreseen the need to create a World Religion which would resolve all the problems associated with religious differences. Robert Muller, the former Assistant Secretary General at UN said:

> We have brought the world together as far as we can politically. To bring about a true world government, the world must be brought together spiritually. What we need is a United Nations of Religions.

This synthetic "world faith" seems to be in the making with the help of Mega-Religionist groups such as the Temple of Understanding and the United Religions Initiative. The process of merging religions together is called "syncretism". Writing in 1948, Marxist Victor Gollancz wrote:

> The ultimate aim should be that Judaism, Christianity and all other religions should vanish and give place to one great ethical world religion, the brotherhood of man.

Neale Donald Walsch and his connection with the URI

Neale Donald Walsch (author of the highly dubious *Conversations with God* books) attended the URI summit meeting at Stanford in 1997 and was given the leadership of its "Committee on Spirituality and the Global Social Agenda", a task force that assisted in URI planning in 1997-1998. He was also involved in the early 1998 discussion of the draft URI Charter. Walsch told readers of *Magical Blend* magazine to expect "the creation of a United Religions organization, similar to the United Nations, with delegates from each of the world's religions, spiritual movements, and indigenous cultures" between 2000 and 2015.

The three basic principles of Satanism, namely that you can do all that you wish, no one has the right to command you, and that you are the god of yourself seem to be the bedrock of Walsch's philosophy.

His god states:

> "All wisdom asks you to do is trust This Process. That is, *trust God*. Or if you wish, trust *yourself*, for Thou Art God."

Again,

> "There is no hell . . . "

In the same book:

> "There's no such thing as the Ten Commandments . . . God's Law is No Law . . . ;"

In Book 3, *Conversations With God*:

> "There's no such thing as right and wrong . . . "

In the first chapter of *Tomorrow's God* entitled "The Greatest Blasphemy" Walsch's god states:

> "the God in whom you believe *isn't real.* The God in whom you believe is *made up.* It is a God you *created* out of *thin air,* having nothing to *do with Ultimate Reality.*"

Like the androgenous Baphomet, the entity that Walsh refers to as God can be addressed using "he" or "she".

In his *Conversations with God* books, Walsch's "god" is an evolving "God" of good and evil who demotes Jesus to "highly evolved being" and who denies death and praises the "cosmic wheel". According to his "god" Hitler went to heaven because there is no hell. His relativist, utilitarian, "God" promotes a libertine theology and libertine practices such as free love, communal parenting, and euthanasia. His teachings are in stark contrast to Jesus's. Walsch's "god" wants to overthrow the churches and proclaims a new gospel. His "god" supports the idea of communism and a world government, claiming that this is how the heavenly beings interact.

Neale Donald Walsch's heroes and allies number Robert Muller, Barbara Marx Taylor and other prominent supporters of United Religions Initiative. He also extols Deepak Chopra and Matthew Fox, whose New Age philosophy is pilloried by Constance Cumbey in *The Hidden Dangers of the Rainbow.*

Walsch has been influenced by Theosophy and has declared that Alice Bailey's book *Spiritual Politics* is one of the most important books in the market. His "god" urges people to read Rudolf Steiner's works and the methods of his Waldorf School.

Walsch's "god" seems to advocate the Catharist practice of mixing the holy with the profane:

> Mix what you call the sacred with the sacrilegious, for until you see your altars as the ultimate place for love, and your bed-rooms as the ultimate place for worship, you will see nothing at all.

Walsh's "god" proposes communism and world government as the solution to our social problems.

Richard Dawkins's war on God

Richard Dawkins blasphemes God in such a similar way to Mikhail Bakunin that he must have been influenced by the Russian anarchist. Dawkins writes:

> The God of the Old Testament is arguably the most unpleasant character in all fiction: jealous and proud of it; a petty, unjust, unforgiving control-freak; a vindictive, bloodthirsty ethnic cleanser; a misogynistic, homophobic, racist, infanticidal, genocidal, filicidal, pestilential, megalomaniacal, sado-masochistic, capriciously malevolent bully.[37]

Richard Dawkins campaigns against the teaching of religion to children. In this he shares the views of the communists. Dawkins writes:

> it still remains within the power of ignorant parents to cripple the minds of their children by teaching them religious fables . . . this freedom of conscience for parents is tantamount to a freedom for them to poison the minds of their children with the opium which when they were young was poured into their own minds by the church.

---

37 *The God Delusion*, R. Dawkins

The introduction to the latest edition of *The God Delusion* tells how the Richard Dawkins Foundation for Reason and Science (RDFRS) is running a campaign called Openly Secular which "encouraged by the earlier success of the gay movement" invites people to "come out" as non-believers.

In this introduction to *The God Delusion*, Dawkins repeats Karl Marx's and Bakunin's view that religion is the opium of the people:

> No wonder the pacifying opium of religion was actively pushed by the oppressors, then and down the ages.

Dawkins then quotes Marx's famous dictum:

> Religion is the sigh of the oppressed creature, the heart of a soulless world, and the soul of soulless conditions. It is the opium of the people.

Another campaign run by the RDFRS has been the Clergy Project which has set up a website for clergy who have become atheists but who are unwilling to break away from the church openly. Daniel Dennett, the co-author of *Caught in the Pulpit*, writes in his Afterword to this latest edition of Dawkins' book that "several of the clergy revealed that it was their decision to read *The God Delusion* that eventually led to their still secret apostasy."

The "Blasphemy Challenge" can be found on the Richard Dawkins Foundation website. This is a campaign launched to "entice" young people to, in the website's own words, "commit what Christian doctrine calls the only unforgivable sin – blasphemy against the Holy Spirit". The website declares that 160 participants have already blasphemed the Holy Spirit and earned free DVDs during the pre-launch phase of the Blasphemy Challenge. The campaign is focused on reaching a young demographic and is targeting sites that are popular with the young. If encouraging people to blaspheme the Holy Spirit is not satanic, then what is?

Dawkins wants to write a new book that specifically targets children, *Atheism for Children*. This would follow on from his earlier book aimed at teenagers entitled *The Magic of Reality*.

Part Eight

SATANIC AND OCCULT SYMBOLISM OF THE RED STAR AND SOVIET EMBLEM

23

OCCULT SYMBOLISM OF RED STAR AND SOVIET EMBLEM

Origins of the Soviet emblem

Vladimir Lenin and Anatoly Lunacharsky held a competition in 1917 to design the Soviet emblem. The winning designer was Yevgeny Ivanovich Kamzolkin (1885–1957). On 6 July 1923 the 2nd session of the Central Executive Committee adopted Kamzolkin's design as the emblem of the Soviet Union.

The Hammer and Sickle represents same gods as those on Tetragrammaton Pentagram

The Hammer and Sickle is often depicted within the Red Star on Soviet insignia.

The points of the Hammer and Sickle represents the points of Eliphas Levi's Tetragrammaton Pentagram, the "Flaming Star"

The insertion of the Hammer and Sickle into the Red Star is evidence of this truth.

The five points of the Pentragram represent the head and limbs of a man, the Microcosm. At each point of the Pentagram, Eliphas Levi has placed the symbols of various planets which each have a specific significance in magick.

Tetragrammaton Pentagram	
Head	Jupiter
Hands	Mars/Venus
Feet	Saturn

The Hammer and Sickle represents these very same gods: Mars, Saturn, and Jupiter:

- The Sickle is a symbol of Saturn (not just of Marduk). Saturn's astronomical symbol represents the god's sickle or scythe.
- The Sickle also represents Jupiter, for in the days of ancient Babylon the planet Jupiter was named Marduk, and the Sickle represents Marduk. (Today, the planet Jupiter is named after a Roman god. In the Hellenistic age, it was named after Zeus.) The Sickle, therefore, represents Saturn and Jupiter (the planet Marduk).
- The Hammer represents Mars.

When placed within the Red Star, therefore, the Sickle is not just a symbol of the Babylonian god Marduk, but also a symbol of the Roman god Saturn, whose symbol is also a sickle. (Saturn was the god of generation, dissolution, plenty, wealth, agriculture, periodic renewal and liberation.)

In 1955 the flag's design was legislated, which gave a clear indication of how to create the flag: the hammer and sickle are in a square; the tip of the sickle lies in the centre of the upper side of the square; and the handles of the hammer and sickle rest in the bottom corners of the square.

It can be seen from this diagram that the tip of the sickle represents the top of the star, the apex. The handles of the hammer and sickle represent the two bottom points of the Pentagram (the "feet"). The head of the hammer is the "right hand" and the furthest extent of the curve in the sickle is the "left hand".

The Hammer and Sickle can face either way. The head of the Hammer will represent the left "hand" when facing one way, the right when facing the other. The same applies of course to the Sickle which can represent Saturn, the right or left "foot," depending upon the direction of the Hammer and Sickle.

The sickle always represents Jupiter as well, regardless of whatever direction the emblem is facing.

Tetragrammaton Pentagram signifies Baphomet

Éliphas Lévi's drawing of Baphomet appeared in his book *Dogme et Rituel de la Haute Magie* ("Dogma and Rituals of High Magic" which came out in two volumes: *Dogme* in 1854 and *Rituel* in 1856.

Baphomet became an important figure within the cosmology of Thelema, the mystical system established by Aleister Crowley

Lévi considered the Baphomet to be a depiction of the absolute in symbolic form:

> The goat on the frontispiece carries the sign of the pentagram on the forehead, with one point at the top, a symbol of light, his two hands forming the sign of occultism, the one pointing up to the white moon of Chesed, the other pointing down to the black one of Geburah. This sign expresses the perfect harmony of mercy with justice. His one arm is female, the

> other male like the ones of the androgyne of Khunrath, the attributes of which we had to unite with those of our goat because he is one and the same symbol. The flame of intelligence shining between his horns is the magic light of the universal balance, the image of the soul elevated above matter, as the flame, whilst being tied to matter, shines above it. The beast's head expresses the horror of the sinner, whose materially acting, solely responsible part has to bear the punishment exclusively; because the soul is insensitive according to its nature and can only suffer when it materializes. The rod standing instead of genitals symbolizes eternal life, the body covered with scales the water, the semi-circle above it the atmosphere, the feathers following above the volatile. Humanity is represented by the two breasts and the androgyne arms of this sphinx of the occult sciences.

Éliphas Lévi states in this passage that the Hermaphrodite in Heinrich Khunrath's *Amphitheatrum sapientiae aeternae* (1595) is symbolically equivalent to his Baphomet. Heinrich Khunrath (c. 1560–1605) was a German physician, hermetic philosopher, and alchemist. His Hermaphrodite holds a globe which equates to the semi-circle found in Baphomet's stomach. Levi noted that Baphomet should be depicted as seated on a cube or a tripod, and no doubt these equate to the triangular and square shapes within the globe held by the Khunrath's Hermaphrodite. In Levi's drawing of Baphomet, the cube is depicted as a throne upon which Baphomet is seated. He omitted the tripod for the sake of simplicity. The multi-coloured feathers of the bird in Khunrath's image equate to the feathers on Baphomet's upper body.

The Hebrew letters of the Tetragrammaton appear in the outermost ring of Khunrath's diagram. This use of the Tetragrammaton is a profanity, for it associates what is holy with magick. The words YAH and *Elohim* also appear in a black sphere at the bottom of Khunrath's drawing, as do the words: "the spirit of the Lord (i*n Hebrew*) hovered on the waters (*in Latin*)". These words refer to the formlessness of the earth at the beginning of creation. Both Levi's and Khunrath's drawing include the Latin words: *solve* and *coagula*.

Eliphas Levi's Tetragrammaton Pentagram represents the same things as the depiction of Baphomet.

Tetragrammaton Pentagram	Baphomet
The arrows on the hands of the Pentagram (the Microcosm)	The fingers pointing up and down
The face (eye and mouth) on the apex of the Pentagram	The face of Baphomet
Symbols of the sun and moon are placed in position of breasts	Baphomet's breasts
Caduceus in place of genitals	Caduceus in place of Baphomet's genitals
The Hebrew word for Adam appears on one arm, Eve on other	Corresponds to male and female arm of Baphomet
The four Platonic elements, earth, water, air, and fire, are represented by teh wand, the cup, the sword/ dagger, and disc symbols	Water: fish scales Aire: semi-circle of atmostphere Fire: Astral Light Baphomet is seated on the Earth
Arms of Pentagram	Moons of Geburah and Chesed are known as the Left and Right arm because of their position on the Kabbalic Tree of Life

Baphomet represents Satan

The striking image of Baphomet immediately evokes a sense of evil. Even the wings of Baphomet suggest Satan, the fallen angel.

Lucifer is the Wiccan name for their Horned God. Another name for their horned god is Pan, the faun-like satyr who is half-man half-goat.

Contemporary Catholics warned Éliphas Lévi that he was unwittingly dealing with demons. Lévi, however, denied the existence of the devil altogether, stating that Satan was merely the personification of all errors and perversities.

In Lévi's writings Lucifer and Satan came to symbolize two opposing tendencies in human nature, which did not exist as independent forces but as positive or negative instrumentations of the Astral Light. Lucifer is depicted as the force of liberty and progress, while Satan stands for perversion and anarchy.

Lévi stated that in black magic, the devil is the great magical agent employed for evil by a perverted will.

Lévi admitted that Baphomet was the object of Devil worship:

> Yes, in our profound conviction, the grand masters of the Order of the Temple have adored the Baphomet and they have made their initiates adore him . . . but the adorers of this sign do not think like us that it is the representation of the devil, but rather that of the god Pan, the god of our schools of modern philosophy, the god of the theurgists of the School of Alexandria and of the Neoplatonic mystics of our days: the god of Lamartine and of Monsieur Hugo, the god of Spinoza and Plato, the god of the primitive Gnostic schools; even the Christ of the dissident priesthood; and this last qualification, ascribed to the goat of black magic, will not astonish those who study the religious antiquities and who are acquainted with the phases of the diverse transformations of the symbolism and dogma, be it in India, be it in Egypt, be it in Judea.

As well as being influenced by Khunrath, it is clear that Levi has based his picture of Baphomet on such drawing as The *Compendium maleficarum* (1608), which shows a goat-headed, winged Devil who bears much resemblance to Lévi's Baphomet. The Tarot card of the Devil is also clearly an influence.

The Tetragrammaton Pentagram profanes the sacred name of God

This use of God's name for occult purposes is a profanity. God condemns sorcerers (Rev. 21:8, 22:15) warning them that their lot shall be **in the lake that burns with fire and sulphur, which is the second death**.

The Tetragrammaton is a name for the four Hebrew letters that spell the name of God (YHVH). The Tetragrammaton has great significance in magick. According to occult teaching, each letter of the Tetragrammaton represents one of the four elements:

- **Yod:** Fire
- **He:** Water
- **Vav:** Air
- **He:** *Earth*

The five point of the pentagram represents Earth, Fire, Air, Water, and Spirit. Eliphas Levi used the pentagram in conjunction with the Tetragrammaton to create a symbol that profanes the sacred name of God. Satan has always desired to debase what is sacred.

The Tetragrammaton Pentagram represents the Divine, the Divine being represented by the four letters of the Tetragrammaton. An Alpha and an inverted Omega also feature in its design. The angel sent by Jesus says:

> **"I am the Alpha and the Omega, the first and the last, the beginning and the end."** (Rev. 22:12)

Placing the Hammer and Sickle within the Red Star makes it explicit that the Tetragrammaton Pentagram is satanic by association. By associating Satan with this symbol of the Divine, the blasphemous inference is made that the Divine is Satan. Since the Hammer and Sickle also represents Karl Marx, there is also the blasphemous inference that Marx represents the Divine too.

In Freemasonry, the five-pointed star is also regarded as a symbol of God. The pentangle is called the pentalpha, with each point representing an alpha. The alpha is perceived by some to represent the Grand Architect of the Universe.

The design of the Masonic Square and Compass may have been an influence in the design of the Hammer and Sickle.

The G that represents God inside the compass and square was replaced with the hammer and sickle in 1877 in Grand-Orient Freemasonry because they objected to this symbol of God, according to John Daniel's *Scarlet and the Beast.*

The pentagram is also associated with the five wounds of Christ: his punctured hands and feet, plus the puncture in his side by the soldier's spear. The symbol is found in many churches. This association gives the Red Star another blasphemous connotation.

The five points of a pentagram also represent the five books of the Pentateuch.

The Tetragrammaton Pentagram represents metals as does Nebuchadnezzar's Statue

It is also pertinent to note how the Tetragrammaton Pentagram represents, amongst other things, some of the metals associated with the Statue that Nebuchadnezzar saw in his dream, namely gold, silver, bronze (an alloy of copper and tin), and iron.

The Tetragrammaton Pentagram has the Sun, Moon, Mercury and Venus portrayed in the center. Mars is found on the upper left point, Venus (again) on the upper right point. Saturn appears on both lower points. Jupiter on the upper point.

These heavenly bodies (Sun, Moon, Mercury, Venus, Mars, Saturn and Jupiter) represent the following metals: Gold, Silver, Mercury, Copper, Iron, Lead, and Tin. The metals Gold, Silver, Bronze (copper/tin) and Iron, the metals of Nebuchadnezzar's Statue are thus represented by the Red Star (which represents the Tetragrammaton Pentagram).

The Fouth Beast has **claws of bronze** and Jupiter (Marduk) represents tin, an alloy of bronze. The fact that the Fourth Beast is described as having **iron** teeth and that Mars represents the metal iron is surely significant.

Lead	Saturn
Tin	Jupiter
Iron	Mars
Gold	Sun
Copper	Venus
Mercury	Mercury
Silver	Moon

USSR's emblem influenced by drawing of Baphomet

The USSR's emblem has borrowed from Eliphas Levi's drawing of Baphomet, published in his book *Transcendental Magic* (1856), and from Heinrich Khunrath's *Amphitheatrum sapientiae aeternae* (1595),

Baphomet	USSR Emblem
Horns of Baphomet	Red ribbons around wheat sheaves look like ridges on horns
Astral Light on Baphomet's head	Sun between horns of wheat
Humanoid shape of Baphomet	Red Star (Pentagram: signifies Microcosm)
Pentagram signifies North, East, South, and West	Longitudes and latitudes depicted on Earth
The five elements: Earth, Air, Fire, Water, Astral spirit	Land, sea, atmosphere with sun's rays, sun, Marxism (Red Star)
Semi-circle at Bapomet's stomach represents the atmosphere	The atmosphere surrounds the Earth
Top half of Earth at bottom	Top half of Sun at bottom
Tetragrammaton Pentagram	Red Star
Crescent moons Geburah and Chesed: "right and left arm" (Tree of Life of Kabbalah)	The handles of hammer and sickle suggest a left and right hand
The caduceus	The Hammer and Sickle
Solve/coagula	These opposites are understood in Red Star/Pentagram
caduceus=Hermes/Mercury	Hammer and Sickle=Mars/Marduk/Saturn
The Earth is Baphomet's throne	The hovering of the Hammer and Sickle above the Earth suggests sovereignty over it
Humanity represented by breasts and arms	Red Star (pentagram=man/humanity)
caduceus=Ningishzida, a Sumerian god depicted with mushussu dragons, Marduk's aminal	Hammer and Sickle=Marduk, a Sumerian word
Light/darkness	Sun/Mars (which can only be seen at night)

The Red Star referred to as "the flaming star"

> **The third angel blew his trumpet, and a great star fell from heaven, blazing like a torch, and it fell on a third of the rivers, and on the fountains of water. The name of the star is Wormwood.** (Rev. 8:10)

Eliphas Levi referred to his Tetragrammaton Pentagram as the "flaming star" and associated it with the great star in Revelation whch fell from heaven (Rev. 8:10).

It may well be that the communists associated the Red Star with this "flaming star" of Rev. 8:10, for the salutation of the officials and the military in the early days of the Soviet Union was always accompanied by a lifting of the right hand to the forehead, the pointing to the communist emblem on their caps or helmets and the fervent cry of "*Plameny pryvyet!*" in Russian which means: "A flaming greeting!"

This metaphor of a star (Rev. 8:10) may have been based on this passage in Isaiah, a taunt against the king of Babylon:

> **"How you are fallen from heaven, O Day Star, son of Dawn! How you are cut down to the ground, you who laid the nations low! You said in your heart 'I will ascend to heaven; above the stars of God I will set my throne on high . . ."** (Isa. 14:12-13)

Since there are strong grounds for interpreting the **great mountain** that burns **with fire** of the earlier verse (Rev. 8:8) to the fall of Babylon the Great, so the "flaming star" may well refer to the destruction of the Beast, an event which will occur after the fall of Babylon the Great.

God warns ancient Babylon that he will make her **a burnt mountain** (Jer. 51:25). In Revelation, a giant angel takes up a stone like a great millstone and throws it into the sea, saying:

> **"So shall Babylon the great city be thrown down with violence, and shall be found no more . . . "** (Rev. 18:22)

These verses have strong resonances with the events ensuing from the second angel's trumpet blast:

> **The second angel blew his trumpet, and something like a great mountain, burning with fire, was thrown into the sea . . .** (Rev. 8:8)

The Red Star (the Tetragrammaton Pentagram) represents Satan

The Red Star symbolizes Satan. Through association, the Hammer and Sickle does too because it is often depicted inside the Red Star.

The two bundles of wheat bound by red ribbon on the Soviet Emblem represent the horns of Baphomet. Between the two horns of the Emblem's cornucopia is the sun, which is a substitute for the Astral Light, the torch that burns between the two horns of Baphomet. In *Dogme et Rituel* Eliphas Levi writes:

> The Astral Light is the universal seducer typified by the serpent in Genesis.

The idea that the Red Star is a satanic symbol has circulated in post-Soviet Russia for a long time. In 2014, the leader of the Liberal Democratic Party of Russia, Vladimir Zhirinovsky, asked the defense ministry to look into its continued use because, he said, the five-pointed red star for "certain Orthodox" Russians "is associated with satanic symbols."

There were some in the White Russian emigration in the 1920s and 1930s who talked about the occult roots of Bolshevism. Some Orthodox radicals even began insisting that overcoming communism required the elimination of all Red Stars. Others have rightly seen a connection between the Red Star and Baphomet, the Sabbatic Goat.

The eyes and mouth of the Tetragrammaton Pentagram represent the Antichrist, the Little Horn of Dan. 7:8

> **. . . and behold, in this horn were eyes like the eyes of man, and a mouth speaking great things.** (Dan. 7:8)

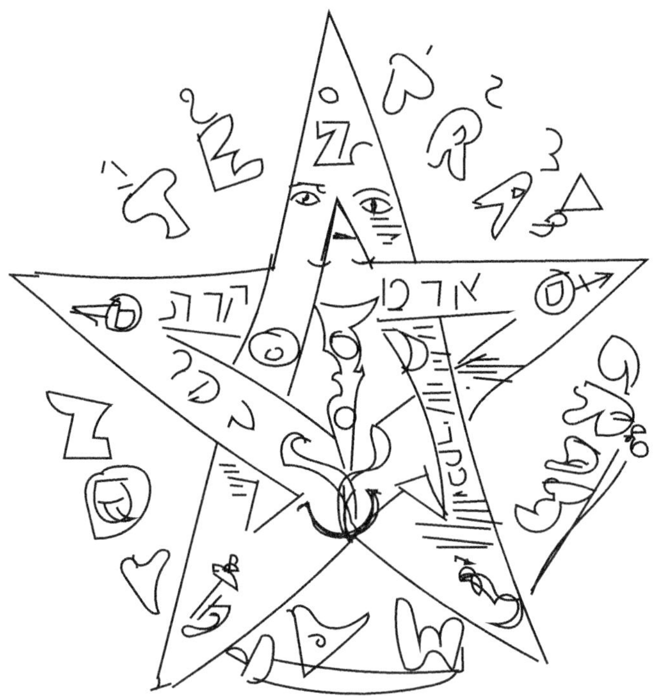

As can be seen from the diagram of the Tetragrammaton Pentagram (*above*), eyes are located on the apex of the Pentagram and a mouth is depicted at the bottom ends of the letter Alpha. Since the Tetragrammaton Pentagram represents Baphomet, these eyes and mouth must represent Baphomet, and therefore Satan.

The two points on the top of an inverted pentagram are said to represent the horns of Baphomet. Through similar reasoning, any point of the Pentagram can be perceived as a horn. (In fact, the Hebrew word *qeren* means both "horn" and "ray (of light)".)

The Little Horn that uproots three of the Ten Horns of the Fourth Beast has the eyes of a man and a mouth that speaks great things (Dan. 7:8). The Red Star, through its connection with the Tetragrammaton Pentagram with its eyes and mouth, represents this Little Horn (RSFSR/Trotzky).

Baphomet: a symbol of the perfect social order

Baphomet is depicted by Éliphas Lévi (Alphonse Constant) as the symbol of a revolutionary heretical tradition that would soon lead to the "emancipation of humanity" and the establishment of a perfect social order, an "*association universelle*".

Éliphas Lévi asserted that the Templars were the torchbearers of the secret tradition of true Christianity, the "champions of humanity" who strived for the establishment of this perfect social order. Thus the Temple was a symbol for a social utopia.

Éliphas Lévi (Constant) believed in the synthesis of man and woman: "The two sexes will be one, according to the word of Christ; the great androgyne will be created, humanity will be woman and man." Baphomet represents this "great androgyne" and is a symbol of the realization of the final universal synthesis.

Lévi's friend Alphonse Esquiros maintained that widespread knowledge about the universal force of magnetism and the "occult" laws of God would emancipate the people and lead to social progress.

Baphomet represents the final synthesis of science, religion, philosophy, and politics: the creation of the Kingdom of God on Earth. This synthesis would be realized through the progressive decryption of the tradition of "true" religion.

Baphomet embodies the "law of opposites"

The fundamental laws of dialectical materialism are:

1. The law of the transformation of quantity into quality, according to which gradual quantitative changes give rise to revolutionary qualitative changes;
2. The law of the unity of opposites, which holds that the unity of concrete reality is a unity of opposites or contradictions;
3. The law of the negation of the negation, which claims that in the clash of opposites one opposite negates another and is in its turn negated by a higher level of historical development that preserves something of both

negated terms (a process sometimes represented in the triadic schema of thesis, antithesis, and synthesis).

Eliphas Levi explained that the feathers on Baphomet expressed "the volatile". Such words might be intended to express the idea of the transformation of quantity into quality.

The depiction of Baphomet certainly embodies one of these fundamental laws, namely the unity of opposites. The idea of polarity, such as dividing the world into male and female energies, was a central concept in occultism.

Polarity can be found in Eliphas Levi's depiction of Baphomet:

- One hand pointing up while the other hand points down, expressing the Hermetic concept "As above, so below" according to which different levels of existence influence one another, whether those levels be intellectual versus physical, the spiritual world versus the material world, or the microcosm versus the macrocosm.
- Chesed and Geburah, the two Sephirot on the Kabbalistic Tree of Life. On opposite sides of the tree, they are commonly understood to be male and female, severity and mercy. Chesed represents kindness and love, while Geburah represents power, strength, and judgment.
- The Latin terms *solve* and *coagula* written upon Baphomet's arms. These translate "dissolve" and "coagulate", opposing alchemical processes.
- Baphomet being both male and female (e.g., breasts and phallus; one male arm, one female arm).

Given how Baphomet represents not only the perfect social order, but also the unity of opposites, it is fair to conclude that Levi's depiction of Baphomet may well have been a key influence in the design of the emblem of the Soviet Union.

It is possible that Trotzky, like so many other Bolsheviks, sported a goatee (a small beard on the end of his chin) in order to resemble Baphomet. Christopher Story asserts that an official portrait of Lenin that appeared in Soviet newspapers deliberately attempted to incorporate features universally attributed to the Devil (this portrait of Lenin is reproduced on page 28 of his book *The European Union Collective*).

Stars represent angels in the scriptures

> **. . . the seven stars are the angels of the seven churches . . .** (Rev. 1:20)

The above verse (Rev. 1:20) illustrates perfectly how stars represent angels.

Thoughout the Bible, stars often represent angels or saints. The twelve stars that crown the Woman (Rev. 12:1) represent both the twelve tribes of Israel and the twelve angels at the twelve gates of New Jerusalem (Rev. 21:12).

In Daniel, the wise shall shine **like the stars** for ever and ever (Dan. 12:3). The righteous will shine **like the sun** in the kingdom of their Father (Matt. 13: 43).

The Red Star and the Tetragrammaton Pentagram likewise represent an angel: Satan. The devil can still be represented by a star, despite the fact that he has been thrown out of heaven, because he is still an angel.

It is clear from the way that the Hammer and Sickle is placed either within the Red Star or just below it that both symbols represent Satan.

Baphomet: the antithesis of the Woman clothed in the sun

> **. . . a woman clothed with the sun, with the moon under her feet, and on her head a crown of twelve stars. . .** (Rev. 12:1)

Baphomet is the antithesis of the Woman clothed in the sun (Rev. 12:1). Instead of the moon under his feet, he has the earth. Rather than being clothed in the sun, he is clothed in darkness, a crescent moon on either side of him.

Instead of a crown of stars, he has one star marked on his forehead. Presumably this star and the Astral Light on his head represent the same thing: Satan, the fallen angel.

Just as the Woman represents the people of God, so Baphomet represents the people of Satan. He is their father.

As noted before, the Red Star may also be interpreted as a representation of Joseph whoss brothers and parents, represented by sleven stars and the sun and moon, bow down before him. In this case the Joseph here would be Stalin.

The Beast is a parody of the Christ

Throughout Revelation, the Beast appears to be a kind of parody of the Christ. Just as the Christ has seven horns (Rev. 5:6), so the Beast has ten horns (Rev. 13:1). Just as Christ is killed and raised again, so the Beast receives a mortal wound and then comes backto life.

The Red Star parodies Christ's designation of himself as the **bright morning star** (Rev. 22:16).

Part Nine

THE SEVENTY WEEKS OF DANIEL

24

CHRIST AND DANIEL'S SEVENTY WEEKS

The seventieth week of Daniel extends from Christ's death until his Second Coming

> **"Seventy weeks of years are decreed concerning your people and your holy city, to finish the transgression, to put and end to sin, and to atone for iniquity, to bring in everlasting righteousness, to seal both vision and prophet, and to anoint a most holy place . . . "** (Dan. 9:24)

These seventy weeks of years are based on the seventy years of Jeremiah:

> **. . . and these lands shall serve the king of Babylon seventy years.** (Jer.25:11).

Several passages in the Book of Daniel divide the final (the seventieth) week into two half-weeks (Dan. 7:25; Dan. 9:27; Dan. 12:7; Dan. 12:11; Dan. 12.12). This division of time is reflected in chapter 11-13 of Revelation. Both prophecies shed light upon each other.

The final week is an elongated week, that endures over many centuries. The final week is an extended period that consists of more than seven calendar years. There is no "Gap" as such, merely an elongation of this final week which is divided into two half-weeks.

It begins at the end of the **seven weeks and sixty two weeks** when the continual sacrifice is taken away at the fall of Jerusalem in AD 70. The first half-week ends with the ascension of the Beast from the abyss (that is, the advent of the USSR) and the restoration of the Temple service. The Beast will have the saints in his power for the second half of this week, that is for **time, times and half a time** (Dan. 7:25).

The final half-week ends with the reappearance of Jesus Christ at the Second Coming.

Christ makes the Covenant that lasts for a week

> **And he shall make a strong covenant with many for one week** . . . (Dan. 9:27)

The covenant referred to in this verse is the New Covenant that Jesus Christ inaugurated at the Last Supper:

> **. . . the Lord Jesus on the night when he was betrayed took bread, and when he had given thanks, he broke it, and said, "This is my body which is for you. Do this in remembrance of me." In the same way also the cup, after supper, saying, "This cup is the new covenant in my blood. Do this, as often as you drink it, in remembrance of me." For as often as you eat this bread and drink the cup, you proclaim the Lord's death until he comes.** (1 Cor. 11:23-26)

When Christ comes, there will be no further need to proclaim his death. The covenant of Holy Communion is only to be observed from the time of Christ's death until Christ's return. This period is the **week** of Dan. 9:27.

Christ's first advent after seven weeks and sixty-two weeks

> **Know therefore and understand that from the going forth of the word to restore and build Jerusalem to the coming of an anointed one, a prince, there shall be seven weeks and sixty-two weeks** ... (Dan. 9:25. *Author's translation*)

There are two different *termini a quo* to pinpoint the date of Christ's advent: the beginning of two projects to rebuild Jerusalem. The first was undertaken by Nehemiah in 454 BC, the second by Herod in 20 BC, 434 (**sixty-two weeks**) years later. Herod's work began **seven weeks** before Christ's advent.

The first building project takes place sixty-nine "weeks" (**seven weeks and sixty-two weeks**) before the advent of Christ, the second building project **seven weeks** before the advent of Christ. Therefore the first building work is undertaken sixty-nine "weeks" (**seven weeks and sixty-two weeks**), that is 483 years, before the advent of Christ.

Nehemiah started the work on the walls of the city in 454 BC, the 20th year of the reign of Artaxerxes, sixty-nine "weeks" (483 years) before the year of Christ's triumphal entry into Jerusalem, the year also of his death.

Upon completion of the work to rebuild the walls of Jerusalem, Nehemiah reinstated the Sabbatical Year, a strong indication that the counting of the sixty-nine weeks should start from this date: **and we will forego the crops of the seventh year and the exaction of every debt** ... (Neh. 10:31). Nehemiah did this to conform comply with the commandments about the sabbatical year found in the Torah (Lev. 25:1-7/Deut. 15:1-11).

Since the practice of observing the Sabbatical Year did not recommence until the time of Nehemiah, it could still be argued that the counting of the "weeks" of years should commence in 454 BC even if one were to take Cyrus's decree as the *terminus a quo.*

Taking the 20th year of Artaxerxes (454 BC) as the starting point for the counting of the "weeks", the **sixty-two weeks** end in 20 BC, the very same year that Herod began his rebuilding of the Temple in Jerusalem. The next period of **seven weeks** follows on immediately, a period which ends in the advent of Christ.

Herod started building a new Temple in 20 BC, forty-nine years (**seven weeks**) before Christ's triumphal entrance into Jerusalem and his subsequent death on the cross that same year. Herod's work on the Temple is mentioned in the Gospel of John:

> **The Jews then said to him, "It has taken forty-six years to build this temple, and will you raise it up in three days?"** (John 2:20)

This conversation occurred in AD 27, three years before the death of Christ in AD 30. Christ was crucified forty-nine years (**seven weeks**) after Herod began his work on the Temple. (The work on the Temple was only completed shortly before its destruction at the hands of the Romans in AD 70.)

When Daniel prophesies that the Christ will be cut off after **sixty-two weeks**, sixty-nine weeks are to be understood, because the **seven weeks** are mentioned before the **sixty-two weeks** in Dan. 9:25. Had the **seven weeks** not been written first, one might have concluded that Christ's first advent would be in 20 BC, 434 years after Nehemiah began work to restore Jerusalem, instead of the correct 483 years. It is perhaps for this reason that the **seven weeks** appear in this verse before the **sixty-two weeks**, despite the fact that historically the period of sixty-two weeks occurred before the period of seven weeks.

Christ's advent is the *terminus ad quem* of both periods: **seven weeks** from Herod's commencement of work to Christ's advent; sixty-nine weeks (the **seven weeks** and **sixty-two weeks**) from the beginning of Nehemiah's work to Christ's advent. It is for this reason that the order in which the two time periods appear in the text is not important – provided one understands that the **sixty-two weeks** until Christ's advent actually represent sixty-nine weeks (**seven weeks and sixty-two weeks**).

Christ did not die in the seventieth week but at the end of the sixty-second

> **And after the sixty-two weeks, an anointed one shall be cut off ...** (Dan. 9:26).

Christ's death and the fall of Jerusalem occur at the end of the sixty-two weeks (Dan. 9:26).

Although Christ is the one who makes a covenant for one week, the subject of the next verb is the Desolator (*meshomem*). The Romans are the ones who cause sacrifice and offering to cease for half a week, not the Christ. Mistaking Christ as the one who makes sacrifice and offering cease, some commentators reason that had Christ died at the beginning of the seventieth week he would have caused the sacrificial system to cease for the entire week, not just half of it. Consequently they deduce (mistakenly) that Christ must have died in the middle of the seventieth week. However, it is plainly written that Christ is cut off at the end of the sixty-two (sixty-nine) weeks, not in the middle of the seventieth.

Some commentators are further inclined to ignore the plain meaning of Dan. 9:26 because it seems incongruous to them that the date of Christ's advent and the date of his death should fall in the same year. They claim that Christ's ministry on earth of three and a half years years must constitute the first half-week of the final seventieth. They also try and justify their placing of Christ's death in the middle of the seventieth week on the grounds that it is written that the anointed one is cut off "**after**" sixty-two weeks. If, however, Christ died in the middle of the final half-week, the scriptures would have stated so.

Two half-weeks (not one) after Christ's death and resurrection

Most commentators presume that only one half-week remains after Christ's death before all seventy weeks expire. They therefore assume that any reference to a half-week in either Daniel or Revelation can only refer to this one half-week. However, far from there being only one half-week between Christ's death and his second coming, there are in fact two half-weeks.

The flawed presumption that there remains only one "half-week" after Christ's death might well explain why so many commentators are convinced that the Roman Empire must be the Beast. The Books of Daniel and Revelation make it clear that the Beast/Little Horn will hold sway for a half-week (time, times and half a time/1260 days). It would follow therefore that if this sole remaining half-week begins immediately upon Christ's death, then the Beast must arise around the time of Christ's death. Hence commentators incorrectly deduce that Revelation is all about the Roman Empire, which it is not.

The Little Horn of Dan. 8:9 was indeed Rome, but the Little Horn of Dan. 7:8 is Russia.

Christ will return during the reign of the restored USSR

> **And in the days of those kings the God of heaven will set up a kingdom which shall never be destroyed, nor shall its sovereignty be left to another people. It shall break in pieces all these kingdoms and bring them to an end, and it shall stand for ever . . .** (Dan. 2:44)

Christ's return marks the end of the seventy weeks.

He will be revealed from heaven with his mighty angels in flaming fire, inflicting vengeance upon the Beast and the Ten Kings. Paul writes:

> **the Lord Jesus will slay him** [the lawless one] **with the breath of his mouth and destroy him with his coming** (2 Thess. 2:9)

When Jesus comes he will destroy the Beast who is represented by the Statue in Nebuchadnezzar's dream:

> **As you looked, a stone was cut out by no human hand, and it smote the image on its feet of iron and clay, and broke them in pieces . . .** (Dan. 2:34)

The kingdom of heaven is the stone cut out by no human hand:

> **But the stone that struck the image became a great mountain and filled the whole earth.** (Daniel 2:35)

The metaphor of a stone reminds one of this passage in Peter where Jesus is described as "a living stone" (2 Peter 2:4-9).

Jesus will instigate this kingdom on his return. He is the one **who is to**

rule all the nations with a rod of iron (Rev. 12:5). His everlasting dominion over all the nations is prophesied in Daniel:

> **. . . and behold, with the clouds of heaven there came one like a son of man, and he came to the Ancient of Days and was presented before him. And to him was given dominion and glory and kingdom, that all peoples, nations, and languages should serve him; his dominion is an everlasting dominion, which shall not pass away, and his kingdom one that shall not be destroyed.** (Dan. 7:13-14)

The Woman and the Dragon

The first few verses in Revelation chapter 12 (Rev. 12:1-6) give a sweeping overview of the future and allude to events that are prophesied about again later in the chapter. The fact that these verses provide an overview of what is to be prophesied about further on can be seen in the repetition of the prophesy about the Woman being nourished for a half-week in the wilderness (Rev. 12:6 and Rev. 12:14), for both verses refer to the same matter. These early verses (Rev. 12:1-6) also allude to Christ's birth and resurrection, and to the Church's protection from Satan during the first "half-week".

The portent of the Dragon standing before the Woman who is about to give birth so that he can consume the child is a reference to Christ's death and resurrection (Rev. 12:4).

The Woman's labour (Rev. 12:2) does not represent the persecution suffered by Israel in the period leading up to the birth of Christ. If this was so, then in terms of covenants, the Woman would have to represent Hagar, and her offspring would have to represent Sarah. This is nonsensical. The Woman must represent the Jerusalem above, and her offspring are children of the Jerusalem above.

The Woman represents the Jerusalem above, the Israel of God where neither circumcision counts for anything, nor uncircumcision, but a new creation (Gal. 6:16). Her offspring, (the first of whom is Christ) are the children of Abraham through faith in Jesus, who like Isaac, are children of promise (Gal. 4:28). Paul uses the allegory of Jerusalem as a mother in Galatians: **But the Jerusalem above is free, and she is our mother** (Gal.

4:26). Here, in Revelation, the Woman does not represent both Hagar and Sarah, but only Sarah.

Satan's fall to earth (Rev. 12:9) marks the point when the prophecy starts to systematically predict events in a sequential manner. No longer just a heavenly portent, the Dragon's actions against the Woman are predictive of the persecutions that the Church will face in the future and of the order in which they will happen.

First half-week of the final week: Christians protected from Satan

> **But the woman was given the two wings of the great eagle that she might fly from the serpent into the wilderness, to the place where she is to be nourished for a time, and times, and half a time. The serpent poured water like a river out of his mouth after the woman, to sweep her away with the flood. But the earth came to the help of the woman, and the earth opened its mouth and swallowed the river which the dragon poured from its mouth.** (Rev. 12:14-16)

In chapter 12, the actions of the Woman and the Dragon represent the Devil's attempts to destroy Christianity from Christ's birth right up to the end of the first "half-week". The prophecy begins with the period of Roman persecution of Christians in the first few centuries after Christ, then refers to the period of relief from persecution that followed when Constantine tolerated Christianity in the Roman Empire, then refers to the fall of Constantinople in 1453 and the rise of the Russian Empire as the Third Rome and the new protector of Christianity.

The first half-week is characterized by the period of time that the Church is spared the onslaughts of Satan (the Woman in the wilderness) and by the trampling of the holy city by the gentiles.

With the establishment of the USSR in 1922 and Israel in 1948, all the signs indicate that the mid-point of the Week has been reached.

The early Roman, and Jewish, persecutions of Christians are represented in these words:

And when the dragon saw that he had been thrown down to the earth, he pursued the woman who had borne the male child. (Rev. 12:13)

The Dragon is thrown down shortly after Christ's resurrection.

The subsequent adoption of Christianity by Constantine the Great is prophesied in these words:

But the woman was given the two wings of the great eagle that she might fly from the serpent into the wilderness, to the place where she is to be nourished for a time, and times, and half a time. (Rev. 12:14)

Wings of an eagle are a metaphor for powerful empires. The use of this metaphor is particularly prevalent in Ezekiel chapter 17 where the wings of an eagle refer allegorically to the empires of Babylon and Egypt in turn:

A great eagle [Babylon] **with great wings, and long pinions, rich in plumage of many colours, came to Lebanon . . .** (Ezek. 17:3)/

But there was another great eagle [Egypt] **with great wings and much plumage . . .** (Ezek. 17:7)

In Rev. 12:14, the wings of the great eagle refers to the Roman Empire (and subsequently to the Russian Empire). The Woman's receipt of these eagle's wings refers to the acceptance and adoption of Christianity throughout the Roman Empire.

This acceptance of Christianity began with Constantine's vision just before the Battle of Milvian Bridge in 312 of a cross with the words "In this sign, conquer" written in Greek. The second key date is 313, when Emperors Constantine and Licinius jointly issued the Edict of Milan to establish religious liberty in the Roman Empire. In 380 Emperor Theodosius I made Christianity the official religion of the Roman Empire.

Satan's efforts to persecute and kill Christians are thwarted during this period when Christianity enjoys the protection of this enormously powerful empire. This is the place prepared by God where the Woman is to be nourished for a half-week (Rev. 12:6; 12:14).

The wings of an eagle are a particularly apt metaphor, for the Byzantine Empire (the Eastern Roman Empire) used the double-headed eagle as its emblem. The wings symbolize the two halves of the Roman Empire, East and West. Constantinople was the capital of the Eastern Roman Empire and Rome of the Western Roman Empire.

The Russian Empire replaces Rome as the Woman's protector

> **The serpent poured water like a river out of his mouth after the woman, to sweep her away with the flood. But the earth came to the help of the woman, and the earth opened its mouth and swallowed the river which the dragon had poured from its mouth.** (Rev. 12:15-16)

The fall of Constantinople in 1453 is prophesied in the words: **The serpent poured water like a river out of his mouth after the woman, to sweep her away with the flood** (Rev. 12:15).

In this "**flood**" (Rev. 12:15), the inhabitants of the city were either massacred or enslaved, and the famous city now became the capital of a huge Islamic empire, the Ottoman Empire. Although the Sultan permitted the Patriarch of Contantinople to retain his post, Orthodox Christians began to look to Moscow as their new religious centre.

Russian Empire

After the fall of the Roman (Byzantine) Empire in 1453, the Russian Empire adopted the double-headed eagle as its symbol too, and became in turn the protector of the Christian religion and the largest centre of the Orthodox Church. These events are prophesied in the words:

> **But the earth came to the help of the woman, and the earth opened its mouth and swallowed the river which the dragon had poured from its mouth.** (Rev. 12:16)

The huge landmass of the Russian Empire ("**the earth**") provided the Church with protection. In a sense, the "**two wings**" had passed from the Roman Empire to the Russian Empire.

Having failed to wash the Woman away in 1453, Satan succeeds in overthrowing the ancien regime of the Tsars in 1917, replacing it with a government that is antagonistic to Christianity. Contrary to the Roman Empire and the Russian Empire, the Soviet Empire is inimical to Christianity. It has adopted a symbol of Satan for its emblem and, empowered by Satan, wages war against all forms of godliness.

The Bolsheviks claimed that their war against Christianity was justified on the grounds that the Church was "counter-revolutionary." What they do not admit is that they deliberately murdered the Tsar to ensure that the protective "**wings**" of a great empire would no longer provide support for Christianity. The god-hating Bolsheviks hated Tsardom because it defended Christianity and was a bulwark against their satanic designs.

The "**wings of an eagle**" surely denote the Holy Roman Empire too.

After constant attacks from barbarians, Rome fell in 476 AD. Romulus Augustulus fell and Odoacer became king of Italy. Zeno became Roman emperor of East and West.

However, Satan failed to wash away the Woman with **the two wings of a great eagle** in the western half of the Roman Empire. In time, the Holy Roman Empire was formed which again maintained the Christian faith as its state religion.

On 25 December 800, Pope Leo III crowned the Frankish king Charlemagne as Emperor, reviving the title in Western Europe, more than three centuries after the fall of the earlier ancient Western Roman Empire in 476. The title continued in the Carolingian family until 888 and from 896 to 899, after which it was contested by the rulers of Italy in a series of civil wars until the death of the last Italian claimant, Berengar I, in 924. The title was revived again in 962 when Otto I was crowned emperor, fashioning himself as the successor of Charlemagne and beginning a continuous existence of the empire for over eight centuries.

Before 1157, the realm was merely referred to as the Roman Empire. In a decree following the 1512 Diet of Cologne, the name was changed to the "Holy Roman Empire of the German Nation".

The exact term "Holy Roman Empire" was not used until the 13th century, but the concept of *translatio imperii*, the notion that the sovereign ruler held supreme power inherited from the ancient emperors of Rome, was fundamental to the prestige of the emperor.

The office of Holy Roman Emperor was traditionally elective, although frequently controlled by dynasties. The mostly German prince-electors, the highest-ranking noblemen of the empire, usually elected one of their peers as "King of the Romans", and he would later be crowned emperor by the Pope; the tradition of papal coronations was discontinued in the 16th century.

Roman Catholicism constituted the single official religion of the Empire until 1555. The Holy Roman Emperor was always a Roman Catholic. Lutheranism was officially recognized in the Peace of Augsburg of 1555, and Calvinism in the Peace of Westphalia of 1648.

Emperor Francis II dissolved the empire on 6 August 1806 following the creation of the Confederation of the Rhine by emperor Napoleon I the month before.

It is significant that all three empires, that is the Byzantine, Holy Roman, and Russian (the "Third Rome") empires all had a double-headed eagle as their symbol, and all three claimed to be "Roman."

History of Roman persecution of Christians: the dragon's pursuit of the Woman (Rev. 12:13)

As noted above, the dragon's pursuit of the Woman (Rev. 12:13) represents the persecution of Christians at the hands of the Romans, and Jews, during the first few centuries after Christ's death.

Some of the persecutions that Christians suffered at the hands of the Jews are found recorded in the Book of Acts.

The following is a brief history of the persecutions that Christians suffered at the hands of Rome. Christians were executed if they failed to sacrifice to the traditional Roman gods and worship the image of the Emperor. There was also a cult of emperor worship running alongside the worship of the traditional pantheon of gods. Correspondence between Trajan and Pliny (governor of Bithynia-Pontus in AD c. 111-113) shows official policy towards Christians. Pliny writes:

> Those who denied that they were or had been Christians, when thy invoked the gods in words dictated by me, offered prayer with incense and wine to your image, which I had ordered to be brought for this purpose together with statues of the gods, and moreover cursed Christ – none of which those who are really Christians, it is said, can be forced to do – those I thought should be discharged. Others named by the informer declared that they were Christians, but then denied it, asserting that they had been but had

> ceased to be, some three years before, others many years, some as much as twenty-five years. They all worshiped your image and statues of the gods, and cursed Christ.

Trajan replies:

> ...if they are denounced and proved guilty, they are to be punished, with this reservation, that whoever denies that he is a Christian and really proves it – that is, by worshiping our gods – even though he was under suspicion in the past, shall obtain pardon through repentance.

The worship of the Emperor's image illustrated in these passages echoes the worship of the Beast and his image.

There were ten major periods of persecution of Christians under the following emperors:

- Nero (64-68)
- Domitian (90-96)
- Trajan (112-117)
- Marcus Aurelius (161-180)
- Septimius Severus (202-210) (193-211) For the first two centuries of the Christian no general laws against Christians had been issued by any emperor. Matters changed in the third century under Septimius Severus. He forbade conversion to either Judaism or Christianity.
- Decius (250-251) Decius demanded that all inhabitants of the empire sacrifice to the gods and eat sacrificial meat, and testify to these acts. There was a mass apostasy during this period.
- Valerian (257-259) In AD 257 and AD 258 Valerian issued edicts punishing Christians who were to face exile or death.
- Maximinus the Thracian (235-238)
- Aurelian (270-275)
- Diocletian and Galerius (303-324).

The Diocletianic Persecution

The Diocletianic Persecution was the most severe. It began in AD 303 and ended with the Edict of Milan in AD 313. It began with a series of edicts demanding that Christians comply with traditional Roman religious practices. All inhabitants were to sacrifice to Roman gods, a policy called universal sacrifice.

Diocletian wanted to preserve the cult of the old Olympian gods and associated himself with Jupiter. His co-emperor associated himself with Hercules. Men such as Porphyry of Tyre and Sossianus Hierocles were ideologically opposed to any toleration of Christians. Porphyry wrote *Against The Christians*. Like Hierocles, he compared Jesus unfavourably to Apollonius of Tyana.

Pagan priests wanted to suppress the threat to their traditional religion. They believed their ceremonies were hindered by the presence of Christians, who were accused of clouding the sight of oracles and stalling the gods' recognition of their sacrifices.

In AD 299 the emperors were engaged in sacrifice and were told that the diviners of omens were unable to read the sacrificed animals because of the interruptions in the process by profane men. The Christians were accused of this. Diocletian and Galerius sent letters demanding that the entire army perform the sacrifices or face discharge. Troops were to sacrifice or lose rank.

Diocletian's "Edict against the Christians" was published in 303. It ordered the destruction of Christian scriptures, liturgical books, and places of worship across the empire, and prohibited Christians from assembling for worship. Christians could not respond to actions brought against them in court, Christian senators, equestrians, veterans and soldiers were deprived of their ranks; imperial freedmen were re-enslaved.

Failure to sacrifice often resulted in execution. Galerius's recommendation – burning alive – was a common method of executing Christians in the East.

This first edict was the only legally binding edict in the West. However, even harsher legislations was announced in the East.

A second edict was published ordering the arrest and imprisonment of all bishops and priests. A third edict would give amnesty to any imprisoned clergyman provided he made a sacrifice to the gods.

According to a fourth edict (around 304), all persons, including children, were to offer a collective sacrifice. If they refused, they were to be executed.

Lactantius, the Christian rhetor, saw in Diocletian's actions the beginning of the apocalypse. Diocletian and his precursors persecuted Christianity out of a misplaced reverence for the ancient gods of Rome and out of a desire to stamp out a religion that threatened the traditional system of worship of these gods.

As noted above, these persecutions ended with the Edict of Milan in AD 313.

First half-week of the Final Week: trampling of the holy city

> **. . . but do not measure the court outside the temple; leave that out, for it is given over to the nations, and they will trample over the holy city for forty-two months.** (Rev. 11:2)

This trampling of the city of Jerusalem is referred to by Jesus as the "**times of the Gentiles**" and he tells his disciples that the Jews will be led captive among the nations after the desolation of Jerusalem (Luke 21:20-24). It is clear that Jesus' words refer to the fall of Jerusalem in AD 70. It must be concluded therefore that the times of the Gentiles, the period of forty-two months (Rev. 11:2), must be the first half-week of the Week of the Great Parenthesis, not the second.

The "times of the Gentiles" covers the same period of time as the Woman's sojourn in the wilderness of 1260 days, which begins immediately upon her child being caught up to God and to his throne (Rev. 12:5). Despite this concurrence, however, the offspring of the Woman of Revelation (chapter 12) are not the Jews, but the children of the New Covenant: Christians, children of the Jerusalem above whom the Woman represents.

Jews were able to buy enough land in Palestine to create the first Jewish city, Tel Aviv, in 1909. With the return of the Jews to the land of Israel, this period of "trampling" has almost come to an end.

The Balfour Declaration was signed in the very same year as the Russian Revolution, the year when control of Palestine passed from the Ottomans to the British during the First World War.

Until the Third Temple has been rebuilt, and the sacrificial system is reinstated, the holy city is still being trampled upon. Dan. 9: 27 implies that sacrifice and offering will only cease for half of the final week. Consequently the building of the Third Temple and the restoration of the sacrificial system marks the beginning of the final half-week. This event corresponds roughly in time with the advent of the Beast, the USSR.

The advent of the First and Second Beast marks the mid-point of the Final Week

> **. . . and [the saints] shall be given into his hand for a time, two times, and half a time.** (Dan. 7:25)

The first half-week comprises the period that the Jerusalem is trampled on by the gentiles. This period runs concurrently with the the period that the Woman (the Christian faithful) enjoy the benefits of being the state religion of both the Roman and Russian Empire (and the Holy Roman Empire).

The second half-week period of the final week is marked by the advent of the Little Horn, Trotzky's kingdom: the USSR.

The saints will have to endure persecution during the period of the final half-week of the Final Week at the hands of the Beast, who **was allowed to exercise authority for forty-two months** (Rev. 13:5). The period of relative freedom from persecution, symbolized by the Woman in the wilderness, will have ended.

The persecution against Christians that occurred during the period of the USSR is an indication of the kind of persecution that Christians will continue to suffer when the USSR is restored. This persecution will culminate at the End when the False Prophet of Israel will enforce all to be marked with the mark of the Beast.

The Third Temple will be restored in the year 2370

> **"For two thousand and three hundred evenings and mornings; then the sanctuary shall be restored to its rightful state."** (Dan. 8:14)

According to Paul, the Beast takes his seat in the Temple of God, proclaiming himself to be God (2 Thess. 2:4). For this prophesy to be fulfilled, the Third Temple must be rebuilt.

Daniel informs us that the Temple will operate again after the land has been trampled on by the gentiles for 2300 days (**evenings and mornings)** (Dan. 8:14). This indicates that the Temple will be restored in the year 2370.

Jews express their desire to see the building of a Third Temple on Temple Mount in the Amidah prayer:

> Be pleased, O Lord our God, with your people Israel and with their prayers. Restore the service to the inner sanctuary of your Temple, and receive in love and with favour the fire-offerings of Israel and their prayers. May the worship of your people Israel always be acceptable to you. And let our eyes behold your return in mercy to Zion. Blessed are you, O Lord, who restores his divine presence to Zion.

Orthodox Jews believe in the rebuilding of a Third Temple and the resumption of Korban (sacrificial worship), but Conservative, Reform and Reconstructionist authorities disavow all belief in the resumption of Korban. In mainstream Orthodox Judaism the rebuilding of the Temple is generally left to the coming of the Jewish Messiah.

Architectural plans for the Third Temple exist in Chapters 40-47 of the Book of Ezekiel.

Two prospective cornerstones for the Third Temple now sit in waiting. The Temple Institute has offered to provide all Jews by the name of Cohen with a priesty garment for the new Temple. Genetic testing of Cohens has already been undertaken. A herd of red Angus cattle is being developed from which a red heifer is expected to come.

Jewish rabbis conducted a rehearsal of animal sacrifices at the Western "wailing" wall during Passover in 1998.

A dozen organizations, including the Temple Institute, the Temple Mount, and Eretz Yisrael Faithful Movement each state its goal is to rebuild the Third Temple on Temple Mount. Some of these organisations receive major funding from the State of Israel. The Temple Insitute have prepared furniture and priestly garments in readiness for the Third Temple. Architectural building plans have been drawn up.

The Temple could be built in less than one year.

Part Ten

ISLAM: MYSTERY BABYLON THE GREAT

25

MECCA (ISLAM) IS BABYLON THE GREAT

Mecca: the metropolis

> "**. . . on her forehead was written a name of mystery: Babylon the great, mother of harlots and of earth's abominations . . .**" (Rev. 17:5)

Mecca is the metropolis, the great holy city of Islam. The word "metropolis" comes from the Greek words for "mother" and "city", hence its meaning "mother city" or "capital". Mecca is Babylon the Great, the "**the great city**" (Rev. 17:18) and represents Islam in general.

During the *hajj* several million Muslims from all over the world, with their different languages, nationalities and cultures, congregate at Mecca. People also visit Mecca during the lesser pilgrimage, the *umrah*, which can take place at any time of the year. Today, more than 15 million Muslims visit Mecca annually.

Babylon and the Kaaba: both a "gate of god"

The Kaaba is called "the Gate of Heaven" (*bab al-Jannah*), for Allah is said to be seated directly above the Kaaba on his throne. This title "Gate of Heaven" strongly echoes the meaning of "Babylon" (Greek: Βαβυλών), a word supposedly derived from the native Babylonian *Bābilim* which means "gate of the god(s)".

The Kaaba is said to be the centre of the world. There is said to be an exact heavenly replica of the earthly Kaaba just above.

The title "Gate of Heaven" reminds one of the passage in Genesis where, in his dream, Jacob saw a ladder ascending into heaven with the angels of God ascending and descending it. Awaking, he exclaimed:

> "**This is none other than the house of God, and this is the gate of heaven.**" (Gen. 28:17).

It is interesting to note that the word *bab* is still used today in Arabic, and that all the gates built by the Muslims in the cities and mosques throughout the world where Arabaic is spoken still bear the word *bab*. This Semitic word does not appear at all in the Hebrew dictionary. The Hebrew word for "gate" used by the Israelites and which appears in the Tanach (the Hebrew Bible) is always *sha'ar*.

The Arabic for "Babylon the Great" is actually *Babil al kabir*. (*Kabir* means "big" or "great"). The assonance between the word *kabir* ("great") and *Kaaba* is possibly significant too.

The name in the Hebrew is *Bavel*. In the Book of Genesis the word is supposedly derived from the verb *bilbel* ("to confuse"). Coincidentally, the Mecca Royal Clock Tower Hotel (*Abraj Al-Bait*) was built on a hill called Bulbul. The bulbul is a common songbird found throughout the Middle East.

Makkah al-Mukarramah: Babylon the Great

The official title of Mecca in Arabic is *Makkah al-Mukarramah*, which means "Mecca the Honoured". In the related Semitic langauge of Hebrew, the word *ram* means "high, tall, exalted", and the word *ramah* means "high place". The impression of being exalted and high up is reflected in the imagery of Babylon the Great being seated on mountains. (In Hebrew, the word *makkar* means "friend, acquaintance".)

The title Babylon the Great is similar to *Babil al-Kabir* and would suggest that Mecca is indeed the city referred to as Babylon the Great. The epithet *al Kabir* ("the great") is one of the ninety-nine names of Allah.

Mecca, Jerusalem, Medinah, Istanbul, Damascus and Baghdad, all have similar titles:

- *Makkah al-Mukarramah*, Mecca
- *al-Quds al-Sharif*, the Arabized name of Jerusalem, meaning "holy" and "high-born" respectively
- *al-Madinah an-Nabawiyyah* or *Medinah al-Nabi*, ("city of the prophet"), Medina
- *Kostantiniyye al-Mahmiyya* ("the well-protected"), Istanbul (formerly Constantinople)
- *Madinat al-Yasmin*, Damascus "*the City of Jasmine*",
- *Madinat al-Salaam*, Baghdad. (When the Abbasid caliph, al-Mansur, founded a completely new city for his capital, he chose the name "*City of Peace*".)

This unique way of naming cities ties "Babylon the Great" to the Arab world.

The origins of the name "Makkah" are not known. Some Islamic scholars have said that the name, Makkah (Mecca), indicates that the city is the centre and middle of the earth. Some state that the name Mecca is derived from the verb *makkaka*, which refers to the action of sucking out marrow from a bone, or the action of a young animal suckling from its mother.

Mecca has had many names. The city was also known as *al-Balad*: simply "the main city"; and as *al-Qaryah*, with a similar meaning. Mecca (*Makkah*) is also known as *Bakkah*, which can be translated as "lack of stream". Mecca was also called *Al-Balad al Amin* (the "city of security"). (*Al-Amin*, "the trustworthy", was a nickname of Muhammad.) Mecca was also known as *Al-Balad al-Haram* ("the holy city").

Mother of Harlots: *Umm al-Qura* ("mother of cities")

> **. . . Babylon the Great mother of harlots and of the abominations of the earth . . .** (Rev. 17:5)

Mecca is called *Umm al-Qura* ("the mother of cities") in the Koran (6:92 and 42:5). The title "**mother of harlots**" may be a dysphemism based on this title of Mecca.

Some say that Makkah was called the "Mother of Cities" (*Umm al-Qura*) because she is the origin of all the cities on earth, and from it the earth spread out. This "spreading out" echoes the biblical story of the Tower of Babel. The ancient city of Babel and its tower was built so that the people could make a name for themselves before they were scattered over the face of the earth (Gen. 11:4).

The root of the Arabic word *ummah* is *amma*, meaning "to go, to go and see". The word *imama* means "to lead", hence the one who leads the prayer is the Imam. Also derived from this root is the word *umm*, which means "mother", "source", or "origin". This connection between *Umm* and *Ummah* again is a pointer towards Mecca as Babylon the Great.

Cities are commonly referred to as daughters throughout the Bible. For example, Babylon is called the daughter of Babylon (Jer. 51:33), and Jerusalem is called the daughter of Zion (Lam. 1:6).

In Ezekiel chapter 16, Jerusalem's father was an Amorite, its mother a Hittite (Eze. 16:3). The metaphor of a harlot enables a city to be identified as a Canaanite. Ezekiel recalls the proverb 'Like mother, like daughter' and predicts that it will be used about Jerusalem. The city is the daughter of her mother (Eze. 16:45), and the sister of her sisters. Her elder sister is Samaria (Eze. 16:46) who lived with her daughters to the north of her. Her younger sister is Sodom (Eze. 16:16) with her daughters. The daughters of Edom and of the Philistines despise Jerusalem.

The word "daughters" can mean "villages" (Num. 21:25) and hence may signify the suburbs of the large cities mentioned in these verses.

Mecca is in the wilderness

> **And he carried me away in the Spirit into a wilderness, and I saw a woman. . .** (Rev. 17:3)

The Hebrew word for "Arabia" is based on the word for "desert" (*arabah*). The angel who showed John the judgment of the great harlot carried him away in the Spirit "**into a wilderness**" (Rev. 17:3), supporting the interpretation that Mecca is indeed Babylon the Great because she is situated in the barren wilderness of Arabia.

The west coast of Arabia where Mecca and Medina are cited is called Tihamah, which allegedly means "severe heat and lack of wind". This area is in fact one of the hottest places on the face of the planet.

The great tower in Mecca

> "**Come, let us build ourselves a city, and a tower with its top in the heavens, and let us make a name for ourselves, lest we be scattered abroad upon the face of the whole earth**." (Gen. 11:4)

The Abraj Al-Bait (which means in Arabic "the Towers of the House"), also known as Makkah Royal Clock Tower Hotel, is the world's fourth tallest building and has the third largest amount of floor area. It towers over the Great Mosque of Mecca.

The Abraj Al-Bait is a complex of seven skyscraper hotels. Again, the number seven is significant. The towers have large prayers rooms capable of holding more than 10,000 people. The main building is topped by a 23 metres high golden crescent.

The building was built after the demolition of the Ajyad Fortress, an Ottoman citadel, sited on Bulbul Mountain, a spur of Jebel Kuda. The fortress was demolished in 2002 and most of Bulbul mount was levelled. The *bulbul* is a kind of bird, but the similarity of this word to *bilbel* ("to confuse"), the word from which Babel is allegedly derived, is striking.

26

THE SEVEN MOUNTAINS UPON WHICH ISLAM IS SEATED

Islam seated on the "mountains" of the seven fallen kingdoms

> **This calls for a mind with wisdom: The seven heads are seven mountains on which the woman is seated. . .** (Rev. 17:9)

The **seven mountains** are those peoples and nations who were formerly subjects of the seven kingdoms represented by the seven heads of the Beast who are now the *ummah*. The *ummah* are Muslims, people of the "mother community" of Islam, whose mother city is Mecca.

The Woman represents not just Mecca in fact, but Islam in general. As the maps below shows so vividly, the main centres of Islam are in the areas of the world that were formerly encompassed within the empires of the seven kingdoms of the Beast. The only exceptions to this rule are Indonesia and Saudi Arabia itself.

The countries with the greatest density of Muslims are those in North Africa, Mesopotamia, Saudi Arabia and Central Asia.

The Babylonian and Medo-Persian Empires ruled over the whole of Mesopotamia which is now Islamic. Alexander the Great conquered all these lands, including most of Central Asia. Much of the Balkans is under Islam, the former territory of the Macedonian kings. The Ptolemies ruled over Egypt and the Seleucids over Syria, both are now Islamic countries. The Romans conquered the whole of the northern part of Africa that bordered the Mediterranean, and now these countries are under Islam. France has a notably high percentage of Muslims. In time, more of Western Europe is likely to fall under Islam to the extent that the whole of the former Roman Empire may have a very high percentage of Muslims. Those who do not submit to Islam may either be killed, or suffer "dhimmitude" and have to pay taxes to avoid being killed.

The Ottoman Empire was responsible for spreading Islam over the Balkans, being an Islamic empire.

Around fifteen per cent of the Russian population are Muslims. Other member states of the CIS (the Beast and the Ten Kings) are Islamic (such as Turkmenistan and Tajikstan).

Babylon is called a "**mountain**" in Jeremiah (Jer. 51:25). These seven **mountains** are not therefore literal mountains, but metaphorical mountains. The fact that many of the seven kingdoms overlapped each other in terms of territory therefore is not significant, for the seven mountains are a concept rather than actual geographical reality.

These seven mountains constitute the land that Islam will be seated upon in the days of the Beast. Islam may suffer from a false sense of security being seated on these seven mountains, but the restored eighth kingdom, the Beast, will hate Islam and destroy it.

In alliance with the Ten Kings, the Beast will wage war against Islam. During this war against Islam, Mecca itself will be destroyed by the Beast.

The imagery of seven mountains gives ancient kingdoms that have long passed away a contemporary significance. This is in keeping with the idea that the **stone** (Dan. 2:34) will break into pieces all the different nations represented by the Statue in Nebuchadnezzar's dream. It is also consistent with the concept of the prolongation of the lives of the other beasts who have had their dominion taken away (Dan. 7:12).

Each mountain is represented by one of the heads of the Dragon, as if the Great City is seated on the Dragon itself. Her seat on the Red Dragon/Red Beast is an indication of the satanic nature of this city. It is no wonder that in her is found the blood of the saints.

Despite the fact that the Harlot represents Islam, the **seven mountains** do not represent the caliphates of Islam, of which there were only four: the

Rashidun, Umayyad, Abbasid, and Ottoman caliphates. These caliphates overlapped in the same way that the Beast's kingdoms overlapped territorially. Like the Beast's "heads", these too have now fallen, but Islam itself has not fallen.

Cairo, Medina, Damascus, Baghdad and Jerusalem are said to be the five historical capitals of Islam, but in a sense they still are centres of Islam. If one added Mecca itself and Istanbul (Constantinople) to this list, one would arrive at seven cities. However, it is surely correct to recognize the seven fallen empires of the Beast as the **mountains** rather than these historic Islamic cities. After all, the **mountains** are an integral part of the seven-headed Beast, not of the Harlot.

Islam is a territorial religion, very conscious of whether or not an area is under Islamic control. Any land once gained is considered sacred and belongs to the *ummah* for ever. Any lost sacred land must be regained, by force of necessary. Lands which were formerly under Islamic control, for example, are Israel, Spain, the Balkans and Chechnya.

The Harlot is not yet fully established on all seven mountains

The Harlot can surely only be considered as seated upon those lands which are called *Dar al-Islam* (the House of Islam). Those lands which are not under Muslim control are called *Dar al-Harb* (the House of War). In his book *Milestones*, Sayyid Qutb wrote:

> Only one place on earth can be called the house if Islam (*dar-al-Islam*), and that is the place where the Islamic state is established and the Shari'ah is enforced and Allah's limits are observed, and where all Muslims administer the affairs of the community with mutual consultation. The rest of the world is the home of hostility (*dar-al-harb*). A Muslim can have only two possible relations with *dar al-harb*: peace with a contractual agreement, or war.

It is evident that despite their large Muslim populations, an Islamic state has not yet been established in Russia, nor in those European countries which once comprised the Western Roman Empire. However, Islam is already fairly well established in Turkey and the Balkans which comprised the Eastern half of the Roman Empire (and the Ottoman Empire). Six of the Beast's Ten Horns are already. predominantly Muslim: Azerbaijan, Kazakhstan, Kyrgyzstan, Tajikstan, Turkmenistan, and Uzbekistan.

The imagery of the Harlot being seated on seven mountains indicates that Islam will indeed succeed in establishing itself as the dominant religion in both the former USSR and most of Europe.

In his book *Russia's Islamic Threat*, Gordon M. Hahn highlights the threat Islam poses to Russia. Not just limited to Chechnya, a network of terrorists is expanding throughout the Caucasus - in particular, to the five other titular Muslim republics: Ingushetiya, Dagestan, Kabardino-Balkariya, Karachevo-Cherkessiya, and Adygeya, under the influence of al Qaeda. This threat could spread to Tatarstan and Bashkortostan.

Jihadists of the Chechen Republic of Ichkeriya have shown interest in small, usually Tatar, Muslim areas as far away as Siberia, presumably to serve as a base for a restoration of the Muslim Khanate there.

The geopolitical significance of the Caucasus region was revealed in a speech Osama bin Laden's chief deputy Ayman al-Zawahiri made:

> The liberation of the Caucasus would constitute a hotbed of *jihad* . . . and that region would [then[] become the shelter of thousands of Muslim *mujaihidin* from various parts of the Islamic world, particularly Arab parts. This poses a direct threat to the United States . . . If the Chechens and other Caucasian *mujahidin* reach the shores of the oil-rich Caspian Sea, the only thing that will separate them from Afghanistan will be the neutral state of Turkmenistan. This will form a *mujahid* Islamic belt to the south of Russia that will be connected in the east with Pakistan, which is brimming with *mujahid* movements in Kashmir. The belt will be linked to the south with Iran and Turkey that are sympathetic to the Muslims of Central Asia. This will break the cordon that is struck around the Muslim Caucasus and allow it communicate with the Islamic world in general, but particularly with the *mujahidin* movement.
>
> Furthermore, the liberation of the Muslim Caucasus will lead to the fragmentation of the Russian Federation and will help escalate the jihad movements that already exist in the republics of Uzbekistan and Tajikstan, whose governments get Russian backing against those jihad movements.
>
> The fragmentation of the Russian Federation on the rock of the fundamentalist movement and at the hands of the Muslims of the Caucasus and

Central Asia will topple a basic ally of the United Sates in its battle against the Islamic *jihadist* reawakening.

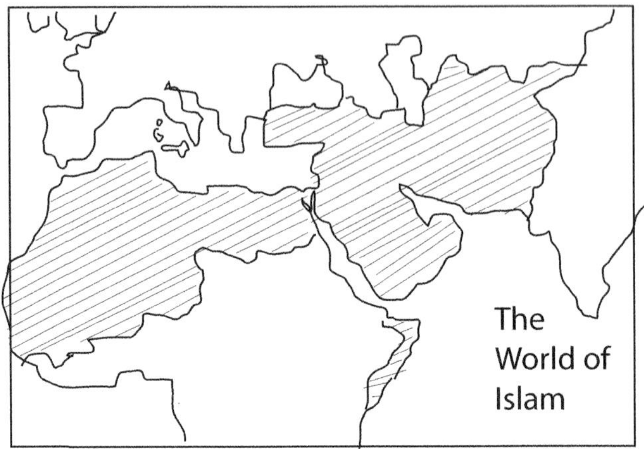

The map (*opposite*) shows how closely the current extent of the World of Islam (*see map above)* corresponds to the empires carved out by Alexander the Great and the Roman Empire.

Alexander conquered the lands of the first two heads of the Beast, the Babylonian Empire and the Medo-Persian Empire. These first two empires correspond to the first two of the five mountains upon which Babylon the Great is currently seated.

The third, fourth and fifth heads of the Beast (the Hellenistic kingdoms) divided up Alexander's huge empire between them. The Harlot is now seated upon these three mountains too (Macedonia, Syria, Egypt).

The sixth "king", the Roman Empire, conquered the land of the three Hellenistic kingdoms and extended its empire into Western Europe and Northern Africa, lands that had not been conquered by Alexander. Many of these new lands have since become *dar-al-Islam* too. However, most of Europe and the lands of the seventh "king", the former Soviet Empire, are yet to fall to Islam completely and currently remain *dar-al-harb.* The sixth and seventh "mountains" therefore are only partially subject to Islam at the present time.

In the map opposite, the route Alexander took during his conquest of Persia and Central Asia is indicated by the thinner of the two lines. The boundary of the Roman Empire at its greatest extent is indicated by the thick black line .

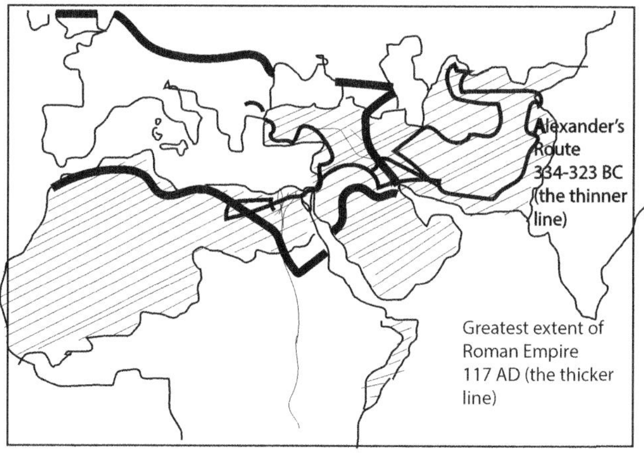

Seven mountains: not actual topography of Mecca itself

Modern building works have changed the original topography of Mecca and hills have been levelled to make way for more buildings and construction work.

The author has found it impossible to find out if Mecca was originally founded in a valley surrounded by seven mountains. Given that there is no such confusion when it comes to the seven hills of Rome, the author is inclined to conclude that Mecca was probably never seated in, or between, seven hills and that the reference to **seven mountains** is not to be understood as pertaining to the actual topography of Babylon the Great.

Although the author may be mistaken, it seems more likely that Mecca was originally seated in a valley surrounded by five mountains, not seven.

"**Mountains**" are purely a convenient metaphor. The city of Babylon, after all, was actually seated in a plain, yet is called a "mountain" in Jer. 51:25.

The "many waters" and the seven mountains: the *ummah*

> **. . . the great harlot, who is seated upon many waters . . .** (Rev. 17:1)

The **waters** upon which the Harlot is seated equate to the **seven mountains** because she is seated upon them both.

The interpreting angel informs us that the **many waters** upon which the Harlot is seated are **peoples and multitudes and nations and tongues** (Rev. 17:15). From this can it can be inferred that the seven mountains also refer to peoples and multitudes and nations and tongues, in particular to those peoples who were once subjects of the seven kingdoms represented by the Beast's heads.

The phrase **peoples, nations, and languages** is used by the herald who summons the subjects of the king of Babylon to worship the image set up by King Nebuchadnezzar (Dan. 3:4). The phrase refers to all the subjects of the king of Babylon. Islam, the great city Babylon the Great, will rule over those **peoples and multitudes and nations and tongues** that had formerly been subjects of the seven kingdoms of the Beast. These seven kingdoms have now fallen, but Islam will rule as queen over all these nations and their peoples.

The interpreting angel explains that the **many waters** (Rev. 17:1) represent **peoples and multitudes and nations and tongues**. These peoples are the *ummah*, the multi-national "nation" or "mother community" of Muslims.

Islam has spread over a huge part of the world. There are 1.6 billion Muslims in the world, forming a fifth of the total world population.

The Muslim World League, a federation of Muslim countries, has fifty members. Of these, twenty-two are Arabic-speaking countries.

The main Islamic countries are found in North Africa, the Middle East, Indonesia, and Central Asia, but many other countries have large Muslim populations.

At his advent, the Beast (the eighth kingdom), along with the Ten Kings, will make war on Islam and destroy her.

27

DOMINION OVER KINGS

Islam is intent on world domination

> **. . . the great city which has dominion over the kings of the earth** (Rev. 17:18)

Jihad is carried out in order to achieve the ultimate goal of Islam, which is to establish Islamic authority over the whole world. As Mark A. Gabriel explains:

> Islam is not just a religion; it is a government, too. That is why it always gets down to politics. Islam teaches that Allah is the only authority; therefore, political systems must be based on Allah's teaching and nothing else.[38]

There is no separation of religion and state in the ordinary Muslim mind-set. It is the very essence of Islam to take control of earthly structures. Power and prestige must be gained at all costs.

38 *Islam and Terrorism*, Mark A. Gabriel

The caliph has dominion over the kings of the earth

> **" . . . the great city which has dominion over the kings of the earth."** (Rev. 17:18)

A caliphate is an Islamic state under the leadership of an Islamic steward with the title of caliph, a person considered a politico-religious successor to the Islamic prophet Muhammad and a leader of the entire ummah (Muslim community).

Historically, the caliphates were polities based on Islam which developed into multi-ethnic transnational empires. There were four major Sunni caliphates: the Rashidun Caliphate (632–661), the Umayyad Caliphate (661–750), the Abbasid Caliphate (750–1258), and the Ottoman Caliphate. The rulers of the Ottoman Empire claimed caliphal authority from 1517-1924. Throughout the history of Islam, a few other Muslim states, almost all hereditary monarchies, such as the Mamluk Sultanate (Cairo) and Ayyubid Caliphate have claimed to be caliphates.

The power over rulers that the Caliph enjoys is illustrated by the demands of the self-proclaimed worldwide caliphate of ISIL. Their self-proclaimed caliph claimed religious, political and military authority over all Muslims worldwide, and claimed that:

> the legality of all emirates, groups, states, and organizations, becomes null by the expansion of the khilafah's [caliphate's] authority and arrival of its troops to their areas.

28

MOTHER OF ABOMINATIONS

Mecca was once a regional centre of idolatry in Arabia

. . .**[mother] of the abominations of the earth** . . . (Rev. 17:15)

Mecca was the regional centre of idol worship. People came from all over Arabia to worship there. Each tribe had an idol in the temple. Some tribes used the name Allah to refer to the moon god. The Kaaba itself used to be the home of 360 pagan gods, presumably one for each day of the lunar year. Allah was the name of one of the gods in the Kaaba, a pagan god who was considered the supreme god over the lesser deities.

Harlotry refers to a city which ceases to practise righteousness and justice. Since the word "**harlots**" in the Harlot's title would appear to refer to cities, it may well be that "**abominations**" refers to idols. Idols are always referred to as "abominations" in the Old Testament. The Torah requires all graven images to be destroyed because they are abominations to the Lord.

The Greek word for "abomination", *bdelugma*, leaves open to doubt whether the word is referring to idols, or merely to abominable actions, or both. In Hebrew the word *shiqutz* always refers to an idol, whereas the word *toevah* refers to an abominable act, such as lying, as well.

Many mistakenly believe that only Jerusalem has a covenant relationship with God, and that therefore only Jerusalem can truly be considered guilty of harlotry. This entirely overlooks the fact that Christianity was already widely spread throughout all the areas that later became subject to Islam. Therefore all those cities which rejected Christianity in favour of Islam can be considered "harlots".

While *shirk*, the Arabic term for the worship of anything other than the one God, is forbidden, the Black Stone is still in the Kaaba, and yet would have been worshipped in the same way as other idols in the pre-Islamic days. Muslims kiss this stone, an act of worship. The Greek word for "worship" is *proskenesis* which is based on the verb "to kiss". One has to wonder why this "detestable thing" has been brought into the House of Allah. It is worth noting that the Black Stone is encased in silver, just as idols of old were covered in silver and gold.

Black stones, usually meteorite stones, were often venerated by pagans. A black stone featured in the idol worship of Venus (Aphrodite) at Paphos, of Cybele in Rome, Astarte at Byblos, and Artemis/Diana of Ephesus. That is why Artemis's "image" in Acts is seen fallen from heaven (Acts 19:35). The veneration of the Black Stone at the Kaaba is a residual tie to the pre-Islamic paganism of the Kaaba. John of Damascus claims that the Black Stone at the Kaaba was from an ancient idol, the head of Aphrodite.

The Black Stone is said to absorb and forgive the sins of those who kiss it. All sins will be wiped clean: touching the Black Stone is an expiation for sins.

It is even said that the Black Stone will become animated, with eyes and a mouth, and stand witness on the day of judgement, condemning or acquitting those whose sins it has absorbed, and that it will testify in favour of those who touched it in sincerity.

Muhammad sanctioned many practices that were performed by the pre-Islamic tribes in Arabia. Such practices include: praying five times a day towards Mecca (Zoroastrians are also expected to recite their prayers at least five times a day having first cleansed themselves by washing); fasting on the 10th of Muharram; walking seven times between the two mounts Tawaf and Safa; *ihram* (a series of procedures like ritual washing before pilgrimage to Mecca); and circumambulation of the Kaaba at Mecca.

Pre-Islamic pagans are alleged to have circumambulated the Kaaba to please the moon god Hubal and the other deities (of which Allah was one). Muhammad himself used to circumambulate the Kaaba, even before the

360 idols inside the Kaaba were removed. (Hinduism and Buddhism also practise circumambulation.)

Muhammad's pagan grandfather almost slaughtered Muhammad's father Abdallah as a human sacrifice to Hubal, the moon god worshiped at the Kaaba.

The pagan origins of Allah

Allah had three daughters, the goddesses Allat, Al-uzzah and Al-Manat, who acted as Allah's intercessors and formed a triad in pre-Islamic Arabia. The three were worshipped as uncut aniconic stones.

The pre-Islamic Arabian goddess Al-lat, whose name is a contraction of al-Illahat, "the Goddess" was called "the Mother of the Gods", or "Greatest of All". She is a goddess of springtime and fertility, the Earth-Goddess who brings prosperity. She was sometimes confused with Al-Uzza, and as one goddess gained in popularity, the other diminished. Allat's symbol is a crescent moon. Herodotus identified Al-Lat with Aphrodite. The Greek historian Herodotus considered Allat the equivalent of Aphrodite:

> The Assyrians call Aphrodite *Mylitta*, the Arabians *Alilat*, and the Persians *Mithra*.

The pre-Islamic Arabs believed Manat to be the goddess of fate.

Some scholars believe that Al-Uzza may even have been the patron deity of Mecca itself. Muhammad himself sacrificed to al-Uzza and is recorded saying:

> "I have offered a white sheep to al-Uzza, while I was a follower of the religion of my people."

Al-Uzza means "the Strong One", "The Most Mighty". She was the virgin warrior and youngest in the triad of goddesses and one of the most venerated Arab deities. She was the goddess of the morning and evening star. Worship of Al-Uzza was originally of Sabean origin (the biblical Kingdom of Sheba in the south of Arabia, present day Yemen), and it worth noting that "Sheba" in Hebrew is spelt with exactly the same letters as the Hebrew word for "seven", though pronounced differently. The woman who is seated upon seven hills therefore may in a sense be Al-Uzza, especially if she was indeed the patron goddess of Mecca.

Despite the "Islamization" of the pagan Arabian religion, Allah did not escape two of his daughters (the third being Manat, the Death or Fate goddess) from appearing on top of almost every mosque and upon many flags of Muslim countries in the form of the Crescent Moon (Allat) and the Star (Al-Uzza). Manat may be implicitly understood, for her symbol, the darkened moon, would not be visible.

These goddesses were associated with Aphrodite or Astarte, whose cults would sometimes involve cult prostitution. Allat was equated with Athena, Manat with Nemesis, and Al-uzza with Aphrodite. Ziaddin Sardar describes Allat as "the mother-goddess"; Manat as "the goddess of fate who represented the darkened moon"; and al-Uzza as "'the she devil', the goddess of love, sex and beauty."

The so-called "Satanic Verses" have been subsequently rescinded, but they prove the point that Allah was a pagan god.

The Koran once read:

> *"Have ye seen Lat and Uzza, and the third Manat? These are the exalted cranes whose intercession is hoped for."* (53:19-22).

The Koran today reads:

> *"Have ye seen Lat and Uzza, and another the third Manat? What! For you the male sex, and for Him, the female? Behold, such would be indeed a division most unfair!"* (53:19-22)

Mecca is a Harlot in the sense that Muslims worship Allah, the god of a strange land, instead of the God of Israel. The Koran errs by stating that Abraham was a true follower of Islam and that he worshiped Allah.

Muhammad's own father Abdullah was named after Allah.

Jehovah, not Allah, is the personal name of the god of Israel

The name "Allah" is derived from *al-ilah*, which means "the god". However, the name Allah is the personal name of the god of Islam, and should not be confused for the word "god". Sadly, even today it is found in the Arabic Bible to translate the word "God" (The name is used by Arab Christians today to mean their heavenly Father.)

Problem arises when people try equate the god Jehovah with Allah. The two different personal names indicate two different gods. The Koran tries to blur this distinction.

The Koran calls Islam "the religion of Abraham". The Koran teaches that Allah rejected the children of Israel because of their sins, and went back to the seed of Abraham and chose a descendant of Ishmael to be the prophet. Islam claims to have superseded Judaism and Christianity.

Whenever God is mentioned in the Koran, the name Allah is used. Muhammad told the Jews and Christians that their prophets were prophets of Islam and that their God is the same God as Islam. In the Koran it states:

> "*Our Ilah and your Ilah is one*" (Surah 29:46).

However, this is not true. Jehovah, not Allah, is the name by which God is to be called to all generations (Ex. 3:15).

The so-called Shema ("hear"), the words which are kept inside the small boxes (*mezuzot* ("doorpost") affixed to the doorposts of Jewish houses contain the fundamental belief in the one god named Jehovah:

> "**Hear, O Israel: Jehovah is our god Jehovah one**." (Deut. 6:4, *author's translation*).

The fundamental belief of Islam is stated in the Shahada ("testimony"):

> "*There is no god but Allah. Muhammad is the messenger of Allah.*"

The Shahadah – ("*There is no God but Allah...*") is a denial that Jehovah is God, since according to Islam, there is no God but Allah. The name Jehovah is not among the ninety-nine names of Allah, which are all mainly epithets like "the great" (*al-Kabir).* The Shahadah is therefore an implicit denial that Jehovah is God.

In the Lord's Prayer, Christians pray "**Father, Hallowed by your name**". The name here being spoken of must surely be Jehovah, a name which God has clearly not rescinded or replaced by any other name, as can be seen from the use of the word "Hallelujah!" in Revelation (Rev. 19:1, 3). In the word 'Hallelujah", the name "Jehovah" has been contracted to "Jah", and *hallelu* means "praise" (in the imperative). The words means "Praise Jehovah!"

The Torah states: **You shall not follow other gods, any of the gods of the peoples who surround you!** (Deut. 6:16), yet Allah was undeniably the god of the Arabs, not of Israel.

God is a jealous God, and would not allow the glory of his name to be shared with another (Isa. 42:8). When Muslims sacrifice to Allah, they break the law of the Torah which forbids sacrifice to any god other than Jehovah (Ex. 22:20). The names of other gods should not even be mentioned (Ex. 23:13). Muhammad's prophecy in the name of Allah is forbidden, for according to the Torah a prophet must not speak in the name of another god (Deut. 18:17).

These truths are self-evident but not endorsed by everyone. Promoting the interfaith movement for the sake of world peace, during an unprecedented papal visit to an Islamic country (Morocco) at the invitation of King Hassan II in 1985, Pope John Paul II said: "We believe in the same God, the one God, the living God." In 2001 in Damascus Pope John Paul II kissed the Koran.

The new Catholic Catechism (1994) includes salvation for Muslims because they claim to worship the god of Abraham (Item 841).

The General Council of the United Church of Canada considered in 2006 a proposal to acknowledge the prophetic witness of Muhammad.

When the *muezzin* calls "There is no god but Allah. Muhammad is his messenger" he is saying that Jesus has been superseded by Muhammad.

The doctrine of the Trinity undermines Christianity

"**Hear, O Israel: Jehovah is our god Jehovah one.**" (Deut. 6:4, *author's translation*)

The doctrine of the Trinity is a stumbling block, not only for Jews and Muslims, but for Christians too. Many Christians have had to wrestle with their consciences over this perplexing, irrational, unbiblical, and indefensible doctrine.

No doubt fear of being burnt at the stake for heresy has discouraged many thousands over the centuries from expressing any dissenting view. No longer threatened with such a cruel punishment, it is difficult to understand though why so many are willing to pay lip service to a doctrine that is clearly false.

This doctrine must account for much of the unwillingness of many Jews and Muslims to convert to Chrstianity. Many Jews are perfectly well aware that at no point did Jesus Christ intimate that he is God, but it is natural for them to be unwilling to participate in a church which does indeed so often equate Jesus with God. The doctrine has led to sermons where the baby Jesus is called God. Such teaching is jarring to most people's ears. Similarly, how often have prayer sessions begun with the words: "Now let's pray to God. Dear Jesus . . . "

There is only one God (Deut. 6:4). The gospels attest that Jesus himself quoted this verse from Deuteronomy (Mark 12:29).

The apostle James undermines the whole doctrine of the Trinity when he states that God is one:

> **You believe that God is one; you do well. Even the demons believe – and shudder.** (James 2:19).

Jesus Christ clearly distinguished himself from God when he said:

> **"Why do you call me good? No one is good but God alone."** (Luke 18:19)

This tenet is confirmed in Revelation, in the song of Moses and the Lamb:

> **For thou alone art holy.** (Rev. 15:4)

Throughout the epistles, the apostles refer to God as the God and Father of Jesus Christ. Here is just one example, but virtually every epistle in the New Testament has a similar formula:

> **Blessed be the God and Father of our Lord Jesus Christ!** (1 Peter 1:3)

Similarly, in Revelation:

> **To him who loves us and has freed us from our sins by his blood and made us a kingdom, priests to his God and Father . . .** (Rev. 1:5)

It is clear and irrefutable from such passages that God is the god of Jesus Christ. Jesus Christ therefore is not God. He is not his own god. The Father is God, Jesus is the Son. This is not mere semantics. Similar reasoning is used by Jesus himself when he argues that the Messiah is not the Son of David, for were he the son of David, David would not have addressed him as Lord (Luke 20:41-44).

The fact that God is the god of Jesus is explicit in Revelation:

> **He who conquers, I will make him a pillar in the temple of my God; never shall he go out of it, and I will write on him the name of my God, and the name of the city of my God, the new Jerusalem which comes down from my God out of heaven, and my own new name.** (Rev. 3:12)

Again, how can Jesus be seated at the right hand of God, if he is God? How can he be seated at his own right hand?

If one looks through the New Testament with unblinkered eyes, one can see that time after time a distinction is made between Jesus Christ and God. For example:

> **But you have come to Mount Zion ... to a judge who is God of all ... and to Jesus ...** (Heb. 12:22)

It is stated in Hebrews that God brought Jesus back from the dead (Heb. 13:20). Clearly God is the subject of this verse, and Jesus is the object.

If Christ is the Son of God, how can he be God? Again, it reads:

> **... Christ was faithful over God's house as a son** (Heb. 4:6).

Clearly there is a distinction here between God and Christ his son.

The following passage makes the distinction between God and Jesus Christ unequivocal:

> **"For God has put all things in subjection under his feet." But when it says, "All things are put in subjection under him," it is plain that he is excepted who put all things under him. When all things are subjected to him, then the Son himself will also be subjected to him who put all things under him, that God may be everything to every one.** (1 Cor. 15:27-28)

It is probably fair to say that on every single page of the New Testament there is an instance where Christ and God are distinguished from each other. Not once is there a reference to any Trinity.

Admittedly there are some verses in the New Testament that appear somewhat ambiguous, but for every one ambiguous verse on the issue regarding the divinity of Christ there are a hundred verses which make it quite clear that Christ is not God.

The Church is simply perpetuating a lie. The Christian life should be based on sincerity, but every vicar must pay lip service to parts of a Creed that they surely cannot truly believe in. The Creed should be amended, so that Christians can recite the Creed with a clear conscience. There is indeed only one God: and his name is Jehovah, not Jesus.

A valuable book which supports this rejection of the doctrine of the Trinity is *The Doctrine of the Trinity, Christianity's Self-inflcted Wound* by A.F Buzzard and C.F. Hunting.

Instead of confronting Islam with the doctrine of the Trinity, Islam should be confronted with this Creed:

There is no god but Jehovah. Jesus of Nazareth is the Messiah, the Son of God.

Abominable practices of Islam

> ... **Mother of the earth's abominations** ... (Rev. 17:5)

The word "abominations" is a reference to both idols and to evil deeds. Abominations are those things that are hated by God, such as murder, lies, and injustice.

Jerusalem was called a harlot in Isaiah because of all the evil that is committed in her (Isa. 1:21).

The title "Mother of abominations" mirrors Jesus' description of Satan: "**a liar and the father of lies**". All lies are hateful to God (Prov. 12:22).

Abominable acts such as female genital mutilation (FMG) are carried out within Arab countries. FMG is practised notably in Somalia, Ethiopia, Sudan and Egypt. 130 million people alive today have undergone this cruel and unnecessary procedure. Muhammad endorsed the practice of cutting a girl's clitoris (*Book 41, Kitab Al-Adab, Hadith 5251*).

In Islam, only men can marry "People of the Book", namely Jews and Christians. Muslims can only marry Hindus or Buddhists if they agree to convert to Islam. It is partly for this reason that Muslims often seek to send their children to single sex schools.

The story about Adam's rib being used to form Eve does not appear in the Koran. A man and wife are not considered "of one flesh" in Islam and consequently marriage is seen in purely contractual terms. This doctrine undermines Jesus' teaching that a man and his wife become one flesh (Matt. 19:4-6)

Some of Muhammad's female companions had up to five husbands during their lifetime, though not at the same time, as polygamy is only permitted to men in Islam.

Men can divorce simply demanding one, but women are often obliged to pay large sums, sometimes the equivalent of a dowry, if they wish to divorce.

If a couple who wish to divorce each other abstain from sexual activity for three menstrual cycles, they are then divorced.

If a couple are divorced and then are reconciled three times, the woman must legally marry another man before she can remarry her first husband. This Islamic practice totally subverts the teaching in the Torah which forbids a man to remarry the same woman after she has been married to another man (Deut. 24:1-4).

Divorce accomplished though the pronouncement of three repetitions of "I divorce you" is still practised in India and Pakistan.

The short-term contracted marriages (*mut'ah*), derives from Muhammad's early teachings and is a commonly accepted practice by Shia Muslims to this day in Iran. The typical *mut'ah* marriage resembles a short-term contractual relationship whereby a man gives something of value to a woman in exchange for the right to have sex with her for the duration of the contractual relationship. It is little more than prostitution.

According to a verse in the Koran, it would appear that sacrifices have no propitiatory value at all:

> *Neither the flesh of animals of your sacrifices nor their blood reaches Allah – it is your righteousness that reaches him.* (Surah 22:37)

This contradicts the Torah which emphasises the importance of blood. This verse also undermines Christianity, which teaches that we are redeemed by the blood of Christ.

In Mecca during the hajj, there is such a surplus of uneaten meat after the sacrifices at Eid that the meat has to be frozen and given to the poor. This is contrary to teaching the Torah which teaches that if the meat has not been eaten by the morrow, it must be burnt (Lev. 7:18).

Eighty lashes is the punishment in Islam for drinking alcohol. Consumption of alcohol is forbidden in the Koran. (5:90) However, righteous Noah drank wine, and Jesus commanded us to remember him whenever we drink wine. By banning alcohol consumption, Islam is banning the commemoration of Jesus' death during Holy Communion.

In Islam, a death sentence imposed on a murderer can be overridden. Family members can accept money (*dijah*) instead. This practice is contrary to the teaching in the Torah which states that the life of a murderer must not be ransomed (Num. 35:31)

Muhammad forbade one of his followers from becoming celibate.

In Islam, the right hand is cut off at the wrist for stealing items over a certain value. Other limbs can be amputated if the thief persists. This punishment is out of all proportion to the crime. The Torah is far more reasonable. A thief must make restitution either by paying double, or even four of five times, depending upon what was stolen (Ex. 22:1).

A Muslim apostate has three days to repent; if he does not repent, he will receive the death penalty.

Jesus taught that a man should pray in secret, and not be like a hypocrite who wants all to see him. Muhammad taught that praying alone was inferior. Muhammad taught that those who pray are closest to Allah when their forehead is on the ground. Yet Jesus clearly expected those who prayed to be standing.

Muslims pray with "many words", contrary to Jesus' teaching.

Muslims wash before prayer. To the contrary, Jesus taught that it was what came out of a man's heart that made him unclean. Jesus did not teach his disciples to wash their hands before eating or praying, yet Muslims have elaborate hand washing and cleaning rituals before they pray (*wudu*). In Islam, cleanliness can be broken for any discharge, urine, faeces, wind, or sleep. Apart from some kinds of discharge, none of the other things make a man unclean according to the Torah. Nowhere in the Torah does it state that a man who is unclean cannot pray. After all, a leper is surely allowed to pray to God, despite the fact that he is unclean.

According to the Torah, if a man is unclean, he must bathe himself and is not clean until the evening. The simple washing of hands does not make an unclean man clean, and even if he bathed, a man would still be unclean during his daily prayers until the evening.

Muhammad taught that if a man had a sexual urge for someone other than his wife, he should have sexual intercourse with his own wife so that his urges would dissipate. This teaching is contrary to Jesus' who taught that a man is committing adultery in his heart when he looks at a woman lustfully (Matt. 5:27).

The Islamic custom to make women cover themselves from head to toe may be the consequence of Muhammad's contradiction of Jesus' teaching. If men are not looking at a women in a lustful manner, there is no need for women to hide their faces and bodies. In Islam, there would appear to be no command that men should not lust after other women.

In the early days of Islam, the majority of Arabs entered Islam so that they would be rewarded with the possessions of those people who would not submit to Islam. The early Muslims profited from slave trading. When invading an enemy country, Muhammad's army killed all the males and took the women and children as slaves. During that time the Arabian Desert became famous for slave trading.

Slave-trading still occurs today. In Sudan, Al-Turabi's Islamic authority has killed Christian men and sold the women and children into slavery. Humanitarian organizations have rushed in to buy them and set them free.

Practically every teaching of Jesus is ignored or contradicted by Islam, despite the fact that the Koran teaches that Jesus was one of the great prophets.

According to Shariah Law, a woman cannot speak alone to a man who is not her husband or relative. In "honour killings", women and girls have been killed for merely speaking to a unrelated man. Often women are killed on the basis of a mere accusation, without any proof.

The concept of "defending Islam", *taqiyya*, is interpreted very broadly and may lead to outright lying. What is said in English to Christians one day might be totally contradicted the next day by the same leaders speaking to Muslims, perhaps in Urdu or Arabic.

Cursing prayers might be said against Christians at Friday prayers and especially during Ramadan night prayers. Death, destruction, disunity and fear are the main things cursing prayers ask for.

To support her claim of rape, a woman needs to be able to provide the testimonies of four males (Surah 24:13). A woman who fails to do so is guilty of adultery, A raped woman cannot testify in court against her rapists. Convicted of rape, a male can have his conviction dismissed by marrying his victim.

Muslim men have sexual rights over any woman not wearing the Hijab.

Christians are often falsely accused of blaspheming Muhammad, a capital offense in Muslim countries.

According to Shariah Law, the following acts are also punishable by death: criticizing any part of the Koran; criticizing Muhammad or denying that he is a prophet; criticizing or denying Allah. A non-Muslim who leads a Muslim away from Islam, or a non-Muslim who marries a Muslim woman must be punished with death. .

A female heir inherits half of what a male inherits.

Islam's denial of the cross

According to Islam, Jesus was a prophet of Allah who taught Islam and who prophesied Muhammad's coming (Surah 61:6).

The Koran teaches that Jesus did not rise from dead, but was taken directly up to heaven. Islamic scholars are in agreement on one issue: he was not crucified. They believe he either survived the crucifixion, or ascended alive into heaven.

Where there has been no death, there can be no resurrection from the dead. The Koran implicitly denies that Jesus rose from the dead. Speaking about the Jews of Jesus' day, the Koran says:

> *That they said [in boast], "We killed Christ Jesus the son of Mary, the Messenger of Allah"; but they killed him not, nor crucified him, but so it was made to appear to them, and those who differ therein are full of doubts, with no [certain] knowledge, but only conjecture to follow, for of a surety they killed him not: Nay, Allah raised him up unto himself; and Allah is exalted in power, wise.* (Sura 4:157-8; Yusuf Ali)

Islam do not acknowledge Jesus as a saviour, and do not acknowledge his death as a ransom. Muslims do not believe that Jesus is the "Son of God" or that he was born to save us from our sins. Muslims still sacrifice animals at Eid at the end of the Hajj.

Muslims do not believe in original sin, but believe that God forgave Adam and Eve, who were reunited on the plain of Ararat. Muslims believe they can receive total forgiveness if they are found on the Mount of Mercy (Mount Arafat) on 9th Dhi'l Hijjah.

You will know them [false prophets] by their fruits (Matt. 7:16)

Muhammad's life and behaviour are important in Islam as they form the *sunna*, or example, that Muslims are supposed to emulate. Many books were written about how Muhammed lived his life by his followers, and his examples and saying as recollected by his followers form the essence of Islam in addition to the Koran itself.

Muhammad was 52 when he contracted to marry Aishah, the daughter of Abu Bakr, when she was only six years old. He had sexual intercourse with her when she was only nine years old. Consequently, according to Shariah Law, a man can cosummate his marriage to an infant when she is 9 years old.

God hates divorce (Mal. 2:16). In Islam, however, a man is permitted to divorce his wife for even trivial reasons.

Muhammad had thirteen wives. Five of Muhammad's wives were divorcees: Zaynab bint Khuzaymah, Zaynab bint Jahsh, Safiyyah, Juwayriyyah and Umm Habibah. Jesus taught that he who marries a woman divorced from her husband commits adultery (Luke 16:18). Israelite priests were forbidden in the Torah from marrying a divorced woman (Lev. 21:7).

Three of Muhammad's four daughters also experienced divorce.

Muhammad was also allowed to have sex with his slaves. Any offspring were not considered to be his sons.

The Bible encourages kindness to orphans, yet Islamic law prohibits adoption. Zaynab, the wife of Muhammad's adopted son, became Muhammad's fifth wife. The marriage was brought about by Muhammad's abolition of adoption:

> *"Allah has not made your adopted sons . . . your real sons"* (Surah 33:4)

Zaid was no longer considered Muhammad's son and so Muhammad was free to marry Zaynab. In marrying his son-in-law's wife, Muhammad had in effect committed incest according to the Torah:

> **If a man lies with his daughter-in-law, both of them shall be put to death; they have committed incest, their blood is upon them.** (Lev. 20:12).

According to Jesus' teaching, Muhammad was also guilty of committing adultery "in his heart" by lusting after another man's wife (Matt. 5:28)..

Islam rejects the Bible as corrupted but perverts it itself

The Koran says that Islam came before Judaism and Christianity and that it was the religion practiced by Abraham.

The Koran states that the Jews corrupted the Torah:

> *A party of them (Jewish rabbis) used to hear the Word of Allah [the Taurat (Torah)], then they used to change it knowingly after they understood it.* (Surah 2:75).

This alleged corruption made it necessary for Allah to send the Koran. Muhammad taught that Christians removed reference of Muhammad's coming from the scriptures.

The Koran perverts many of the biblical stories to such an extent that they barely resemble the original story found in the Bible.

29

JERUSALEM IS NOT BABYLON THE GREAT

Mecca, not Jerusalem, is guilty of the death of the saints

> **. . . in her [Babylon the Great] was found the blood of the prophets and saints and all who have been slain upon the earth . . .** (Rev. 18:24)

The destruction of Jerusalem at the hands of the Romans in 70 AD was retribution for the fact that city had killed the Christ and the prophets (Luke 13:31-34). Jesus prophesied that all the righteous blood from Abel to the blood of Zechariah son of Berechiah will fall upon Jerusalem (Matt. 23:34–35). The fact that Jesus draws the line at the blood of Zechariah son of Berechiah, however, indicates that the blood of those killed later will not fall on Jerusalem.

Surely Jerusalem is innocent when it comes to the deaths of those killed in the name of Islam.

Jerusalem has not been inhabited by Jews for nearly the past two thousand years and is not guilty for the killing of the saints during this period.

Even if one takes Jerusalem to represent Judaism in general, the amount of Christians killed by Jews is dwarfed by the number of saints killed by Muslims. Excluding those killed during battles of *jihad*, around nine million Christians have been martyred by Muslims.

Such facts indicate that Mecca, not Jerusalem, is Babylon the Great.

The "great city" where Christ was crucified is not Babylon the Great

> **. . . and their dead bodies will lie in the street of the great city which is allegorically called Sodom and Egypt, where their Lord was crucified.** (Rev. 11:8)

The terms used to describe this multitude of onlookers are identical to the words used to denote those multitudes over whom the Beast will wield authority (Rev. 13:7). These are the multitudes referred to here in Rev. 11:9, not those that Babylon the Great rules over.

This list of **peoples and tribes and tongues and nations** (Rev. 11:9) reminds one of the represenatives of the **people, nations and languages** from all the provinces governed by the king of Babylon who were commanded to worship the statue set up in the plain of Dura by Nebuchadnezzar (Dan. 3:4). This association with idol-worship again points to Jerusalem, as it is from Jerusalem that the False Prophet will exert his influence and make people worship the image of the Beast.

The above verse (Rev. 11:9) clearly denotes Jerusalem as the **great city** where the two Lampstands will be killed by the Beast, for it is the city where Jesus Christ was crucified (Rev. 11:8). However, Jerusalem is not Babylon the Great, the Harlot city. Despite the fact that Babylon the Great is likewise described as the **great city** (Rev. 17:18) and rules over **peoples, multitudes and nations and tongues** (Rev. 17:15), Jerusalem is not Babylon the Great.

Jerusalem here is allegorically called Sodom and Egypt (Rev. 11:8). This title points away from the Harlot city, for that city is allegorically called Babylon (the Great), not Sodom or Egypt.

A precedent has already been set in Ezekiel for using the metaphor of Sodom for Jerusalem:

> **Behold, this was the guilt of your sister Sodom: she and her daughters had pride, surfeit of food, and prosperous ease, but did not aid the poor**

and needy. They were haughty and did abominable things before me... (Eze. 16:49-50)

It must be remembered that the False Prophet, who will be an Israelite, will exercise the same authority as the Beast in his presence. The Beast sits in the Temple to show that he is God. The Beast and False Prophet will at some point exercise their authority from Jerusalem.

The Table below illustrates these correlations.

Rev. 11:9	Rev. 13:7	Rev. 17:15	Dan. 3:4
peoples	**tribes**	**peoples**	**peoples**
tribes	**peoples**	**multitudes**	**nations**
tongues	**tongues**	**tongues**	**tongues**
nations	**nations**	**nations**	

Islam: drunk with the blood of saints

And I saw the woman, drunk with the blood of saints and the blood of the martyrs of Jesus (Rev. 17:6).

Nine million Christians have been martyred by Islam. This figure does not include the 50 million Christians who have died in wars by jihad.

Christians have faced increasing levels of persecution in the Muslim world. A report by Aid to the Church in Need said that the persecution of Christians is so severe that they are set to disappear completely from parts of the Middle-East within a decade. A report commissioned by the British foreign secretary Jeremy Hunt and published in May 2019 stated that the persecution of Christians in the Middle East is arguably coming close to meeting the international definition of genocide, according to that adopted by the UN.

Around 200 million people in total are estimated to have been killed by Muslims through jihad and persecution according to *World Christian Trends* (D. Barrett & T. Johnson).

30

JIHAD AND ISLAMIC CONQUESTS

Jihad

Ninety per cent of all the fighting in the world involves radical Islamic terrorist groups. Islam is primarily a politico-military enterprise. As Mark Gabriel, writes in *Islam and Terrorism*, the history of Islam could only be characterized as "a river of blood."

Muhammad washed his followers' swords, Jesus their feet. Muhammad personally led 27 battles. He also sent his army out 47 times without him.

Within four years of Muhammad's death, roughly a third of a million Christians were slaughtered. Over the next ten years another million were killed. Within one hundred years of the birth of Islam, half of global Christianity was under Islam.

Muslims believe that the only way to know for sure that you will get into Paradise is to die in jihad, fighting the enemy of Islam.

Many of the milder verses found in the Koran have been cancelled out by the Islamic doctrine of *Naskh*: where there is a contradiction, new revelations override previous. If a verse is *nasikh* (overridden), it is as if that verse does not even exist.

The Koran states:

> *"When you meet the unbelievers in the battlefield, strike off their heads and, when you have laid them low, bind your captives firmly"* (47:4)

Surah 9:5, known as the verse of the sword, cancelled out previous verses:

> *Fight and slay the Pagans wherever you find them, and seize them, beleaguer them, and lie in wait for them in every stratagem (of war); but if they repent, and establish regular prayers and practise regular charity, then open the way for them: for Allah is Oft-forgiving, Most Merciful.*

Sixty per cent of the Koranic verses talk about jihad, the driving force of Islam.

Killing innocent people in the name of Allah is a continual practice of Islam worldwide and is happening even today to millions of Christians in the south Sudan, Egypt, Nigeria and other countries.

The greatest curbs on religion freedoms take place in Muslim-majority countries. Pondering whether the notion of jihad is more embedded in Islam than other religions, Rupert Shortt writes in *Christianophobia*:

> we must confront directly a question which has haunted a large portion of this book. Is there a problem with Islam as such . . . ?

Jihad is carried out in order to achieve the ultimate goal of Islam: to establish Islamic authority over the whole world. Judaism, Christianity and Communism are seen by Muslims as the three main ideologies standing in the way of the worldwide Islamic revolution. Muslims believe there are only two types of nations: the house of Islam and the house of war. Jihad is fighting anybody who stands in the way of spreading Islam, or fighting anyone who refuses to enter into Islam (based on Surah 8:39). Christians are a target of the world conquest because they resist conversion.

All political systems must be based on Allah's teachings and nothing else. Jihad has succeeded in its mission when a nation declares Islam both their religion and their form of government. Such a government has been accomplished in Iran (Ayatollah Khomeini's revolution), Sudan (under Hasan al-Turabi) and Afghanistan (under the Taliban).

Since the revolution, Iran has supported all of the Islamic fundamentalist groups that have terrorized the world.

Muslims believe that war requires deception and that lying is an important element of war. Muslims will lie if doing so would help Islam. Their loyalty is to Islam, not to the nation where they are living. All the fundamentalist movements in the Arab countries forbid their members from joining the military.

True Muslim Palestinians, like members of Hamas, are willing to die for Islam and the holy sites. One group might fight for land in order to establish a communist government, but diehard Muslims like Hamas look at the other group as betrayers of Islam.

Egypt is the centre of modern terrorism, being the capital of Islamic education for the entire world. Al-Azhar sends missionaries everywhere. Though the terrorists in Egypt did not succeed in overturning their own government initially, they influenced radical groups in other countries such as Libya, Tunisia, Algeria and Sudan.

Over the last decade in Algeria, more than 150,000 people have been killed in the attempt to keep fundamentalist Islam from ruling their nation.

In the 1974 Turkish invasion of Cyprus, Greeks were ordered to move out in 24 hours. Churches were burnt down or converted into mosques.

The Armenian Genocide

In the 1822 massacre of Chios by Muslim Turks, thousands of islanders were either killed or sold into slavery by Istanbul. Only 2,000 Greeks were left on the island, 25,000 had been killed, and 40,000 enslaved.

Between 1915 and 1921 the Ottoman Empire conducted a series of massacres against ancient indigenous Christian populations of what is today western and eastern Turkey, and northern Iraq. The Armenian Genocide accounted for the deaths of 3,500,000 Armenian, Assyrian, Greek and Maronite Christians, and the deportation and destitution of many more.

During the Armenian Genocide, torture was commonplace. Crucifixion was treated as a sport, the victims mocked. Policemen and soldiers ransacked Christian churches and handed bishops and priests over to the mob. Doctors and teachers were hanged in batches on gallows in the town squares. Men were beheaded with swords, hanged or shot, simply for being Armenians. Some were hacked to death by Turkish peasants with scythes and spades. Convicts were let out of prison to join in the killing. On one particular death march, virtually all 18,000 were dead within a week of setting out. Women had to readily submit to sex or were whipped. In her home town, one Armenian girl witnessed 20 Armenian women being forced to dance while being whipped across their breasts so that their clothes fell off. Their own children were forced to clap faster and faster or they were whipped themselves, crying pitifully. Smartly-dressed Turkish townspeople clapped along delightedly. Two soldiers then doused the women in kerosene and burnt them to death in front of their children, some of whom were as young as two. On the death march out into the desert, the same girl witnessed a policeman slash off the breasts of a girl who resisted him with his sword. She bled to death next to her breasts.[39]

Beheadings and other atrocities perpetrated by Islamic State

> **Also I saw the souls of those who had been beheaded for their testimony to Jesus ...** (Rev. 20:4)

During the period 2014-2017, the Islamic State of Iraq and Syria (ISIS), (also known as the Islamic State of Iraq and the Levant (ISIL)), beheaded around 100 Syrian soldiers as well as several Iraqi, Lebanese, and Kurdish fighters.

Islamic State also beheaded two American journalists (James Foley and Steven Sotloff), one American (Peter Kassig) and two British aid workers (David Haines and Alan Henning), 30 Ethiopian Christians, 21 Egyptian Coptic Christians in Libya, a French mountaineering guide (Herve Gourdel) and a Japanese national (Haruna Yukawa). Islamic State has beheaded many other people besides these.

Islamic State have murdered tens of thousands of civilians and kidnapped several thousand people. The organization has committed torture and mass rapes. It has sanctioned forced marriages and practiced ethnic cleansing. It has committed mass murder, genocide and robbery, and has engaged in extortion, smuggling and slavery. In its adherence to Shariah law, Islamic State has carried out crucifixions, mutilations, the stoning of adults and children, and the burning of people alive.

---

39 "Genocide of the Christians", *Daily Mail*, 18.04.2015

Islamic State has engaged in public mass executions of Syrian and Iraqi soldiers and civilians, sometimes forcing prisoners to dig their own graves before shooting them. Islamic State executed up to 1,700 Shia Iraqi Air Force cadets from Camp Speicher near Tikrit on 12 June 2014. Islamic State executed 250 Syrian soldiers captured at the Al-Tabqa air base between 27 and 28 August 2014. In Palmyra up to 280 Syrian soldiers and government loyalists were shot in the head or beheaded in a public square on 22 May 2015 and in Deir ez-Zor Islamic State killed at least 300 Syrian soldiers, pro-government militiamen and their families on 16 January 2016. ISIS executed 600 Shia prisoners in Mosul in June 2014.

In November 2014, there were reports that Islamic State fighters massacred more than 630 members of the (Sunni Arab) Albu Nimr tribe in Iraq. In 2014 Islamic State executed at least 150 women from the Albu Nimr tribe in Falluja for refusing to marry ISIS militants.

In northern Iraq, Islamic State shot around 5000 Yazidi men, bulldozing their bodies into mass graves. 7000 Yazidi women were held in detention centres to be offered as slaves.

This section is by no means a comprehensive record of all the atrocities committed by Islamic State. These are so numerous that several books could be filled just to record each one.

Ancient Babylon: type for Babylon the Great

The Greek words used in Revelation for "Babylon the great", Βαβυλων η μεγαλη, appear only once in the Septuagint (Dan. 4:20), in the chapter where King Nebuchadnezzar aggrandizes himself in his own eyes when he beholds the glory of Babylon.

The prophet Jeremiah describes Babylon as the "**hammer of the whole earth**" (Jer. 51:20-23), an appropriate term for Islam given its conquest over so many nations and lands. The Muslim conquerors were like a hammer too, destroying all the nations around them who would not submit to Islam.

The fate of Babylon the Great in Revelation echoes the fate of the Babylon of Belshazzar. Just as Jeremiah ordered Seraiah to bind a stone to the book containing his prophecies against Babylon and to throw it into the midst of the Euphrates (Jer. 51:63), so an angel takes up a great stone and throws it into the sea to represent the violence with which Babylon the Great shall be thrown down in Revelation (Rev. 18:21)

Like Babylon the Great, Nebuchadnezzar's Babylon was seated on many waters: **O ye who dwells by many waters.** (Jer. 51:13)

Life of Muhammad

Medina, where Muhammad fled in 622 is the second holiest site in Islam and Muhammed is buried there. This flight, or *hegira*, marks Year One of the Islamic calendar. Before Muhammed's day, it was a Jewish city, called Yathrib.

Muhammad, born around 570 in Mecca, the prophet and founder of Islam.

Muhammad was orphaned at an early age; he was raised under the care of his paternal uncle Abu Talib. Aged forty, he reported being visited by Gabriel in a cave, where he received his first revelation. Three years later, Muhammad started preaching these revelations publicly, proclaiming that he was a prophet.

Muhammad gained few early followers, and met hostility from some Meccans. To escape persecution, Muhammad and his followers migrated from Mecca to Medina (then known as Yathrib) in the year 622. This event, the Hegira (*Hijra*) marks the beginning of the Islamic calendar, known as the Hijri Calendar.

In Medina, Muhammad united the tribes under the Constitution of Medina. In December 629, after eight years of intermittent conflict with Meccan tribes, Muhammad gathered an army of 10,000 Muslim converts and marched on the city of Mecca. The attack went largely uncontested and Muhammad seized the city with little bloodshed. Before his death on 8 June 632, most of the Arabian Peninsula had converted to Islam

History of Muslim conquests

The Muslim conquests brought about the collapse of the Sassanid Empire and a great territorial loss for the Byzantine Empire. In the space of a hundred years the Muslim armies were able to establish the largest empire until that time.

The Arab conquest of the Levant occurred in the first half of the 7th century, later to become the Islamic Province of Bilad al-Sham. The real invasion began in 634 under the Rashidun Caliphs Abu Bakr and Umar ibn Khattab, with Khalid ibn al-Walid as their most important military leader.

Arab Muslim forces had laid control of Mesopotamia (638), Syria (641), Egypt (642), and had invaded Armenia, all previously territories split between the warring Byzantine and Persian Empires.

In 644 at Madinah, Caliph Umar (Omar) was succeeded by Uthman ibn Affan (Othman), during whose twelve-year rule Armenia, Cyprus, and all of Iran, would be added to the growing Islamic empire; Afghanistan and North Africa would receive major invasions; and Muslim sea raids would range from Rhodes to the southern coasts of the Iberian Peninsula. The Byzantine navy would be defeated in the eastern Mediterranean.

In a series of three stages, the conquest of the Byzantine-controlled North Africa commenced in 647 and concluded in 709 with the "Byzantine" Roman Empire losing its last remaining strongholds to the Umayyad Caliphate.

Arab Muslims first attacked the Sassanid territory in 633, when Khalid ibn Walid invaded Mesopotamia. The Muslim conquest of Persia, led to the end of the Sasanian Empire in 651 and the eventual decline of the Zoroastrian religion in Persia.

The Islamic conquest of Afghanistan (642–870) began after the Islamic conquest of Persia was completed. By 667, the Afghan area was under invasion by the Arabs but in 683 Kabul and other parts of Afghanistan fought with resistance and completely routed the invading army which was led by the Governor of Seistan. The near-complete conversion of Afghans to Islam was during the period of the Ghaznavids in the 10th century with Kafiristan holding out until Emir Abdur Rahman Khan conquered and forcibly converted them in the 1890s.

The Umayyad conquest of Spain was the initial expansion of the Umayyad Caliphate over Spain extending from 711 to 788. The conquest resulted in the destruction of the Visigothic Kingdom and the establishment of the independent Emirate of Cordoba under Abd ar-Rahman I, who completed the unification of Muslim-ruled Iberia, or al-Andalus

(756–788). The conquest marks the westernmost expansion of both the Umayyad Caliphate and Muslim rule into Europe.

Muslim conquests on the Indian subcontinent mainly took place from the 12th to the 16th centuries, though earlier Muslim conquests made limited inroads into modern Afghanistan and Pakistan as early as the time of the Rajput kingdoms in the 8th century. With the establishment of the Delhi Sultanate, Islam spread across large parts of the subcontinent.

Prior to the rise of the Maratha Empire, which was followed by the conquest of India by the British East India Company, the Muslim Mughal Empire was able to annex or subjugate most of India's kings.

From the time of the Umayyad Dynasty to the last Mughal, Bahadur Shah Zafar (1858), entire cities were burnt down and hundreds of thousands killed in every campaign, with similar numbers deported as slaves. Every new invader made hills of Hindu skulls.

The conquest of Afghanistan in the year 1000 was followed by the annihilation of the Hindu population; the region is still called the Hindu Kush, which means "Hindu slaughter."

The Muslim invasions into the Indian subcontinent began with the invasion of India by Mahmud Ghazni about 1000 AD, and they lasted for several centuries.

Contemporary records boasted about and glorified the crimes that were committed – and the genocide of tens of millions of Hindus, Sikhs, Buddhist and Jainist, mass rapes of women and the destruction of thousands of ancient Hindu and Buddhist temples.

The conquest of India is probably the bloodiest story in history. The Islamic historians and scholars have recorded the slaughters of Hindus, abduction of Hindu women and children to slave markets and the destruction of temples carried out by the warriors of Islam during 800 AD to 1700 AD. Millions of Hindus were converted to Islam by the sword during this period.

The Afghan ruler Mahmud of Ghazni invaded India no less than seventeen times between 1001– 1026. Entering Somnath on one of his annual raids, he slaughtered all 50,000 inhabitants.

The biggest slaughters also took place during those of Mohammed Ghori and his lieutenants and those under the Delhi Sultanate (1206-1526). When Qutb-ul-Din Aibak, the First Sultan of Delhi (1194-1210), conquered Meerat, he demolished all the Hindu temples of the city and erected mosques in their place. In the city of Aligarh, he converted Hindu inhabitants to Islam by the sword and beheaded all those who adhered to their own religion. He killed and enslaved hundreds of thousands.

When the Alaul-Din Khilji (1295-1316) captured the city of Kambayat he killed the adult male Hindu inhabitants and made about twentv thousand Hindu women his private slaves.

Timur, the Turkic conqueror and founder of the Timurid Dynasty, executed 100,000 Hindu prisoners of war during his Indian campaign (1398 – 1399). Timur describes the scene when his army conquered the Indian city of Delhi:

> In a short space of time all the people in the [Delhi] fort were put to the sword, and in the course of one hour the heads of 10,000 infidels were cut off. The sword of Islam was washed in the blood of the infidels, and all the goods and effects, the treasure and the grain which for many a long year had been stored in the fort became the spoil of my soldiers. They set fire to the houses and reduced them to ashes, and they razed the buildings and the fort to the ground . . . All these infidel Hindus were slain, their women and children, and their property and goods became the spoil of the victors. I proclaimed throughout the camp that every man who had infidel prisoners should put them to death, and whoever neglected to do so should himself be executed and his property given to the informer. When this order became known to the ghazis of Islam, they drew their swords and put their prisoners to death.

The Mughal emperor Babur (who ruled India from 1526 -1530) wrote:

> I attacked Chanderi and by the grace of Allah captured it in a few hours. We got the infidels slaughtered and the place which had been Daru'l-Harb (nation of non-muslims) for years was made into a Daru'l-Islam (a muslim nation).

The Bahmani sultans in central India (1347-1528) would set the killing of a hundred thousand Hindus as a minimum goal whenever they felt like punishing the Hindus.

The atrocities of the Mughal ruler Shah Jahan (1628 – 1658) are mentioned in the contemporary record:

> he carried on a ruthless war in the Hindu territory beyond Indus . . . The

> sword of Islam yielded a rich crop of converts . . . Most of the women (to save their honour) burnt themselves to death. Those captured were distributed among Muslim Mansabdars (Noblemen)

The Afghan ruler Ahmad Shah Abdali attacked India in 1757 and made his way to the holy Hindu city of Mathura, the birthplace of Krishna. The atrocities that followed are recorded thus:

> Abdali's soldiers would be paid 5 Rupees for every enemy head brought in. Every horseman had loaded up all his horses with the plundered property, and atop of it rode the girl-captives and the slaves. The severed heads were tied up in rugs like bundles of grain and placed on the heads of the captives . . . Then the heads were stuck upon lances and taken to the gate of the chief minister for payment.
>
> It was an extraordinary display! Daily did this manner of slaughter and plundering proceed. And at night the shrieks of the women captives who were being raped, deafened the ears of the people . . . All those heads that had been cut off were built into pillars, and the captive men upon whose heads those bloody bundles had been brought in, were made to grind corn, and then their heads too were cut off. These things went on all the way to the city of Agra, nor was any part of the country spared.

It is estimated that the Hindu population in India decreased by 80 million between 1000 AD and 1525 AD. The holocaust of the Hindus in India lasted roughly 800 years, till the brutal regimes were effectively overpowered by the Sikhs in the Panjab and the Hindu Maratha armies in other parts of India in the late 1700s.

A thorough examination of the history of Islamic *jihad* and of its negative impact on the vanquished nations can be found in *Global Jihad*, a book by Patrick Sookhdeo. It covers all aspects of *jihad* in great depth.

In Babylon the Great was found t**he blood of prophets and of saints, and of all who have been slain on earth** (Rev. 18:24). The endless slaughter will be requited by God:

> **Babylon must fall for the slain of Israel, as for Babylon have fallen the slain of all the earth.** (Jer. 51:49)

Jihadis motivated by false assurance of entry into heaven

Dying in jihad is the only way a Muslim can be assured of getting into Paradise. According to Islam, when a man dies during jihad, he goes to heaven and Allah rewards him with enough energy to enjoy sex with seventy vrigins the first night. This expectation of sexual gratification in heaven is erroneous, for no kind of marital relations takes place in heaven. Jesus taught:

> **. . . in the resurrection they neither marry nor are given in marriage, but are like angels in heaven.** (Matt. 22:30)

31

MECCA: THE COUNTERFEIT CITY

The Harlot's attire is likened to the High Priest's

> **. . . clothed in fine linen, in purple and scarlet, bedecked with gold, with jewels, and with pearls!** (Rev. 18:16)

Islam is a counterfeit to the true religion which is why the Harlot's attire reflects the Jewish priestly colors of scarlet, purple, and gold.

The garments worn by Babylon the Great are similar to that of a High Priest whose breastplate of judgement is made of **gold, blue and purple and scarlet stuff, and fine twined linen** (Ex. 28:15). Also made out of these same materials were the High Priest's girdle, his ephod, and the stitched pomegranates on his garments.

Many of the items for the tabernacle were made out of similar materials: the curtains of the tabernacle, the veil of the temple, the hanging for the door of the tent with lampstands, the hanging for the gate of the court and the cloths of service.

It is fitting that Babylon the Great is described in terms befitting that of a High Priest because Islam declares that it is the only true religion. It wishes to replace Judaism and Christianity, and destroy all remnants of these religions.

Mecca has set itself up as a replacement to the Temple in Jerusalem, with Muslims having to pray in the direction of the Kaaba in Mecca (the *qibla*) instead of towards Jerusalem.

It is appropriate therefore that Mecca is compared to the Temple through the description of the Harlot's attire, for Mecca has taken upon herself the attributes of the Temple in Jerusalem.

The writing on the Harlot's forhead is like the writing on the High Priest's crown

> **And they made the plate of the holy crown of pure gold, and wrote upon it an inscription, like the engraving of a signet, "Holy to the Lord." And they tied to it a lace of blue, to fasten it on the turban ...** (Ex. 39:30, 31)

With words enscribed on her forehead, the Harlot city is being compared unfavourably with the High Priest. Babylon the Great's attire is similar to that of the High Priest, and just as the High Priest wears a plate of gold on his forehead which has an inscription, so the Harlot has an inscription on her forehead.

It should be noted that the Greek for Babylon (Βαβυλον) sounds very similar to the Greek word βεβηλον which means "profane".

Babylon the Great is profane and unholy, but the High Priest should be holy: **[the High Priest] shall not profane** (βεβηλωσει) **the sanctuary of his God ...** (LXX Lev. 21:12). The priests must be ceremonially clean in order to perform their duties. Priests cannot marry a divorced woman or a prostitute. A High Priest must marry a virgin. No descendant of Aaron with even a blemish can offer the offerings.

The contents of the golden cup in the hand of the Harlot is full of abominations and uncleanness. These things are in total violation of the sanctity expected of the High Priest with whom Babylon the Great is being compared. The great city is not fit for priesthood.

Reference to the Harlot's forehead recalls the verse in Jeremiah:

> **... you have a harlot's brow, you refuse to be ashamed ...** (Jer. 3:3).

Mecca: counterfeit of the New Jerusalem

Mecca is a counterfeit to the heavenly New Jerusalem.

The Zamzam well in Mecca is like the river of the water of life (Rev. 22:2).

Just as "**nothing unclean shall enter, nor anyone who practices abomination or falsehood**" the New Jerusalem (Rev.21:27), so no non-Muslim can enter Mecca or Medina.

Kaaba means "cube" in Arabic. The holy city Jerusalem coming down out of heaven has the dimensions of a cube too (Rev. 21:16)

New Jerusalem is described as "**the holy city, new Jerusalem**." "The Holy City" is one of Mecca's names.

The New Jerusalem is "**prepared as a bride adorned for her husband**" (Rev. 21:2). The Kaaba too is described in a similar way, with its veil compared to that of a woman. During Hajj the huge black drape is lifted. Similarly, on Hajj, women must unveil their faces.

The Harlot is contrasted unfavourably with New Jerusalem

Babylon the Great is compared unfavourably with the New Jerusalem.

The city's title itself contrasts the offspring of the Harlot with the seed of the Jerusalem above, whose offspring keep the commandments of God and bear testimony to Jesus (Rev. 12:17).

Twelve stones with the names of the sons of Israel are set into the High Priest's breast-piece of judgment (Ex. 28: 17-2). These foreshadow the twelve different jewels that adorn the foundations of the holy city's wall (Rev. 21: 19-20). In this way the High Priest himself represents the holy city New Jerusalem.

The contents of the Harlot's golden **cup** (ποτηριον) are to be contrasted with the **river** (ποταμος) **of the water of life** found in the New Jerusalem (Rev. 22:2).

Likewise, **the gold and jewels and pearls** with which the Harlot is bedecked are to be compared to the description of the New Jerusalem. The New Jerusalem's wall is built of **jasper**, and the city is **pure gold**. The foundations of the city's wall are adorned with **every jewel**. The gates are **pearls**. The streets of the city are **pure gold** (Rev. 21: 18-21).

Whereas the Harlot's cup is full of abominations, **nothing unclean** shall enter the New Jerusalem, nor any one who **practises abomination or falsehood** (Rev. 21:27).

New Jerusalem is foreshadowed in the description of the Woman, who represents the Jerusalem above, and hence all those who fear God and bear witness to Jesus. She is **clothed with the sun, with the moon under her feet, and on her head a crown of twelve stars** (Rev. 12:1). These twelve stars represent not only the twelve tribes of Israel as envisioned in Joseph's dream (Gen. 37:9), but also the **angels** (Rev. 21:12) who are found at the **twelve gates** which are inscribed with the names of the twelve tribes of Israel.

The description of the Woman who finds refuge in the wilderness does not entirely translate across to the description of the New Jerusalem, for the New Jerusalem has no need for sun or moon. Night shall be no more, God being the light of his servants (Rev. 22:5).

The Harlot is arrayed in purple and scarlet. Scarlet is the colour of sin

> **. . . though your sins are like scarlet, they shall be white as snow; though they are red like crimson, they shall become like wool.** (Isa. 1:18)

The Bride of the Lamb, the New Jerusalem, to the contrary is "**clothed with fine linen, bright and pure**". The fine linen is the righteous deeds of the saints (Rev. 19:8).

The Woman gave birth to the Church, but the Harlot attempts to exterminate the Church.

Babylon the Great is compared with the harlot city Tyre

> **The woman was arrayed in purple and scarlet . . .** (Rev. 17:4)

The reference to **purple and scarlet** points to the city of Tyre, a city famed for its purple.

Tyrian purple (aka Royal purple or Imperial purple) is a dye extracted from the murex shellfish. Its difficulty of manufacture, striking purple to red colour range, and resistance to fading made clothing dyed using Tyrian purple highly desirable and expensive. The Tyrians gained great fame as sellers of purple and exported its manufacture to its colonies, notably Carthage. Tyrian purple was adopted by the Romans as a symbol of imperial authority and status.

The Greek for Tyrian purple is πορφύρα, *porphura*. This is the same word that is found in Revelation that is translated "purple".

The Old Testament phrase corresponding to **purple and scarlet** is: *blue, purple, scarlet and fine twisted linen*, as found for example in this verse:

> **"Moreover, you shall make the tabernacle with ten curtains of fine twined linen, and blue, and purple, and scarlet stuff; with cherubim skilfully worked shall you make them."** (Ex. 26:1)

Almost everything in the service of the Temple that was made from cloth was made out of these colours. However, the absence of the colour blue in the description of the Harlot's attire shows that this city has more in common with Tyre, than with the Temple in Jerusalem.

In Ezekiel chapter 27 the same three groups express sadness over Tyre's demise as here in Revelation chapter 18: kings of the earth, merchants, and the mariners. The description of Babylon the Great in chapter 18 of Revelation is based upon the lamentation over Tyre in Ezekiel chapter 27 and 28.

The Tyre metaphor in Isaiah is the closest verbally to the text in Revelation:

> **[Tyre] will return to her hire, and will play the harlot with all the kingdoms of the world upon the face of the earth.** (Isa. 23:17)

Tyre is one of the few cities in the Bible which is called a harlot, other than cities of Israel.

The repeated reference to the Ezekiel 26-28 pronouncement of Tyre's judgment in Rev. 18:9-22 and the specific allusion to Isa. 23:8 in Rev. 18:23 also points to Tyre.

Purple and scarlet represent splendour and magnificence, and wealth. Great wealth accumulated to the capital cities of the caliphates of Islam. In its day, Cairo was the largest city in the world. Istanbul was reckoned one of greatest cities in the world, renowned for its wealth, its harems, and its slave trade.

This list of products in Revelation (Rev. 18:12-13) is based almost entirely on the lamentation against Tyre in Ezek. 27:7-25, and there are in fact very few discrepancies between the two.

The probable inspiration for the double woe in Rev. 18:16 (**"alas, alas"**) is Exek. 16:23, where the prophet announces "**woe, woe**" to Jerusalem because of her idolatry.

Satanic nature of the Harlot

> **. . . behold, a great red dragon, with seven heads . . .** (Rev. 12:3)

That each hill upon which Islam (Babylon the Great) is seated should be represented by a head of the Red Dragon indicates how closely this city is associated with Satan. The city and the Red Dragon are almost as one. The great city Babylon the Great is thus of a satanic nature.

One should not be surprised to find that **in her was found the blood of prophets and of saints, and of all who have been slain on earth** (Rev. 18:24).

Christian C. Sahner has written the first book ever written about Christian martyrdom in the first centuries (7th to 9th) after the rise of Islam entitled *Christian Martyrs Under Islam*. Named "neomartyrs" at the time, hariogaphies number these martyrs at 270.

The execution of Perfectus is one example of such a martyrdom that occurred in Spain. He had confessed to a group of Muslims that he viewed Muhammad as a false prophet, that he saw him as a carnal man, as evidenced by his lust for Zaynah, the wife of his adopted son. Hauled before a court, he was given the chance to repent but said:

> I have reviled and do revile your prophet as a man of demons, a sorcerer, an adulterer and a liar.

He was executed in front of the praetorium.

32

ISLAM'S CURRENT WAR AGAINST THE CHRISTIANITY

The Organization of Islamic Cooperation (OIC): operates like a caliphate

The Organization of Islamic Cooperation (OIC) is the closest thing to a caliphate in existence today. The Secretary of the Organization of Islamic Cooperation (OIC) is on record saying that the "OIC fulfils the function of a Caliphate".

The OIC is an international organization founded in 1969, consisting of 57 Muslim or Muslim-majority member states, with a collective population of over 1.6 billion as of 2008. It is the second largest international organization after the UN. (56 of its members are also member states of the United Nations.)

The OIC controls the lion's share of global energy resources. Some of its member states are the richest in the world. The Muslim world will continue to become increasingly powerful through its wealth, oil power and systems of using wealth, which do not rely on the traditional Western banking systems.

The OIC is the collective voice of the Muslim world, claiming to "safeguard and protect the interests of the Muslim world in the spirit of promoting international peace and harmony". Its beginning was brought about by a fire in 1969 started in the Al-Aqsa Mosque in Israel-controlled Jerusalem which Israel blamed on a Christian fundamentalist called Denis Michael Rohan. Amin al-Husseini, the former Mufti of Jerusalem, called the arson a "Jewish crime" and called for all Muslim heads of state to convene a summit.

The OIC is close to the Muslim World League of the Muslim Brotherhood.

Networks that spread global governance overlap where the influence of the OIC at the UN is paramount, such as the EAD, Medea, the Barcelona Process, the Anna Lindh Foundation, the Alliance of Civilizations (AoC), EMPA (Euro-Med Parliament Associaton), and UNRWA.

The transformation of independent nation states into a unified Europe is integrated with international organizations like the UN, UNESCO, the OIC, and so forth.

The OIC promotes human rights for fellow Muslims that are not reciprocated to non-Muslims in the countries of OIC member states because two completely different Declarations of human rights are being used. Arab nations subscribe to the OIC's 1991 Cairo Declaration on Human Rights in Islam in which all humans are united in submission to Allah. The 1948 Declaration and the Cairo Declaration on Human Rights in Islam are two totally different concepts.

The OIC was the body behind the CAIRO Declaration of Human Rights—essentially Human Rights according to the Islamic *Sharia*. Whereas the 1948 UN Charter of Human Rights gave Muslim women equal rights to men for example, the 1990 CAIRO Declaration maintains women as inferior as per the Sharia. The Cairo Declaration of Human Rights has been signed by all 57 Islamic Nations and submitted to the United Nations to represent the views of these Islamic Nations, despite what the UN Charter maintains about tolerance and equality.

The term "Islamophobia" was created by the Muslim Brotherhood and then adopted by the OIC to hold anyone to account anywhere in the world that was opposed to Islam. In the 2005 OIC Summit a ten-year Action Program was created which included combating Islamophobia. Section three of that plan moved that they involve the UN to "adopt a UN international resolution to counter Islamophobia and get all of its member states including the West to enact laws to counter Islamophobia including deterrent punishments". The OIC is actually forcing Sharia onto the West using the United Nations.

Islamic lobby groups pressurize their adopted country to expand their Judaeo-Christianbasis to include Islam, thus creating a society with a Judaeo-Christian-Islamic basis. They then seek for Islam special priveleges.

The OIC is supportive of jihadist movements that are resisting "foreign occupation", including those in "occupied" Indian Kashmir, and condemns the "humiliation and oppression" of Muslims in India.

The OIC has an Islamic International Court of Justice with an international mandate that could try foreigners, both Muslim and non-Muslim (blasphemers, apostates) who have broken laws of sharia anywhere.

Jerusalem will not be the seat of the next caliphate

At the Rabat and Amman conferences organised by ISESCO, a major organ of the OIC and is responsible in the fields of education and cultures, denial was made of any trace of Judaism in the lands of the Bible. The objective of the Amman conference was to establish a global strategy for the re-Islamization of Jerusalem (al-Quds) because as one lecturer explained:

> Jerusalem is the cornerstone of the spiritual edifice of the Zionist Jewish identity. Were it to be dislodged, the whole edifice and the Zionist entity itself would crumble like a deck of cards . . .

Jerusalem is not Babylon the Great, nor will it become the seat of the next caliphate despite plans to make it so.

In its Charter, the OIC has stipulated that the future Palestine, with Jerusalem (*Al-Quds al-Sharif*) as its capital, will be crowned as the seat of the caliphate. Article 21 of the OIC's Charter declares:

> The Headquarters of the General Secretariat shall be in the city of Jeddah until the liberation of the city of al-Quds so that it will become the permanent headquarters of the Organisation.

Since the caliphate is the guarantor of sharia and world jihad, the OIC envisages a Jerusalem purged of Jews and Christians. The demise of Israel is essential for the OIC and its conquest of the Christian West. However, the imagery in Revelation indicates that any future caliphate will not actually be based in Jerusalem.

Firstly, the imagery in Revelation shows Islam (Babylon the Great) seated on the First Beast, not on the Second Beast (Israel). From this one can must conclude that Jerusalem will not become the seat of Islam.

The fact that the Harlot is not merely a different way of representing the Second Beast (Israel) can be deduced from the fact that the Beast and the False Prophet are united in purpose. Such a relationship is quite different from the relationship between the Beast and the Harlot where the Beast hates the Harlot. In the last days, Jerusalem actually serves the Beast's purpose for in this city he will declare that he is God by taking his seat in the Temple of God. The Beast has no motive therefore to destroy Jerusalem, and there is no indication in Revelation that the False Prophet will encourage him to do so.

Secondly, the fact that there is still a Temple in Jerusalem also indicates that Jerusalem has not become the seat of the caliphate. No caliph would ever permit the Jews to worship God in their own Temple, but instead would be obliged to wage *jihad* against them and to destroy the Temple.

Members of OIC discriminate against their own native Christians

The 52 member and 5 observer states of the Organization of the Islamic Cooperation (OIC) have 1.77 billion inhabitants.

Roughly two thirds of the non-Muslims are Christians (around 300 million), which is about 18 per cent of the inhabitants of the member states.

As the OIC by definition only speaks on behalf of Islam and Muslims alone, more than half a billion people are represented by an organization that denies their rights. It would appear that the OIC just counts the non-Muslim citizens as Muslims. OIC members do not work for the interests of their non-Muslim citizens, but have them pay for the expansion of Islam via their taxes.

The OIC's intensive actions within the United Nations is only in favour of Islam.

Benin, Cameroon, Cote d'Ivoire, Gabon, Guyana, Mozambique, Nigeria, Surinam, and Uganda, like Russia, have non-Muslim majorities. One must question why these states have applied to become members of the OIC. Their membership works for the expansion and protection of Islam and against the interests of the majority of their citizens.

Campaigns for a new caliphate throughout the world

The eventual conquest and complete Islamization of the earth is a natural expectation for most Muslims. They see the modern Muslim states in the Middle East as a product of the evil of the Western powers who divide the Islamic Caliphate.

The pro-caliphate movement is functioning across the whole of the earth.

In 2007 over 100,000 Muslims gathered in Indonesia for the Hizb-ut-Tahrir's pro-Caliphate conference. 50,000 gathered in Israel, and tens of thousands in London.

In February 2006, Sheikh Ismail Nawahda of Guiding Helper Foundation, preached to a gathering of Muslims on the Temple Mount in Jerusalem calling upon them to restore the Caliphate.

A few months later, Sheikh Raed Salah of the Islamic Movement in Israel, addressing of 50,000 Muslims just outside the Israeli city of Haifa, declared:

> Jerusalem will soon be the capital of the Moslem Arab Caliphate....soon Jerusalem will be the capital of the new Muslim caliphate, and the caliph's seat will be there.

The pro-Caliphate group Hizb-ut-Tahrir is often a gateway into other more violent pro-Caliphate groups like al-Qaeda or the Muslim Brotherhood (*Al-Ikhwan*).

The National Intelligence Council released a study entitled *Project 2020, Mapping the Global Future* in which it stated:

> political Islam will have a significant global impact leading to 2020, rallying disparate ethnic and national groups and perhaps even creating an authority [the Caliphate] that transcends national boundaries.

On Sept 17, 2005, the Iranian President Mahmoud Ahmadinejad in his address to the UN asked his god to hasten the emergence of the long-awaited Mahdi. In the same year Ahmadinejad proclaimed that his mission as President was to "pave the path for the glorious reappearance of Imam Mahdi". In 2004 Iranian leaders set up an institute for the study and dissemination of information about the Mahdi. Over $20 million dollars was spent refurbishing the Mosque in Jamkaran just outside the "holy city" of Qom to receive the new Mahdi.

Iran's Hojjatieh Society is governed by the conviction that the twelfth Imam's return can be hastened by the creation of a period of chaos on earth. Israeli PM Netanyahu described Hojjatieh as "the cult of the Mahdi".

Because of Iran's firm stand against America and Israel, as well as Hezbollah's alleged successes against Israel in 2006, many radically minded Muslims are siding with Iran and turning against the Saudi power block, which they see as compromised with the West. This is seen not only by Libya's Gaddafi, but also many Sunni Muslims who convert to Shi'a Islam.

Gaddafi called publicly for the establishment of a Fatimid Caliphate on Easter weekend, 2007. The Fatimids were a Shi'a group that controlled much of North Africa during the 10th Century. The fact that Libya, which is a Sunni majority nation, would call for a return to a Shi'a Caliphate is significant. It was an appeal for an Iranian/Libyan axis to stand against the Saudi/Sunni power block. In other words, Libya is trying to side with Iran. The Iranian revolution has made some strong appeals for Sunni/Shi'a unity.

"Eurabia": how the European Union and the UK is being undermined by Islam

Melanie Phillips's book *Londonistan* investigates the use of the United Kingdom for terrorist activities. The British government has tried to appease Islam, failing to realize that it is dealing with a religious ideology that will only see this as a sign of weakness. "Multiculturalism" and "Islamophobia" are being used by Islamists to promote Islam and undermine any reaction to the spread of Islam.

Philips also looks at how the Christian church has also tried to appease Islam, with its liberal leadership joining the attack on Israel.

Islam's growth rate is four times faster than Christian's. Muslims account for one fifth of world's population. Europe will soon become "Eurabia". By 2025, one third of all Europeans will be Muslim. In the UK, Mohammed is already the most popular name for boys.

Bat Yeor argues that what she calls the "Palestinization of Europe" has already brought the caliphate into the cities of Europe through the extinction of basic freedoms, thought-control, subversion of democratic laws by sharia, fatwas, self-censorship and fear. Citizens of the Europe suffer "dhimmitude" and are obliged to accept the demographic and cultural colonization of their own territory through massive immigration.

In her book *Le Dhimmi* (*The Dhimmi: Jews and Christians Under Islam*), Bat Yeor depicts how Islamic Jihad infiltrated, overthrew and subjugated indigenous peoples in pre-Islamic lands. Those who survived rape, pillage and murder, and who did not convert, lived in perpetual fear for their lives, avoided only by payment of the *jizya*, the onerous poll tax that saved them from being beheaded.

Bat Yeor argues that the OIC is restoring the Caliphate, the supreme controlling body for all Muslims.

Bat Yeor accuses the European Union (EU) of creating transnational structures that will bring a worldwide caliphate to power as a result of the OIC's preponderance within the United Nations (UN) and in particular within the 118-state Non-Aligned Movement which the OIC effectively controls. By building up a UN counterforce to the United States, the EU is paving the way for the domination of the UN by a universal caliphate. The EU is weakening the influence of rule-of-law states by transferring their sovereignty to international organizations.

The Parliamentary Association for Euro-Arab Cooperation (PAEAC) is the cornerstone of the "Eurabia" network. The PEAC program was anti-American and anti-Israel. It pushed Muslim emigration giving migrants the same rights as EU citizens. The PAEAC was created in 1974 in response to Palestinian terrorism and the oil boycott decreed by the Arab League after the Yom Kippur war. Bat Yeor describes the parliamentarians of the PAEAC as "loyal agents and disseminarians of OIC policy in Europe."

The Euro-Arab Dialogue (EAD), the founding body of Eurabia, is an offshoot of the PAEAC. The influence of the OIC is spread by EU politicians who, despite being discredited by their fellow citizens are "put back into the circuit through the OIC networks to carry on their work of termites." Massive waves of Muslim immigration were encouraged by the official policy of the Euro-Arab Dialogue and expanded in the Barcelona Process (1995).

Convergence between the policies of the EU and the OIC is ensured by the PAEAC which passes on to the European Council and its Commission the demands of the Arab League. The PAEAC is behind the spread of anti-semitism in Europe. Supported by the Commission, it functions as the European instrument of Islamic proselytising.

Without their consent, the historic peoples of France and Germany, Italy and Spain, have lost their identity as the European Union has acceded to almost every Islamic demand, especially regarding immigration. Dependent on Middle East oil and hoping to profit from immigrant labour, the EU has provided ways for Muslims to settle in Europe without forfeiting their Islamic culture. Second and third generations insist on the teaching of Arabic and pro-Islamic materials in the schools. Leaders from Muslim communities must be included in the political system and where possible *sharia* law must be established to settle intra-Muslim issues. Slowly, through demographic growth, Muslims hope to gain power in various places.

The OIC claims to be the guardian and protector of Muslim immigrants living in all countries that are not members of the OIC. This implies an extension of its jurisdiction and political influence over all the Muslims of Europe, North and South America, and the other non-Member States. This situation exacerbates the danger incurred by non-religious European Muslims, whether atheists, apostates, or free thinkers.

The EU has absolutely no influence in the Muslim world whatsoever despite having aligned itself with the Muslim world against the United States and Israel. In an attempt to gain influence, the EU permitted a massive Muslim immigration into Europe, paid billions to the Mediterranean Union and Palestinian Authority, and undermined the unity of the European states. It has wrapped itself in the flag of Palestinian justice, thereby hoping to be spared global jihad.

How the United States is being undermined by Islam

Robert Chandler dedicates an entire chapter of his book *Shadow World* to the issue of the emerging caliphate, entitled "Restoration of a world Islamic

Caliphate". He examines how the US is being destroyed by Islam from within by Saudi Arabia.

The Muslim Brotherhood (*Ikhwan*) aims to destroy Western civilization from within through infiltration.and multiculturalism. The Muslim Brotherhood consists of about seventy US national organizations. A network of Wahhabi-sponsored propaganda organisations underwrite the Muslim Brotherhood's goal of developing a fifth column of support for militant Islam in the United States and establishing an Islamic caliphate. Eight in particular provide the basis:

- Council for American-Islamic Relations (CAIR)
- Islamic Society of North America (ISNA)
- Muslim Students Association
- Islamic Circle of North America (ICNA)
- Muslim American Society (MAS)
- Muslim Public Affairs Council (MPAC)
- Arab-American Institute (AA)
- American-Arab Anti-Discrimination Committee (ADC)

The Saudis placed about $1 million in the Nation of Islam's coffers. The HRH Prince Alwaleed Bin Talal Center for Muslim-Christian Understanding at Georgetown University fosters civilizational jihad, destroying American culture from within and preparing for a time when Islam will emerge dominant over other religions in the United States. The Saudis have seized control over Middle Eastern and Islamic studies in the United States with ease. Saudi money funds "educational materials" that praise and promote Islam, and criticize Judaism and Christianity.

Around 60,000 Americans may be converting to Islam annually.

Both Russia and Islam understand the West's weakness, namely its political correctness. The West has voluntarily fallen into this trap which was invented by Leftists. Political correctness makes it impossible for the West to resist the Islamic onslaught.

Russia is closer to Islamic society than the United States. Women are openly discriminated against in Russia and its society is vertical and paternalistic. Anti-American moods are widespread. As freedom shrinks in Russia, the more Russia resembles an Oriental despotic kingdom. For this reason, Russia may escape the fate awaiting the United States, which is likely to fall to Islam. The United States is a gigantic piece for Islamic terrorists to conquer and Russia might survive at the expense of America.

Islamists hope their actions will lead to the following chain of events:

- the collapse of the US economy by the year 2020 under the strain of multiple engagements in numerous places;
- the consequent collapse of the worldwide economic system;
- global political instability leading to a global jihad led by al-Qaeda;
- the installation of a Wahhabi Caliphate across the world, following the collapse of the US and the rest of the Western world countries.

Al-Qaeda's Osama bin Laden and Ayman al-Zawahiri were both admirers of Yale historian Paul Kennedy's book *The Rise and Fall of Great Powers*, which observes that great empires fall in large part because they overstretch themselves militarily abroad and in maintaining security at home.

The Red-Black alliance

The "The Red-Black Alliance" is aimed at weakening the West's foundations based upon the Mosaic code. There is an affinity between Islam and Communism, which is not surprising as both are of a satanic nature and enemies of Christianity.

Leftists and Muslims have a mutual short-term interest in keeping Leftist parties in power, and a mutual long-term interest in weakening the traditional culture of Europe. Chris Harman, of the Socialist Workers Party, argued that the revolutionary capacity of Islam 'could be tapped for progressive purposes.'

Leftists from all over Europe seem to be opening the gates of Europe, allowing it to be conquered from within by Islam, in return for votes, the destruction of capitalism, and the eradication of our Christian heritage.

Examples of this "Red-Black Alliance" in action are:

- Stop the War Coalition: Islamists and leftists jointly formed the Stop the War Coalition, whose steering committee includes the Communist Party of Britain and the Muslim Association of Britain.

- The Respect Party: this party amalgamates radical international socialism with Islamist ideology.
- International Solidarity Movement: Leftists founded the International Solidarity Movement to prevent Israeli security forces protecting themselves from Hamas.

Multiculturalism advocated by Left-wing professors, journalists, and politicians have weakened Western resolve. To "divide and conquer," multiculturalism pits ethnic and cultural groups against each other to destroy the coherence of Western society. Multiculturalism is a concept contrived to support the radical Left's assault on Western culture. Islamists support multiculturalism, employing the concept as a weapon against the West.

Norway's largest "anti-racist" organisation, SOS Rasisme, was heavily infiltrated by Communists in the late 1980s around the time of the downfall of communism in Eastern Europe, suggesting that multiculturalism is a continuation of communism by other means.

Islamo-Marxism

Islam has been redefined as anti-Americanism.

Ali Shariati, the intellectual behind the Iranian revolution of 1978-79, was a prominent ideologue of the Islamic Revolution and was an Islamo-Marxist. Under Ali Shariati's influence, Iranian radicals became Marxists and interpreted the Koran according to the theory of the class struggle. According to the Iranian analyst Azar Nafisi:

> [Islam] takes its language, goals, and aspirations as much from the crassest forms of Marxism as it does from religion. Its leaders are influenced by Lenin, Sartre, Stalin, and Fanon, as they are by the Prophet.

Intelligence expert Angelo Codevilla explains how the essence of Marxism-Leninism can be found in Islam. He tells of a conversation he had with the Ayatollah of Iran who interpreted the Koran "in ways that were really quite indistinguishable from those of Vladimir Lenin". When this was pointed out to the Ayatollah, he was dismayed.

The Constitution of the Islamic Republic of Iran contains clauses which reveal an ideology that is of Leninist origin such as the clause which speaks of an "American conspiracy known as the 'White Revolution'", a conspiracy which was intended "to reinforce the political, cultural, and economic dependence of Iran on world imperialism."

The Soviet's harnessing of Islamic fundamentalism against the United States

The Iranian revolution of 1979, with its anti-US overtones, led the Soviet leaders to conclude that the liberation struggle could also be waged under the banner of Islam. The harnessing of Islamic fundamentalism, given its anti-US stance, opened up possibilities for undermining the pro-Western regimes in Saudi Arabia and the Gulf states.

Brezhnev said:

> under the banner of Islam, the liberation struggle can be deployed.

Referring to the Surikov Document, a report intended for use in developing the military doctrine of the Russian Federation and authored in 1995, Representative Curt Weldon (R-PA) said:

> [The Surikov Document] says . . . that in the end America is always going to be a threat to Russia's sovereignty. In the end, the Russian government should look to establish linkages with emerging rogue Islamic nations and it names them. It names Libya. It names Iraq, Syria, as those allies of Russia that should be nurtured and where technology should be transferred to benefit a mutual relationship.

Through "Muslims" in so-called "independent" Muslim states in the CIS, the Soviets intend to consolidate the concealed Russian influence over Islamic fundamentalism, in order to complement the influence that the Chinese were openly seeking. They will thus swing the balance of power in their favour in the oil-producing Arab/Iranian areas of the Middle East. The Azeris will ally with Iran and the Arab states.

Putin has refused to consider Hamas a terrorist organisation because it is still under the control of Russian intelligence.

The KGB have some agents in the Taliban leadership, like Abd al-Rashid Dustum who had studied at the KGB school in Tashkent in the early 1980s.

The FSB also trained Juma Namangoniy, a native of Soviet Uzbekistan. He was an Uzbek Islamist militant with a substantial following who co-founded and led the Islamic Movement of Uzbekistan. He received substantial Taliban patronage and was allowed to operate freely in northern Afghanistan. Namangoniy was in charge of the Taliban's northern front in Afghanistan. He was once a student of the Saboteur Training Center of the First Chief Directorate of the KGB in 1989-94.

According to former Israeli Prime Minister Benjamin Netanyahu, modern terrorist organizations would not have got very far had they not been actively supported by states that were built on the foundations of Marxism and radical Islam. Russia is behind Iranian, Syrian and other terrorist groups, with the ultimate aim of targeting Israel for destruction.

Intelligence expert Angelo Codevilla notes how terrorist activity around the world declined around the time of the so-called "collapse" of the Soviet Union, and then how around the beginning of 1993, the very same people who had been involved in anti-American terror under the Soviet banner returned to their task but under the Islamic banner. These people are using the same weapons from the same Russian sources.

Ion Pacepa, the high-ranking Romanian defector and author of *Disinformation*, recalls how the Kremlin established a "Socialist Division of Labour" for persuading the governments of Iraq and Libya to join the terrorist war against the United States.

The Soviets stoked up hatred of Jews through the wide dissemination of the *Protocols of the Elders of Zion* throughout the Middle East.

A jihadist hacking group linked to ISIL is believed to be a front for a Russian government cyber warfare programme (*Daily Telegraph*, 20 June 2016). German intelligence services also believe the Russians may be behind other cyber attacks ascribed to the Cyber Caliphate.

Supyan Abdullayev, a Soviet/Russian-trained asset and founder of the Soviet-authorized Islamic Revival Party, became a leading commander and ideologue for the Caucasian Emirate.

Writer and researcher Christian Gomez traced the roots of ISIS to the Islamic Revival Party, created by the KGB during the final days of the old Soviet Union.

On December 6, 2015, in a televised interview with the Ukrainian news program TSN.Tyzhden a Russian FSB officer claimed that radical Islamist groups are staffed with Russian agents and that Moscow has a real influence on what they do. The FSB agent claimed that Moscow is actively involved in terrorist groups such as ISIS, despite the fact that Russia is supposedly waging war them. This Russian FSB officer said that among the vast number of refugees entering Europe were certain Russian operatives whose task it was to infiltrate the Muslim communities. Financed by the FSB, these undercover Muslim operatives would rise to prominence within their respective communities. The operatives would provide the Kremlin with intelligence about Muslim activities in Europe, allowing Moscow to exert influence over these communities. The Russian security services would supply funds to these operatives who in turn could make financial donations to the Muslim community they were in, thereby acquiring prestige and a higher status in the hierarchy. The FSB agent identified the son and two nephews of Abdul Hadi Hamadi, Hezbollah's head of counterintelligence, as operatives who received money in order to destabilize the situation. The Russian Federation does not recognize Hezbollah as a terrorist organization.

The Russian special services set up ISIS as an alternative terror organization to al-Qaeda. The defector from the FSB confirmed that those former officers of the Iraqi army and Arab Socialist Ba'ath Party members who created ISIS had all graduated from Moscow-based educational institutions. This was during the period when Saddam Hussein's regime was in close alliance with the Soviet Union. Moscow had signed a Treaty of Friendship and Cooperation with the regime.

Mohammed Atta, one of the 9/11 terrorists, met with a senior Iraqi intelligence officer agents in Prague, Czech Republic, five months before the 9/11 attack. Since the Iraqi intelligence was a client of Russia's intelligence service it is is fair to conjecture that Putin knew what was going to happen. Ion Pacepa, former head of the Romanian secret service, sees significance in the date 9/11, it being Felix Dzerzhinsky's birthday. Articles in *The Morning Star* have drawn attention to the "other 9/11", the date of the overthrow of the Allende government in Chile.

The Soviets would commonly use an act of provocation for strategic purposes. 9/11 was a provocation to forge a partnership with the United States in a war against Islamic terrorism.

33

THE BEAST AND TEN HORNS WILL HATE THE HARLOT

The Beast and Ten Horns will hate Islam

> **And the ten horns that you saw, they and the beast will hate the harlot . . . and burn her up with fire.** (Rev. 17:16)

The Ten Horns and the Beast will hate Islam and will destroy her. The alliance between the Beast and the Ten Kings gives the Beast the manpower he needed to defeat Islam.

The Caliphate confers legitimacy to jihad. According to Islamic law, without a Caliphate it is not possible to declare a genuinely sanctioned pan-Islamic jihad. Once a Caliph is in office, however, it is actually a legal obligation for him to engage the non-Muslim world in war in order to spread Islam. The land with whom the Caliphate was at war was referred to as *Dar al-Harb,* "land of war" in contrast to "land of peace", *Dar al-Salam.*

According to Islamic law, anyone who disobeys a seated caliph should be beheaded.

It may be that Russia, despite its Observer Status at the OIC will be considered a *Dar al-Harb,* land of war"and therefore a country that Muslims must make war against. In such a scenario, the Beast may go on that attack, on the basis that attack it the best form of defence.

USSR's double standards regarding Islam

The Soviet Union followed a double standard regarding Islam, dividing it into good and bad. The bad one was domestic Islam, which was doomed to annihilation. The good was "foreign Islam" which could be utilized for destroying the West, the strategic goal of world communism.

The Bolsheviks appealed to the Muslims from the beginning. In 1920, at the Second Congress of the Communist International, Grigory Zinoviev called in his speech five times for "holy war" against the British and the French "colonialists" and "the rich in general - Russian, German, Jewish, French."

Support of Islam was considered a part of Russian-based anti-colonialism. Lenin saw a way using bourgeois nationalist revolutions as a way to deprive imperialist powers of the raw materials and markets necessary for their survival.

The Soviet infiltration of Islam involved the cultural phenomenon called "The Islamic name and communist heart". Former KGB agent Konstantin Preobrazhensky asserts that this phenomenon was embodied in Karim Khakimov, the first Soviet Ambassador to Saudi Arabia. Khakimov, an expert in the Muslim religion, was actually a communist. To win the sympathy of the ruling elite, he had done the *Umrah* (the little pilgrimage) to Mecca. He was considered a zealous Muslim, but was in fact a member of the Communist Party and had vowed to destroy religion.

It was Khakimov who initiated the World Muslim Congress in 1926 in Mecca, which discussed how to liberate Muslims from colonial independence on the West.

The phenomenon of a Muslim in name only – but with a communist heart – was especially prevalent among the Tatars. The Soviet Union preferred to appoint Tatars as ambassadors to Muslim countries. Their names gave then a pass to local society, but their communist hearts served world communism, not the world of Islam. There were many quasi-Muslim officers in the KGB.

The USSR has a long history of using Islam for its own political ends and trod carefully when dealing with Muslims.

After World War II, Islam was used as a tool for political influence, especially in Xinjiang, China, Afghanistan, Iran, Syria and Iraq, resulting in pro-Soviet influence on the pro-Islamic East.

Muslims of the Uzbekistan and other Central Asian republics' elite joined the KGB intelligence to spy on fellow Muslim countries. They all have former class mates of the KGB schools in Moscow and appreciate such friendship. These KGB officers are the main tool of Russian intelligence influence in Central Asia, from where its influence spreads to other Muslim countries.

The communists were exercised over what to do about the Islamic festival of Ashura, where the worshipers whip themselves. Preobrazhensky has uncovered documents that shows that Islamic fatwas were issued on this matter by order of the Central Committee of the Communist Party.

Muslim Communist Party members were given privileges that were not given to other religions. Muslim Party members were allowed to circumcise their sons, but Christians were forbidden from baptizing their children. Party members were not reprimanded for practising Islam secretly, but a practising Christian would be deprived of "political trust". Colleagues in the Middle East were not deprived of "political trust" and these colleagues are still ruling in the former Soviet republics of Central Asia. This indulgence spread to ordinary Muslims too, whereas members of the underground True Orthodox Church could be imprisoned for 15 years. Even today, Muslims enjoy privileges. The Russian Minister of Healthcare, Mikhail Zurabov, is a Chechen.

How Islam was suppressed internally in the USSR

Internally, vigorous anti-Islamic propaganda was carried out. Independent Islamic institutions were dissolved forcefully. Extensive territorial reorganizations divided Muslim peoples into ethnic units and stressed differences in language and history. The aim being to discourage the sense of religious solidarity which is one of Islam's stonrgest characteristics. Rebellions were suppressed, with mass population transfers to remote areas during World War II.

The Soviet leaders had an unconditional hostility to all religions including Islam. The goal was to destroy religion within the Soviet state. Any accommodation with religion was purely tactical.

Those Muslim national communists who pointedly called for Lenin to employ Soviet Muslim cadres to carry the revolution into the Muslim world were systematically removed from positions of influence after 1921, and after 1923, were dismissed, imprisoned, and, finally, liquidated under Stalin.

Soviet policy reflected a deep fear of conservative Islam at home as a dangerous adversary. Soviet Muslims were considered too untrustworthy to represent Soviet interests abroad faithfully.

The Soviets concluded that any promotion of Muslim national self-determination abroad, even if it disrupted the empires of the major European powers, might result in compromises having to be made with regard to Muslim national self-determination at home.

Beginning in 1923 Stalin launched a strong anti-nationalist offensive against the Muslim national communists, which by the late 1930s had resulted in their virtual extinction. In 1928 Stalin augmented the systematic elimination of the Muslim intellectual elite with a frontal assault on the USSR's Islamic infrastructure. Mosques were closed and destroyed by the thousands, clerics were arrested and liquidated as 'saboteurs' and after 1935, as spies. By 1941, of the 25,000-30,000 mosques open in 1920, only about 1000 remained. All of the 14,500 Islamic religious schools were forcibly shut down, and fewer than 2000 of the approximately 47,000 clerics survived. By the outbreak of Word War II the traditional Muslim religious establishment in Central Asia and the Caucasus had been destroyed.

With the exception of Karim Khakimov, a Tatar, who was the first Soviet Consul-General in Jeddah and representative at the court of the Imam Yahya in Yemen (1928), Stalin avoided using Soviet Muslim diplomats abroad in visible positions. At home Islam was vilified continuously by Soviet propaganda as the most reactionary of religions.

In the official *Great Bolshevik Encyclopedia* (1953) Islam is described thus:

> In the USSR, Islam is a vestige of the society of exploiters, and [abroad] is a weapon in the hands of the local reactionaries and of foreign imperialism.

Under Khrushchev, anti-Islamic propaganda was increased massively, with the new themes centring on the objective of destroying Islam in one generation. Soviet authoriites again closed working mosques, the number dropping from about 1500 at the time of Stalin's death to about 500 in the early 1960s.

The message from the Soviets to their guests was that the USSR is an important Muslim country and that the Soviet Muslims enjoy extraordinary freedoms.

The anti-Islamic campaign was toned down upon Khrushchev's departure from office, but the official Soviet Marxismt-Leninism and the theoretical writings about religion, including Islam, inside the Soviet state for the most part remained uncompromisingly hostile. Moderation of the Kremlin's behaviour was predicated upon the realization that Khrushshev's policies were counterproductive. However, the anti-Islamic campaign was never completely abandoned. The anti-clerical propaganda was abandoned in favour of the propaganda of 'scientific atheism' and the denunciation of Islamic 'fanatics'.

The Soviet leadership moved to develop a Janus-like strategy which stressed the dangers of unrestrained Islam at home while simultaneously, albeit cautiously, advancing the notion that Islam abroad could be a progressive, even a revolutionary factor.

A typical statement to this effect was by G M Kerimov:

> Islamic socialism may be used by reactionary circles as a new ideological weapon against Marxism-Leninsim; it may also become a new bourgeois illusion concerning socialism, but it may become a revolutionary anti-capitalist reformist movement, for instance as was the case in Syria, Algeria or in the United Arab Republic.

Efforts to control Islam after the collapse of the USSR

In Tajikistan, where jihadi organizations were prominent in the civil war that swept across the country immediately after the fall of the Soviet Union, Yeltsin quickly ordered the deployment of a locally based Russian garrison to help the Tajik side confront the Islamist fundamentalists. The war dragged on, and Russian policy was geared to establishing conditions of peace.

All the former Muslim-majority former Soviet Republics have full membership of the OIC. They are listed here [with date of OIC membership in brackets]:

- Azerbaijan [1991]
- Kyrgystan [1992]
- Tajikstan [1992]
- Turkmenistan [1992]
- Kazakhstan [1995]
- Uzbekistan [1995]

Former Eastern bloc country Albania was granted full membership of the OIC in 1992. Bosnia and Herzegovina was granted Observer status in 1994.

It was evident back as 1994 that key communist implementers were still in control over the predominantly Islamic former Soviet Republics.

- **Azerbaijan** was under the thumb of KGB General Gaidar Aliyev, formerly a member of Brezhnev's Politburo;
- **Kazakhstan** was ruled by Nursultan Nazarbayev, former member of Gorbachev's Politburo;
- **Tajikstan** was controlled by Rakhmon Nabiyev, the Tajik Communist Party leader;
- **Turkmenistan** was run by Saparmurat Miyazov, a member of Gorbachev's Politburo;
- **Uzbekistan**, under Islam Karimov, operated an unaltered Communist state.

Russia will continue to be a powerful force as far as the Central Asian states and Azerbaijan are concerned. Iran, Turkey and Afghanistan will only be able to increase their influence gradually in a limited diplomatic space. Russia is the leader of the Commonwealth of Independent States (CIS) to which these countries belong (excepting Azerbaijan). Russia has multilateral and bilateral cooperation treaties in culture economics, military and security matters with these states.

Russian minorities in these republics will remain important. This will be obvious in Kazakhstan, owing to the sheer size of its Slavic population. Even in Tajikistan, where the Russian population is now less than five per cent, Moscow has decided to take a strong stand in the context of bilateral and multilateral military agreements, thereby safeguarding the country from the advance of Islamists from Afghanistan. Kyrgyzstan is economically so weak that it continues to rely on hand-outs from Russia. Russian will hence continue to be the inter-ethnic language in all Central Asian republics and the inter-state language in the region.

The president of each of the Muslim-inhabited member states of the CIS engaged with Islam by making a personal profession of their faith and by providing funds to build mosques and Islamic schools. This was done as a way of outflanking the jihadis and gaining approval for their arrest. The persecution of Islamist fundamentalists was strengthened.

Kremlin leaders cannot depend on the permanent stability of states in Russia's own "near abroad." There is no guarantee that the anti-jihadist Muslim dictatorships in ex-Soviet Central Asia will always be able to crush their internal fundamentalist enemies.

Putin's efforts to stamp out Islamic fundamentalism

Russia is losing 900,000 people annually, who are being replaced by Muslims from the Caucasus and Central Asia. There are up to 28 million adherents of Islam in the Russian Federation, which is why it was granted Observer Status in 2005 of the OIC. While in the chair of the OIC, Iran promoted Russia's observer status. The GCC countries, Turkey, Iran and central Asian republics also emphatically supported the Russian request. Pakistan, though initially reluctant, went along with it.

The OIC's acceptance of Russia as a permanent observer proves that Russia is more important to the Islamic world than Chechnya. Observer status was granted, despite the fact that the Russian Orthodox Church is the largest religious association in the country. Muslims represent only the second largest religious community in Russia and number 19 million - that is one in seven of the population.

Russia's interest is seen as lying with the eradication of real and potential jihadists. The concern for Russian politicians is that violent Islamism in the "near abroad" could leach into the territories of the Russian Federation. The adjacent Muslim-majority states had to become a sanitary cordon. Not only the North Caucasus but also Tatarstan were to be quarantined from the fundamentalist contagion.

Putin stamped out violent Islamism wherever it raised its head. He expressed surprise that President George W. Bush and Prime Minister Tony Blair did not recognize the international ramifications of jihadism when they advised him to put an end to the atrocities in Chechnya. Putin urged the leaders of the United States and Europe to sympathize with Russia's efforts to tranquilize Chechnya.

Putin argued that it was the other European countries rather than the Russian Federation that found themselves having to tackle unpleasant questions about Islam. He points out that the United States, Britain, and France have been the objects of recurrent Islamist terrorism. In his opinion, they have permitted terrorist groups to flourish in their own countries while censuring Russia's policy in Chechnya.

Putin derided the West for its refusal to copy Russian methods. His own preference has been to combine a positive appeal to moderate forms of Islam in Russia and around the world with a ruthless campaign to crush militant jihadism. Putin recommends Western countries abandon their alleged Russophobia and join with Russia in extirpating jihadis everywhere.

Putin announced the wish for a country whose Muslims are peaceful, loyal citizens who abide by moderate versions of Islam. He appeared in public with Chief Mufti Tadzhuddin. In Tatarstan, he endorsed the surge of mosque building. Putin put forward Russia as a model pluralistic society where tolerance of every traditional major religion is the norm.

To prove his pro-Islamic credentials, Putin attended the Organization of the Islamic Conference in October 2003. With Saudi Arabia's sponsorship, Russia acquired associate status two years later.

Putin's priority is securing the Russian Federation and its allies in the "near abroad" against the growth of jihadism.

Seeking to expunge the jihadi threat from Russia, the Federal Security Service (FSB) hit on the idea of making an offer to known militants in the North Caucasus to travel to Turkey at official expense. Would-be jihadis were sent to Iraq, where they could fight for the Islamist cause. The thinking behind this was that Russia itself would be made safer by the exodus of militants. Whether this was prudent is open to doubt. The FSB did not allow for the possibility that those who went could come back better trained and more determined to destabilize the Russian state order.

Beijing, confronted with its own Muslim insurgency in Xinjiang, was just as firm as Moscow in its determination to snuff out the fires of jihadism.

After the annexation of the Crimea, protests by the Crimean Tatar minority were suppressed. This largely Muslim minority had nursed grievances against Soviet power since 1944, when Stalin had deported the Tatars from their peninsular homeland.

There was a degree of cooperation between Russia and the United States in the crushing of the Islamic State in Iraq and Syria in 2017.

The Kremlin cannot be sure that Russia's millions of Sunni citizens will never oppose Russian foreign policy in the Middle East, especially when it transparently favours a Shia power such as Iran.

Moscow still covets the Middle East

Russia has long wished for control of the Middle East, giving it access to the Mediterranean and the Persian Gulf. Control over the oil of Saudi Arabia, a long-term objective of Moscow, would give her huge leverage over the whole world, given that oil reserves are running out in the G7 countries.

Through its intervention in Syria to save President Assad of Syria, the Russians have now regained their influence in the Middle East

Russia's influence in Middle East had weakened after President Sadat of Egypt turned away from Moscow towards Washington in the late 1970s. The 1973 war against Israel went so badly that Cairo sought peace with Israel. This culminated in the Camp David agreement in 1978. President Sadat abrogated the treaty with the USSR and suspended repayment of debts to Moscow.

Ira Hirschmann warned of the danger of Moscow's influence over the Middle East in those days in his book *Red Star over Bethlehem* (1971):

> There are two conflicts crisscrossing in the Middle East: the minor one between the Arabs and the Israelis; the major one, the Russians versus the United States. A few more such moves, and the Soviet Empire will stretch from the North Pole to the Persian Gulf, and capture the Middle East without firing a shot. The more than two-hundred-year-old dream of Peter the Great and Catherine II will have become a harsh reality, and the world will witness a Red Star over Bethlehem.

Hirschmann observed how, in less than fifteen years, the Russians were instrumental in helping break American alliances. He noted how the Russians had under their control the populations of more than 80,000,000 Arabs in Egypt, Sudan, Algerian, Syria, Libya, Iraq, and Yemen. These statistics proved that Russia was building up a Russian rampart against the West, an insuperable wall for the United States to surmount, which would turn the Middle East into an impregnable Soviet-Red Crescent.

The Middle East is of major importance in the struggle for world balance of power and an area the Soviets want to control. Hirschmann believed that it was only Israel which prevented the Russians taking over Suez and preventing further consolidation of Russia's hold on the Middle East.

Part Eleven

THE SECOND BEAST: ISRAEL AND THE FALSE PROPHET

34

THE FALSE PROPHET

The Second Beast represents both Israel and the False Prophet

> **Then I saw another beast which rose out of the earth; it had two horns like a lamb and it spoke like a dragon.** (Rev. 13:11)

The Second Beast represents Israel and the False Prophet.

The imagery of chapter 13 of Revelation is clearly taken from chapter 7 and 8 of Daniel. The First Beast is a composite of the four beasts that rise from the sea in Daniel chapter 7, of which three are wild carnivorous animals. The fourth is even fiercer. The Second Beast is like a lamb, a ruminant like the the Ram and He-Goat of Daniel chapter 8. Every beast in these chapters of Daniel represent nations and so it must follow that the lamb-like Second Beast must also represent a nation. That nation is Israel.

Whereas the Second Beast is like the beasts of Daniel chapter 8, the First Beast is a hybrid of the animals of both chapters 7 and 8. It is comprised of the wild beasts of Daniel chapter 7, but also has horns like the ruminant animals of chapter 8.

At the time of Daniel had his visions (which he received during the reign of Belshazzar king of Babylon) the kingdoms that are foreseen in the visions had not yet come into being (with the exception of the kingdom of

Babylon itself). In other words, his visions looks forward in time, not back in time. In Revelation however, the two Beasts that arise from the land and sea look both forward and back in time and represent some kingdoms that have already fallen and some that are yet to come into existence. The Second Beast represents both Israel's past and its future. Despite this, it is only correct to envisage both Beasts of Revelation as arising out of the sea and land at the same that John had his vision.

The fate of Israel is entwined with those of the kingdoms represented by the heads of the Beast.

Towards the end of the restored Soviet Empire, the Beast himself arises who will declare himself to be God. The False Prophet will arise out of Israel around the same time to make the inhabitants of the world worship the Beast.

The False Prophet

> **It works great signs, even making fire come down from heaven to earth in the sign of men ...** (Rev. 13:13)

The Second Beast is actually denoted the False Prophet in Rev. 16:13 and Rev. 19:20. This Second Beast is lamb-like, and therefore reminiscent of the Lamb of God himself (Rev. 5:6). The False Prophet appears righteous, but speaks "**like a dragon**" and is thus of satanic origin (Rev. 13:11). The nature of the Second Beast is actually more like Mushushshu, the dragon-like beast with two horns that accompanied Marduk, the god of Babylon.

Making fire come down from heaven is a sign that would associate the False Prophet in the minds of men with Elijah (1 Kgs 18:38-39; 2 Kgs 1:10-14). It is likely therefore that the advent of the False Prophet will be seen as a fulfilment of the prophecy in Malachi about Elijah:

> **"Behold, I will send you Elijah the prophet before the great and terrible day of the Lord comes."** (Mal. 4:5)

John the Baptist however was the **Elijah who is to come** (Matt. 11:14), according to Jesus.

The False Prophet will repudiate Jesus of Nazareth and may claim that he is the Messiah in his stead. Jesus Christ warned his disciples that false prophets would arise who will show **show great signs and wonders** (Matt. 24:25).

The False Prophet will cause everyone to be marked on their forehead or right hand, despite the fact that the law prohibits the making of tattoos on one's body (Lev. 19:18). He will introduce idolatry and emperor-worship, and will slay those who do not receive the mark of the Beast.

Just as the First Beast represents both the eighth kingdom and the Beast ("the Antichrist"), so the Second Beast represents both Israel and the False Prophet. The two Beasts only take on the meaning of the Antichrist and the False Prophet respectively at the End, just before the second coming of Jesus Christ and the battle of Armageddon.

The False Prophet himself is not represented by either of the two horns of the Second Beast, just as the Beast himself is not represented by any of the ten horns of the First Beast. The Beast and the False Prophet are represented by the First and Second Beast respectively, not by their horns.

The dual partnership of the Beast and the False Prophet continues right to the bitter end. Three fouls spirits like frogs issue from the mouth of the Dragon, the Beast and the False Prophet which are demonic spirits that perform signs, who gather the kings of the whole world for the battle of Armageddon (Rev. 16:13). Captured, the Beast and the False Prophet are thrown into the lake of fire (Rev. 19:20).

The two horns of the Second Beast represent the two kingdoms of Israel

> **. . . it had two horns like a lamb . . .** (Rev. 13:11)

The two horns of the Lamb represent the two former kingdoms of Israel, the kingdom of Israel (Samaria) and Judah. Between them, the two kingdoms ruled over all twelve tribes of Israel.

Commentators often compare the Second Beast with its two horns to the Ram (Dan. 8:3), but it is more pertinent to compare the two horns of the Second Beast to the horns of the He-Goat. Just as Alexander the

Great's great kingdom became divided and is represented by four horns, so the kingdom of David and Solomon was divided up into the kingdoms of Judah and Israel. The first three Javanic kingdoms were absorbed within the last, the Roman Empire, yet the Javanic Kingdom (the Leopard) is still portrayed as having four heads (four horns), rather than just one. So likewise, despite the fact that Israel became reduced to one kingdom (Judah), Israel is still represented by two horns, rather than one.

Israel was united under one king during the reigns of David (1003-970) and Solomon (970-930). After the first three years of Rehoboam's reign, however, it became divided into two. The Neo-Assyrian Empire conquered and exiled the ten tribes of the northern kingdom of Israel in 722 BC. The southern kingdom of Judah fell in 586 BC when the Babylonians conquered Jerusalem and took away the Jews to Babylon. (The Babylonians are represented by the first head of the seven–headed First Beast.) For a brief period just before the destruction of Jerusalem at the hands of the Romans (the sixth head of the Beast), Judah became a kingdom again. Judah Aristobulus I (104-103) was the first Jew in 483 years to establish a monarchy since the return from the Babylonian Captivity. The Hasmonean dynasty lasted until 37 BC. The Herodian dynasty followed, the last king over Judea being Herod Agrippa whose reign ended in 44 AD.

Israel had no king for most of the period spanned by the seven kingdoms represented by the seven heads of the First Beast. It is therefore apt that Israel should be represented by a beast that appears to be lacking two mature horns. The Second Beast's horns are "like" those of a lamb in that they are small and resemble stumps. Stumps signify the absence of these two horns, rather than their imminent growth to maturity. The stumps serve as a reminder of the history of Israel when it was divided into two kingdoms.

Just as the seven heads of the First Beast represent kingdoms that go back in time to the exile of the Jews in 586 BC, so the lamb-like Second Beast also represents the same period of time during which Israel was deprived of its two kings. However, the Second Beast represents the modern State of Israel, just as the First Beast represents the USSR/neo-Russian Empire. The modern state of Israel will not be ruled by any king, which is why it is represented by a beast which lacks any fully formed horns.

In the latter days, the False Prophet will gain enormous authority, equalling that of the First Beast himself. In those days, the authority of the

False Prophet will be as great as that of any king, and his authority will not just extend over Israel, but over the entire world.

Israel is depicted as a lamb in Jeremiah

> **. . . [the Second Beast] had two horns like a lamb . . .** (Rev. 13:11)

The scriptures themselves confirm that Israel is indeed the Second Beast, for Israel is actually called a lamb (Hebrew: *seh*) in Jeremiah:

> **"Israel is a hunted lamb** (RSV: sheep) **driven away by lions. First the king of Assyria devoured him, and now at last Nebuchadnezzar king of Babylon has gnawed his bones . . . I will restore Israel to his pasture, and he shall feed on Carmel and in Bashan, and his desire shall be satisfied on the hills of Ephraim and in Gilead."** (Jer. 50:17)

Israel's history is entwined with the kingdoms represented by the Beast's heads

> **So I will be to them like a lion, like a leopard I will lurk beside the way. I will fall upon them like a bear robbed of her cubs, I will tear open their breast, and there I will devour them like a lion, as a wild beast would rend them.** (Hos. 13:7-8).

In this verse in Hosea, God declares that he will destroy the kingdom of Israel (Ephraim) and compares himself to the three wild beasts seen in Daniel's vision. Such imagery indicates that to a certain extent the kingdoms represented by the Beast are fulfilling God's designs against Israel.

Like a sheep devoured by a lion, Israel fell victim to the kingdoms represented by the Beast's heads. Jerusalem fell under the control of Babylon, the Persians, Alexander the Great and the Antigonids of Macedonia, the

Ptolemies, the Seleucids, and the Romans, each in turn. The following history shows how each kingdom in turn took control of Jerusalem:

Babylonian Empire

The Babylonians conquered Jerusalem and exiled its inhabitants in 586 BC.

Medo-Persian Empire

Cyrus the Great captured Babylon in 539 BC. It was during his reign that an edict went out allowing the Jews to rebuild the Temple.

Greece (Javan)

Alexander the Great: Jerusalem capitulated to Alexander the Great in 332 BC, during his six-year Macedonian conquest of the empire of Darius III of Persia. Despite having initially refused Alexander the Great provisions for his siege Tyre, Jaddus, the High Priest in Jerusalem, was able to win Alexander over. When Alexander saw Jaddus dressed in the robes of the High Priest he saluted him, for in a dream he had seen the High Priest who had assured him that he would be victorious over the Persians.

Antigonids of Macedonia:

The Antigonid dynasty gained control of Jerusalem in 315 BC after Ptolemy I Soter withdrew from Syria and Antigonus I Monophthalmus invaded during the Third War of the Diadochi. In 312 BC Jerusalem was re-captured by Ptolemy I Soter after he defeated Antigonus' son Demetrius I at the Battle of Gaza.

In 311 BC the Antigonid dynasty regained control of the city after Ptolemy withdrew from Syria again following a minor defeat. In 302 BC Ptolemy invaded Syria for a third time, but evacuated again shortly thereafter following false news of a victory for Antigonus against Lysimachus.

In 301 BC Coele-Syria (Southern Syria) including Jerusalem was re-captured by Ptolemy I Soter after Antigonus I Monophthalmus was killed at the Battle of Ipsus.

Ptolemies

The Ptolemies ruled over Judea from 301-198 BC when the Seleucids wrested control of Judea away from them.

Seleucids

In 198 BC King Antiochus III wrested Southern Syria and Palestine from Egyptian control. They ruled over the Jews for around sixty years, from 198-142 BC.

Antiochus IV Epiphanes led the Jewish people into deep apostasy. In 167 BC the Syrians used the Temple in Jerusalem as a pagan temple. Some mistake him for the Beast, others mistake him for the Little Horn of Dan. 8:9.

Roman Empire

Rome's involvement with Judea dates from 63 BC when Rome made Syria a province at the end of the Third Mithridatic War. Pompey the Great captured Jerusalem that same year.

The former king Hyrcanus II was confirmed as ethnarch of the Jews by Julius Caesar in 48 BC and under Julius Caesar Judaism was officially recognised as a legal religion. The ruling Hasmonean dynasty was deposed and in 37 BC the Herodian Kingdom was established as a Roman client kingdom. In 6 AD Judea proper, Samaria, and Idumea, became the Roman province of Judea.

In AD 70 the Romans destroyed the Temple in Jerusalem, and enslaved many Jews. At least half a million Jews died during the siege.

In AD 130 Publius Aelius Hadrianus had Temple Mount ploughed by the Roman governor of Judea to signify the utter destruction of the Jewish city and to signal the birth of Jerusalem as the Roman colony *Aelia Capitolina*. In AD 132 arose the Bar Kokhba rebellion and in AD 135 Hadrian retook Jerusalem. Hadrian desecrated Temple Mount by erecting a statue of himself on the site of the Holy of Holies. A pagan temple was constructed on Temple Mount. Few Israelites were left in the Holy Land and Judea was renamed *Palestina*.

The Beast and the False Prophet will both reside in Jerusalem

It exercises all the authority of the first beast in its presence . . . (Rev. 13:12).

The False Prophet must have such huge miraculous powers that the Beast himself is deceived by him along with the rest of mankind.

The fact that the False Prophet will flatter the Beast and have him worshipped as God will only endear the Beast all the more to the False Prophet. The Beast will most likely believe that the False Prophet is the true Messiah.

Since the Second Beast also represents Israel, one can conclude that the False Prophet will hold sway in Jerusalem. It would be extraordinary for a prophet like one of the Israelite prophets of old to live in any other country other than Israel.

The fact that the False Prophet is in the presence of the First Beast shows that the Beast will also reside in Jerusalem. This conclusion agrees with Paul's statement that the Beast will take his **seat in the temple of God** and proclaim himself to be God (2 Thess. 2:4). Since the Beast's seat will be the Temple in Jerusalem, it follows that Jerusalem will be his capital city.

The False Prophet is allowed to work its signs **in the presence** of the Beast (Rev. 13:14). The words "in the presence" suggests presence before the Beast's throne. The Greek word means "face to face", suggesting close physical proximity between the False Prophet and the Beast.

That the theomachistic Beast should share his rule with a Jewish False Prophet seems incongruous. One would naturally assume that if the Beast was to pervert any religion to suit his purposes, it would be the Christian religion, not Judaism. However, it would appear that the False Prophet has such great miraculous powers, that the whole world is deceived by him. Presumably most Christians (except for the elite) are deceived by him too, and disown Jesus. No longer recognizing Jesus of Nazareth as the Messiah, it is quite likely that the masses will recognize the False Prophet as the Christ. This is the great apostasy referred to by Paul (2 Thess. 2:3).

Through his miracles, the False Prophet deceives the whole world into worshipping the Beast as God, and the Beast takes his seat in the Temple of God to show that he is God. The Temple service may be put in place to worship the Beast rather than the true God. Since the Beast takes his seat in the Temple of Jerusalem, it would make no sense for the False Prophet to be found in any city other than Jerusalem.

An image of Lenin will be given the breath of life

> **. . . and [the False Prophet] was allowed to give breath to the image of the beast so that the image of the beast should even speak . . .** (Rev. 13:15)

The False Prophet will make everyone worship an image of Lenin.

The False Prophet enables the image of the Beast to even speak. The False Prophet appears to be exercising the power of God by breathing life into an inanimate object:

> **. . . then the Lord God formed man of dust from the ground, and breathed into his nostrils the breath of life; and man became a living being.** (Gen. 2:7)

Worshipers of the Beast and its image receive the mark, the **mark of its name** (Rev. 14:11), the Hammer and Sickle.. Stalin will be chosen to represent the First Beast.

The fact that the False Prophet has to command the people to make an image (Rev. 13: 14) indicates that by this time Lenin will have been given a state funeral and his body will no longer be on display. If Lenin's body was still on display in his Mausoleum, the False Prophet would surely have breathed life into his body, rather than a statue.

Stalin's body was embalmed and lay in rest next to Lenin's in the Mausoleum until 1961.

Lenin's Mausoleum: a precedent for worship of Lenin's image

The cult of Lenin has set a precedent for the worship of the image of the Beast. Lenin's body is already an icon to the communist world.

The words "**wounded by the sword and yet lived** (Rev. 13:14)" strongly resonate with the assassination attempt upon the life of Lenin in 1918. Lenin was shot in the neck, but survived. Lenin's cult grew after this failed assassination attempt by Fania Kaplan, who was referred to as a "murderess" despite the fact that she did not succeed in killing Lenin.

The cult of Lenin shows a propensity for Marxism to worship its leader, just as the Beast will be worshipped. After his death, even the members of Lenin's family were canonized into a holy family. Lenin became the man-god of communism. After this failed assassination attempt, Lenin was often treated in the same reverential way as Christ. Phrases like "The mortal man exposed himself to danger, but Lenin cannot be harmed" exhibit a striking parallel with Christ. Lenin's wounding appears as a voluntary sacrifice of a man who consciously made himself vulnerable. Much was made of Lenin's recovery from the bullet wound. Some literature immediately following the incident attributed his physical survival to a miracle. Lenin was called a "martyr", "a passion-sufferer" and treated as a cross between Christ and St George. Lenin had become a "passion-sufferer" resembling the medieval saintly princes whose sanctity derived from the tragic ends they met as princes. In an article published in a provincial weekly of the Military-Revolutionary Committee of the Moscow-Kiev-Voronezh railroad calls him "the sole idol and divinity of the working class". Lunacharsky wrote a poem on Lenin in which he calls him the "guide of the world".

Upon his death, literary works for him were addressed: "To our father" in the same manner in which the Tsar had been. He was described as "a herald, prophet, a leader", and treated as a Bolshevik god.[40]

Lunacharsky was placed in charge of the cult of Lenin as a member of the Immortalization Commission which attempted to deify Lenin by trying to preserve his body.[41] In those days, there was a popular belief that the body of saints were incorruptible. Upon his death, there ran a theme of Lenin's immortality. A play on words was made with his name: LENIN–NETLENEN: "Lenin is imperishable".

Alexander Bogdanov believed that eternal life could be achieved through the transfusion of blood. Leonid Krasin believed in the possibility of physical resurrection and immortality through science and it is therefore quite likely that Krasin believed Lenin should be preserved intact for such a resurrection. Like Nikolai Fedorov, Krasin had faith in the miracle working powers of technology. Shortly after Lenin's death he wrote an article on "The Immortalization of Lenin" and proposed a monument containing Lenin's corpse that would become a centre of pilgrimage like Jerusalem or Mecca. Krasin, along with Anatoly Lunacharsky, announced a contest for

40 *Lenin Lives*, Lina Tumarkin

41 *The Immortalization Commission*, John Gray

designs of the permanent monument, which became the mausoleum. Krasin also attempted unsuccessfully to cryogenically preserve Lenin's body.

Upon Lenin's death refrains such as "He has not died, He will never die" and "Lenin is more alive than all the living!" became popular, along with the words from Maiakovsky's poem "Lenin lived – lives – will live". At the centenary of Lenin's birth in 1970, Brezhnev's speech included these words from Maiakovsky's poem of 1924.

The Lenin cult of the 1960s was even more extensive than the 1920s. To this day, many see Lenin as someone sacred.

The "Internationale" was played at Lenin's funeral. There were no last rites.

Some of those involved in creating the Lenin's cult thought that the cube had a spiritual significance. The use of a cube for the cult may have been attempt to draw in Muslims to the cult, who may have felt echoes of their faith in the cube given the shape of the Kaaba ("cube") in Mecca.

The stones from which the mausoleum was built were red and black, the colours of the Lenin cult. The grey stones were said to represent the workers. Red corners, which had originally housed sacred icons, were renamed Lenin corners. Other elements to the Lenin cult were the Lenin tents and Lenin evenings. There was an annual commemoration of Lenin on 21 January, the date of his death and the Sparrow Hills were renamed the Lenin Hills after Lenin's death in 1924. A yearly Lenin "subbotnik", a day of work given to the state, was held on the Saturday closest to Lenin's birthday, 22 April. Petrograd was renamed Leningrad.

Earth Day falls on the same date as Lenin's birthday. No doubt socialists hope that Earth Day will supplant Easter as the key day in the calendar. This year (2019) Earth Day fell on the first day after Easter Sunday, and several bishops and influential clergyman called for action to combat climate change.

Even during the Soviet Period statues of Lenin were venerated along with statues of Karl Marx and Friedrich Engels. In fact, during the Soviet period, 14,000 statues of Lenin were made.

Communism is the creed of the False Prophet, and Lenin is a great representative of this creed.

In F.A. McKenzie's book *The Russian Crucifixion* there is a photograph of a huge bust of Karl Marx in place on the altar of the Church of St Pimen in Moscow, a strong visual reminder of Communism's intention to replace Christ with Marx and the worship of God with the worship of Satan. In the same book are photographs of posters which mock and blaspheme not only Christ, Archbishops, God, and capitalists, but the Holy Spirit too.

Since 1929, there have been 100 million visitors to the Mausoleum. Recently, Putin has said: "Lenin was placed inside a mausoleum. How is that different from holy relics?"

In 2018, Vladimir Petrov, a member of the legislative assembly of Leningrad oblast, proposed that a Special commission be set up to remove the body of Lenin and replace his corpse with a copy made of synthetic resin.

The golden image that Nebuchadnezzar set up in the plain of Dura is a type for worship of the image of the Beast. **All the peoples, nations, and languages** (Dan. 3:7) worshipped the golden image, just as all must worship the image of the Beast or be killed.

Lunacharsky's God-building

God-building was the process of generating myths and rituals, the development of faith in communism, without lapsing into god-worship.

Lunacharsky (1875-1933) was chief exponent of "God-building". He proposed a new religious sentiment which accommodated the world-view of communism, one that was compatible with science and which was not based on any supernatural beliefs. He believed religion, the psychological and moral basis of millions of people, should be transformed into positive humanistic values. Lunacharsky wanted to propagate a Marxism as an anthropocentric religion whose god was Man, raised to the height of his powers. He wanted to utilize music-dramas of Wagner in the process.

Lunacharsky saw in socialism a kind of religion:

> Scientific socialism, is the most religious of all religions, and the true Social Democrat is the most deeply religious of all human beings.

God-building was based on Empiriomonism and Energeticism, doctrines which could be assimilated into a quasi-occult paradigm.

In is book *Religion and Socialism*, Lunacharsky endeavours to locate socialism within other world religion systems. He speaks of his "conversion to Marxism" and of his response to socialism as a "deeply emotional impulse of the soul". He calls Marx "the greatest prophet of the world" in the tradition of the Hebrew prophets, of Zoroaster, and of Jesus. He speaks of Marxism as a new religion, the most complete synthesis, the fifth great religion that emerged out of Judaism. (Roland Boer notes that Lunacharsky's book *Religion and Socialism* is not included in the eight volume Collected Works of Lunacharsky. It is as though the Soviets did not want this particular work to be widely known. Boer explains how very hard it was for him to get hold of a copy of this book.)

Lunacharsky was impressed by Feuerbach's *Essence of Christianity.* Feuerbach, who also had an enormous influence on Karl Marx, wrote:

> I am to change the friends of God into friends of man; believers into thinkers, worshippers into workers, candidates of the other world into students of this world; Christians, who, on their own confession are half-animal and half-angel, into men, whole men.

Lenin blamed Lunacharsky's God-building on the philosophy of Avenarius (which claimed, for example, that angels were real to those who saw them). Lenin debunked this philosophy in his work *Materialism and Empirio-criticism* (1909).

Lenin however gave control of all religious organizations to Narkompros, including all records, book, buildings, land and librarires. In 1922 Narkompros began publishing the daily newspaper *Bezbozhnik* ("Godless"). By 1938, more than 100 million pieces of anti-religious literature had been disseminated.

Deification of Communist leaders and the Party

Marxist heads of state oppose and exalt themselves against every so-called god or object of worship. Benjamin Gitlow, writes in *The Whole of Their Lives* about how communists worship the Party:

> Chicanery, intrigue, conceit, tricks of the sycophants and doubled-dealers – the black attributes of Satan and his fallen angels – constitute the stock in trade of the communists not only in dealing with their enemies but also in their relations with each other and with their friends.

> In the place of the spiritual, the eternal God, the communists have installed a God dressed in red robes and wielding the sceptre of the hammer and sickle – the God of Power. The communist God is above morality and law. It recognizes as good, as honest, as justifiable, as commendable, conduct and actions, no matter how reprehensible, which enhance communist power. Power is the one basic principle – the religion of communism.

> In the eyes of Communist party members, Party decisions are vested with supernatural omniscience. Here we have the strange paradox of modern times: that communists, Marxian materialists, with a pronounced atheistic outlook on life and history, adopt a profoundly religious attitude towards a temporal man-made organization. To the communist the Party is Godly and fanatically worshipped as such.

Lenin revealed Marxism's determination to oppose God and anything that is called God when he said:

> Every religious idea, every idea of God – even flirting with the idea of God – is unutterable vileness of the most dangerous kind, contagion of the most abominable kind. Millions of sins, filthy deeds, acts of violence, and physical contagion, are far less dangerous than the subtle, spiritual idea of a God.

Paul explains that Jesus Christ will not return before the apostasy comes and the man of lawlessness is revealed:

> **. . . the son of perdition, who opposes and exalts himself against every so-called god or object of worship, so that he takes his seat in the temple of God, proclaiming himself to be God.** (2 Thess. 2: 3-4)

Communists have a history of treating its leaders like gods. The communists are constantly building statues to honour the gods of communism.

Recently a giant statue of a sitting Mao was built in farmland in Tongxu county, Henan Province. This province was the centre of a famine in the 1950s due to Mao's policies. The statue is 37 metres high (120 foot) and gold-painted. Taking a cubit as 22 inches, it can be worked out that Mao's statue is 10 feet taller than Nebuchadnezzar's statue was – and Mao is sitting down! It is clear that Nebuchadnezzar's statue was not sitting, but standing, because the statue was only 6 cubit wide. [Mao's statue: 120x12=1440 inches; Nebuchadnezzar: 60x22=1320 inches]. The biblical text is as follows:

> **King Nebuchadnezzar made an image of gold, whose height was sixty cubits and its breadth six cubits.** (Dan. 3:1)

It is fair to say that Nebuchadnezzar is a type of the worship of the Beast of Revelation, because just as the Beast demands worship of itself on pain of death, so those who did not worship the statue made by Nebuchadnezzar would also die (Dan. 3:4,5).

On learning of Christianity, North Koreans maintain that attributes usually ascribed to the Almighty are instead projected on to their founding leader. This cult is enforced through the use of song, incantations, and Stalinist holy writ. He records the comments of a former guard at a number of political prison camps:

> One is meant to worship only the political leaders and any other worship is a deviation from loyalty to the regime. When North Koreans hear about God, they think they are talking about Kim Il-Sung. All North Koreans have this confusion. If anyone embraces Christianity in North Korea, they are called a crazy guy. No one could understand or imagine someone wanting to become a Christian. It is very unlikely one could find a descendant of Christian still living . . . The purpose of the camps I was involved in was to kill the prisoners. Instead of killing them by shooting, the intention was to force them to work until the last minute. The intention was to kill, not to extract labour.[42]

There has been a marked propensity in communist countries to attribute god-like qualities to some of their leaders

Vincent Miceli argues in his books that the divinising of the Party leader is not foreign to the spirit of Marxism-Leninism but indeed natural to it. Miceli notes how Berdyaev wrote that Russian atheism is "*an inverted theocracy*". He notes how the Party leader evolves from being an atheist humanist to becoming a despot God. This divinising cult is the logical and

---

42 *Christianophobia*, Rupert Shortt

inevitable fruit of man's madness to displace the true God. Miceli argues that the cult constitutes the basis of the Party's power. Atheism is an idolatry which worships that strange God – absolute Man.

Stalin's personality cult veered towards worship. His brother-in-law, Kaganovitch, said: "[Stalin] occupied a position previously reserved only for God".

In North Korea, the atheist state turned its political leader into its own distorted version of God. In 1997 it officially withdrew from the Christian calendar and put itself on "juche time" which marks the beginning of history, Year Zero, as 1912 – the year of Kim Il-sung's birth. After his father's death, Kim Jong-il passed an amendment to the Constitution in 1998 declaring Kim Il-sung the "Eternal President" of North Korea. He built an enormous mausoleum in which his father is entombed.

April 15, the birthday of Kim Il-Sung's birthday, is basically Christmas in North Korea, although no presents are exchanged.

Victor Cha notes in *The Impossible State* that *juche* was transformed from a political ideology into a cult of personality and semi-religion from 1949. The one statue of Kim Il-sung grew to an omnipresent 30,000 statues by 1982 and over 40,000 by 1992.

The North Korean state took draconian measures to erase any influences, political and religious, which might detract from fidelity to Kim. Over 2000 Buddhist temples and Christian churches were burned. The persecution of Christians was especially intense given the success of missionaries in Korea compared with other parts of Asia. Kim imprisoned over 100,000 Christians and spread rumours that missionaries were Western spies who branded Korean children with hot irons and sold their blood. Kim was replacing God with himself in the minds of North Koreans. Through destroying others, he made himself the Creator of everything material and spiritual in the North Korean state. Nothing existed before him. State propaganda thereafter referred to Kim as superior to Christ in love, Buddha in benevolence, Confucius in virtue, and Mohammed in justice.

There are five main gulags in North Korea, each holding between 5000 and 50,000 prisoners. Some are sent there for merely allowing a portrait of the Great Leader to collect dust.

The law of laws in communism is this: whatever you do in thought, word or deed, do all for a communist victory under the leadership of the

Communist Party. In *Red Masquerade*, Angela Calomiris, an agent for the American government assigned to infiltrate the Communist Party, wrote:

> It is hard for anyone outside the Party to realize that Communism is more than a physical or military threat. It is an assault on the minds of men, as the Party prophets claim. In order to do their work, the shock troops of the revolution must be pure in heart. Sins of word and thought are counted, and even the faithful sin. An off phrase could be a booby trap.

Communism's demand for total allegiance is a form of worship, according to Dr W. Steuart McBirnie:

> The reason why many Christians do not fight communism, or fight it effectively, is that they do not understand it. Communism is a spiritual way of life that demands total and ultimate allegiance. And what is that but worship? Worship is your admission that someone or something has total authority over you. When you worship God, you believe that God has ultimate authority.

Inability to buy or sell in USSR without the mark (the Hammer and Sickle)

> **And it causes all . . . to be marked on the right hand or the forehead, so that no one can buy or sell unless he has the mark, that is, the name of the beast or the number of its name.** (Rev. 13:16-17)

The False Prophet will cause all to be marked with the Hammer and Sickle.

Louis Richard Patmont noted how international communism restricted "the commercial activity of those who do not bear its mark." In a passage which has sharp echoes of the Book of Revelation, Patmont writes:

> The privilege to buy and sell is extended only to those who have accepted the Bolshevik regime and have given their unquestioning loyalty to the communistic scheme. Food cards are issued only to members of the party, pro-bolsheviks, and such other workers who have not incurred the suspi-

> cion of the Soviet henchman. The disfranchised are not only deprived of the privilege to buy and sell, but according to official decree are not entitled to living quarters or employment except those who are in prisons or exile.[43]

> It is significant that the Soviet emblem which these cards bear is a five-pointed star, with hammer and sickle in the centre. Even those who are not members of the communist party, but have registered as pro-communists, must show their cards bearing these emblems before they are able to obtain anything at the commune. The salutation of the officials and the military is always accompanied by a lifting of the right hand to the forehead, pointing to the communist emblem on their caps and helmets. "Plameny pryvyet!" ("A flaming greeting!") they cry with fervour.

Communist monopoly of commodities enabled the state to browbeat the masses into submission, "withdrawing food and clothing card privileges from those who refuse to deny openly their faith in God." As Trotzky put it:

> In a country where the sole employer is the State, opposition means death by slow starvation. The old principle: who does not work shall not eat, has been replaced by a new one: who does not obey shall not eat.

The wearing of military caps bearing the Hammer and Sickle is, in a way, a partial fulfilment of the prophecy that the beast would make his worshipers be marked on the forehead or the right hand with his mark. From this, it can be deduced that when the Beast himself appears, it is possible that his worshippers will literally bear the mark of the Beast on their forehead or right hand in the physical sense, and not just the spiritual sense.

However there is the spiritual side to this as well, and the comparison must be made between the mark of the Beast and the use of phylacteries (*tephillin*) in Hebrew) worn by the Israelites on their hand and forehead (Deut. 6:4-9). The worshippers of the Beast have forsaken the God of Israel, and worship the Beast who will proclaim to be God himself. Their faith therefore is not belief in the one God of Israel according to the Shema which is to be written upon the tablet of their heart, and upon their forehead and

---

43 *The Mystery of Iniquity*, L.R. Patmont

hand, but in the Beast, who is signified by the mark on their head and right hand.

Modern Israel and Russia

It is the False Prophet himself who speaks like **a dragon** (Rev. 13:11), and not Israel. However, it is pertinent to note the huge influence that Marxism has had on the history of modern Israel, and similarly the huge influence that Jews have had on Marxism. Given this propensity for Marxism, Israel may be particularly susceptible to the deceptions of the latter-day False Prophet.

Jews were found in disproportionately large numbers in Socialist, Social democratic and Communist parties across Europe and North America in the latter part of the nineteenth century. It is estimated that in the late 1940s and early 1950s, a tenth of activists in the Communist Party of Great Britain were Jewish, despite the fact that Jews formed less than 1% of the UK population.

Many Jews dedicated their lives to the socialist revolution: Karl Marx, Leon Trotzky, Grigory Zinoviev, Lev Kamenev, Leonid Krassin, Yakov Sverdlov, Yemelyan Yaroslavsky, Karl Radek, Rosa Luxemburg, Julius Martov, Moisei Uritsky, Grigory Kaminsky, Lazar Kaganovich, Maxim Litvinov, and Genrikh Yagoda. In Hungary, Communism was led by Bela Kun and Tibor Szamuely, and later by Matyas Rakosi and Erno Gero.

Many Jews also contributed in a large measure to the erection of Communism in Romania. Richard Wurmbrand wondered how Jews could ever be rejudaized:

> There is not much chance that they [the Jews in the Soviet Union] will be allowed to go to Israel. Even if allowed, how could Israel take in a short time over three million new inhabitants? And how will they rejudaize three million men and women who certainly hate Communism, but have been indoctrinated only with Marxism? They know no other teaching than that of fierce atheism, wherewith they have been brainwashed.[44]

---

44 *On The Christian Road*, Richard Wurmbrand

Israel was founded largely by a group of Russian Jews such as Ben Gurion, Moshe Sharet, and David Remez. They came to Israel around the turn of the nineteenth century and were extremely influenced by Karl Marx and socialist ideas.

The culture of Jewish society in Mandatory Palestine was socialist. Mapai, Ben Gurion's "Workers' Party of the Land of Israel", was a centre-left political party in Israel, and was the dominant force in Israeli politics until its merger into the modern-day Israeli Labor Party in 1968. During Mapai's time in office, a wide range of progressive reforms were carried out: the establishment of a welfare state, provision of a minimum income, security, and free access to housing subsidies and health and social services. To get a job, you had to bare Mapai's "Red Notebook".

In the opening years of Israel, each major party's electoral symbol was a letter of the Hebrew alphabet. The aleph of Mapai was clearly based upon the Hammer and Sickle itself. The logo of Mapam (an acronym for "United Workers Party") was also based on the Hammer and Sickle, with a stem of wheat substituted for the sickle, and with a sword intersecting the hammer and sheaf.

The socialist ideas of the founding fathers were the foundations for Israel's entire infrastructure. Every 1st of May, the entire country celebrated International Workers' Day. When Stalin died in 1953 the newspapers mourned.

The Histadrut (General Organization of Workers in Israel) was originally Israel's national trade union centre, representing the majority of trade unionists in the State of Israel. Established in December 1920 in Mandatory Palestine, it soon become one of the most powerful institutions in the Yishuv (the body of Jewish residents in the region prior to the establishment of the state). As late as 1983, most wage earners were Histadrut members. It owned huge industrial conglomerates and Israel's largest bank.

The kibbutz-oriented and labour-oriented left both in the Land of Israel and worldwide dominated the political spectrum from the birth of Israel as a modern nation for roughly thirty years, though always, in the multi-party system, in coalitions (Mapai (Labour Party), Mapam (very leftist but Zionist) and others.

Some of the kibbutzim were radically socialist farming collectives that not only shared the output of production but even, in some cases, went so far as to raise children collectively. Kibbutzim could even be described as communist since there was absolute equality of wages and an almost total ban on private property. Buying anything from outside the kibbutz canteen without committee permission was forbidden.

The moshavim were similar in many ways but made some effort to reward more productive farmers. They were a type of cooperative agricultural community of individual farms pioneered by the Labour Zionists during the second wave of *aliyah*.

In the 1970s Menachem Begin started carrying out capitalist reforms.

Gradually the Histadrut lost its grip on the economy and the kibbutzim were forced to embrace capitalism and privatization.

Purpose of notifying mankind of the mark

At the End, the mystery will not be the identity of the man in whose likeness the image of the Beast is made. This will be plain to see since the icon will be in the man's likeness. The purpose of being able to recognize the mark is to ensure that no Christian worships the icon and the Beast through ignorance. Recognition of the mark will fortify the Christian to endure persecution, and to reassure himself that Christ's return is imminent.

The Beast's icon is not necessarily made in the image of the Beast who will make war on the Lamb at Armageddon. The text reads that the icon is made "to" or "for" the Beast, rather than "of" the Beast. This is indicated by the use of the dative, a case which may indicate that something is being done to someone's advantage or disadvantage.

The description of the mark (Rev. 13:17-18) also enables one to identify the eighth kingdom, the Beast: the USSR, not Rome.

POSTSCRIPT

"A city set on a hill cannot be hid. Nor do men light a lamp and put it under a bushel, but on a stand, and it gives light to all in the house." (Matt. 5:14)

Despite the fact that some ancient manuscripts have 616 at Rev. 13:18 in their main text, no modern version of the Bible does. However, eight out of the fifteen most significant English versions of the Bible have footnotes at Rev. 13:18 which note 616 as a variant reading. These eight versions are:

- RSV – Revised Standard Version, 1946
- NRSV – New Revised Standard Version, 1990
- ESV – English Standard Version, 2001
- NASB – New American Standard Bible, 1964, 1995
- NJB – New Jerusalem Bible, 1986
- NAB – New American Bible, 1984
- NLT – New Living Translation, 2004
- HCSB – Holman Christian Standard Bible, 2004

Conscious of his own fallibility and of the curse that will befall anyone who adds to the words or takes away from the words of Revelation (Rev. 22:18-19), the author does not advocate changing the main text of Rev. 13:18 until a thorough investigation into this issue has been conducted by all those responsible for editing Bibles. Editorial committees of each and every version of the Bible should look afresh at the documentary evidence without any preconceptions and reconsider which number is the correct one in the light of the material contained in this book and all other factors. Irenaeus' testimony should be given due weight, but should not be allowed to determine the issue. After all, some of his testimony, such as the date of Christ's crucifixion, is demonstrably false. In the meantime, a footnote should be added to every version of the Bible at Rev. 13:18 with notification of the variant reading 616.

Just as a prophet is proven false through the failure of his prophecy to come true (Deut. 18:21-22), so the number 666 has been proven false. A true prophet is revealed through the coming to pass of the words of his prophecy. The words of Revelation have come to pass (and are still coming to pass) and John has proven to be a true prophet. The number 616 has proven to be the true number.

On these grounds, it seems right that if the documentary evidence remains equivocal despite further investigations into this matter by those responsible, then the variant reading 616 should replace 666 in the main text, for it has been proven to be the true number in exactly the same way that a prophecy is proven to be true: through its fulfilment. There is no better way of discerning truth from falsehood than this.

No one has yet been marked with the emblem of the USSR on his forehead or right hand, and an emblem is not the same things as a mark (*charagma*). However, one can safely conclude that the Hammer and Sickle will be the mark, for it fulfils all the criteria of the mark of the Beast.

The words of Revelation encourage the hearer to calculate the number of the Beast so that the Christian can be prepared in advance. To resist being marked is to evade eternal damnation.

The final half-week of Daniel's seventieth week began in 1917 with the advent of Lenin, the Little Horn (Dan. 7:8)/Beast. From 1917 until Christ's return, the saints will be given into the hand of the Beast. The advent of the False Prophet in the final days only heralds the most intense period of persecution of the saints. It is only appropriate therefore that Christians should be able to identify the Beast at the beginning of this half-week period of persecution, and not just only at the very end.

The Bolsheviks only intended the Hammer and Sickle to represent the Workers' and Peasants' Government. Unwittingly, they fulfilled the prophecy of Revelation by creating a symbol that can be perceived as a monogram of the number "616" in both Hebrew (TRTZ) and Greek letters (ChIV).

The Hammer and Sickle is Lenin's number, because it is a monogram of the letters that comprise the number 616 and, through transliteration, the name: "Beast". Since Lenin is the "Beast", 616 is his number.

Constantine's Chi Rho is not a number, but it represents Jesus in a similar way to the way that the Hammer and Sickle represents Lenin. The letters

XP are a cipher for the name "Christ" (ΧΡΙΣΤΟΣ) in the same way that the letters ΧΙϚ and תריו are ciphers, through transliteration, for the name "beast"(*cheivah/therion*).

Constantine's vision of the cross above the sun emblazened with the words Εν τουτω νικα ("By this conquer!") and his marking of his soldiers' shields with the mark of the cross marked the beginning of the first half-week period when the Woman had respite from the Dragon (Rev. 12:14) under the protective wings of the Roman Empire. The advent of the Hammer and Sickle marks the beginning of the final half-week, the half-week of persecution.

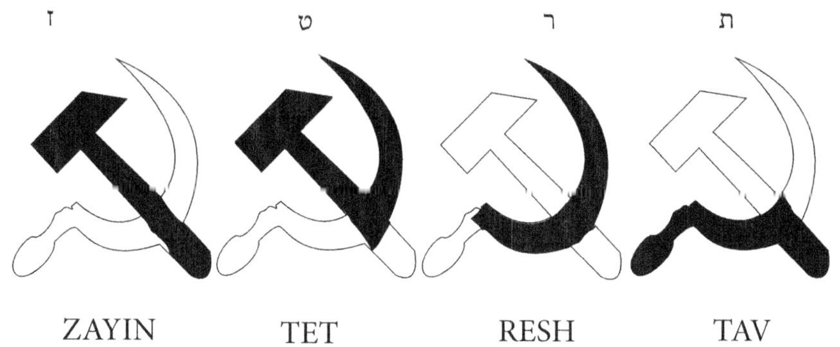

TRTZ=616

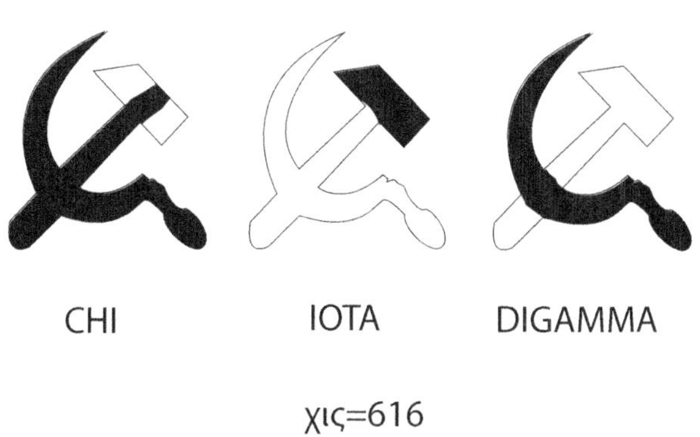

χις=616

APPENDIX 2: GREEK AND HEBREW ALPHABETICAL NUMBER SYSTEM

1	Α	α	alpha	א	aleph
2	Β	β	beta	ב	bet
3	Γ	γ	gamma	ג	gimel
4	Δ	δ	delta	ד	dalet
5	Ε	ε	epsilon	ה	he
6	Ϛ	ς	digamma	ו	vav
7	Ζ	ζ	zeta	ז	zayin
8	Η	η	eta	ח	chet
9	Θ	θ	theta	ט	tet
10	Ι	ι	iota	י	yod
20	Κ	κ	kappa	כ(ך)	kaf
30	Λ	λ	lamda	ל	lamed
40	Μ	μ	mu	מ(ם)	mem
50	Ν	ν	nu	נ (ן)	nun
60	Ξ	ξ	xi	ס	samech
70	Ο	ο	omicron	ע	ayin
80	Π	π	pi	פ(ף)	pey
90	Ϙ	ϙ	koppa	צ(ץ)	tzade
100	Ρ	ρ	rho	ק	qof
200	Σ	ς	sigma	ר	resh
300	Τ	τ	tau	ש	shin/sin
400	Υ	υ	upsilon	ת	tav
500	Φ	φ	phi	תק	
600	Χ	χ	chi	תר	
700	Ψ	ψ	psi	תש	
800	Ω	ω	omega	תת	
900	Ϡ	ϡ	san	תתק	

Five Hebrew letters change their form when they are the last letter in a word. These are the kaf, mem, nun, pey, and tzade (These final (*sofit*) letters are shown in brackets.) These five *sofit* letters were once, for a brief period of time, used to supply the shortfall of Hebrew letters to make 500, 600, 700, 800, and 900, respectively, instead of the system shown in the Table above.

The yod/he and yod/vav (15 and 16) are invariably substituted with tet/vav and tet/zayin nowadays.

In Greek, the number 616 is represented by the letters XIϹ (ChIV)=600+10+6=616.

In Hebrew, the corresponding letters are:

תריו (TRTZ)=400+200+9+7/תריו (TRIW) = 400+200+10+ 6=616

Printed in Great Britain
by Amazon